Aquatic Instruction, Coaching, and Management

COACHING · TEACHING · LIFE GUARDING · EVALUATING · POOL MANAGEMENT

SWIMMING
DIVING
LIFESAVING

John A. Torney, Jr.
University of Washington

Robert D. Clayton
University of North Dakota

Illustrations by
Barbara J. Sanborn
University of North Dakota

Burgess Publishing Company

426 South Sixth Street · Minneapolis, Minn. 55415

Library of Congress Catalog Card Number 78-120-288

ISBN 8087-2031-7

Preface

The art of swimming is known to be at least nine thousand years old. Writings from both the Near and the Far East refer to the use and enjoyment of this activity two thousand years before the birth of Christ, and since that time a continuous stream of evidence throughout the centuries has indicated man's interest in this water sport. Swimming has been extolled for reasons of health, pleasure, utility, and survival.

Special organizations foster enjoyment of the sport and promote competition and instruction. Other organizations emphasize swimming as an essential component of the programs they sponsor. Schools, government agencies, and private groups construct pools and adapt beach sites to provide opportunity for the pursuit and enjoyment of aquatic activities. Such sports as water skiing, scuba diving, and water polo are only possible because participants know how to swim.

Millions of people of all ages take part in such aquatic pursuits, and it is critically important that they know how to swim. If their needs are to be met, instructor training programs must be provided, improved, and expanded. A great many aquatic teachers, coaches, and program managers must be trained.

This book is designed as a tool for the accomplishment of this task. It is not meant to be all-inclusive, although all necessary skills and related matters are treated in sufficient depth, but is intended to be used in conjunction with instructor training programs in colleges, universities, and established organizations.

In order to assist both the teacher and student of swimming, diving, and lifesaving skills, possible flaws and errors have been identified and illustrated in addition to the description and portrayal of correct performance techniques.

To complete a project such as the writing of this text requires more than a mere reshuffling of the normal work schedule. It means a radical departure from the usual family and social life which we enjoy. To us, the merit of the project justifies this radical change; however, on occasion our spouses and families have wondered just how much longer the work would continue. Now that the task is done, we gratefully acknowledge the patience, understanding, and even the gentle prodding of Marian Torney and Joyce Clayton.

John A. Torney, Jr.
Robert D. Clayton

August, 1970

Contents

Tables and Charts

Chapter 4   Performing and Teaching Other Aquatic Strokes and Skills

Chapter 5   Performing and Teaching Springboard Diving Skills

Chart 6 – Performing and Teaching Lifesaving Skills

Chapter 7   *The Skills and Knowledges Needed by Lifeguards*

Chapter 8   *Organization and Administration of Aquatic Programs*

CHAPTER 1

Becoming a Competent Aquatic Worker

Definitions and Abbreviations
Minimum Competencies of Prospective Aquatic Workers
Do You Need This Text?
How Should You Use This Text?
What Can This Text Do for You?

Everyone has a desire to become competent in certain areas of work or play. The fact that you are reading this book implies that you wish to become more competent as a lifeguard, a swimming teacher, a swimming coach, or pool manager. But how are competent aquatic workers trained? Usually the young person begins by joining a swimming team or synchronized swimming group. Then a period of time is often spent helping teach swimming classes and/or lifeguarding. When the person is older he undertakes formal training (a Red Cross Water Safety Instructor course, a YMCA Aquatic Leader-Examiner course, etc.), so that certification may be earned. Finally, after some years of preparation, a competent aquatic worker develops.

This text is designed to aid in this preparation—whether the reader is a young swimmer interested in correct stroking, a beginning lifeguard or coach or pool manager, a student seeking instructor certification, or a veteran instructor keeping abreast of all that is published on aquatics.

DEFINITIONS AND ABBREVIATIONS

Throughout this text we will mention "certified aquatic workers" or "certified aquatic instructors." This term refers to those who have earned some recognized national certificate as a teacher of swimming and diving, usually the Water Safety Instructor (Red Cross) or Aquatic Leader-Examiner (YMCA). Many references will be made to the ARC and YMCA programs; these are abbreviations for the American National Red Cross or Young Men's Christian Association, respectively.

MINIMUM COMPETENCIES OF PROSPECTIVE AQUATIC WORKERS

Even though this text is potentially valuable to many persons, we feel that its greatest value will be to those who are beginning their formal aquatic worker training. Each of the national groups has its own tests which "screen" those who are applying for training. A modified test (Table 1:1) has been developed for use in a college or university situation. The level of skill performance is expected to be the same, whether the instruction is given in a week-long aquatic school or in a school term. However, the much longer school term permits students to overcome initial shortcomings by additional practice.

Table 1:1 is presented in the form of a self-rating test. If you are seeking to enroll in a formal course for aquatic workers, rate yourself on each item. Your instructor may have you demonstrate any or all of the physical skill items, or perhaps even add more. Meeting these standards would be the first step toward becoming a certified aquatic worker.

1

TABLE 1:1
SELF-TEST FOR PROSPECTIVE CERTIFIED AQUATIC WORKERS

	YES	NO
1. Are you at least 17 years of age?		
2. Do you have a current senior lifesaving certificate?		
3. Do you have the ability to perform these physical skills?		
a. Correct flutter kick (no bicycle action)		
b. Correct scissors kick (not inverted)		
c. Correct whip or wedge kick		
d. Acceptable breathing in crawl stroke (face in water, rhythmic)		
e. Swim 500 yards nonstop (any combination of strokes: 11½ minutes or less for girls, 9½ minutes for boys)		
f. Carry a person of equal size with the cross-chest carry (25 yards)		
g. Enter water head first (1-meter board)		
4. Do you have these vitality and attitudinal skills?		
a. Energetic enough to demonstrate and teach aquatic skills for at least 45 minutes at one time		
b. Conscientious enough to read and think about written material in this course		
c. Enthusiastic enough to master all aquatic skills (including diving) in those classes you may teach		

DO YOU NEED THIS TEXT?

If you meet the physical, vitality, and attitudinal requirements given above, you may wonder if you need this text. Consider the scope of knowledge a well-trained aquatic instructor is supposed to have mastered. A glance at the Table of Contents reveals that this text discusses the background information for teaching aquatic skills. It next gives suggestions for performing and teaching almost all aquatic strokes and skills, including six of the basic dives. The text presents material which will enable you to perform lifesaving skills and to be a better lifeguard. For those of you who want to become pool managers there is advice on water and pool sanitation; on the organization and administration of aquatic programs; and on the organization and coaching of a swimming team. Finally, suggestions concerning the evaluation of skills in the aquatic program are presented.

Thus it is apparent that there are many areas about which one needs to be knowledgeable before being judged a truly competent aquatic instructor. Experience *is* a good teacher—but this text will help you learn some things others have learned by bitter experience.

HOW SHOULD YOU USE THIS TEXT?

Every chapter begins with a brief introduction that serves to provide an outline of the material and, we hope, make you eager to read on. Next, the chapter presents appropriate material, utilizing various combinations of written text, illustrations, tables, and charts. At the end of each chapter is found a section entitled "Behavioral Objectives" which is to be read before beginning the study of that chapter. These objectives specify what is expected of students in our aquatic certification classes. The final chapter in this text discusses behavioral objectives that are designed to motivate the student because he knows exactly what is expected of him.

It is important that you know the objectives and *then* study the material with the help of one or more of these techniques: redraw the diagrams; rephrase important points; add your own comments in the margin. In addition, some students will complete the written assignments at the end of the chapters. They will use the teaching suggestions with novice students and retain those suggestions which are effective. Finally, these students will gain experience now in all phases of the swimming program.

When using this book in classes in which you assign grades to students, a just and sound method of evaluation must be employed to measure the extent to which each student has achieved the behavioral objectives identified in each chapter. A conventional method may be used (A — 95-100%; B — 85-94%; C — 75-84%; D — 65-74%; E — 0-64%) or other methods may be chosen. Refer to Chapter 11 before undertaking to rate student attainment of behavioral objectives.

WHAT CAN THIS TEXT DO FOR YOU?

This text presents a summary of the experiences of the authors and other swimming teachers. It will give you information about the great majority of those problems facing the beginning instructor. This information will be detailed enough to make your first years as an aquatic instructor less traumatic and embarrassing, but you should not regard this text as the complete source for all information you may need; other publications, especially those of the Red Cross and YMCA, should be consulted also. What works well for one may not work quite so well for others. The competent instructor is distinguished by his ability to combine the lessons of experience with new ideas and use them as a guide. We hope this book will help you to make a good start on the road toward excellence.

CHAPTER 2

Foundations of Successful Aquatic Instruction

What Are the Characteristics of a Competent Swimming or Diving Teacher?
What Are the Values of Teaching Progressions?
Must Lesson Plans Be Made?
What Is Meant by a Sound Teaching Approach?
Demonstrating and Correcting Errors
How Can Fear Be Overcome?
Of What Value Are Drills and Formations?
Essential Considerations Before Teaching a Swimming or Diving Class

The evolution of a novice into a veteran aquatic worker usually begins by observing persons already active in the field. After presenting what we feel are the characteristics of a competent swimming or diving teacher, we will discuss how these people teach—the progression they use from one part of the stroke to the other, and their lesson plans. Since effective teaching is based in part on psychology, the discussion of a sound teaching approach includes material in this area. Correction of errors and elimination of fear of the water are difficult problems in some instances; we hope our comments will provide practical help for you. Patterns for practicing strokes will be diagrammed. Finally, the five basic things to consider before teaching a class will be listed and discussed.

WHAT ARE THE CHARACTERISTICS OF A COMPETENT SWIMMING OR DIVING TEACHER

The list of desirable characteristics found in superior swimming and diving teachers (Table 2:1) appears to be formidable. However, each of these points is truly important; training given by national groups to certified instructors requires at least minimum exposure to the first seven. It seems necessary to add one more characteristic—that of patience—to this list. Patience is an absolute necessity when instructing in aquatics. Some students just do not "catch on" to a needed skill even after many sessions of instruction. The teacher's temptation is to cease instruction of the skill—and this is sometimes done. However, most competent instructors alter their explanation, devise a new drill, and/or organize practive in a different fashion in order to accomplish the task. Some instructors naturally have patience, others must cultivate it. However it is gained, it is essential.

WHAT ARE THE VALUES OF TEACHING PROGRESSIONS?

A teaching progression may be defined as the sequential steps in which a certain skill is taught. For example, when teaching the crawl stroke with the progressive-part method, the usual progression is to have students practice the flutter kick, then the arm stroke, and then combine them. Breathing is then practiced and added to the skills that have already been learned. There are no universally accepted progressions for any stroke; some teachers probably reverse the steps and still succeed. Beginning instructors are handicapped in formulating their own progressions because they have forgotten how they

4

TABLE 2:1
DESIRABLE CHARACTERISTICS OF A SWIMMING OR DIVING TEACHER*

Characteristics	Where Discussed in This Text
1. Knowledge of subject matter	Chapters 3, 4, 5, 6
2. Knowledge of logical teaching progressions	Chapters 2, 3, 4, 5, 6 (selected portions)
3. Ability to formulate complete lesson plans	Chapter 2
4. A sound teaching approach	Chapter 2
5. A photographic eye	Chapters 2, 3, 4, 5
6. Ability to correct mistakes	Chapter 2
7. Ability to demonstrate	Chapter 2
8. Patience	Chapter 2

*Items 1-7 from: The American National Red Cross. *Swimming and Water Safety Courses: Instructor's Manual,* 1968, pp. 2-4. Used by permission.

learned the stroke or dive. Teaching progressions are of importance to the student because they lead him from the simple to the complex skills; they are of even greater importance to the instructor because they enable him to teach with the confidence that comes from knowing what the next step will be. The instructor's confidence is evident to the student, and this in turn makes the progression more effective.

The most complete reference on teaching progressions is *Teaching Progressions for the Swimming Instructor* (Brown, 1948).† Although now out of print, a copy might be found in some bookstores; if so, it is well worth purchasing. Throughout the next four chapters of the present text, however, the reader will find suggested progressions for every stroke, skill, and dive discussed. The beginning instructor would be well-advised to use these progressions until experience leads to the formulation of new ones. Development of new progressions is desirable, providing the following guidelines are considered:

1. The progression should begin with an explanation, and preferably a demonstration, of one part of the skill. (In diving, it is sometimes impossible to demonstrate an individual part of a dive. The learner is then instructed to concentrate his attention on one part only.) This explanation should be complete and in language the student can understand.
2. Correct physical practice of the first part is done enough times to ensure reasonably consistent performance.
3. The next part is explained and demonstrated.
4. This second part is practiced until it can be done.
5. Steps 1 and 2 are again repeated for each additional part until the whole stroke, dive, or skill is learned.

MUST LESSON PLANS BE MADE?

"Ability to formulate complete lesson plans" was given as a characteristic of competent teachers. Experienced teachers might smile at this axiom, because very few ever appear on the pool deck with a carefully formulated, written lesson plan. However, the competent teacher *does* have lesson plans formulated in his mind. These plans are composed primarily of the teaching progressions which are habitually used, plus the skill sheets which list all the skills needed by students at the end of the course. The American Red Cross has prepared some lesson plans to guide the teacher *(Swimming and Water*

†See Bibliography at end of chapter.

Safety Courses: Instructor's Manual, 1968, Sections 5-9). However, experienced instructors tend to develop their own plans. Only the poor instructor truly has no lesson plan to follow.

Table 2:2 summarizes the elements of a lesson, together with a description and approximate time allotment for each element. Even though the ages of students, their skill levels, and the complexity of the new material will cause plans to vary from situation to situation, the elements presented below should be the basis for virtually all class sessions.

TABLE 2:2
THE ELEMENTS OF A LESSON PLAN, DESCRIPTION AND TIME ALLOTMENT

Element	Description of Element	Percentage of Time Devoted to this Element
Introduction	What will be done today. Why it will be done.	Should take less than 5% of the time.
New Material*	Explanation of new material. Demonstration of new material. Directed practice of new material.	Should take 25-40% of the time, depending upon complexity of skill, ease of learning, etc.
Old Material*	Review skills taught previously.	Should take 50-60% of the time.
Individual Practice	Not free play, but supervised practice of previously taught skills.	Should take 5-20% of the time.

*Quite often, the new material is a continuation of the old, e.g., the back glide and standing up have been taught before, and now the arm stroke for the elementary backstroke will be taught. Thus, the explanation and demonstration include the old material, or perhaps the old material is practiced before the new material is presented.

WHAT IS MEANT BY A SOUND TEACHING APPROACH?

"Teaching approach" is a vague, ill-defined term having to do with a number of issues based upon research into teaching methods. Our view is that a sound teaching approach implies that the instructor is aware of the results and implications of methodology research, plus understanding the reasons why good teachers do certain things.

Methods of Teaching — Whole, Part, Progressive-Part, and Whole-Part-Whole

At some time in his teaching career, each instructor will encounter persons who maintain that the only way to teach a person to swim is to "throw him in the water," (the "whole" method). While this is not a recommended procedure, it does have some slight basis in the psychology of teaching. In the "whole" method of teaching the person is asked to swim the entire stroke. As this is attempted, the teacher points out flaws in the stroke and gives corrections.

The counterpart of the "whole" method is the "part" method, wherein the instructor requires the beginner to practice one part of the stroke separately (the kick, for example). The arm action is practiced next. When all parts have been practiced separately, they are put together into one whole stroke.

To compound the problem, there is the "progressive-part" method (one part is practiced, then another part, the two parts are practiced together, then a third is added to the first two, etc.) and the "whole-part-whole" method (the whole is practiced, then the parts which need more work are singled out for more work, and finally the whole practiced again). Numerous research studies have attempted to decide which of these four methods is superior. Unfortunately, the evidence does not clearly indicate that any one method is definitely superior to the others in all situations (Singer, 1968, pp. 213-216).

6

Most swimming instructors recommend either the part or the progressive-part approach. They feel that either method works well because concentration can be focused on one part at a time. The principles of teaching progression are based on either the part or progressive-part methods, and for this reason it is recommended that beginning instructors select one or the other to use. However, it is often possible to teach skills to intermediate or advanced students more quickly with the whole-part-whole method. This alone is reason enough to try it. Also, the easier the skill, the better the whole-part-whole method seems to be.

Frequency and Length of Practice Periods

Regardless of the method of teaching you are using, you must consider the length of time to practice each part or stroke. The merits of the "massed" and "distributed" practice have been studied at length, but again we can come to no clear-cut, universal opinion (Singer, 1968, pp. 190-3). "Massed" practice is when a certain amount of practice is given at one time, whereas "distributed" practice occurs when the same amount of time is divided into several days of practice.

Research suggests that for people learning a skill, distributed practice over a several-day period seems to be the best. On the other hand, experienced performers (such as advanced swimmers) perhaps benefit most if they have massed practice on a stroke. The age of the learners is related to the length of time a swimmer should practice one stroke. It may be necessary for a young beginner group to take four five-minute sessions to practice floating while an older group could profitably accomplish this in two ten-minute sessions.

The Quality of Practice

One of the most popular myths of all times is "Practice makes perfect." A moment's reflection will reveal that this simply cannot be true. If so, why can't experienced bowlers consistently roll games of 250-300? Why can't all veteran golfers consistently shoot close to par? The most obvious aquatic example is the diver who cannot learn a certain dive. He tries the dive over and over, but seldom with success. It should be obvious that practice alone will not make a perfect performance. This concept of practice should be rephrased to read, "Correct and sufficient practice leads toward perfection." The key words in this phrase are "correct" and "sufficient." The primary job of the teacher, then, is to make certain that his students are practicing correctly. His secondary job is to enable them to practice this correct form a sufficient length of time. Because skills can be practiced either correctly or incorrectly, sufficient practice on incorrect skills will result in incorrect performance.

Learning Plateau

As learning progresses, there will be times when the rate of learning slows or stops (learning plateau). This is especially true of beginners, who appear to make very slow progress for a few sessions, but suddenly seem to cease learning, thus becoming discouraged, and quite often (among adults especially) cease coming for lessons. The experienced instructor expects this plateau and avoids discouragement by such devices as:

1. Introducing a new stroke or skill even though the person has not mastered the previous stroke.
2. Spending more time in review than on new skills.
3. Using distributed practice periods rather than massed.
4. Using varied explanations of the same stroke or skill.

The Location of Practice

Where should students practice? The usual procedure is for them to get into the water and practice—and this seems to make sense. However, land drill (standing or lying on the pool deck or beach) has been recommended since 1798. It is also possible to practice mentally. However, swimming research (Clayton, 1963, pp. 188-9) has not shown that either land drill or mental practice were significantly beneficial to beginning male swimmers when either was used in conjunction with water practice. It is conceivable that either or both methods would aid in the learning of aquatic activities, but instructors will continue to believe that the best place to learn to swim is in the water, until they are shown that this is untrue. In learning to dive, however, it is common to use diving sand pits, trampolines, and visual aids.

Analysis of Performance

A "photographic eye" implies the ability to watch any part of a stroke or dive and instantly know what is right or what is wrong. A beginning instructor cannot easily separate the parts of a performance in his mind—or relate exactly what should be done to better the performance. This is an acquired trait developed only when the instructor can analyze or dissect a performance. Even though only teaching experience will develop the photographic eye to its sharpest degree, acquiring this ability should begin as early as possible.

Skill analysis sheets are specialized forms developed for the express purpose of analyzing the form of a swimmer or diver. Usually they contain a diagram of the skill, plus common errors listed alongside. As the student demonstrates a skill, the instructor notes on the sheet exactly what is satisfactory and what is not, and then shows it to the student. Analyzing the form of fellow students is excellent training for all members of a class, and especially important for those who are becoming certified aquatic instructors. The use of the analysis sheet is much superior to the usual method of watching a swimmer and then mentioning one or two faults. Performance analysis sheets are presented for every stroke and dive described in this text; they should help develop the photographic eye that is a desirable characteristic of aquatic instructors.

Introduction of New Skills

Teaching involves a judicious addition of new skills to those previously learned. When to add new skills is puzzling to beginning teachers. Not everyone in the class will master a skill at the same time, because of the plateaus that occur in learning. To complicate matters, the average class contains a marked deviation in skill level. Some instructors add new skills rather often, their theory being that the students will become bored if this is not done. The other view is that the students will become discouraged if skills are added too rapidly, before the previous ones have been thoroughly learned. There is no universally accepted rule as to when to review, and when to teach a new skill. Many instructors progress to new skills when 65-70% of the class members can perform the old skill satisfactorily. The old skill is reviewed in subsequent sessions until virtually everyone can master it and then it is not practiced again on a class basis.

DEMONSTRATING AND CORRECTING ERRORS

The abilities to demonstrate and correct mistakes have previously been cited as characteristics of competent teachers. These, too, are acquired traits. Some national certifying groups require that their instructors be able to demonstrate most of the strokes, dives, and skills shown in Chapters 3, 4, 5, and 6. Actual practice is thus required. There is a universal feeling (but no research to prove it) that instructors who can demonstrate are better teachers than those who cannot. However, the practical view is that it makes little difference whether a correct demonstration is given by the instructor or by a student.

The ability to correct mistakes begins when they are recognized. A photographic eye, combined with a knowledge of what correct performance should be, is the starting point. The error should be explained, using language appropriate to the maturity of the student. Next, the correct movement is demonstrated, followed by practice. It is better to use praise ("good" or "that's right, but. . .") more often than adverse criticism. "Positive" teaching (demonstrating what is being done right) is likewise recommended over negative teaching. The manner in which the correction is made is often more important than what is said. Above all, the teacher must not merely say to the learner, "That is wrong." He should tell the learner precisely how he erred and then indicate specifically how the performance can be improved.

HOW CAN FEAR BE OVERCOME?

Overcoming a student's fear is an essential task, because fear among swimmers or divers is a tremendous detriment to learning. There are no hard and fast rules, but a combination of these techniques will be effective.

1. Try to remember when you were faced with learning a new skill. What inspired you?
2. Demonstrate the skill yourself (or at least have a student or film demonstration).
3. Encourage, but don't force, students to attempt the skill.
4. Use workable teaching progressions, making certain most students are successful before proceeding.
5. Build confidence day-by-day, not with an all-out effort one day.
6. Remember that success breeds confidence and vice versa.
7. Make use of devices which tend to eliminate the bases for fear (floating aids, sweat shirts when learning new dives, etc.).
8. Distribute practice time on difficult skills.
9. Use a variety of teaching methods. Don't give up and don't let the student do so.

OF WHAT VALUE ARE DRILLS AND FORMATIONS?

A drill is a specific movement or series of related movements whereby the student practices a single aspect of a stroke or dive. For example, one drill for improving the crawl stroke would be flutter kicking with a board. One student may perform a particular drill by himself, or an entire class may be engaged in the same drill at the same time. When several students are involved in the same drill, practice is more effective and use of water space is more economical if those students practice in some type of formation. A formation is defined as a pattern made by a class. Thus, formations are devised so that students may drill on certain parts of a stroke. There are numerous formations, but they are all variations of the basic patterns shown in Chart 2:1.

CHART 2:1
BASIC FORMATIONS FOR SWIMMING PRACTICE

Description

1. *Wave formation.* The group is formed into one or more lines (counting off if necessary). One line at a time is sent to the opposite side of the pool. This is especially good for kicking, pulling, and breathing drills.

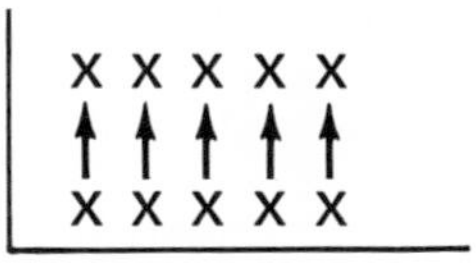

2. *Stagger formation.* The group is formed into lines, as in the wave formation, but the individual members leave from the side one at a time. This is useful when individual appraisal must be made.

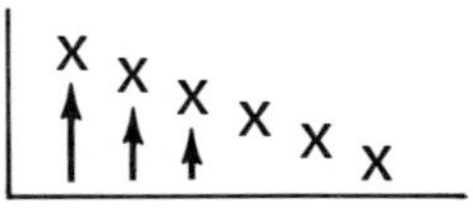

3. *Circle formation.* The group is in either a small or large circle and all are performing the same skill at the same time. This is useful when swimming lengths or for individual appraisal.

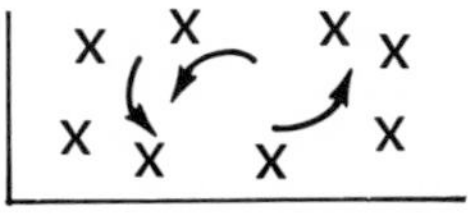

4. *Single file formation.* The individual follows the person in front of him. This is useful for individual appraisal.

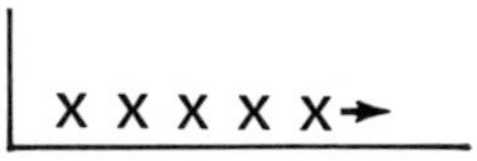

5. *Corner formation.* The group is formed into a semicircle in one corner of the pool. This is especially useful for stroking practice or when the instructor needs to demonstrate to a group.

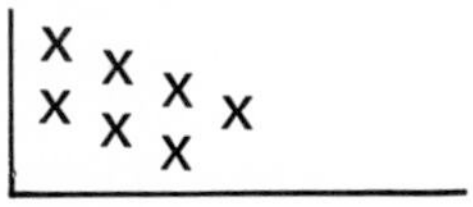

ESSENTIAL CONSIDERATIONS BEFORE TEACHING
A SWIMMING OR DIVING CLASS

Regardless of what or where you are teaching, you must know the answers to five pertinent questions when you meet the class on the first day of instruction. If you have not based your planning on the answers to these questions, problems certainly will arise later.

What Is the Age Level of the Students?

Usually, preschoolers and adults do not learn as rapidly as the students of in-between ages. Each age group possesses unique characteristics which will affect the method of teaching skills. The ARC text, *Swimming and Water Safety* (1968, Chapter 3) summarizes succinctly those important considerations concerning the different age groups. Table 2:3 is based on this source, but contains additional comments.

TABLE 2:3
GUIDELINES FOR TEACHING DIFFERENT AGE LEVELS*

Age Level	Main Comments
Preschool children	Use imitation, not explanation, as the source of learning. Water temperature should be higher than for others; activity prevents shivering! Keep lessons short; make drills gamelike and fun. Competition sometimes encourages a child who is afraid to try a new skill. Use swimmer aides; have parents help, if they will. Don't expect significant aquatic skills to develop in all the students; forewarn each parent of this possibility.
Elementary school children	Demonstration and much student activity yield greatest results. Make instruction fun. Use swimmer aides for those who are not making sufficient progress. Watch for show-offs who attempt a skill they cannot do.
Teen-agers	Beware of embarrassing a student. Allow more free time for practice (not free play). Demonstration by fellow students is sometimes more effective than demonstration by the instructor.
Adults	The primary task is to build confidence. Stress drownproofing and swimming on back. Even though they listen politely, avoid talking too much. Distributed practice is usually more successful than massed practice. Expect great variations in skill level after the third or fourth session.

*Adapted from *Swimming and Water Safety,* ARC, 1968, Chapter 3. Used by permission.

What Do You Plan To Accomplish?

What are the objectives and/or standards of the course? When teaching a Red Cross, YMCA, etc. course, the objectives and standards are given. These are clearly defined for each class and you are expected to follow them as presented. Your job is to represent the group as faithfully as possible and to make your course exactly like one offered in any other sector of the country.

Teaching in a school situation presents certain other problems. What is the purpose of the course? And what skills will be taught? The usual practice is to follow the Red Cross program, with certificates being given. Parents and students expect this and the cooperation of the local chapter makes this feasible. However, if a progressive physical education program is to be followed, then provision must be made for different levels of aquatic instruction in the same class. This is a difficult problem to solve. Using the skilled students as teacher aides is common practice, but you also have an obligation to help these students acquire new aquatic skills. At any rate, the program must be organized, and before that can be done, the objectives and standards must be considered.

What Skills Do Your Students Already Possess?

One of the first things a beginning aquatic instructor will learn is that the mere possession of a certificate (intermediate swimmer card, for example) does not mean that the person is capable of performing all the skills required to earn that card. Therefore, it is a certainty that you must have some way of evaluating your class to see exactly what skills each student possesses. Consider the following ways of assessing skill level before, or at least during, the first class period.

1. Give the final skill test that you plan to use. Obviously, any student who can satisfactorily perform the skills should not be in that class. After the test, you will know exactly how skilled each student is.
2. Select the three or four most difficult skills from the final test. If these can be done by a student, it is probable that he is in the wrong group.
3. Have each student swim a width (or less) of these strokes:
   a. Backstroke (If he cannot do so, he is probably a beginner.)
   b. Craw stroke (If he cannot do this or the backstroke, he is probably a beginner.)
   c. Breaststroke (If the kick is not correct, he is probably an intermediate. If the stroke is correct in all details, he is almost always in the advanced swimmer stage.)
4. The breaststroke is the one best single stroke to rate students. An overall rating for form could be used, awarding points on this basis:
   0-1 points—no conception of the stroke—Beginner category
   2-3 points—poor form in both arms and legs—Advanced beginner
   4-5 points—incorrect kick, but arms reasonably good—Intermediate
     6 points—form acceptable, but no power—Advanced
   7-8 points—form and power acceptable, but no glide—Advanced
   9-10 points—good form—Advanced
5. Have each student swim the basic strokes and demonstrate any other aquatic skills that you desire (such as surface dive, floating, etc.). Rate each student on a 1 (poor) to 4 (excellent) scale. Determine the maximum number of points that can be scored and place each student in the beginner, etc. category. Chart 2:2 presents one such device.

CHART 2:2
AN EXAMPLE OF A SCALE FOR RATING STUDENTS

Directions: Demonstrate the skill, then ask each student to perform it. Rate students as follows: 0 (cannot perform); 1 (poor); 2 (average); 3 (good); 4 (excellent).

NAME	Crawl				Back			Side				Drown-Proofing			Etc.*
	Arms	Kick	Breath	Coor.	Arms	Kick	Coor.	Arms	Kick	Breath	Coor.	Arms	Kick	Coor.	
Pete Salmon	4	4	3	3	2	2	1	4	4	4	4	1	1	1	
Will Dolphin	2	2	1	2	4	4	4	3	1	3	2	3	2	3	

*Strokes and skills appropriate to the level of instruction can be used, or the same rating scale can be used for all levels. The fewer points scored by a student, the less proficient he is.

How Much Time and Help Will You Have?

The overall length of all the class periods is easily known, but how much of that time will be spent in instruction? Teaching assistants will permit the class to be segregated by ability levels. Will such help be used? The answer to these questions will greatly affect the worth and organization of your program.

How Will You Test and How Much Time Can You Devote to Testing?

Chapter 11 presents a detailed discussion of evaluation devices in aquatics. If you teach for one of the national groups, its skill sheets are fairly explicit and the standards should be known to you. In a school situation, you must consider this before you finish your class organization.

CLASS ASSIGNMENTS

1. Observe a swimming teacher as he or she instructs a class.
   a. Does he or she use sound teaching progressions?
   b. Is there any evidence (not necessarily written) of a lesson plan?
   c. What type of teaching method (whole, part, etc.) is used?
   d. Does he or she seem to use massed or distributed practice?
   e. Does he or she seem to have a photographic eye?
   f. What is used more—praise or criticism? Are these more positive than negative teaching methods?
   g. What drill formations are used?

2. Talk to a swimming instructor at an elementary, junior high, or senior high school.
   a. Does he or she follow the ARC program? The YMCA? A locally developed program?
   b. How are students evaluated?
   c. What sort of objectives are there for the class?
   d. Are there student aides to help in teaching the classes?

3. Observe a swimming class at the YMCA and at a community recreation pool. What are teaching problems found here that are unique to this type of situation?

BEHAVIORAL OBJECTIVES

Quite often, the aquatic leader's course (WSI or Leader-Examiner) is taught in a situation where it is possible for students to spend more time than in the concentrated weekend or week-long aquatic school. Also, many colleges and universities have aquatic courses as part of their regular curricula. In these situations, it is expected that students will study this text more thoroughly—and quite often the instructor will test more thoroughly!

Below will be found specific objectives for Chapter 2. If desired by the instructor, these could be used as the basis of the examination on this chapter.

After study of this chapter, students should be able to complete successfully an examination that requires them to list important points, to diagram formations, and to respond correctly to questions calling for brief answers. They should be able to perform any or all of the tasks listed below:

1. . List the eight characteristics found in a competent swimming or diving teacher.

2. Discuss the value of teaching progressions to the beginning instructor and the guidelines to follow when devising progressions.

3. Discuss the value of lesson plans and the component parts of such plans.

4. Define and explain such parts of a sound teaching approach as:
   a. Whole, part, and progressive-part learning
   b. Massed and distributed practice methods
   c. Correct and sufficient practice
   d. Plateaus
   e. Mental, land, and water practice
   f. Photographic eye
   g. Introduction of new materials

5. Discuss the value of praise and positive teaching, when correcting errors.

6. List at least four ways to minimize students' fear of water.

7. Diagram any of the basic formations for swimming practice and explain the value of each.

8. List and discuss the essential considerations which instructors should heed before beginning a class.

BIBLIOGRAPHY

The American National Red Cross. *Swimming and Water Safety.* Washington: The American National Red Cross, 1968, Chapters 2 and 3.
_____. *Swimming and Water Safety Courses – Instructor's Manual.* Washington: The American National Red Cross, 1968.
Brown, Richard L. *Teaching Progressions for the Swimming Instructor.* New York: A. S. Barnes and Co., 1948.
Clayton, Robert D., "The Efficacy of the Land-Drill, Implicit Rehearsal, and Water-Practice Methods in Teaching the Breast Stroke and Crawl Stroke to College Men," Microcarded Ed. D. Dissertation, University of Oregon, 1963.
Singer, Robert N. *Motor Learning and Human Performance.* New York: The MacMillan Co., 1968, Chapters 6 and 7.

CHAPTER 3

Performing and Teaching the Essential Aquatic Skills

The goal of all aquatic teachers is to make each student safe in the water. A "safe" swimmer is one who has these characteristics: the ability to stay afloat for at least five minutes; the ability to enter the water either head- or feetfirst; and finally, the ability to safely help himself or others when trouble arises. If a swimmer can meet these requirements, the teacher can be fairly confident that almost any aquatic activity can be enjoyed with a reasonable degree of safety.

To reach the goal of safety in the water, a certain number of skills need to be taught. The American National Red Cross, the YMCA, and similar groups have established definite skills for their beginning courses. This chapter will present those major skills which are required for the beginning courses of the national aquatic groups, plus one other skill deemed essential. A school program of beginning swimming should include these skills. Unless each student can perform all of these skills to the standard indicated he is not ready to pass from the beginner stage.

WHAT ARE THE ESSENTIAL AQUATIC SKILLS?

The skills shown in Table 3:1 represent standards (or objectives) for a beginner course in swimming. Even though these standards are somewhat different for the various age groups, we recommend that these skills be given to all swimming classes. For beginners, the standards would serve as a final examination; for all other classes, the items would serve as a screening device.

FLOATS AND GLIDES

Floating is defined as a means of staying at or near the surface of the water with a minimum amount of effort for an indefinite period of time. Because a greater proportion of their weight is made up of nonfloating substances (muscle and bone), almost all males are poorer floaters than females. Even

14

TABLE 3:1
STANDARDS FOR BEGINNING SWIMMERS

Skills	Ages of Beginners		
	5-10	11-16	17+
1. Vertical floating (face-up—motionless or nearly so)	30 seconds	1 minute	1 minute
2. Rhythmic breathing and bobbing	1 minute (6 feet of water)	1 minute (7 feet of water)	1 minute (8 feet of water)
3. Kicking (flutter, scissors, breaststroke)	30 feet each	45 feet each	60 feet each
4. Drownproofing	2 minutes	5 minutes	7 minutes
5. Treading water (using hands and feet)	30 seconds	1 minute	1 minute
6. Front crawl stroke	30 feet	45 feet	60-75 feet
7. Stroke on back (finning, elementary backstroke, or crawl)	30 feet	60 feet	60-75 feet
8. Water entry and swim (any stroke)	Standing or running entry, swim 30 feet	Standing or running entry, swim 30 feet	Standing or running entry, swim 30 feet
9. Use of life jacket	Demonstrate	Demonstrate	Demonstrate
10. Release of cramps (calf and arch)	Demonstrate	Demonstrate	Demonstrate
11. Mouth-to-mouth resuscitation	Explain	Explain	Explain
12. Reaching Assists	Demonstrate	Demonstrate	Demonstrate

though only about 2% of male Caucasians and 30% of male Negroes, are thought to be absolute nonfloaters (Lanoue, 1963, p. 105), the majority of males consider themselves nonfloaters because they cannot keep their feet at the surface while lying on their backs. Our definition makes no mention of where the legs must be; common sense indicates that the position of the head is more important than that of the feet. If the head stays at or near the surface, with no more than an intermittent arm press or kick, for at least 10 seconds, the body is floating.

The ability to float is insurance that in case of fatigue or an aquatic accident the swimmer can remain at or close to the surface while gathering strength and his wits—both of which are essential to survival. Therefore, beginning swimmers should be able to float because of the confidence they gain when they realize that they do not have to strain constantly to remain afloat.

Performing the Tuck Float

Exactly what floating skills to teach is an unsettled question among instructors. Traditionally, the tuck, the prone, and the supine floats are all taught—but as a means to an end. The tuck float is generally taught first, because the instructor can quickly know which students can float. Furthermore, this position is the one taken when regaining the feet after the prone glide and also assumed when removing clothing in the water. Chart 3:1 shows the tuck float—the floating position and the method of regaining the feet.

CHART 3:1
PERFORMANCE TECHNIQUES FOR THE TUCK FLOAT

Techniques	Illustration	Major and/or Common Performance Errors
A. Begin with shoulders in water and large amount of air in lungs; place face in water, look downward.	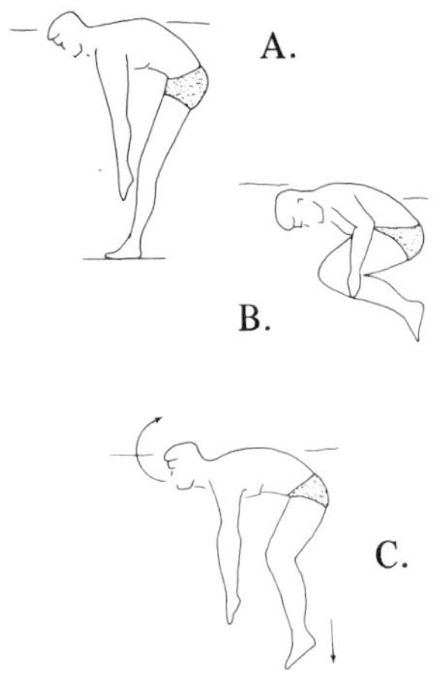 A.	A. Failing to submerge face. Failing to look downward.
B. Tuck chin close to chest; wrap arms around tucked legs. Float in this position.	B.	B. Failing to pull knees up to chest (instead, shoulders forced down). Failing to hold floating position long enough (3-6 seconds for beginners).
C. To regain feet, raise head as the feet are lowered.	C.	C. Raising head before feet are lowered.

Teaching the Tuck Float

Other than having the group where the instructor can see everyone, there is no special teaching technique for the tuck float. Doing this with a partner standing by, in case of trouble, is a desirable method of instilling confidence in beginners.

Performing the Prone Float

The prone (or stomach-down) float is usually taught after the tuck float. This is a necessary skill because it is the basic position for the front crawl stroke, the breaststroke, and the trudgen strokes. Chart 3:2 depicts this float.

CHART 3:2
PERFORMANCE TECHNIQUE FOR THE PRONE (FACE-DOWN) FLOAT

Techniques	Illustration	Major and/or Common Performance Errors
A. Begin with tuck float.	 A.	A. Failing to submerge face. Failing to look downward. Failing to pull knees up to chest.

16

B. Extend arms and legs in opposite directions.
　Float in this position.

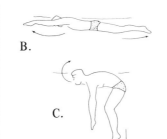

B.

C.

B. Failing to keep face submerged.
　Failing to keep ears between extended arms.
　Failing to float long enough (3-6 seconds).

C. To regain feet, resume tuck float first and then stand.

C. Failing to bend hips and knees before attempting to stand.

Teaching the Prone Float

The teaching progression for the prone float is ordinarily based upon learning the tuck float first and then extending the arms and legs as described above. However, some instructors find that the progression shown in Chart 3:3 is useful, especially with students who do not seem to perform the tuck float with ease.

**CHART 3:3
TEACHING PROGRESSION FOR THE PRONE FLOAT (SHALLOW WATER)**

Step 1	Step 2	Step 3
Have partner face student grasping his hands; student faces shallow water.	Have student take breath, place face well into the water.	Have student lift feet off bottom; partner retains grip.

Step 4	Step 5	Step 6
Have partner help student regain feet.	After student is at ease in Step 3, have partner release grip. Student assumes standing position without help.	Have partner observe, but not touch, student floating in prone position.

Performing the Supine (Face-up) Float

The supine, or face-up, float must be taught before any type of back stroke can be attempted. Chart 3:4 presents the techniques, illustrations, and major and/or common performance errors of this float.

CHART 3:4
PERFORMANCE TECHNIQUES FOR THE SUPINE (FACE-UP) FLOAT

Techniques	Illustration	Major and/or Common Performance Errors
A. Begin with arms at sides, legs bent enough so that shoulders are in water. Place back of head in water, lean backward and push gently with feet to place body in horizontal back-down position.	A.	A. Failing to submerge shoulders. Keeping entire head out of water. Throwing body backward with vigor.
B. Float on back with ears in water, face up, arms at sides, feet well off bottom.	B.	B. Raising head or hands above the surface. Failing to look upward at sky or ceiling.
C. Slowly move arms sideward and then beyond head, causing feet to rise toward (but not to) surface. Float in this position.	C.	C. Moving arms too quickly. Expelling air in lungs. Overarching the body. Letting hips bend and sink.
D. To regain feet, return arms to body sides and lift face out of water as knees are bent. Swing feet under knees and toward hips. Arms may be pressed downward and backward if desired.	D.	D. Raising arms above water surface. Attempting to stand while body is straight. Moving vigorously.
E. When feet are under hips, raise head and come to standing position.	E.	E. Attempting to stand before feet are under hips. Raising head before feet are under hips.

Teaching the Supine Float

Chart 3:5 depicts and describes the teaching progression that may be used in the supine float. As with the prone float, this progression is designed to utilize a partner until the student gains confidence.

CHART 3:5
TEACHING PROGRESSION FOR SUPINE (FACE–UP)FLOAT

Step 1

Have partner stand behind student, both facing deep water. Partner supports back of student's head as it is placed in water. Student looks at sky or ceiling.

Step 2

Have student *gently* push off bottom, arms at side. Partner retains support. Partner helps student regain feet.

Step 3

Have student slowly move arms sideward and forward (next to ears); arms stay in water at all times; partner retains support.

Step 4

After floating position is reached, have partner withdraw support but remain available for help.

Step 5

Have student move arms back to side and regain feet by putting feet under buttocks and face toward stomach. Partner helps by lifting student's upper back.

Step 6

Have partner observe, but not touch, student floating in supine position and then regaining feet.

Performing the Vertical Floats

Two methods of vertical floating—face-down and face-up—are shown in Chart 3:6. Women and most children can usually perform either one with equal ease, but men who are not good floaters find the face-down method better. The face-down float ("dead man's" float) is not what most people consider to be a desirable skill; however, it is the essential lead-up position for drownproofing.

CHART 3:6
PERFORMANCE TECHNIQUES FOR THE VERTICAL FLOATS

Techniques	Illustration	Major and/or Common Performance Errors
FACE DOWN A. Following a deep breath, extend arms forward (as in prone float); tuck chin. Float in this position 5-10 seconds.	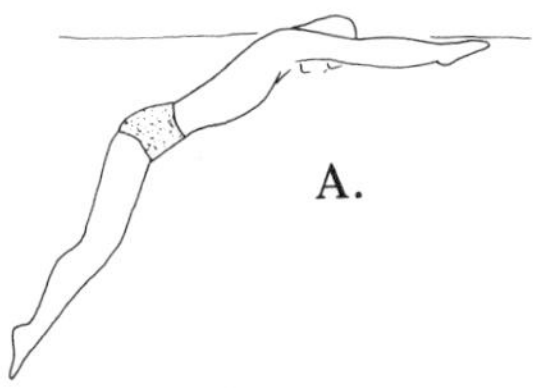 A.	A. Failing to submerge face. Holding float position too briefly. Exhaling breath.
FACE UP B. Extend legs with feet below hips, extend arms sideward, take and hold a deep breath, press chest upward, place back of head in water, and look upward.	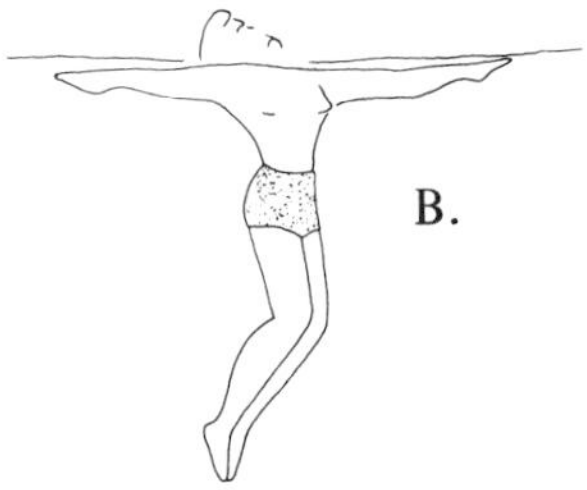 B.	B. Failing to arch back, press hips forward and place back of head in water. Failing to place feet under hips. Failing to assume floating position slowly and gently.
C. Hold breath for 3-5 seconds, exhale one-half of air in lungs and quickly inhale a like amount. On succeeding trials, lengthen to 10-15 seconds the time the breath is held.	C. See B above.	C. Breathing out slowly. Breathing out more than one-half of air in lungs. Failing to breathe in immediately after breathing out.

20

Teaching the Vertical Floats

The vertical floats may be taught in shoulder-deep water, using a partner to provide support if needed. However, we recommend that these be taught in deep water if possible, using the progression shown in Chart 3:7.

CHART 3:7
TEACHING PROGRESSION FOR VERTICAL FLOATING (DEEP WATER)

FACE-DOWN FLOAT

Step 1	Step 2	Step 3

Have partners on either side of student. Student puts hands on trough, feet underneath. Arms are wide, with chest next to wall.	Have student take breath, put face in water. Partners support (not lift) student by placing near hand under his shoulder. Student removes his hands from trough and floats.	Have partners observe the floater; help only if needed.

FACE-UP FLOAT

Step 1	Step 2	Step 3
	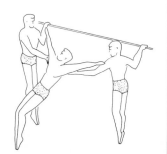	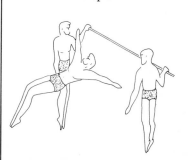
Have two partners on either side of student. Student has back to wall, arms outstretched grasping deck, feet underneath (not out).	Have student take breath, look at sky or ceiling, remove hands from wall; partners support student with near hand under shoulder. Student holds breath, then exhales and inhales quickly.	Have partners observe the floater; help only if needed.

Performing and Teaching the Glides

A glide is merely a float with motion. Because the forward movement aids the student in floating, the glides are considerably easier for some students. For this reason, certain instructors teach the glides before the floats. Charts 3:8 and 3:9 describe and illustrate the teaching progressions for the prone and supine glides.

CHART 3:8
TEACHING PROGRESSION FOR THE PRONE (FACE-DOWN) GLIDE

Step 1	Step 2	Step 3
Have student face shallow water. Partner grasps hands of student, who leans forward, takes breath, and puts face in water.	Have partner walk backward; student "stretches" out.	Have student regain feet by bringing knees underneath, raising head and pressing down with arms; partner provides support.

Step 4	Steps 5 and 6
Have student *gently* push off wall as shown (or off bottom by leaning forward and pushing), and glide to partner who is 6-10 feet away.	Have partner back up 3-5 feet each time student adds length to glide. Partner aids student in regaining feet. Have student perform glide; partner ready to assist if needed.

CHART 3:9
TEACHING PROGRESSION FOR THE SUPINE (Face-up) GLIDE

Step 1	Step 2	Step 3
Have student grasp wall as shown, back of head in water. Partner supports head. (If no wall, bend knees so shoulders are in water.)	Have student gently press with feet, stretch out with arms at sides; partner walks backward, supporting head. Student must look at sky or ceiling.	Have student regain feet as in supine float; partner assists.

Step 4	Steps 5 and 6
Have student push off wall and glide to partner who is 6-10 feet away. Partner helps student regain feet if necessary.	Have partner back up 3-5 feet each time student adds length to glide. Have student perform glide; partner ready to assist if needed.

RHYTHMIC BREATHING AND BOBBING

While the term "rhythmic breathing" is self-explanatory, it is frequently associated with "bobbing." Bobbing is a method of alternately rising above and sinking below the surface. Since it is virtually impossible to bob more than four or five times without breathing, these two skills are frequently combined into one drill.

Rhythmic breathing is extremely important because proper and efficient form in several strokes requires that the face be in the water most of the time.

Performing Bobbing

Chart 3:10 illustrates the techniques for bobbing, both in shallow water and in deep water. Rhythmic breathing is obviously a part of this skill.

PERFORMANCE TECHNIQUES FOR BOBBING

Techniques	Illustration	Major and/or Common Performance Errors
SHALLOW WATER A. Take a breath; sink below surface by bending knees and raising arms overhead. B. Extend legs to push off bottom. C. As face emerges above the surface, lower the arms, exhale and inhale. D. Repeat Steps A, B, and C rhythmically and in sequence.		A. Failing to submerge completely. B. Leaning too far forward or too far backward from vertical. C. Exhaling before emerging above surface. D. Pausing for longer than 2 or 3 seconds between submersions.
DEEP WATER E. After taking a breath, descend to bottom by extending arms overhead (very buoyant persons may have to expel some air). Variations include: 1. Using a sculling action with the hands overhead (a continual upward-pushing motion with the palms). 2. Using a reverse pull (lowering the arms to the thighs and then pulling sideward and upward with palms facing upward). F. Push off bottom and pull arms down to thighs. (If a lake bottom is soft mud, it probably is better to omit push-off). G. To move forward, incline body slightly forward when pushing off bottom. H. Emerge at surface. Exhale and inhale. Thrust arms overhead. I. Repeat Steps E, F, G, and H rhythmically and in sequence.		E. Bending at hips or knees. Extending the feet backward or forward from vertical. 1. Failing to push upward with palms. 2. Thrusting the arms upward instead of exerting a pull upward. F. Failing to pull arms through to thighs. Failing to execute a vigorous pull. Failing to execute a vigorous push-off. G. Inclining body forward too much. H. Exhaling before reaching surface. Failing to rise high out of water on emerging. I. Failing to perform actions in sequence.

Teaching Bobbing and Rhythmic Breathing

Both of these skills are taught together, for obvious reasons. Before beginning, it is wise to remind swimmers that water will not go up the nose if a "trickle" of air is allowed to escape while the body is submerging. Nose clips are acceptable, but we recommend that a swimmer first try to keep water out of his nose by the method described above or even by holding his nose.

To practice bobbing, have the students stand in chest-deep water, face the instructor, and then bob up and down in the same place. When most have mastered this, a single file of students can cross the pool (or a given distance), again in chest-deep water.

Bobbing in deep water is more difficult to master, hence our recommendation of distributed practice sessions. The students should try, one at a time, to go as far into deep water as they can. They should go close to the side of the pool or dock (Chart 3:11A). If instruction is taking place in open water, a line of advanced swimmers may be placed along the intended route (3:11B). These "lifeguards" tread water, and only move if needed. Whether in a lake or in a pool, traveling from the shallow to the deep water is easier for most beginners. They should have some experience in starting in the deep water, however.

CHART 3:11
TEACHING BOBBING IN DEEP WATER

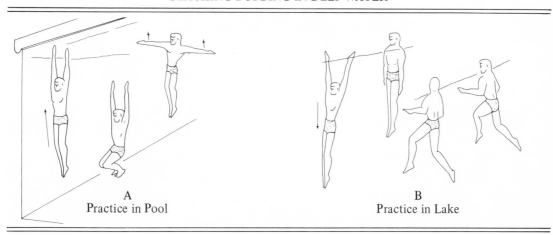

A
Practice in Pool

B
Practice in Lake

Rhythmic breathing should also be practiced while standing in waist-deep water because it relates directly to the breathing action for the various strokes. Chart 3:12A shows a swimmer with one ear in the water and the face to the side. After inhaling, the face is rolled so that it goes under water where exhalation takes place (3:12B). The head is rolled back to the original position (3:12A). A useful drill for the breaststroke and butterfly stroke is to bring the face forward until the chin is out of the water (3:12C) and then lower it while the arm movement continues.

CHART 3:12
BREATHING DRILLS

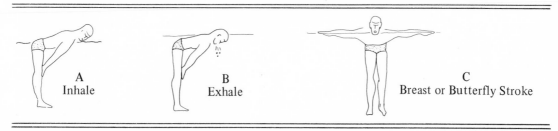

A
Inhale

B
Exhale

C
Breast or Butterfly Stroke

KICKING

Kicking may be defined as propelling the body through the water by means of some movement of the legs. Even though many beginners seldom use their legs, their importance is soon realized as the novice learns that some strokes depend upon the legs for their primary source of power. Many instructors spend more time in the beginner course on kicking than they do on any other single phase. Because the flutter kick is less efficient, these instructors devote most of their efforts to the scissors and breaststroke kicks.

Performing the Flutter Kick

The flutter kick on the stomach begins by pointing the toes. If the toes are not pointed, the kick will be too weak to be effective. (As a matter of fact, it is possible to move backward if the toes are hooked enough!)

CHART 3:13
PERFORMANCE TECHNIQUES FOR THE FLUTTER KICK

Techniques	Illustration	Major and/or Common Performance Errors
STOMACH (PRONE) POSITION A. Extend legs, point toes. 　Move feet alternately up and down 12-15 inches. 　Have slight bend at knees, bring heels to surface, limit the amount of splash. 　Emphasize "down" beat and kicking from hips.	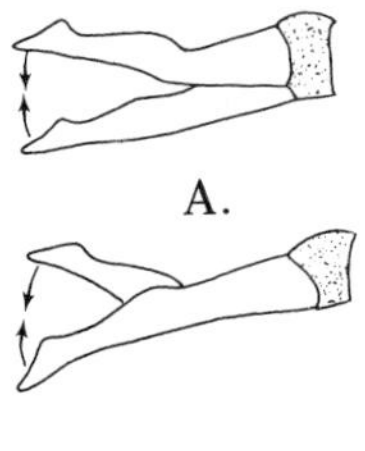 A.	A. Bending too much at knees (causing bicycle-riding movement). 　Causing too much splash. 　Bending too little at knees. 　Using a kick that is too narrow and tense. 　Failing to point toes.
BACK (SUPINE) POSITION B. Extend legs, point toes. 　Move feet alternately up and down 12-15 inches. 　Have slight bend at knees, limit the amount of splash. 　Emphasize "up" beat and kicking from hips.	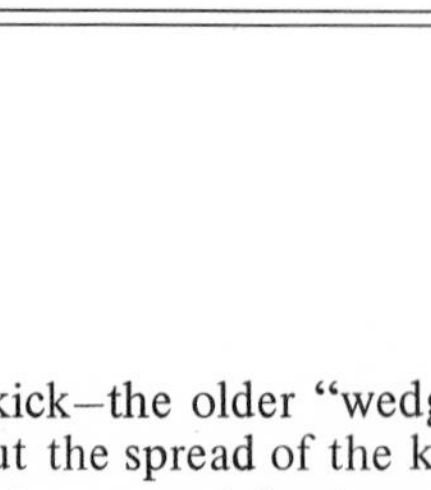 B.	B. Bending too much at knees (causing knees to be above surface). 　Having feet too low in the water. 　Using a kick that is too narrow. 　Failing to point toes.

Performing the Breaststroke Kicks

There are two types of breaststroke kick—the older "wedge" kick and the competitive "whip" kick. Both kicks begin and finish the same, but the spread of the knees during the kick is different. The whip kick is now considered to be the first choice to teach beginners. Chart 3:14 depicts these kicks, either of which can be used on the back (i.e., inverted).

CHART 3:14
PERFORMANCE TECHNIQUES FOR THE BREASTSTROKE KICKS

Techniques	Illustration	Major and/or Common Performance Errors

WEDGE
 	
A. Extend legs and point toes backward.
 	
B. Move knees sideward, bring heels toward buttocks (heels are almost touching toes, point outward).
 	
C. Move heels to outside, partially straighten legs, point toes outward.
 	
    Actions in steps A, B, and C should be gentle, drifting actions.
 	
D. Press legs backward and squeeze together.
    Point toes backward at end of the press.
 	
E. Glide for 3-6 seconds with legs extended and toes pointed.
	A.
	
	 B.
	
	 C.
	
	 D.
	
	 E.
		A. Bending the knees.
		    Failing to point toes.
		
		B. Pointing the toes of one foot inward (causing scissors kick).
		    Lowering knees toward bottom instead of outward.
		
		C. Continuing to point toes backward.
		
		    Recovering the legs too quickly and too vigorously.
		
		D. Applying too little effort during the press.
		    Underemphasizing the press and overemphasizing the squeeze.
		    Pointing toes backward during press.
		
		E. Failing to glide.

WHIP
 	
F. Keep knees close together as they are lowered downward.
 	
G. Move heels outward, keep knees close together.
    Partially straighten legs, point toes outward.
 	
    Movements in F and G should be gentle.
 	
H. Press legs backward and squeeze together.
 	
I. Glide for 3-6 seconds with legs extended and toes pointed.
	F.
	
	 G.
	
	 H.
	
	 I.
		F. Bringing knees forward and under stomach.
		
		G. Drifting knees apart.
		    Pointing toes backward.
		
		    Recovering the legs too quickly and too vigorously.
		
		H. Applying too little effort to backward press and squeeze.
		
		I. Beginning next kick without pause for glide.

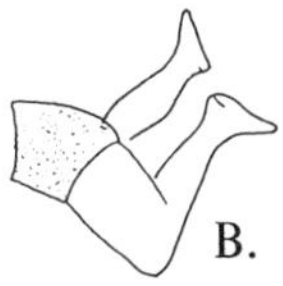

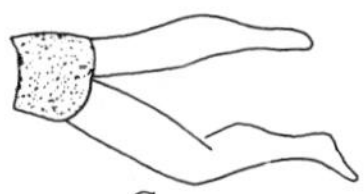

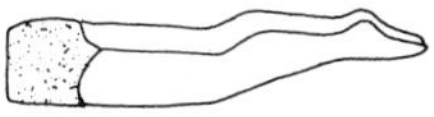

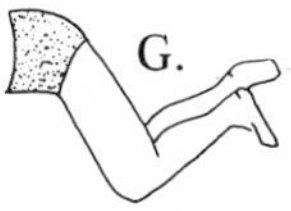

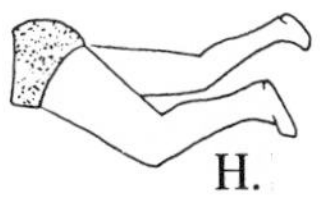

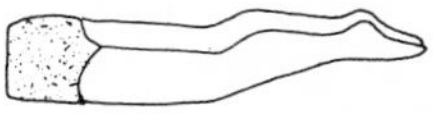

27

INVERTED KICK (WEDGE)

J. Spread knees 15-18 inches.
  Lower heels downward, keeping knees just below surface.

K. Extend lower legs by moving feet outward.
  Point toes outward.

L. Straighten legs as they are pressed backward and squeezed together.
  Point toes back by end of press.

M. Glide for 3-6 seconds.

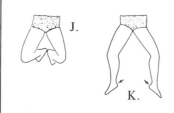
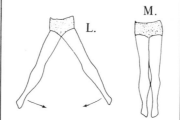

J. Bringing knees above surface.

K. Extending legs by lowering thighs.
  Pointing toes upward.

L. Expending too little effort on press or squeeze.
  Pointing toes backward.

M. Recovering legs for next kick without pause for glide.

INVERTED KICK (WHIP)

N. Drop heels toward bottom, keeping knees just below surface.
  Keep knees together (toes pointed outward).

O. Extend legs by bringing feet diagonally outward and toward surface (toes remain pointed outward).

P. Straighten legs as they are pressed back and squeezed together.
  Point toes back by end of press.

Q. Glide for 3-6 seconds.

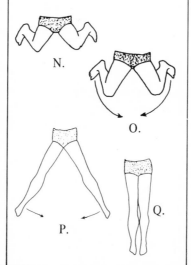

N. Failing to keep thighs at surface.
  Pointing toes backward.

O. Lowering thighs as legs are extended.

P. Applying too little effort to press or squeeze.

Q. Failing to glide.

Description of the Scissors Kick

The scissors kicks, used in the sidestroke and in lifesaving, are shown in Chart 3:15

CHART 3:15
PERFORMANCE TECHNIQUES FOR THE SCISSORS KICKS

Techniques	Illustration	Major and/or Common Performance Errors
REGULAR A. Rest the upper leg directly upon the lower, with both legs extended and toes pointed.	A.	A. Bending at the knees and ankles (body position is not streamlined).

B. Bend the legs at the knees and bring the heels up to just behind the buttocks.

C. Move the legs into a striding position, the upper leg forward.
  Make leg actions parallel to surface.
  Point toes of upper leg outward in front of body, toes of lower leg to rear of body.
  Movements in A, B, and C should be gentle.

D. Straighten legs as they are squeezed rearward and together.
  Point toes during squeeze.
  Stop the squeeze when legs are together.

E. Assume a stretched, streamlined position.
  Glide for 3-6 seconds.

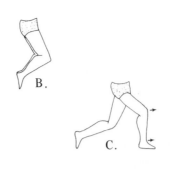
B.

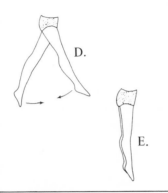
C.

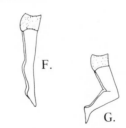
D.

E.

B. Bringing the knees too far in front (near stomach).
  Failing to bend knees.

C. Extending lower leg forward.
  Lowering the under leg toward bottom.

  Making actions too quick and vigorous.

D. Using a breaststroke kick.
  Failing to straighten legs before the squeeze.
  Expending too little effort.
  Squeezing legs past each other (as in flutter kick).

E. Failing to glide.

INVERTED ^

F. Rest the upper leg directly upon the lower, with both legs extended and toes pointed.

G. Bend the legs at the knees and bring the heels up to just behind the buttocks.

H. Move the legs into a striding position, with the *lower* leg *forward* and the *upper* leg *backward*.
  Make leg actions parallel to surface.
  Movements in F, G, and H should be gentle.

I. Straighten legs as they are squeezed rearward and together.
  Point toes during squeeze.
  Stop the squeeze when legs are together.

J. Assume a stretched, streamlined position.
  Glide for 3-6 seconds.

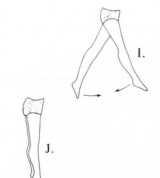
F.
G.
H.
I.
J.

F. Bending at the knees and ankles (body position is not streamlined).

G. Bringing the knees too far in front (near stomach).
  Failing to bend knees.

H. Extending upper leg forward.
  Lowering the under leg toward bottom.
  Making actions too quick and vigorous.

I. Using a breaststroke kick.
  Failing to straighten legs before the squeeze.
  Expending too little effort.
  Squeezing legs past each other (as in flutter kick).

J. Failing to glide.

Teaching the Kicks

The usual pattern of teaching any kick is to start with the student hanging on to the trough and wall (Chart 3:16A) or bracing himself in shallow water (3:16B).

Practicing the scissors kick requires a different method of grasping the wall (3:16C). The instructor moves back and forth on the deck, observing everyone's kick. Occasionally, it is desirable for the instructor to enter the water, grasp the ankles of a student, and control the leg movement himself. Make corrections to the entire group after they have kicked a while and need a rest, but individual corrections can be made while the other students are still kicking. The use of the prone or back glide (with or without a kickboard) is usually recommended by veteran instructors. Some instructors, however, do not advocate use of kickboards for beginners, saying that the form of the kick is more important than the distance covered. The matter is debatable. If a kickboard is used, Chart 3:16D shows how to hold it without destroying the desired position of the body in the water.

CHART 3:16
POSITIONS FOR KICKING PRACTICE

DROWNPROOFING

Drownproofing, developed by Fred Lanoue, is a technique of staying afloat and/or moving in the water. It has become world-famous because "...it guarantees that (unless you are: 1) held or pinned underwater; 2) dazed or unconscious in the water; 3) so badly cramped or injured you are useless in the water; or, 4) faced with an impossible problem in thickness of foam, rate of heat loss, etc.) you will survive any water accident regardless of age, sex, or condition." (Lanoue, 1963, p. 13).

This is quite a claim, but in the opinion of the writers, it is entirely justified. No technique yet devised "drownproofs" people as well as Lanoue's method. The importance of drownproofing is so obvious that it need not be dwelled on; we feel that everyone who enters the water, from beginner to certified aquatic worker, should master this technique. The YMCA evidently agrees, because this statement is printed on all its aquatic skill sheets. "At this, and at every, grade level, instruct and review: drownproofing techniques and mouth-to-mouth resuscitation." (YMCA Skill Sheets, Revised, 1966). Every national aquatic group now includes drownproofing in its teaching program; unfortunately, most of the current instructors have not even tried the technique, much less mastered the teaching procedures.

Performing Drownproofing

The following drownproofing technique (Chart 3:17) is suitable for use by almost all women and young children, and by those men who are naturally good floaters.

PERFORMANCE TECHNIQUES FOR DROWNPROOFING (WOMEN AND YOUNG CHILDREN)

Techniques*	Illustration*	Major and/or Common Performance Errors
A. *Rest:* vertical floating position, arms and legs dangling, face in water. Hold an ordinary amount of air in the lungs.		A. Raising face out of water.
B. *Get ready:* Slowly raise the arms so that they are at the surface. *Position* the legs for a scissors kick.		B. Raising arms too fast. Failing to move legs into position for delivery of a scissors kick.
C. *Exhale and rise:* Press the hands down toward bottom; at same time, exhale through nose.		C. Failing to exhale. Pushing hands and arms backward rather than downward.
D. *Stay at surface:* Inhale as soon as chin is at surface. Continue to press arms and legs downward.		D. Trying to rise too far out of water.
E. *Rest:* Place face in the water. Remain motionless as body settles underwater and then regains floating position.		E. Failing to lower the face into the water. Moving before the body regains floating position.

*Adapted from Lanoue, *Drownproofing* (Prentice-Hall, 1963). pp. 15-18. Used by permission.

Most men are not sinkers, but yet do not float as well as women. The techniques described and illustrated in Chart 3:18 are designed for them.

PERFORMANCE TECHNIQUES FOR DROWNPROOFING (BUOYANT MEN)

Techniques*	Illustration*	Major and/or Common Performance Errors
A. *Rest:* With lungs full of air, assume position with head forward and face in water, arms and legs dangling, floating with back of head at surface.	A.	A. Raising or holding the face out of water.
B. *Get ready to breathe:* Raise the forearms leisurely to surface in front of head. Place forearms parallel to each other. Prepare to scissors kick.	B.	B. Raising the forearms too vigorously. Failing to place arms and/or legs into correct position.
C. *Exhale:* Without moving the arms or legs from their position, raise the head so the chin just nears the water's surface. As head is raised, exhale through the nose. Finish exhaling just as the chin reaches the surface.	C.	C. Failing to exhale. Moving the hands and/or legs.
D. *Inhale:* The instant the chin clears the surface, begin the inhalation through the mouth. Kick with the feet and sweep out with palms of hands until the arms are extended sideward. The inhalation should be finished just as the arms are extended sideward and the kick is finished.	D.	D. Treading water (to take 2-3 breaths). Pressing arms toward bottom. Inhaling through the nose. Kicking and moving arms too vigorously, thus causing body to rise too high in the water.
E. *Stay at surface:* As inhalation is finished, body will sink. As head settles below the surface, force arms downward (legs may be kicked). Place face in water.	E.	E. Failing to lower the face into the water.

*Adapted from Lanoue. *Drownproofing* (Prentice-Hall, 1963). pp. 24-29. Used by permission.

Finally, Lanoue has adapted his technique for the people who need it most, the nonfloaters. The basic difference is that there is no resting phase for nonfloaters. They must continually be moving forward, sinking, or coming back to the surface.

PERFORMANCE TECHNIQUES FOR DROWNPROOFING (NONFLOATERS)

Techniques*	Illustration*	Major and/or Common Performance Errors
A. *Get to the top:* As soon as the head settles underwater, lower the face into the water, bend the elbows and hold arms close to chest. Ready the feet for a scissors kick. Deliver the kick to propel the body toward the surface.		A. Failing to lower the face into the water. Failing to deliver the kick.
B. As soon as the kick is completed, sweep the arms slowly but forcefully backward until they reach the sides. Sweep the arms slightly downward to push the body to the surface while traveling 3-5 feet forward.		B. Failing to travel (concentrating on up and down movement instead).
C. *Get ready to inhale:* Allow legs to settle as forward momentum is lost. Place legs into scissors kick position as arms are gently recovered toward surface.		C. Failing to let legs settle before moving them into position for delivery of scissors kick. Moving arms to surface too quickly and vigorously.
D. *Exhale:* Deliver scissors kick as arms are pressed downward and air is exhaled. Expel air just as chin reaches water surface.		D. Exhaling before the chin reaches the surface.
E. *Inhale and sink:* Press with palms as arms move outward. Allow body to settle after breath is taken and face is placed in water.		E. Raising the mouth too far above the surface of the water. Failing to lower the face into the water.

*Adapted from Lanoue, *Drownproofing* (Prentice-Hall, 1963), pp. 29-32. Used by permission.

Teaching Drownproofing

This involves basically the same steps as outlined previously for floating. Lanoue (1963, pp. 74-77) advocates that this be done in deep water, but we prefer to begin in shoulder-deep water. Chart 3:20 discusses and illustrates our technique.

CHART 3:20
TEACHING PROGRESSION FOR DROWNPROOFING

Step 1	Step 2	Step 3
Have students stand in shoulder-deep water, facing shallow end. Practice coordination of arm press-exhalation-head lift-inhalation-head drop.	Have students travel across pool in shoulder-deep water. (Identify those who are poor floaters; they will need more help than others.)	Have students enter deep water, with partner on each side. Student faces wall and practices. Add kick where needed. Partners keep student close to wall. (If in lake, use advanced swimmers as guards.)

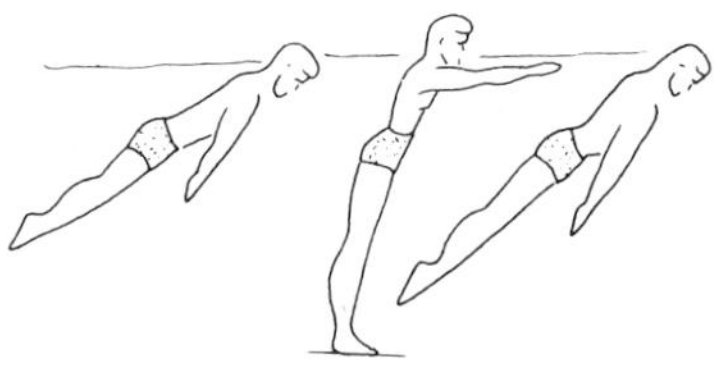

Step 4	Step 5	
		NOTES: Practice Step 1 during the first two or three sessions. Set goals (30 consecutive, successful breaths, for example). Add Step 2. When virtually everyone can do Step 2, go to deep water for remainder of steps.
Have students go across pool staying next to edge. Then go length of pool, again next to edge.	Have students drownproof in one place for a period of time.	

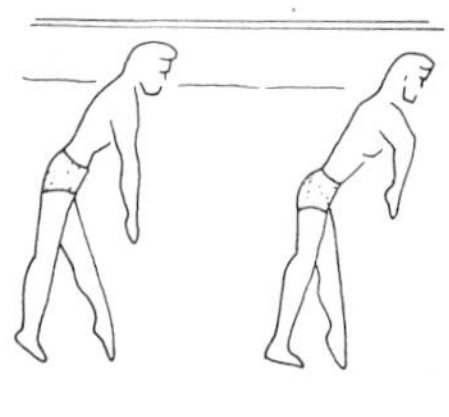

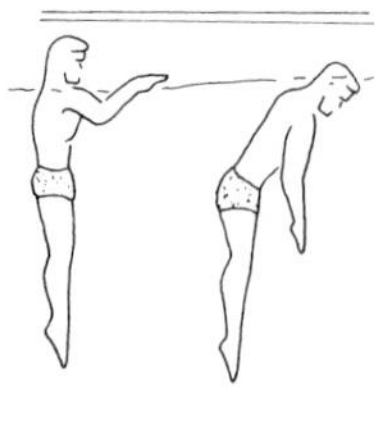

TREADING WATER

Treading water is a way of remaining at the surface of the water while the head is out of the water. Its importance is readily apparent the first time a swimmer needs to orient himself or has to take three or four breaths while clearing his air passage of extra water.

Treading Water

Chart 3:21 describes and depicts the skills involved in treading water.

CHART 3:21
PERFORMANCE TECHNIQUES FOR TREADING WATER

Techniques	Illustration	Major and/or Common Performance Errors
ARM MOVEMENTS A. With palms facing downward and with elbows bent so that hands are 12 inches in front of chest, tilt thumb down, move hand sideward (as in spreading butter on piece of bread). B. After hands have moved about 24 inches outward, reverse the tilt; return hands to original position.	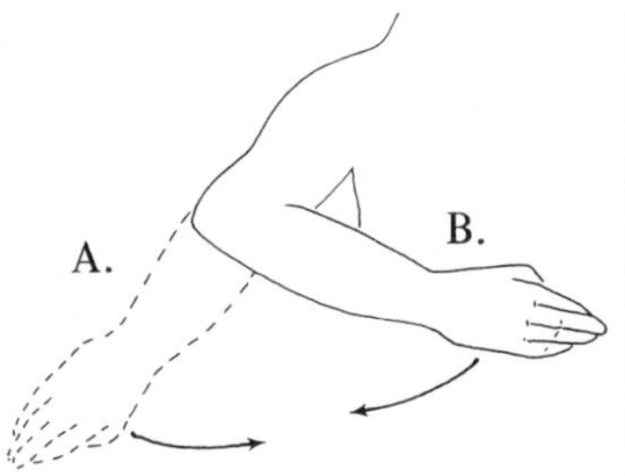	A. Failing to tilt hands. Facing palms more upward than downward. B. Failing to reverse tilt of hands.

LEG MOVEMENTS
 	
C. Use any of these kicks:
 	
    1. Wide, slow flutter
 	
    2. Scissors
 	
    3. Breaststroke
	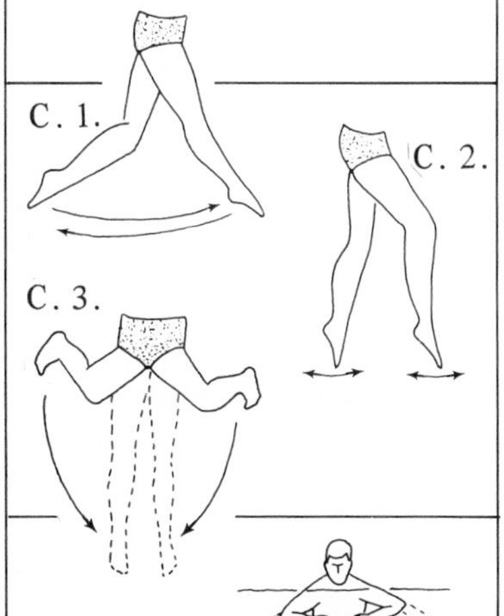	C.
		
		    1. Making the kick too fast or too narrow.
		    2. Kicking too hard or too fast and causing expenditure of too much effort.
		    3. Kicking too hard, causing body to surge out of water and sink down.

COORDINATION
 	
D. Move arms and legs simultaneously.
    Keep head erect.
    Retain one-half of air in lungs or more.
    Make movements as slow as possible without losing effectiveness.
	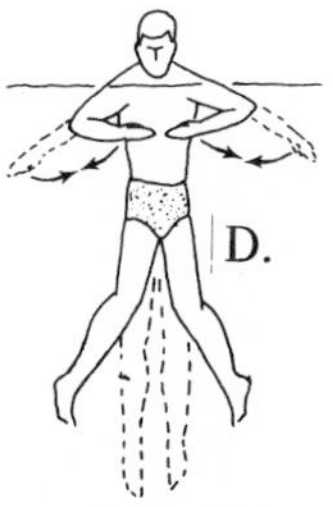	D. Allowing the body position to deviate from vertical.
		    Failing to hold air in the lungs.

Teaching the Treading of Water

Treading water is taught in the same fashion as described for vertical floating or drownproofing. Practice in shoulder-deep water, first by standing on the bottom and then with knees bent. This will enable students to master the arm movements. In deep water, hanging on the wall while practicing *all* the kicks (to see which one is preferred) will prove beneficial. Finally, the student attempts to tread while facing the wall and his partner.

SWIMMING ON THE STOMACH

Swimming on the stomach is best described as a simultaneous kicking of the legs with some form of arm pull. Its importance lies in the fact that virtually everyone wants to learn to swim on the stomach; it is considered the "only" way to swim! Additional and more practical values are that it permits the swimmer to see where he is going and to avoid being surprised by waves when trying to breathe.

Whether to teach the human stroke (one arm pull to one flutter kick) or the dog paddle (one arm pull to three flutter kicks) depends, for the most part, on the age of the learner. Many youngsters find the crawl stroke breathing difficult to combine with the over-water recovery of the arms; these students will learn the dog paddle readily. Ordinarily, teen-agers and adults dislike to be taught the dog paddle but will respond to instruction in crawl stroke or elementary backstroke. We are, therefore, unwilling to recommend either the human stroke or dog paddle as a stroke to be taught to everyone.

Performing the Front Crawl Stroke

Chart 3:22 describes and illustrates the front crawl stroke and points out common and/or major performance errors.

CHART 3:22
PERFORMANCE TECHNIQUES FOR THE FRONT CRAWL STROKE

Techniques	Illustration	Major and/or Common Performance Errors
A. Extend legs, point toes. Move feet alternately up and down 12-15 inches. Have slight bend at knees, bring heels to surface, limit the amount of splash. Emphasize "down" beat and kicking from hips.	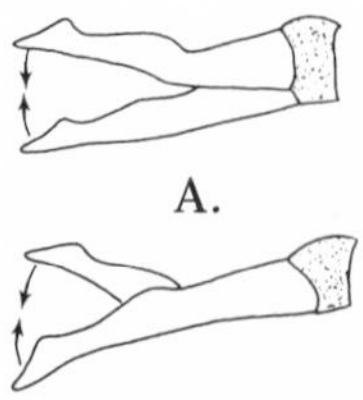 A.	A. Bending too much at knees (causing bicycle-riding movement). Causing too much splash. Bending too little at the knees. Using a kick that is too narrow and tense. Failing to point toes.

ARM ACTION

B. Arms are always opposite each other. Extend one arm, fingers entering water first directly in front of shoulder (as other arm pulls).

B.

C. "Settle" hand and forearm 8-12 inches below water.

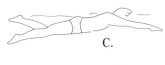
C.

D. Bend arm, pull, and then push it back until nearing hips.

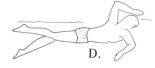
D.

E. Lift elbow out of water; bring forearm forward; extend arm to original position.

E.

B. Permitting elbow to enter water prior to hand entry.
Entering hand in front of opposite shoulder.

C. Entering hand in front of face and pushing hand forward before pulling backward.

D. Failing to bend arm to obtain best leverage.
Failing to pull completely through.

E. Keeping arm straight.
Thrusting arm forward instead of swinging from the shoulder.
Failing to relax arm during recovery.

COORDINATION

F. Combine, usually, 6 kicks to one arm cycle (one stroke with each arm).

F.

G. Keep kicking and pulling action continuous.

G. See F above.

F. Failing to deliver the same number of kicks to each arm pull (inserting a scissors kick with one arm pull).

G. Executing the kicking and pulling actions independently of each other.

BREATHING

H. Position the face to "look ahead" underwater (water line at hairline).

H. See C above.

I. Exhale during pull and push of one arm. Roll head to that side; keep lower ear in water.

I. See D above.

J. Inhale during recovery of same arm; return head to "look ahead" position.

J. See E above.

H. Carrying head above water or too low in the water.

I. Exhaling during arm recovery.
Lifting head rather than rolling it for breathing.

J. Trying to inhale after arm on breathing side is entering the water.

Teaching the Crawl Stroke

A progressive-part method for teaching the crawl stroke is shown in Chart 3:23. Many instructors begin their progression with a demonstration of the whole stroke and then a demonstration of the part to be practiced during the class session. It must be remembered that all students will not progress at the same rate. Some will have improved rapidly, but for some learning will have stagnated at one stage or another (see Learning Plateau, Chapter 2). Although the teaching progression will be appropriate for all in the class, the instructor must accommodate his teaching to the skill differences between individuals. Moreover, he must be aware that some skills in the progression will be acquired quickly and others (e.g., breathing) may require extensive practice.

CHART 3:23
TEACHING PROGRESSION FOR THE FRONT CRAWL STROKE

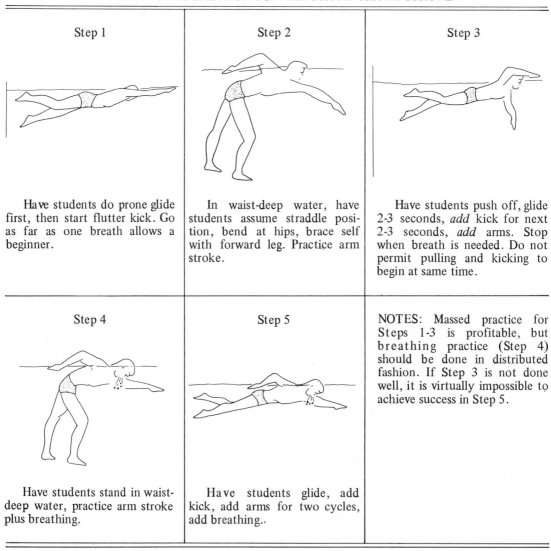

Step 1	Step 2	Step 3
Have students do prone glide first, then start flutter kick. Go as far as one breath allows a beginner.	In waist-deep water, have students assume straddle position, bend at hips, brace self with forward leg. Practice arm stroke.	Have students push off, glide 2-3 seconds, *add* kick for next 2-3 seconds, *add* arms. Stop when breath is needed. Do not permit pulling and kicking to begin at same time.
Step 4	Step 5	NOTES: Massed practice for Steps 1-3 is profitable, but breathing practice (Step 4) should be done in distributed fashion. If Step 3 is not done well, it is virtually impossible to achieve success in Step 5.
Have students stand in waist-deep water, practice arm stroke plus breathing.	Have students glide, add kick, add arms for two cycles, add breathing.,	

38

SWIMMING ON THE BACK

The greatest advantages of swimming on the back are ease of learning and simplicity of performance. It is entirely possible for a group of beginners (age 7 or more) to learn to swim 50 feet on their backs (flutter kick, finning combination) in the first class session.

Performing a Backstroke

There are two possible strokes on the back which can be mastered by beginners. The easiest one (but not universally accepted as the best one for beginners to learn first) has no formal name but is a combination of flutter kicking and hand finning. Finning is a movement whereby the forearms are moved from the side to a position about 18 inches from the body and then pushed back until they touch the sides again. A continuous flutter kick, combined with finning, will effectively move the body through the water. Because the face is out of the water all the time, breathing presents no particular problem. See Chart 3:24 for this stroke.

A second way of swimming on the back is by use of the elementary backstroke (Chart 3:24 also). In the performance of this stroke, the swimmer combines an inverted whip or wedge kick with a simultaneous underwater recovery and pull-and-push with both arms.

Correct form requires that the stroke be performed with an inverted whip or wedge kick. However, at times when form is not a factor, a swimmer with a strong scissors kick may choose to use this kick if it is more effective than the inverted whip or wedge kick.

CHART 3:24
PERFORMANCE TECHNIQUES FOR SWIMMING ON THE BACK

Techniques	Illustration	Major and/or Common Performance Errors
FINNING A. Recover arms from position alongside thighs to position with hands about 18 inches outward from body. Point fingers outward, face palms backward.	A.	A. Facing palms downward. Bringing hands to less than 18 inches from sides. Failing to point fingers outward.
B. Push palms forcefully backward toward feet and thighs.	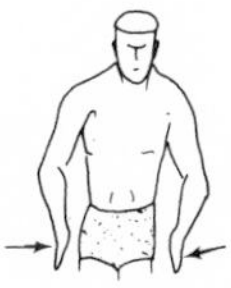 B.	B. Pushing hands downward rather than backward and toward thighs.
C. Repeat the pull-push in continuous action. Add an inverted flutter kick for faster progress.	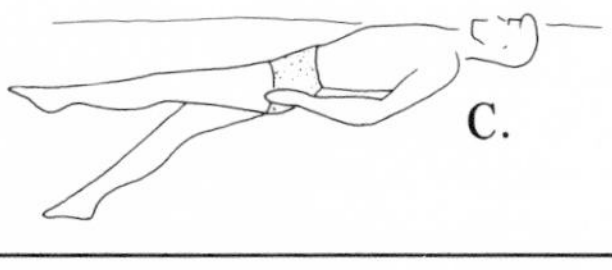 C.	C. Failing to push backward vigorously.

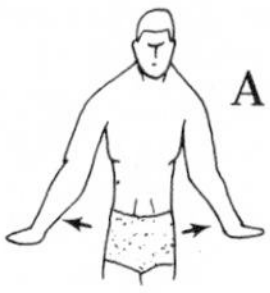

ELEMENTARY BACKSTROKE

D. Assume glide position on back with eyes looking straight upward, ears underwater, arms at side, legs together, hips at surface, and body in straight, streamlined position.

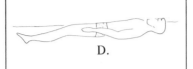

D. Sagging at hips.
Raising head upward and/or forward.
Raising hands above surface.

E. Bend elbows as fingers move up (tickling) the side.
Bend knees and draw legs downward.

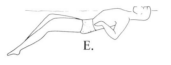

E. Keeping arms straight.
Bringing arms above surface.
Bringing hands over chest.
Recovering arms and legs too abruptly and vigorously.

F. When fingers reach armpit, draw elbows in to ribs and point fingers forward and outward (to bisect the angle between neck and shoulders).
Continue wedge kick leg recovery or begin whip kick leg recovery.

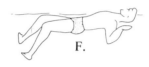

F. Bringing hands out of the water.

G. Extend arms diagonally outward and forward.

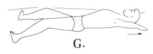

G. Extending arms within the angle between shoulders and lower body.

H. Pull the arms backward to the hips, bending at elbows if better leverage desired.
Deliver kick at same time as arms are pulled.
Exhale and inhale immediately.

H. Failing to kick and pull at the same time.
Executing a leg kick and arm stroke in manner either too gentle or too forceful.

I. Glide for 2-4 seconds.

I. See D above.

I. Inclining head too far forward or backward.
Failing to glide.

Teaching a Backstroke

Even though different methods of swimming on the back are presented above, the instructor will find that the elementary backstroke is so quickly mastered by supine floaters that it might as well be taught first. If a student has difficulty with this stroke, however, the flutter-finning stroke is recommended.

TEACHING PROGRESSION FOR THE ELEMENTARY BACKSTROKE

Step 1	Step 2	Step 3
Review inverted breaststroke kick and supine glide.	Have students do supine glide for 2-3 seconds, then begin inverted breaststroke kick. Emphasize glide between kicks.	Have students stand in waist-deep water, practice arm stroke. After arm stroke practice, add one leg (to emphasize coordination).

Step 4	Step 5	Step 6
Have students supine glide 5 feet, then kick and pull at same time. Take only one stroke. Glide as far as possible. Regain feet.	Permit those who do one stroke correctly to add 1-2 strokes as long as they glide between movements.	Have students swim distances, emphasizing glides between strokes.

STANDING DIVE

Diving is any means of entering water headfirst. Its value is primarily to the younger swimmer, but the utilitarian importance is that at some time or other any swimmer might want to enter the water quickly and cover a distance rapidly. The student must be reminded that if the feet are placed higher than the head during the dive, there is little danger of landing on the stomach.

CHART 3:26
PERFORMANCE TECHNIQUES FOR THE STANDING DIVE

Techniques	Illustration	Major and/or Common Performance Errors

A. Stand, toes curled over edge of deck.
 	
B. Bend at knees and place extended arms over ears.
   Focus eyes on spot under the surface and about 5 feet outward from edge of deck.
 	
C. Lose balance; keep arms over ears.
		A. Failing to curl toes over edge of deck or raft.
		
		B. Bending knees at more than 60 degree angle.
		   Extending arms in front of chest.
		   Focusing eyes on distant spot on surface.
		
		C. Failing to fall forward off balance.
		   Taking spot on surface, instead of on bottom, as point of aim.

D. Push vigorously with legs, causing feet to rise upward; arms remain straight and over ears.		D. Falling off balance without extending legs.
		   Raising head from between the arms.
		   Bending at hips and knees after take-off.

E. Enter water with hands about 3 feet from deck or dock; arms, body, and legs straight; toes pointed. F. After feet enter water, rise to surface by pointing diagonally upward with fingers and raising head slightly.		E. Bending knees and raising head as body enters water. F. Arching back and inclining hands upward too much. Pulling arms backward to thighs.

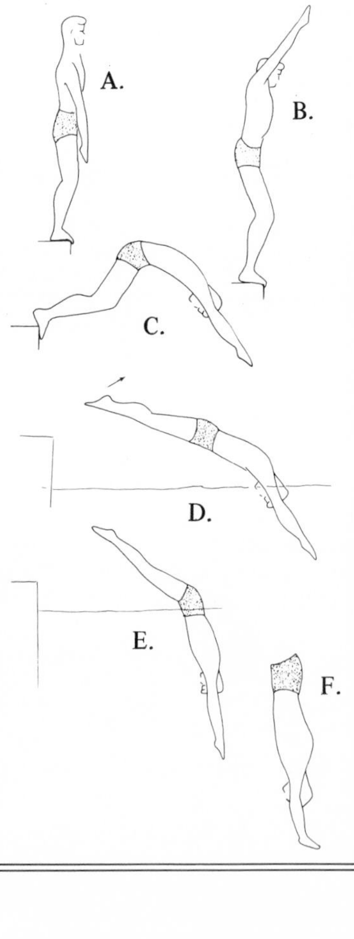

Teaching Diving

Very few people dive successfully on the first attempt. Therefore, most teachers advocate a definite progression, beginning with a sitting dive and including a kneeling and one-legged standing dive.

CHART 3:27
TEACHING PROGRESSION FOR THE STANDING DIVE

Step 1	Step 2	Step 3
Have students sit, aim for a spot 3 feet ahead. Fall forward. Hands enter water as legs are pushed vigorously.	Have students kneel, aim for spot 5 feet ahead. Fall forward. Hands enter water as one leg (braced against solid object) pushes vigorously.	Have students stand on one leg, keep other leg straight as it is raised behind body. Bend forward at the hips as the leg is raised behind the body. Enter water about 5 feet in front.
Step 4	Step 5	Step 6
Have students crouch, bend both knees. Fall forward and push back with legs by straightening knees as balance is lost.	Have students do beginner standing dive, but beginning with arms extended overhead (Chart 3:26).	Have students begin with arms at side. As balance is lost, arms are raised overhead and dive is completed as before (Chart 3:26).

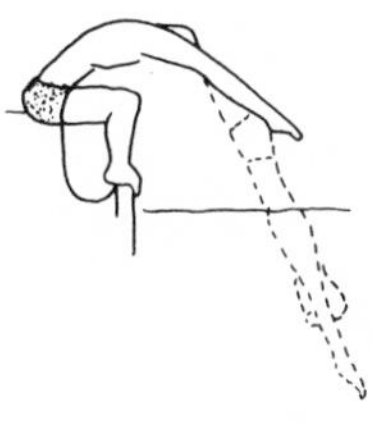

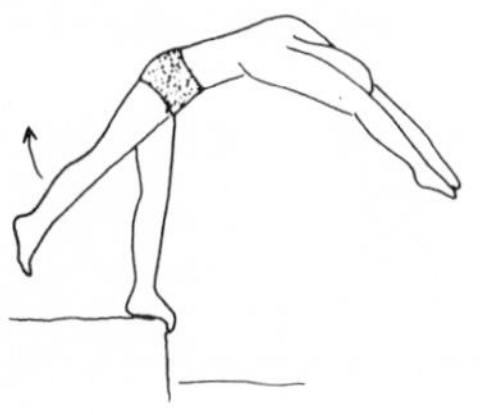

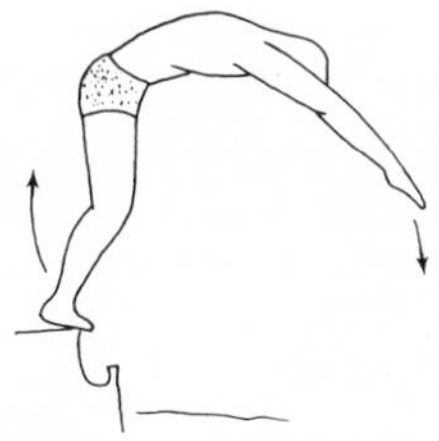

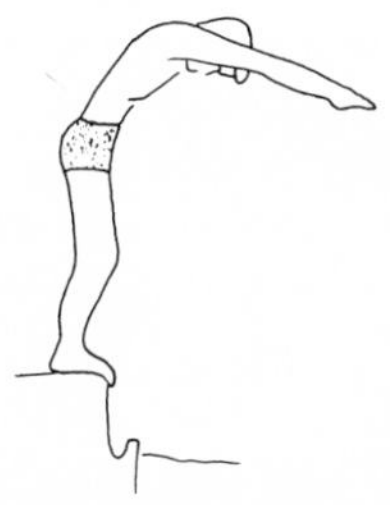

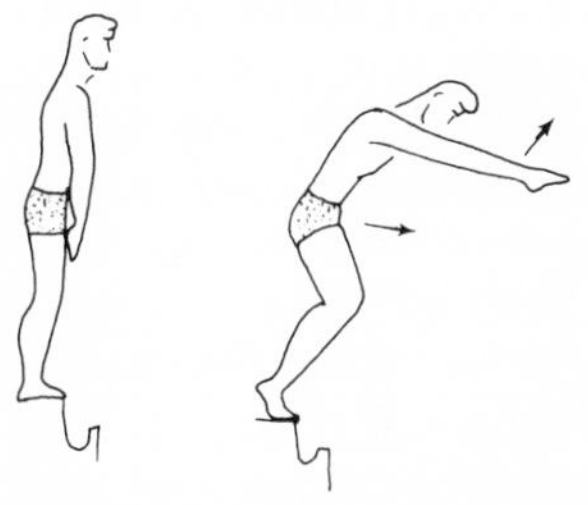

FLOATING AND SWIMMING WITH LIFE JACKETS

Today, thousands upon thousands of people spend much leisure time in boats of all types. Many states now require life jackets to be available in all aquatic craft, and thus it is important that instructors make sure that their students know what to do should the jackets be needed. Instructors should point out that only Coast Guard approved life jackets should be worn. However, instructors should likewise know that even some of these approved jackets are not safe, because they would hold an unconscious victim in a face-down position (see Lagemann, 1965, pp. 215-218). Students should have actual practice floating with a life jacket. After this has been done, they should swim a short distance, keeping arms underwater at all times. Finally, they should practice jumping into the water (Chart 3:28). Do not leave your students with the idea that they should try to swim to safety after a water accident; even when wearing a life jacket, it is still wise advice to stay with the craft or in the immediate vicinity.

CHART 3:28
WATER ENTRY WHILE WEARING A LIFE JACKET

Techniques	Illustration	Major and/or Common Performance Errors
A. Keep arms crossed over the chest, hands grasping top of jacket.		A. Failing to grasp jacket firmly (thus causing jacket to hit the chin).

CRAMPS

Cramps are described by the layman as "knotting of a muscle." This can be crucial, since the swimmer cannot use the affected body part if the cramp is severe. Despite what you hear, virtually all cramps occur in limbs or fingers; stomach cramps are apparently very rare and thus need not be of great concern to swimmers (Lanoue, 1963, pp. 97-98).

Treatment for Cramps

Since cramps occur when a muscle is contracted (or knotted), the logical treatment is to cause the muscle to stretch. Kneading or massaging with the hand is sometimes effective, but stretching the muscle is all that really needs to be done. Most authorities recommend that swimmers float and massage the affected muscle very forcefully even after a cramp has disappeared, because cramps are seldom completely eliminated in a short time. For cramps in the calf or instep, gentle and steady pulling of the toes toward the knee while the other hand is massaging the affected part seems effective. Chart 3:29 illustrates these various massaging positions.

CHART 3:29
TREATMENT FOR CRAMPS

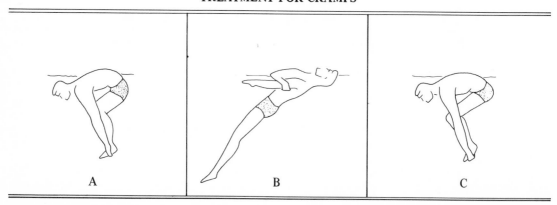

A   B   C

Teaching about Cramps

When the students are attentive (which usually means not chilled or exhausted) the instructor can explain what a cramp is and demonstrate how a limb is stretched and/or massaged. Students should then float in various positions in the water and practice the kneading movements.

ARTIFICIAL RESPIRATION

Death by suffocation (as occurs in drowning) is always a danger in an aquatic environment. Artificial respiration is defined as a means of keeping a person alive by artificial means until he resumes his own breathing. The YMCA, ARC, and the American Medical Association all recommend the mouth-to-mouth method as the most effective for the semitrained layman to use. It is easily learned; in fact, there is an instance where a six-year-old boy successfully revived his younger brother by this method.

Chart 3:30 describes and illustrates mouth-to-mouth resuscitation. This is the official publication by the American National Red Cross and thus should be considered the standard technique.

CHART 3:30
PERFORMANCE TECHNIQUES FOR MOUTH-TO-MOUTH RESUSCITATION*

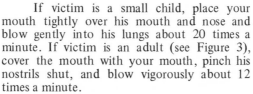

If victim is not breathing, begin some form of artificial respiration at once. Wipe out quickly any foreign matter visible in the mouth, using your fingers or a cloth wrapped around your fingers.

MOUTH-TO-MOUTH (MOUTH-TO-NOSE) METHOD

Tilt victim's head back. (Figure 1). Pull or push the jaw into a jutting-out position. (Figure 2).

If victim is a small child, place your mouth tightly over his mouth and nose and blow gently into his lungs about 20 times a minute. If victim is an adult (see Figure 3), cover the mouth with your mouth, pinch his nostrils shut, and blow vigorously about 12 times a minute.

If unable to get air into lungs of victim, and if head and jaw positions are correct, suspect foreign matter in throat. To remove it, suspend a small child momentarily by the ankles or place child in position shown in Figure 4, and slap sharply between shoulder blades.

If the victim is adult, place in position shown in Figure 5, and use same procedure.

*Adapted from ARC, *Saving A Life by Artificial Respiration,* Poster 1002. Revised October 1959. Used by permission.

Teaching About Artificial Respiration

When the students are dry, warm, and attentive, the instructor should explain and show a movie which demonstrates this technique. The American National Red Cross does not recommend actual practice of the mouth-to-mouth resuscitation, saying that it is such a simple technique and the unhygienic aspects outweigh any possible advantage of actual practice. Some instructors disagree and use such aids as a special dummy (ResusciAnne), or plastic devices made for the purpose, or handkerchiefs over the victim's mouth to eliminate the spread of germs during actual practice. We recommend that the movie, *Rescue Breathing,* be shown once to the group, then the technique explained to them; then the movie shown a second time. Beginning instructors may think it a waste of time to show the movie twice, but audio-visual methods experts say that the first showing has limited value.

REACHING ASSISTS

Reaching assists are simple methods whereby a person who is not a skilled swimmer may safely aid a person who is in trouble in the water. (Actually, skilled swimmers also use these assists if at all possible). Extending an arm, a branch, an oar, a towel, a rope, etc. is always preferable to actual contact with the victim. There is no real technique necessary for reaching assists, other than that the rescuer must maintain his position by lying down or by grasping some immovable object with his free hand. Instructors should have students practice extending arms, towels, tree branches, kick boards, sweat shirts—anything that is available in the pool or beach area.

CLASS ASSIGNMENTS

1. Locate a friend who cannot swim and teach him any three of the twelve essential aquatic skills.

2. Talk to a local swimming instructor. How many of the skills mentioned in this chapter does he or she teach to beginners? Which 2-3 skills does he or she regard as most important for beginners?

3. Talk to a local instructor. What problems does he or she have in teaching skills to beginners?

4. Using the analysis sheets at the end of this chapter, evaluate the elementary backstroke and the crawl stroke of a swimmer.

BEHAVIORAL OBJECTIVES

Virtually every instructor will teach beginners; therefore, we expect our students to master all the material in this chapter.

1. Describe a certain number (specified in parentheses) of the major and/or common performance errors usually found in the following skills:

    A. Supine floating (2)
    B. Crawl stroke (4)
    C. Elementary backstroke (4)
    D. Standing dive (2)
    E. Scissors kick (2)
    F. Whip kick (2)

2. Be able to explain and/or diagram how to perform these skills:

    A. Drownproofing (nonfloaters)
    B. Treading water
    C. Flutter kick
    D. Release cramp in the arm or calf
    E. Artificial respiration
    F. Reaching assist
    G. Bobbing (deep water)
    H. Jump into water wearing a life jacket

3. Be able to describe a suitable teaching progression (not necessarily the one given in this text, but conforming to those principles given in Chapter 2) for:

    A. Supine floating (shallow and then deep water)
    B. Crawl stroke
    C. Elementary backstroke
    D. Standing dive

4. Meet the minimum standard for certified aquatic workers for each of the essential aquatic skills given on the next page.

Skill	Standard*
Vertical float	Motionless (or nearly so) for 60 seconds.
Bobbing	8 feet of water; 60 seconds.
Drownproofing	4 minutes arms alone
	4 minutes legs alone
	12 minutes combined
Treading water	1 minute arms alone
	1 minute legs alone
Kicks: Flutter	30 feet
Whip	30 feet
Wedge	30 feet
Scissors	30 feet
Inverted whip	30 feet
Inverted flutter	30 feet
Crawl stroke	30 feet
Elementary backstroke	30 feet
Standing dive	Legs straight, toes pointed, body in straight line, little splash.

*Form for all skills to be as described in this text.

BIBLIOGRAPHY

American National Red Cross. *Swimming and Water Safety.* Washington: American National Red Cross, 1968. Pages 9-35, 55-57, 62-66.

American National Red Cross. *Swimming and Water Safety: Instructor's Manual.* Washington: American National Red Cross, 1968. Pages 30-54.

Boy Scouts of America. *Aquatic Program.* New Brunswick, N. J.: Boy Scouts of America, 1965. Pages 25-39.

Lagemann, John K. "Drowned Wearing Life Preserver," *Reader's Digest,* July, 1965, Pages 215-218.

Lanoue, Fred R. *Drownproofing.* Englewood Cliffs, N.J.: Prentice-Hall, Inc., 1963, Chapter 1.

Movie on artificial respiration. *Rescue Breathing.* Available through the local Red Cross office or perhaps other local groups (schools, fire department, civil defense, etc.).

PERFORMANCE ANALYSIS SHEET FOR THE ELEMENTARY BACKSTROKE*

DIRECTIONS: Check √ all items that apply to the performance of this skill. Add other noted errors in the spaces provided.

NAME_____
                (performer)

NAME_____
                (analyzer)

Illustrations of Correct Techniques	Analysis of Performance

BODY POSITION

_____The form *is* acceptable.

_____The form is *not* acceptable because:
    _____Ears not in water.
    _____Eyes not looking upward.
    _____Arms not at sides.
    _____Body not straight (_____hips sag;_____knees are bent; ___toes not pointed; ___arms not straight).
    _____(Other)_____

LEGS

_____The form *is* acceptable.

_____The form for inverted whip kick is *not* acceptable because:
    _____Knees above surface during recovery.
    _____Toes not pointed backward during recovery.
    _____Thighs drop downward as legs extend.
    _____Feet not turned outward during press.
    _____Too little effort on backward press.
    _____(Other)_____

_____The form for inverted wedge kick is *not* acceptable because:
    _____Knees come above surface during recovery.
    _____Knees not spread enough during recovery.
    _____Thighs drop downward as legs extend.
    _____Toes not pointed outward during kick.
    _____Too little effort on backward press.
    _____Legs not straight as they are squeezed.
    _____(Other)_____

ARMS

_____The form *is* acceptable.

_____The form is *not* acceptable because:
　_____Arms recovered too forcefully.
　_____Arms recovered above the surface.
　_____Arms not recovered close to body.
　_____Arms not extended to bisect angle of shoulder and neck.
　_____Pull and kick too forceful.
　_____Stroke incomplete (___Legs do not press-squeeze until together; ___arms end pull before hands are at thighs).
　_____(Other)_____

COORDINATION AND BREATHING

_____The form *is* acceptable.

_____The form is *not* acceptable because:
　_____Recovery of arms and legs too forceful.
　_____Arms and legs not extended diagonally outward at same time.
　_____Pull and kick not done at same time.
　_____Glide poor (___no glide; ___too brief).
　_____Breath not expelled as arms finish pull.
　_____Breath not taken in immediately after exhalation.
　_____(Other)_____

*Method by Barbara J. Sanborn.

PERFORMANCE ANALYSIS SHEET FOR THE FRONT CRAWL STROKE*

DIRECTIONS: Check √ all items that apply to the performance of this skill. Add other noted errors in the spaces provided.

NAME _____
(performer)

NAME _____
(analyzer)

Illustrations of Correct Techniques	Analysis of Performance

BODY POSITION

_____The form *is* acceptable.

_____The form is *not* acceptable because:
_____ Face not looking ahead underwater.
_____ Head too deep in the water.
_____ Head held above the surface.
_____ Back overarched.
_____ Hips higher than the legs.
_____ (Other)_____
_____

LEGS

_____The form *is* acceptable.

_____The form is *not* acceptable because:
_____ Too much bend at the knees.
_____ Not enough bend at the knees.
_____ Kick range too narrow (less than 12-15").
_____ Too much splash.
_____ Toes not pointed with ankles extended.
_____ (Other)_____
_____

50

ARMS

_____The form *is* acceptable.

_____The form is *not* acceptable because:

    _____Arm not bent during recovery.

    _____Arm not relaxed during recovery.

    _____Arm thrust rather than swung from shoulder.

    _____Elbow not higher than hand during recovery.

    _____Elbow enters water before hand enters.

    _____Hand enters water in front of opposite shoulder.

    _____Hand enters water in front of face and pushes forward before pulling back.

    _____Arm does not pull through under body.

    _____Elbow not bent when pull-push is executed.

    _____Pull-push of arms too short.

    _____(Other)_____

    _____

COORDINATION AND BREATHING

_____The form *is* acceptable.

_____The form is *not* acceptable because:

    _____Arms and legs work independently.

    _____Arm action not rhythmic (swimmer gallops).

    _____Head lifted for breathing rather than rolled to side.

    _____Breath taken in during late stage of arm recovery.

    _____Kick and arm stroke stopped while breath is taken.

    _____Head turned from side to side.

    _____(Other)_____

    _____

*Method by Barbara J. Sanborn.

CHAPTER 4

Performing and Teaching Other Aquatic Strokes and Skills

What Additional Skills Are Needed?
Front Crawl and Elementary Backstrokes
Sidestroke and Overarm Sidestroke
Breaststroke
Butterfly Stroke
Back Crawl Stroke
The Trudgen Strokes
Inverted Breaststroke
Turning at Pool Ends
Surface Diving
Underwater Swimming
Diving from Board
Clothing Inflation

The skills presented in this chapter must be taught to all who would consider themselves competent in the water. Younger swimmers probably will be less skillful, but they nevertheless should receive the instruction. The essential aquatic skills presented in Chapter 3 must be learned by everyone before more advanced skills are presented. This implies that every class above the beginner level should begin with a quick review, or screening test, to determine if the essential skills have been mastered. This initial screening test will take a small amount of time, but will accomplish two important things: (1) quickly tell the instructor exactly what essential skills he must teach; and (2) remind the student of the important things he must remember in time of need. After this initial test and instruction, the skills presented in this chapter should be taught.

WHAT ADDITIONAL SKILLS ARE NEEDED?

The skills and techniques presented in this chapter correspond roughly to those required in swimming classes above the beginner level. Since many of our readers now teach or will teach swimming courses in a school situation, we have indicated logical content and standards which can be applied to two different levels of instruction (Table 4:1). For those readers who will be teaching Red Cross or YMCA courses, the content is already established by the organization and must be followed exactly.

Students seeking aquatic certification have already achieved a relatively high level of aquatic skill and are sometimes tempted to pay only cursory attention to this chapter. However, our experience tells us that it is rare for even one student in an instructor's class to correctly demonstrate each of the skills and techniques in this chapter without additional practice. For example, are you absolutely sure that you can swim the breaststroke correctly? Many of our students in an instructors' class cannot. What about demonstrating correct form in the butterfly stroke? The single and double trudgen strokes? The trudgen crawl? Can you inflate clothes quickly?

You might ask, "Why must I be able to demonstrate all the skills in this chapter?" The practical answer is that aquatic certification standards require (or strongly suggest) it; this is based on the belief

CONTENT AND STANDARDS FOR INTERMEDIATE AND ADVANCED SWIMMING COURSES

SKILLS	STANDARDS OF PERFORMANCE		
		Intermediate	Advanced
1. Flutter kick on stomach	No Major Errors	40-50 yds.	- - - - - - - - - - - - - - -
2. Crawl stroke arm action	No Major Errors	20-25 yds.	- - - - - - - - - - - - - - -
3. Front crawl stroke	No Major Errors	40-50 yds.	100 yds.
4. Elementary backstroke	No Major Errors	40-50 yds.	100 yds.
5. Scissors kick	No Major Errors	40-50 yds.	- - - - - - - - - - - - - - -
6. Sidestroke arm action	No Major Errors	20-25 yds.	- - - - - - - - - - - - - - -
7. Sidestroke (preferred side)	No Major Errors	40-50 yds.	100 yds.
8. Overarm sidestroke (preferred side)	No Major Errors	- - - - - - - - - - - - - - -	100 yds.
9. Breaststroke kick (wedge, whip)	No Major Errors	40-50 yds. (one type)	40-50 yds. (both types)
10. Breaststroke arm action	No Major Errors	20-25 yds.	- - - - - - - - - - - - - - -
11. Breaststroke	No Major Errors	40-50 yds.	100 yds.
12. Dolphin kick	No Major Errors	20-25 yds.	- - - - - - - - - - - - - - -
13. Butterfly arm action	No Major Errors	10-15 yds.	- - - - - - - - - - - - - - -
14. Butterfly stroke	No Major Errors	- - - - - - - - - - - - - - -	50 yds.
15. Flutter kick on back	No Major Errors	20-25 yds.	- - - - - - - - - - - - - - -
16. Back crawl stroke	No Major Errors	- - - - - - - - - - - - - - -	100 yds.
17. Single trudgen stroke	No Major Errors	- - - - - - - - - - - - - - -	100 yds.
18. Double trudgen stroke	No Major Errors	- - - - - - - - - - - - - - -	100 yds.
19. Trudgen crawl stroke	No Major Errors	- - - - - - - - - - - - - - -	100 yds.
20. Inverted breaststroke	No Major Errors	- - - - - - - - - - - - - - -	100 yds.
21. Turning at pool ends (stomach, back, side)	No Major Errors	Demonstrate all	- - - - - - - - - - - - - - -
22. Surface dives (tuck, pike, feet first)	No Major Errors	Demonstrate any one	Demonstrate all
23. Underwater swim	No push off	10 ft.	30 ft.
24. Dive from board	No Major Errors	Standing (front)	Running (front) Standing (back)
25. Clothes inflation (wearing shirt, pants, shoes)	Float (any position) for 2 min. after inflation.	Inflate shirt while wearing other clothes.	Inflate shirt and pants.
26. Continuous swim (any combination of strokes).	No time limit	200 yds.	500 yds.
27. 200 yd. continuous swim (50 yds. each of breaststroke, sidestroke, elem. back, crawl or trudgen).	No Major Errors	- - - - - - - - - - - - - - -	6:40 or less (girls) 5:30 or less (boys)

that ability to demonstrate enables a person to become a better teacher. Even more to the point, however, is that this chapter presents teaching progressions for eleven different strokes, plus discussions and diagrams of open turns, surface dives, underwater swimming, and clothing inflation. Even though you may have had extensive teaching experience, we think that this chapter can help you. Specific behavioral objectives for certified aquatic instructors will be found at the end of the chapter.

FRONT CRAWL AND ELEMENTARY BACK STROKES

The front crawl and the elementary back strokes have been discussed in Chapter 3. It would be wise for the instructor to review the basic techniques of these strokes, because both are a part of the intermediate and advanced swimming courses.

SIDESTROKE AND OVERARM SIDESTROKE

The sidestroke is primarily a resting stroke, featuring a powerful scissors kick followed by a long glide. The glide is an essential characteristic of the stroke. This stroke is comparatively easy to teach and is especially useful in instructing adults because the breathing problems inherent in the crawl and breaststrokes are absent. Children and younger adults are not especially keen on learning the sidestroke because it is not a racing stroke. Even though the overarm sidestroke was used in international swimming meets until 1904, basically it is not suited for speed.

Performing the Sidestroke

The scissors kick, arm action, coordination, and breathing used in the sidestroke are shown and discussed in Chart 4:1. The use of the inverted scissors kick, and the lack of a glide, are very common errors.

Performing the Overarm Sidestroke

The overarm sidestroke is basically the same as the sidestroke, except that the arm recovery has been altered for the sake of speed. See Chart 4:2.

Teaching the Sidestroke and Overarm Sidestroke

It is much easier to teach these strokes to a beginner than to one who has learned them incorrectly. The major problem is that the person who has learned to swim the strokes incorrectly usually has an inverted scissors kick, and he cannot "get the power" from the correct kick. Even though he practices on the wall or with a kickboard, it "still doesn't feel right." The easiest way to overcome this problem is to simply have the student roll over to his opposite side; he will then be doing the same kick, but it will be the correct one.

When instructing students, it will be helpful to remind students that the sidestroke can be considered in three distinct movements. The first is the pull with the leading arm. When this is finished (e.g. down to the chest), the legs and other arm are brought up, out, and pushed back. The last (and most important part) is the glide. Beginners will make much quicker progress if the instructor will constantly emphasize that the strokes start with the leading arm, not with the kick.

The arm action of the sidestroke has been likened to picking one apple out of a tree, transferring the apple from the picking hand to the other hand, putting the apple in a sack at the hip at the same time the picking hand goes back for another apple. This analogy has proved very useful in implanting the concept of the leading arm pulling first to keep the body moving, before the remaining arm and the legs are recovered (see Chart 4:1, Illustration F). Another analogy would be that water is pulled down to the chest area with the leading arm, and then the same water is pushed down to the feet with the other arm.

Chart 4:3 presents a usable teaching progression for the sidestroke. The overarm sidestroke is not taught until the sidestroke is mastered; since it is the same stroke except for the over-the-water recovery, no different progression is called for.

PERFORMANCE TECHNIQUES FOR THE SIDESTROKE

Techniques	Illustration	Major and/or Common Performance Errors
SCISSORS KICK A. Rest the upper leg directly upon the lower, with both legs extended and toes pointed. B. Bend the legs at the knees and bring the heels up to just behind the buttocks. C. Move the legs into a striding position, the upper leg forward. Make leg actions parallel to surface. Point toes of upper leg outward in front of body, toes of lower leg to rear of body. Movements in A, B, C should be gentle. D. Straighten legs as they are squeezed rearward and together. Point toes during squeeze. Stop the squeeze when legs are together. **ARM ACTION** E. Assume glide position with trailing arm extended over hip, leading arm extended forward, body on side, head turned to bring chin toward upper shoulder so mouth is out of water. F. Pull leading arm outward, downward, and inward toward chin. Bend elbow of trailing arm and bring hand toward chin. G. Place the hand of the trailing arm over the hand of the leading arm as they meet in front of chin. H. Lower the elbow of leading arm, point fingers forward, extend arm forward with palm facing downward. Push trailing arm completely back to thigh.		A. Bending at the knees and ankles (body position is not streamlined). B. Bringing the knees too far in front (near stomach). Failing to bend knees. C. Extending lower leg forward. Lowering the under leg toward bottom. Making actions too quick and vigorous. D. Using a breaststroke kick. Failing to straighten legs before the squeeze. Expending too little effort. Squeezing legs past each other (as in flutter kick). E. Allowing trailing arm to drift in front of or behind body line. Bending either arm at elbow. Failing to be perfectly on the side. F. Pressing the leading arm toward pool bottom rather than pulling parallel to water surface. Ending the pull of leading arm too soon. G. Failing to have hands meet in front of chin. H. Pulling trailing arm to thigh before extending leading arm. Pulling both arms toward feet at the same time.

COORDINATION AND
BREATHING

Techniques	Illustration	Errors
I. Begin the stroke by pulling with leading arm.	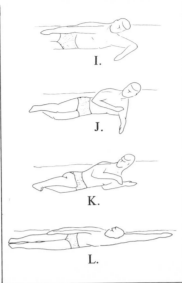 I.	I. Beginning leg recovery before leading arm begins to pull.
J. After leading arm has begun pull, begin recovery movement with other three limbs.	J.	J. Beginning the movement of all four limbs at the same time. Pulling leading arm and kicking at same time.
K. Finish pull of leading arm, extend leading arm forward, pull with trailing arm, and deliver kick. Exhale.	K.	K. Kicking before leading arm is in position to be extended forward.

L. Streamline the body.
    Inhale.
    Glide for 2-3 seconds.
	L.	L. Failing to glide.
		    Turning the entire body onto the back to raise the face to breathe.

CHART 4:2
PERFORMANCE TECHNIQUES FOR THE OVERARM SIDESTROKE

Techniques	Illustration	Major and/or Common Performance Errors
SCISSORS KICK		
A. Rest the upper leg directly upon the lower, with both legs extended and toes pointed.	A.	A. Bending at the knees and ankles (body position is not streamlined).
B. Bend the legs at the knees and bring the heels up to just behind the buttocks.	B.	B. Bringing the knees too far in front (near stomach). Failing to bend knees.

C. Move the legs into a striding position, the upper leg forward.
    Make leg actions parallel to surface.
    Point toes of upper leg outward in front of body, toes of lower leg to rear of body.
 	
    Movements in A, B, C should be gentle.
	C.	C. Extending lower leg forward.
		    Lowering the under leg toward bottom.
		
		    Making actions too quick and vigorous.

D. Straighten legs as they are squeezed rearward and together.
    Point toes during squeeze.
    Stop the squeeze when legs are together.
	D.	D. Using a breaststroke kick.
		    Failing to straighten legs before the squeeze.
		    Expending too little effort.
		    Squeezing legs past each other (as in flutter kick).

ARM ACTION

E. Assume glide position with trailing arm extended over hip, leading arm extended forward, body on side, head turned to bring chin toward upper shoulder so mouth is out of water.

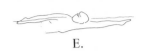

E.

E. Allowing trailing arm to drift in front of or behind body line.
    Bending either arm at elbow.
    Failing to be perfectly on the side.

F. Pull leading arm outward, downward, and inward toward chin.
    Bend elbow of trailing arm and recover it over the surface to a point in front of face.

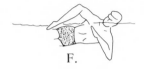

F.

F. Recovering trailing arm underwater.
    Pounding trailing arm into water.
    Overreaching with trailing arm (causing body to roll onto stomach).

G. Place the hand of the trailing arm over the hand of the leading arm as they meet in front of chin.

G.

G. Failing to have hands meet in front of chin.

H. Lower the elbow of leading arm, point fingers forward, extend arm forward with palm facing downward.
    Push trailing arm completely back to thigh.

H.

H. Pulling trailing arm to thigh before extending leading arm.
    Pulling both arms toward feet at the same time.

COORDINATION AND BREATHING

I. Begin the stroke by pulling with leading arm.

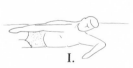

I.

I. Beginning leg recovery before leading arm begins to pull.

J. After leading arm has begun pull, begin recovery movement with other three limbs.

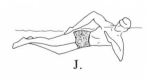

J.

J. Beginning the movement of all four limbs at the same time.
    Pulling leading arm and kicking at same time.

K. Finish pull of leading arm, extend leading arm forward, pull with trailing arm, and deliver kick.
    Exhale.

K.

K. Kicking before leading arm is in position to be extended forward.

L. Streamline the body.
    Inhale.
    Glide for 2-3 seconds.

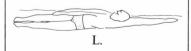

L.

L. Failing to glide.
    Turning the entire body onto the back to raise the face to breathe.

CHART 4:3
TEACHING PROGRESSION FOR THE SIDESTROKE

Step 1	Step 2	Step 3
Have students practice the kick hanging on the wall or in shallow water. Be sure student is on side, not back.	Have students push off, float on side. Glide until feet sink; regain feet. A partner can tow the student if desired, or a kickboard can be used by the student.	Have students push off, glide, then kick, and glide. Have student take one kick, glide, then stop. When this is correctly done, permit 2 or more kicks.

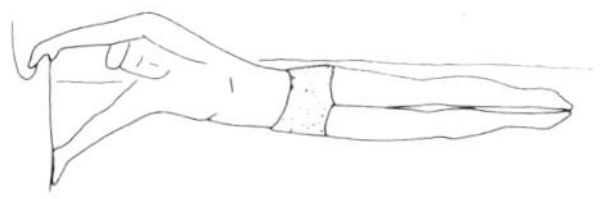

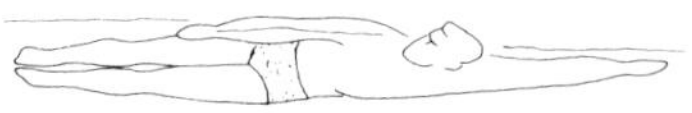

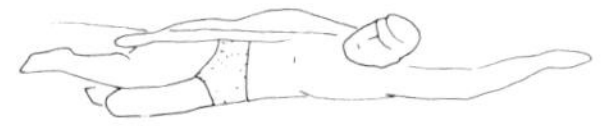

Step 4	Step 5	Step 6
Have students stand in water, practice trailing arm movement coordination with top leg.	Have students push off, glide, kick and use trailing arm. Continually emphasize the glide between kicks.	Have students stand in water, practice leading arm movement alone. Then, move both arms and top leg while standing.

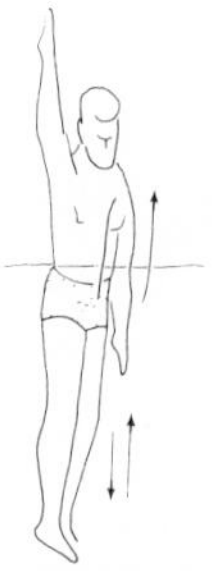

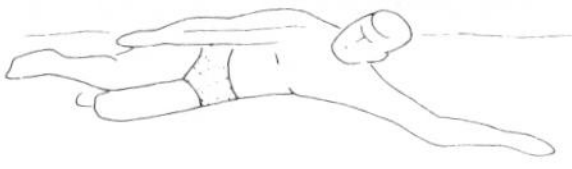

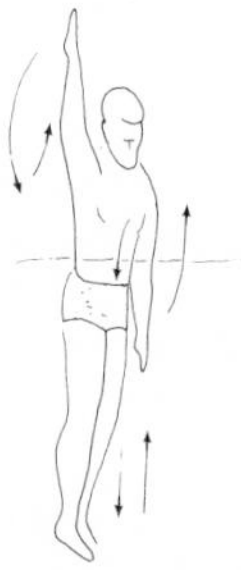

Step 7	Step 8	Step 9
Have students push off, glide, take one stroke, glide. Be sure stroke is correct in all respects.	Permit those students who perform one stroke correctly to do three.	Have students swim a given distance in as few strokes as possible.

58

BREASTSTROKE

In the United States, most instructors teach the crawl stroke, the backstroke, and the sidestroke before they teach the breaststroke. Conversely, Europeans usually teach the breaststroke first. Perhaps this delay in instruction accounts for the fact that, on the average, Europeans perform the stroke much better than we do. Because it is not a very fast stroke, most American swimmers are not motivated enough to learn it correctly. It requires a powerful kick, and if this is lacking, the arm pull of the stroke has to be wrong (i.e., all the way back to the hips) in order to achieve satisfactory momentum.

Performing the Breaststroke

The two types of kick (whip and wedge) which are used in the breaststroke were shown first in Chapter 3. The kicks, arm stroke, coordination, and breathing are shown in Chart 4:4 below.

The stroke as we describe it can be continued by the swimmer for long distances without undue effort, provided the kick is reasonably effective. The swimmer is resting while he glides and he gets good distance from each stroke. This could be called "form" stroking to distinguish it from the competitive breaststroke. When swum by a competitor in good physical condition, the glide is eliminated in order to travel a comparatively short distance in the shortest possible time.

CHART 4:4
PERFORMANCE TECHNIQUES FOR THE BREASTSTROKE

Techniques	Illustration	Major and/or Common Performance Errors
WEDGE KICK A. Extend legs and point toes backward.	A.	A. Bending the knees. Failing to point toes.
B. Move knees sideward, bring heels toward buttocks (heels are almost touching, toes point outward).	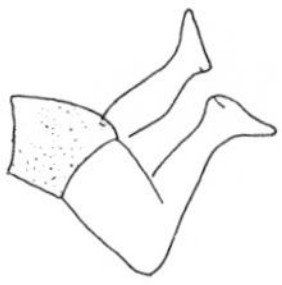 B.	B. Pointing the toes of one foot inward (causing scissors kick). Lowering knees toward bottom instead of outward.
C. Move heels to outside, partially straighten legs, point toes outward.	C.	C. Continuing to point toes backward.
Actions in steps A, B, C should be gentle.	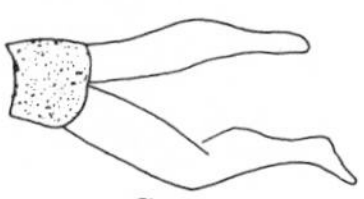	Recovering the legs too quickly and too vigorously.
D. Press legs backward and squeeze together. Point toes backward at end of the press.	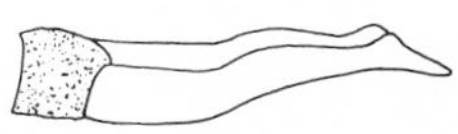 D.	D. Applying too little effort during the press. Underemphasizing the press and overemphasizing the squeeze. Pointing toes backward during press.
E. Glide for 3-6 seconds with legs extended and toes pointed.	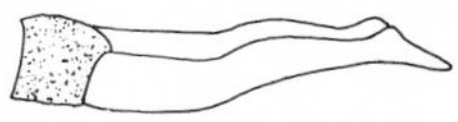 E.	E. Failing to glide.

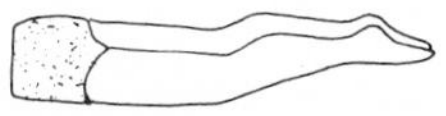

WHIP KICK

F. Keep knees close together as they are lowered downward.

G. Move heels outward, keep knees close together.
     Partially straighten legs, point toes outward.

     Movements in F and G should be gentle.

H. Press legs backward and squeeze together.

I. Glide for 3-6 seconds with legs extended and toes pointed backward.

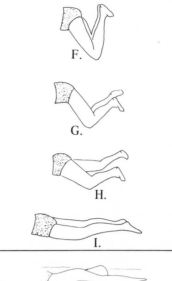

F. Bringing knees forward and under stomach.

G. Drifting knees apart.
     Pointing toes backward.

     Recovering the legs too quickly and too vigorously.

H. Applying too little effort to backward press and squeeze.

I. Beginning recovery of legs without pause for glide.

ARM ACTION

J. Glide with face down and ears between extended arms.

K. Bend elbows and press arms backward and downward; keep elbows close to surface.

L. As elbows reach the shoulder line, move them inward to a point in front of chest and under chin.

M. After hands reach position under chin, extend them forward to gliding position.

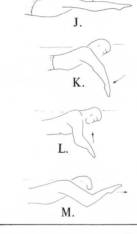

J. Holding head above surface.
     Failing to glide.

K. Pulling arms outward (as in rowing a boat).
     Pulling arms under center of body.

L. Pressing the hands back to the hips or thighs.

M. Failing to stretch arms to full extension.
     Failing to lower head to position between arms.

COORDINATION AND BREATHING

N. After glide, press arms backward.
     Maintain extension of legs.
     Inhale as arms begin pull.

O. As hands move inward toward chest, begin leg recovery.
     Lower face into water.

P. Kick with legs as arms recover to gliding position.

Q. Glide with entire body in straight line.
     Exhale at end of glide.

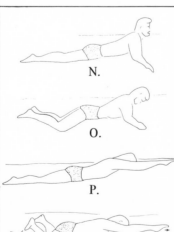

N. Recovering legs while arms are pulling.
     Raising head too late.
     Performing the leg kick and arm pull at the same time.

O. Holding head up, with face not in water.

P. Extending the arms after kick has been delivered.

Q. Beginning arm pull immediately after extending the arms.

Teaching the Breaststroke

Stressing the correct kick cannot be overdone. At least one-third of our aquatic instructor candidates come to us thinking that they are swimming the breaststroke correctly, but in fact they are using a scissors kick. Many students will say that they get more power from the scissors kick. While this is often true, it is no reason why an instructor should permit the stroke to be done incorrectly. Likewise, many of our students do not glide at the end of the stroke. While this error can be corrected very easily, the use of the scissors kick is extremely difficult to overcome.

Chart 4:5 presents the teaching progression for the breaststroke that we have found to be effective.

CHART 4:5
TEACHING PROGRESSION FOR THE BREASTSTROKE

Step 1	Step 2	Step 3
Have students review the breaststroke kick on the wall or in shallow water. Kick distances using board or glide position. Practice both the wedge and whip kicks. Let students use either, provided it is correct.	Have students stand, practice arm action. Placing one foot well ahead of other will make it possible to stroke without being pulled off balance.	Have students push off, glide, pull once, recover, glide again. No leg action is permitted. When done correctly, repeat two or more times, emphasizing the glide.
Step 4	**Step 5**	**Step 6**
Have students stand, practice arm action standing on one leg. Emphasize timing between kick and arm recovery.	Have students push off, glide, take one complete stroke, glide. When done correctly, repeat two or more times.	Have students stand, practice arm action and breathing. Emphasize raising head to breathe just as the arms begin pressing.
Step 7	**Step 8**	**Step 9**
Have students swim one complete stroke and then stop. Do not permit incorrect movements to go uncorrected.	Permit those students who perform one stroke correctly to do three strokes.	Have students swim a given distance in as few strokes as possible.

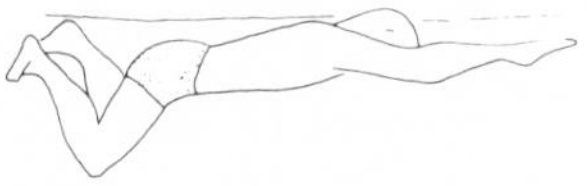

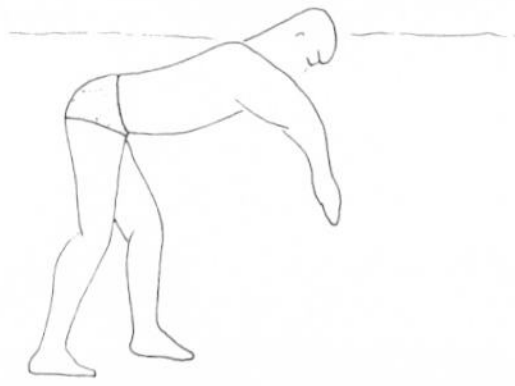

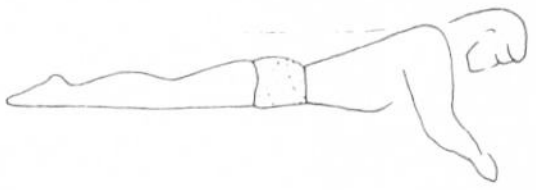

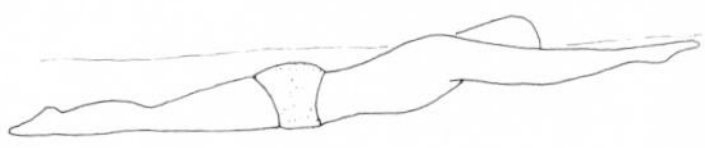

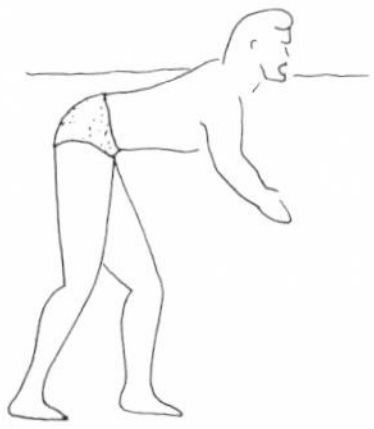

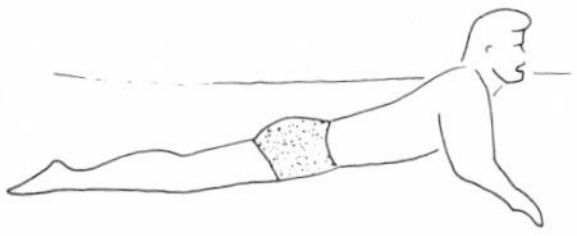

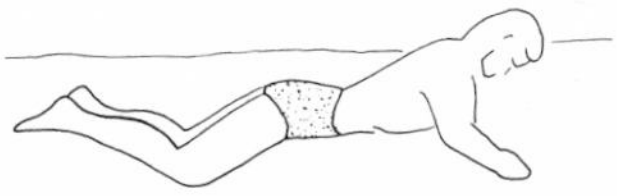

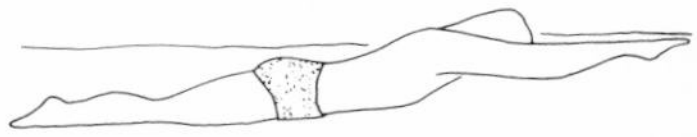

BUTTERFLY STROKE

The butterfly stroke is the only stroke invented by an American, David Armbruster, a former swimming coach at the University of Iowa. Although first demonstrated in 1935, it was not accepted as an official stroke until nearly twenty years later. It is the second fastest swimming stroke, ranking just behind the crawl. Because this stroke requires so much strength in the arms, most beginners and intermediates find it extremely difficult to do, and for the same reason, it has limited value for life-saving.

Performing the Butterfly Stroke

The dolphin kick is best described as a double-leg flutter kick, while the arm action likewise can be pictured as a double-crawl stroke movement. Chart 4:6 diagrams and explains the kick, arm action, coordination, and breathing of this stroke.

CHART 4:6
PERFORMANCE TECHNIQUES FOR THE BUTTERFLY STROKE

Techniques	Illustration	Major and/or Common Performance Errors
KICK A. Assume face-down position with legs together, toes pointed. Bend slightly at knees.	A.	A. Bending too much at the knees (causing feet to come out of water).
B. Press feet vigorously downward and backward, keeping thighs at about same level in water.	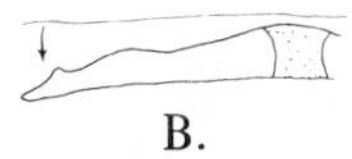 B.	B. Pressing feet backward and with no downward emphasis.
C. Force legs upward. Keep legs extended until near end of rise.	 C.	C. Moving hips downward rather than forcing legs upward. Having too much up-and-down movement of hips.
D. Bend knees slightly in preparation for downward and backward press.	 D.	D. Bending too much at the knees.

ARM ACTION

E. Extend arms, with slight bend at elbows.
  Submerge arms 10-12 inches in water.

E.

E. Pressing down too far or too hard (causing head to rise too high and feet to sink).

F. Bend at elbows. Pull and push hands backward toward feet until arms are extended along sides.

F.

F. Failing to bend arms to obtain best leverage.
  Gliding with arms at sides.

G. Begin arm recovery by lifting elbows upward.
  Swing arms forward over the water.
  Lower chin toward chest.

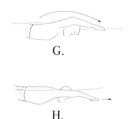
G.

G. Pushing arms forward instead of swinging from shoulders.
  Dragging arms in water.

H. Enter hands in water in front of shoulders.
  Glide briefly.

H.

H. Placing elbows in water before hands enter.

COORDINATION AND BREATHING

I. Raise chin out of water and inhale during arm press.
  Deliver one major kick during the late part of backward press of arms.

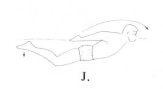
I.

I. Raising head too high in order to breathe.
  Raising head as kick is delivered.

J. (Usually) deliver a second (weaker) kick during the late part of arm recovery.
  Lower face into water.
  Exhale slowly or hold breath until just prior to inhalation.
  Undulate the spine and legs to obtain a porpoiselike action.

J.

J. Failing to return the face into the water.
  Being stiff in the spine and legs.

Teaching the Butterfly Stroke

The instructor will find that unless students are permitted to swim widths (or comparatively short distances) of the butterfly stroke, they become so arm-weary that correct practice is impossible. Swimming without breathing is essential before the leg and arm coordination can be mastered; thus swimming more than 15 yards is not advised. The "one-stroke kicking" drill may be used effectively; that is, the swimmer kicks lengths while in a gliding position without a board. When he needs a breath, only one arm stroke is taken, and then the kicking continues. This drill has two advantages: (1) the legs are given the practice they need, and (2) the swimmer does not have to be continually thinking about his legs, arms, and breathing all at once. At first, the distance kicked should be short (10 yards) but as soon as a strong dolphin kick is developed, the distance should be lengthened.

Chart 4:7 depicts a teaching progression for the butterfly stroke.

CHART 4:7
TEACHING PROGRESSION FOR THE BUTTERFLY STROKE

Step 1	Step 2	Step 3
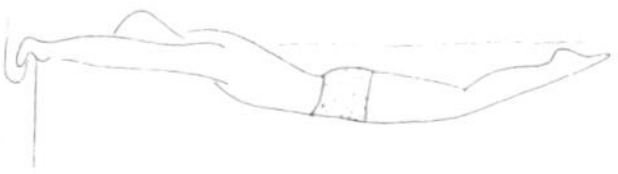 Have students practice the kick on wall. Emphasize down and back action; no thumping, very little splash.	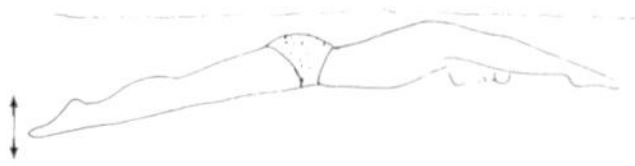 Have students duck underwater, push off, kick a distance underwater. Sometimes turning on the side will help students grasp idea of "dolphin" motion.	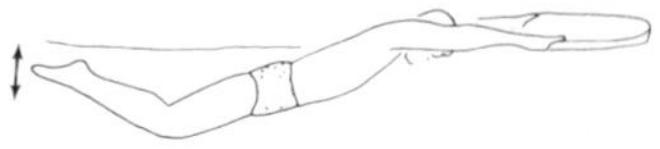 Have students kick on top of the water (with or without kickboard). Do not permit thumping.

Step 4	Step 5	Step 6
 Have students stand, practice arm movement (no breath). Emphasize "push back," not press down.	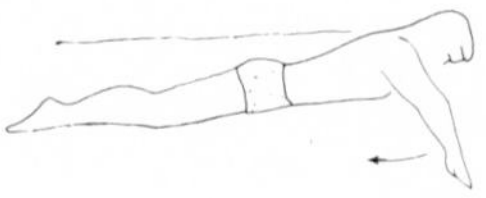 Have students push off, practice arm action (no breathing).	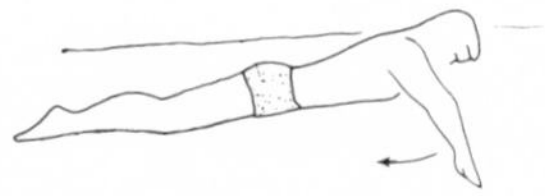 Have students push off, kick four or six times; then add arms on kicks numbers 5 and 7. Stress two kicks to one arm action; no breathing.

Step 7	Step 8	Step 9
 Have students stand, practice arm action with breathing. Emphasize chin just clearing water, with no shoulder rise.	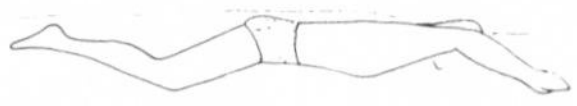 Have students push off, glide, do one complete stroke (including breathing), stop. Permit those who do this correctly to take three strokes.	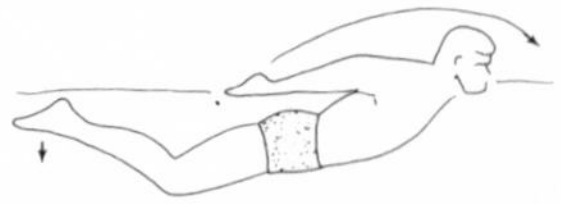 Have students swim a given distance. Emphasize form, not speed.

BACK CRAWL STROKE

The back crawl stroke is comparatively easy for most swimmers, young and old, to learn. It is a good stroke for beginners because breathing poses no problems; however, this is counterbalanced for most adults because they prefer to see where they are swimming. Since swimming is most often taught in pools, instruction in the open turn should also accompany this stroke.

Performing the Back Crawl Stroke

The flutter kick on the back (first described in Chapter 3) is used for this stroke.

The arm stroke, coordination, and breathing for the back crawl are discussed and diagrammed in Chart 4:8.

CHART 4:8
PERFORMANCE TECHNIQUES FOR THE BACK CRAWL STROKE

Techniques	Illustration	Major and/or Common Performance Errors
KICK A. Extend legs, point toes. Move feet alternately up and down 12-15 inches. Have slight bend at knees. Limit the amount of splash. Emphasize "up" beat and kicking from hips. **ARM ACTION** B. Extend leading arm forward and extend trailing arm along side.	 A. B.	A. Bending too much at knees (causing knees to be above surface). Having feet too low in the water. Using a kick that is too narrow. Failing to point toes. B. Crossing the leading arm behind the head.
C. Bend leading arm at elbow and pull (parallel to surface) to a point opposite the shoulder. Begin recovery of trailing arm (little finger leading).	 C.	C. Pulling too deeply (causing lunging from side to side). Delaying recovery of trailing arm.
D. Continue pull of leading arm toward hips, extending wrist so push is toward feet. (Some bend at elbow may give better leverage.) Continue the recovery of trailing arm.	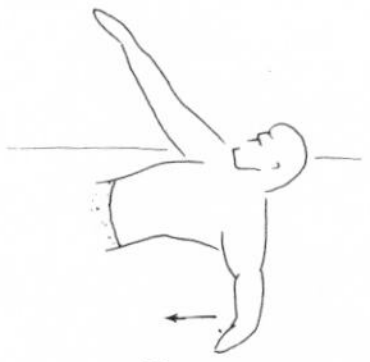 D.	D. Pointing the elbow toward the feet (thus causing hand to slip through water). Failing to lift entire arm above water surface.
E. As hand of pulling arm nears side, rotate wrist to face palm downward. Enter the recovering arm into water above the shoulder. (Some instructors encourage limited side-to-side roll as an aid in arm leverage and recovery.)	 E.	E. Failing to keep arms opposite one another (letting one remain at side until other catches up). Entering elbow before hand. Pounding arm into water. Rolling into an on-side position.

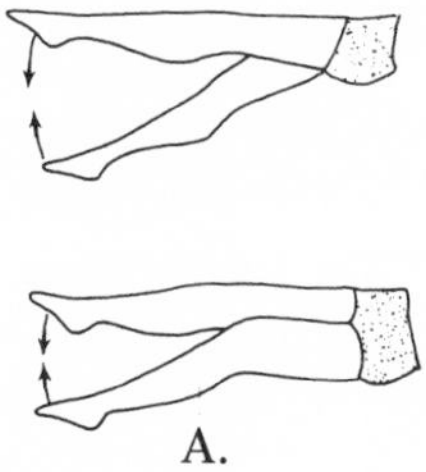

Chart 4:8 - Performance Techniques for the Back Crawl Stroke (continued)

COORDINATION AND
BREATHING

F. (Usually) deliver six flutter kicks to the pull-push-recovery cycle of both arms (three up-kicks to one arm pull).

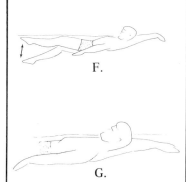

F.

F. Kicking less than two times to each complete arm pull.
    Permitting arms and legs to work independently of each other.
    Letting hips sag (causing "sitting down" in water).

G. Keep back of head in water, with eyes looking upward.
    Breathe when convenient and need is felt.

G.

G. Raising head and looking toward feet.
    Inclining head too far back (causing water to surge over face).

Teaching the Back Crawl Stroke

    Once the swimmer can float and kick on his back, this stroke may be taught. A teaching progression is shown in Chart 4:9.

**CHART 4:9
TEACHING PROGRESSION FOR THE BACK CRAWL STROKE**

Step 1	Step 2	Step 3
Have students practice the kick by hanging on the wall or in shallow water. Emphasize no knees out of water, top of foot kicking only to surface.	Have students push off, flutter kick on back. A kickboard can be used but it is easier to leave arms at side or extended forward.	Have students stand, practice arm stroke. Emphasize push down toward feet.
Step 4	Step 5	Step 6
Have students glide and practice arm stroke only.	Have students practice the complete stroke (arms, legs, breathing) for a short distance. Emphasize form, not speed.	Have students swim a longer distance to refine techniques and attain smooth coordination.

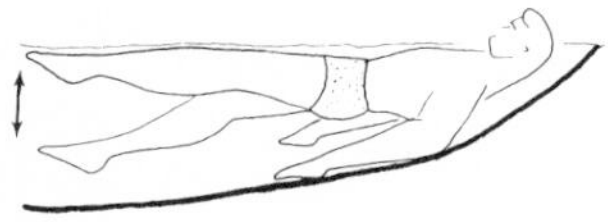

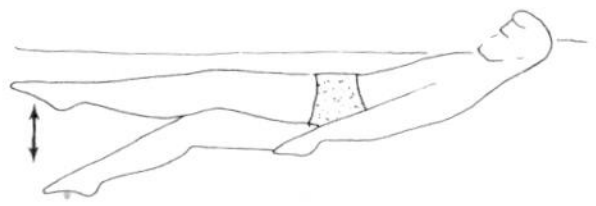

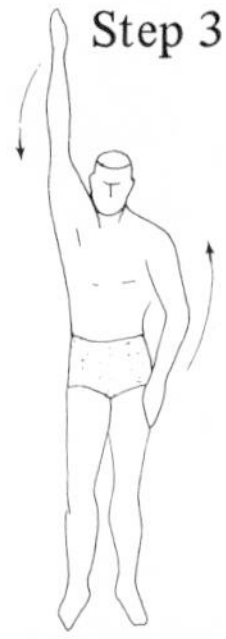

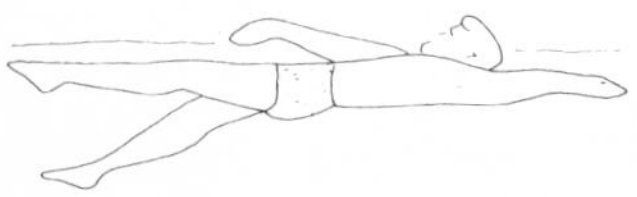

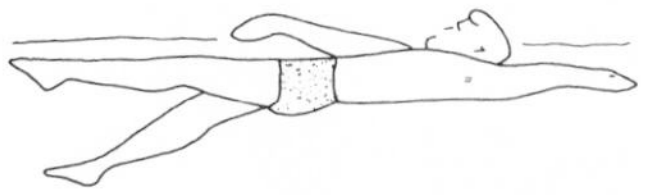

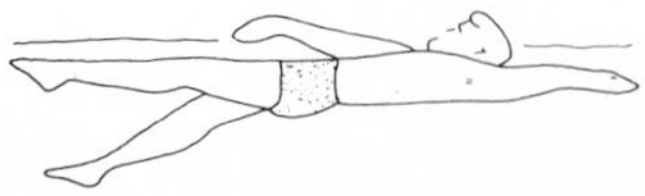

THE TRUDGEN STROKES

So far as we know, the trudgen is the only stroke named after a definite person — John Trudgen, of England. Although it is not taught very often in beginning or intermediate classes, it still is quite common because many people have taught themselves the stroke. The trudgen stroke features an extreme body roll and glide (akin to the gliding position of the sidestroke), with the arm action of the crawl stroke. Those who have taught themselves to swim find it easier to breathe by rolling the entire body than to roll the head. This body roll is accompanied by a scissor or breaststroke kick. It has three advantages: (1) it is an overhand stroke, which both adults and children like to be able to do; (2) it permits more time for breathing; and (3) it is less tiring, permits more rest and relaxation, and yet is faster than the elementary backstroke, sidestroke, or breaststroke. All in all, it is often advisable to perfect the trudgen stroke of adults rather than have them spend excessive time trying to master the crawl stroke.

Performing the Single and Double Trudgen Strokes

In the single trudgen stroke only one kick is delivered in conjunction with a complete arm cycle. The double trudgen features two kicks to each arm cycle, delivered as each arm recovers. A narrower scissors kick is preferred, but a swimmer with a good breaststroke kick can sometimes move more easily with the latter leg action. Chart 4:10 depicts the single trudgen stroke, and Chart 4:11 the double trudgen stroke.

CHART 4:10
PERFORMANCE TECHNIQUES FOR THE SINGLE TRUDGEN STROKE

Techniques	Illustration	Major and/or Common Performance Errors
KICK A. Deliver a scissors kick as learned for sidestroke but make the stride separation of the legs narrower.	A.	A. Making stride too narrow. Making stride too wide. Failing to kick vigorously.
ARM ACTION B. Assume a gliding position on the side as learned for side-stroke.	B.	B. Failing to assume the correct gliding position.
C. Execute simultaneously a crawl stroke pull with leading arm and a crawl stroke recovery with trailing arm.	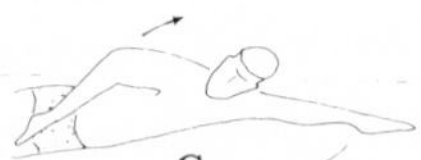 C.	C. Thrusting the trailing arm forward instead of swinging the arm forward over water from the shoulder.
D. Recover leading arm as trailing arm pulls.	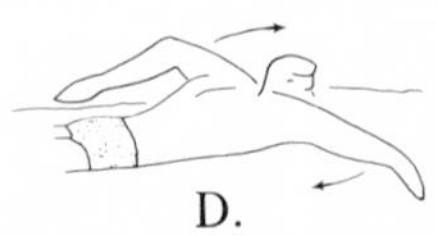 D.	D. Failing to recover trailing arm over water.

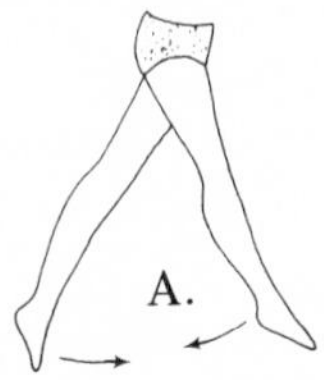

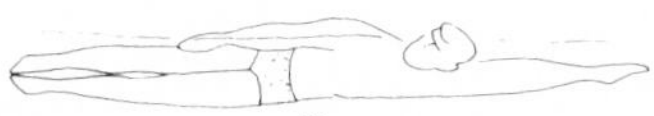

COORDINATION AND BREATHING		Major and/or Common Performance Errors
E. Assume a gliding position on one side.	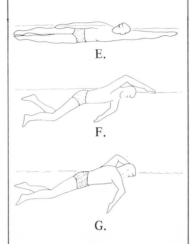E.	E. Gliding on stomach. Gliding on back.
F. Roll onto stomach as leading arm pulls and trailing arm recovers.	F.	F. Failing to roll far enough onto stomach for trailing arm to be lifted clear of the water. Kicking during recovery of trailing arm.
G. Recover leading arm forward and bring legs into position for scissors kick as body is rolled from stomach to side and as trailing arm begins pull. Deliver kick and complete pull of trailing arm. Exhale. Glide on side and inhale.	G.	G. Pulling trailing arm through to thigh before recovering the legs for kick. Lifting trailing arm for recovery immediately after pull to thigh.

CHART 4:11
PERFORMANCE TECHNIQUES FOR THE DOUBLE TRUDGEN STROKE

Techniques	Illustration	Major and/or Common Performance Errors
KICK A. Deliver a scissors kick as *each* arm is recovered.	A.	A. Executing a kick that is too narrow. Failing to kick with equal vigor on each side.
ARM ACTION B. Execute the crawl stroke recovery and pull of the arms.	B.	B. Making the pull and/or recovery of one arm shorter than that of the other arm.
COORDINATION AND BREATHING C. Assume a face-down gliding position with one arm extended forward and other arm trailing at thigh. Execute a scissors kick as leading arm is pulled backward to thigh and trailing arm is recovered forward. (NOTE: Some instructors permit a breath to be taken as each arm is thrust forward.) Glide in on-side position. (Length of glide may be long for resting or may be brief.)	C.	C. Permitting the kick to precede or to follow the arm pull.

D. Roll onto stomach and to opposite side.

During the roll, recover the arm that now is at the thigh, pull with the opposite arm and execute a second scissors kick.

(NOTE: Some instructors permit a breath to be taken as each arm is thrust forward.)

Glide in on-side position (may be long or brief).

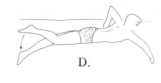
D.

D. Permitting the kick executed. when rolling to one side to be weaker than the kick executed when rolling to the other side.

E. Substitute a breaststroke kick for each scissors kick (limited or no body roll is induced). This variation is especially beneficial to a swimmer with a strong breaststroke kick.

E.

E. Failing to pull the arms through completely.

Failing to clear arms over surface on recovery.

Teaching the Single and Double Trudgen Strokes

Most instructors are not too eager to teach the trudgen strokes because they themselves do not swim them well. If it is remembered that the basis for these strokes is the overarm sidestroke, the following progression (Chart 4:12) will be easy to use.

CHART 4:12
TEACHING PROGRESSION FOR THE SINGLE AND DOUBLE TRUDGEN STROKES

Step 1	Step 2	Step 3
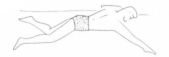		
Have students review the overarm sidestroke, but consciously rolling more on the stomach with each stroke. Emphasize glide and body roll.	Have students switch to single trudgen by recovering both arms above water. Be sure both arms are pushed all the way back, and that glide is present.	To prepare for double trudgen, have students practice scissors kick on alternating sides. Exaggerate body roll if necessary, but don't permit inverted scissors.

Step 4	Step 5

Have students swim single trudgen but exaggerate roll to stomach. (Glide between arm pulls if going to use breaststroke kick.)	Have students add second kick as second arm is recovered. Students can say to themselves, "Kick and glide, kick and glide" as each arm is recovered.

Performing the Trudgen Crawl Stroke

It is not uncommon to see self-taught swimmers use the trudgen crawl stroke. They have seen other swimmers use a flutter kick so they try it, but because they roll their body to breathe, the natural tendency is to use the trudgen crawl rather than the crawl stroke. The trudgen crawl is thus a combination of three flutter kicks, one scissors (or breaststroke) kick, and two arm strokes. A pronounced glide follows the scissors kick. The breathing is the same as described earlier. See Chart 4:13 for these skills.

CHART 4:13
PERFORMANCE TECHNIQUES FOR THE TRUDGEN CRAWL STROKE

Techniques	Illustration	Major and/or Common Performance Errors
KICK A. Deliver three flutter kicks as one arm is pulling.	A.	A. Bending too much at knees. Failing to point toes.
B. Deliver a single scissors kick as other arm is pulling.	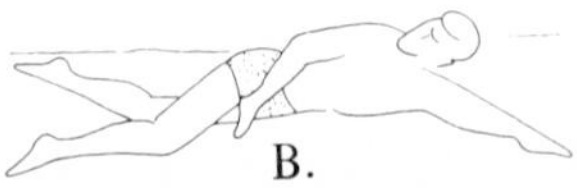 B.	B. Performing a wide flutter kick instead of a scissors kick.
ARM ACTION C. Execute the arm action as learned for the single trudgen stroke.	C.	C. Failing to recover each of the arms above the surface.

COORDINATION AND BREATHING
 	
D. Assume a sidestroke glide position.
    Execute three flutter kicks as the leading arm pulls backward and trailing arm recovers forward.
    Execute the scissors kick and arm action of single trudgen stroke.
    Exhale and inhale.
    Glide on the side.
	D.	D. Executing too many flutter kicks (causing interference with recovery of the legs for delivery of scissors kick).

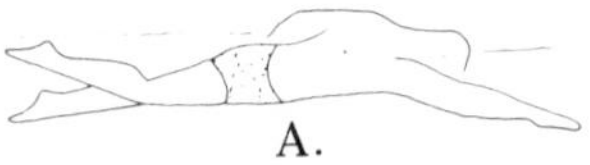

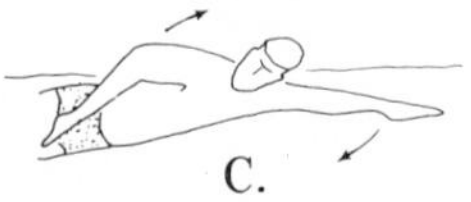

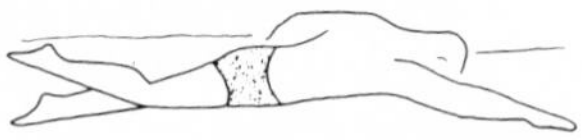

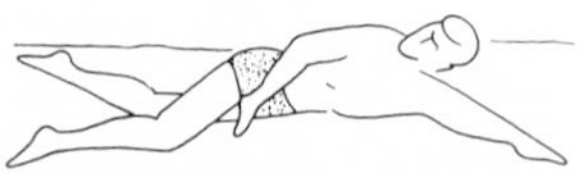

Teaching the Trudgen Crawl Stroke

As mentioned earlier, if students have taught themselves the trudgen, it is almost always the trudgen crawl. The whole method of instruction is suitable for use with such students. When teaching the stroke to persons who have never tried it, the progression shown in Chart 4:14 is suitable.

CHART 4:14
TEACHING PROGRESSION FOR THE TRUDGEN CRAWL STROKE

Step 1	Step 2	Step 3
Have students use kickboards to practice three flutter kicks, followed by a body roll and one scissors kick. Emphasize the body roll for scissors kick.	Have students swim the single trudgen stroke.	Have students swim the single trudgen, adding the three flutter kicks as the arm pull between glides is made.

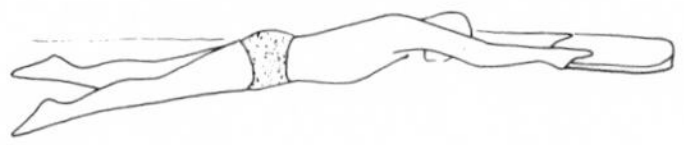

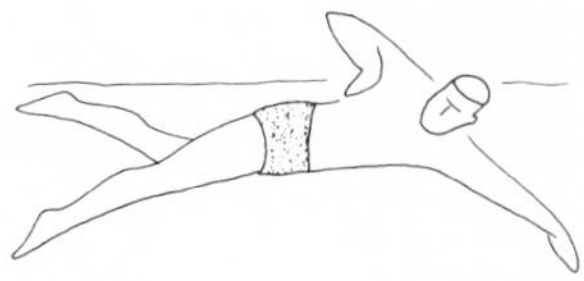

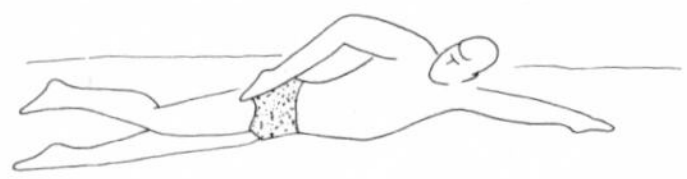

INVERTED BREASTSTROKE

This stroke is primarily a resting stroke and can be done most easily by those swimmers who possess a good wedge or whip kick. It is usually performed with a single glide following the kick, but a variation (shown below in Chart 4:15) is much superior in terms of efficient movement through the water. This variation, also called the double-gliding backstroke, emphasizes an arm pull followed by a glide and then an arm recovery followed by a glide.

Performing the Inverted Breaststroke

Both the whip and the wedge kicks have been described earlier in Chapter 3. When done on the back, the technique is essentially the same as when done on the stomach. Chart 4:15 presents the kick, arm action, coordination, and breathing of the inverted breaststroke.

CHART 4:15
PERFORMANCE TECHNIQUES FOR THE INVERTED BREASTSTROKE

Techniques	Illustration	Major and/or Common Performance Errors
KICK A. The inverted whip kick is preferred, but the inverted wedge is acceptable.		

INVERTED KICK (WHIP)

1. Drop heels toward bottom, keeping knees just below surface.

   Keep knees together (toes pointed outward).
2. Extend legs by bringing feet diagonally outward and toward surface (toes remain pointed outward).
3. Straighten legs as they are pressed back and squeezed together.

   Point toes back by end of press.
4. Glide for 3-6 seconds.

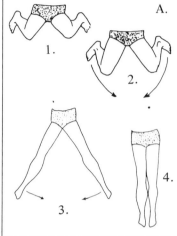

A. 1. Failing to keep thighs at surface.

   Pointing toes backward.

2. Lowering thighs as legs are extended.

3. Applying too little effort to press or squeeze.

4. Failing to glide.

INVERTED KICK (WEDGE)

5. Spread knees 15-18 inches.

   Lower heels downward, keeping knees just below surface.
6. Extend lower legs by moving feet outward.

   Point toes outward.
7. Straighten legs as they are pressed backward and squeezed together.

   Point toes back by end of press.
8. Glide for 3-6 seconds.

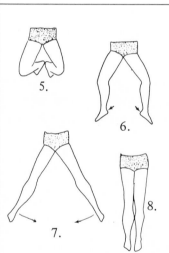

5. Bringing knees above surface.

6. Extending legs by lowering thighs.

   Pointing toes upward.
7. Expending too little effort on press or squeeze.

   Pointing toes backward.

8. Recovering legs for next kick without pause for glide.

ARM ACTION

B. Assume gliding position with arms extended in direction of progress.

C. Pull arms down to shoulder level, continue pushing them to hips.

D. Recover arms by bending at elbows, hands close to body, elbows slowly leading hands toward the shoulders.

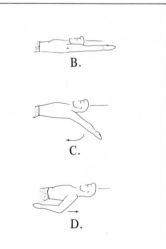

B. Failing to extend arms.

C. Failing to apply sufficient force with pull and push of arms to provide momentum.

D. Recovering arms so forcefully that momentum is retarded.

   Recovering hands over the chest rather than outside of shoulders.

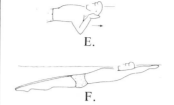

E. When hands reach shoulders, drop elbows toward bottom, push hands to extended position.	E. Causing water to be splashed over the face by not dropping elbows or by moving arms too fast.
F. Glide until legs start to drop.	F. Failing to hold glide long enough.

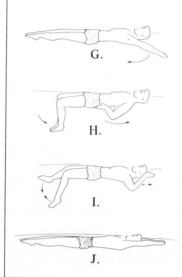

COORDINATION AND BREATHING

G. Pull (and push) with arms. Legs remain in streamlined gliding position. Exhale and inhale at the end of the pull.	G. Bending legs immediately after completion of the kick.
H. As the hands approach shoulder level, recover the legs.	H. Recovering the legs before beginning the recovery of the arms.
I. Kick as the arms are extending forward into gliding position.	I. Kicking before the hands begin their move into the gliding position.
J. Glide, and hold breath.	J. Failing to hold glide until feet start to drop.

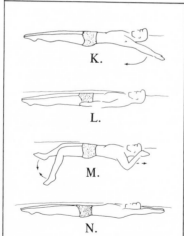

VARIATION

K. Pull (and push) with arms, legs remaining in gliding position. Exhale and inhale.	K. Bending legs immediately after completion of the kick.
L. Glide until feet start to drop.	L. Failing to hold glide long enough.
M. Recover arms and deliver leg kick as shown in Illustration I.	M. Kicking before the hands begin their move into the gliding position.
N. Glide and hold breath.	N. Failing to hold glide until feet start to drop.

Teaching the Inverted Breaststroke

Since this stroke normally will not be taught until the swimmers are skilled in the other basic strokes, it is usually easy to teach. A suggested progression is shown in Chart 4:16.

When doing this stroke for a test, the correct arm action must be used. However, for practical purposes, advise the swimmer to use whichever arm action gives him the best distance for the number of strokes taken.

CHART 4:16
TEACHING PROGRESSION FOR THE INVERTED BREASTSTROKE

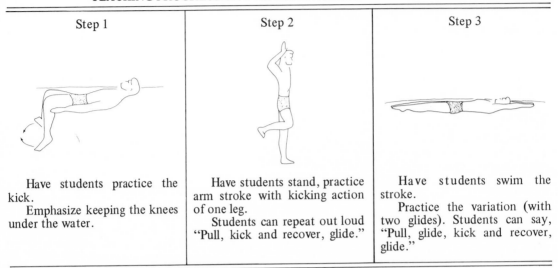

Step 1	Step 2	Step 3
Have students practice the kick. Emphasize keeping the knees under the water.	Have students stand, practice arm stroke with kicking action of one leg. Students can repeat out loud "Pull, kick and recover, glide."	Have students swim the stroke. Practice the variation (with two glides). Students can say, "Pull, glide, kick and recover, glide."

TURNING AT POOL ENDS

Swimming lengths in a pool requires that some efficient way of turning must be known. Open turns are taught to all swimmers; closed turns (see Chapter 10) are taught to those who have a possible racing career ahead of them. The essential difference between these turns is that the swimmer takes a breath during an open turn, and does not do so during a closed turn.

Performing the Crawl, Side, Back, and Breaststroke Open Turns

Charts 4:17 and 4:18 depict the skills needed for the crawl stroke, sidestroke, and backstroke open turns. The competitive breaststroke turn is essentially that one shown here in Chart 4:19, but the underwater action is much more demanding. If the skill of the group warrants, it is better to teach the competitive turns right away; see Chart 10:5 for this explanation.

CHART 4:17
PERFORMANCE TECHNIQUES FOR THE CRAWL STROKE AND SIDESTROKE OPEN TURNS

Techniques	Illustration	Major and/or Common Performance Errors
CRAWL STROKE A. Roll on one side, with lead arm extended toward wall.	A.	A. Failing to roll on side.
B. Bend lead arm upon contact; begin to tuck legs.	B.	B. Failing to bend arm upon contact with wall.
C. Swing legs under body; swing upper body in opposite direction; inhale.	C.	C. Failing to tuck legs enough. Failing to breathe. Raising head too high.

D. Submerge 12-15 inches; legs and arms bent.

E. Remain on side; extend arms and extend legs.

F. Push off in streamlined position (arms over ears).

G. Gradually roll over to stomach; begin flutter kick.

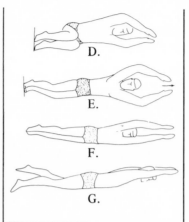

D.

E.

F.

G.

D. Failing to sink down well underwater.

E. Extending legs before arms are extended.

F. Failing to tuck head.
Pushing off on stomach.

G. Failing to begin kick while underwater.

SIDESTROKE

H. Exactly the same as the crawl stroke open turn.
  1. Roll on one side, lead arm extended toward wall.
  2. Bend lead arm upon contact; begin to tuck legs.
  3. Swing legs under body; swing upper body in opposite direction; inhale.

  4. Submerge 12-15 inches; legs and arms bent.
  5. Remain on side; extend arms and extend legs.
  6. Push off in streamlined position (arms over ears).
  7. After brief glide, pull arm closest to surface down to thigh.
  (OR, if wishing to swim on same side as before, roll over to other side after push-off).

I. Alternate turn.
  1. Reach to contact wall with trailing hand, rather than with leading arm.
    Bend trailing arm.
    Turn around by dropping shoulder of leading arm, tucking knees and hips.
  2. Submerge and push off on proper side. Pull uppermost arm down while underwater.

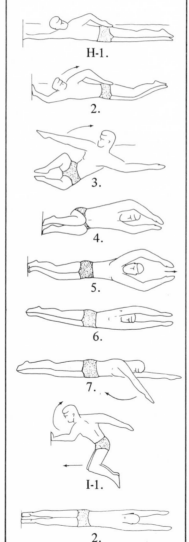

H-1.

2.

3.

4.

5.

6.

7.

I-1.

2.

H.

  1. Failing to roll on side.

  2. Failing to bend arm upon contact with wall.
  3. Failing to tuck legs enough.
    Failing to breathe.
    Raising head too high.
  4. Failing to sink down well under water.
  5. Extending legs before arms are extended.
  6. Failing to tuck head.
    Pushing off on stomach.
  7. Pulling through with leading arm.
    Pulling through with both arms during glide after push-off.

I.

  1. Failing to bend arm on contact.
    Failing to tuck tightly.
  2. Failing to submerge.
    Pulling through with leading arm or with both arms.

PERFORMANCE TECHNIQUES FOR THE BACKSTROKE OPEN TURN

Techniques	Illustration	Major and/or Common Performance Errors
A. Contact the wall with leading hand directly in front of its shoulder.		A. Placing the hand too outside of shoulder.
B. Bend leading arm, begin to tuck knees. Drop shoulder of leading hand, causing slight body roll toward that side.		B. Failing to roll toward proper side.
C. Swing tucked legs to wall as upper part of body goes in opposite direction.		C. Failing to tuck tightly.
D. Inhale; submerge 12-15 inches; place feet on wall; arms bent alongside head.		D. Failing to submerge deeply enough.
E. Extend arms, push off under water in a streamlined position.		E. Pushing off on top of the water. Pushing off before arms are extended.
F. Begin flutter kick before surface is reached.		F. Failing to begin kick as momentum decreases.

PERFORMANCE TECHNIQUES FOR THE BREASTSTROKE OPEN TURN

Techniques	Illustration	Major and/or Common Performance Errors
A. Contact wall with both hands at same time on same plane.		A. Failing to touch wall as rules prescribe (both hands touch simultaneously on same plane).
B. Bend arms; tuck knees.		B. Failing to get close to wall.
C. Push body (head leading) to one side or the other. Inhale.		C. Raising head too high. Failing to tuck head before turning.
D. Submerge 15-20 inches. Place bent arms under chest and face. Roll over on stomach.		D. Failing to get body deep enough before push off.
E. Extend arms and legs as push-off is performed. Attain streamlined position.		E. Completing push-off from wall before arms are extended.
F. Incline body upward to surface.		F. Having body inclined downward (feet higher than head).

Teaching the Turns

The push-off and the glide should be taught first before interjecting the more difficult elements of the turn. This is done by having practice on these skills alone. When these have been mastered, the swimmer should then stand about 8 feet from the wall in the shallow water, push off and glide into the wall. He then practices the turn itself, omitting the push-off. All swimmers have a favorite hand, and it is wise to let them practice more with this hand at first than the other. They must have a feeling of confidence in use of that hand before they are ready to try the other hand. However, once they can do the turn fairly well, then they must be forced to practice with both hands. Swimming widths, making them use whichever hand comes up, is an effective way of accomplishing this.

SURFACE DIVING

Surface diving appeals greatly to younger swimmers, but not so much to adults. Experience has shown that most adults will not surface dive voluntarily, but since these skills are part of the ARC and YMCA courses, everyone should know how to do them. We are continually amazed at the number of aquatic instructor candidates who cannot do these dives correctly; being able to get underwater with acceptable form is a requirement they all had to pass at one time or another.

Performing the Feet-First, Tuck, and Pike Surface Dives

Charts 4:20, 4:21, and 4:22 present descriptions and diagrams of these dives.

CHART 4:20
PERFORMANCE TECHNIQUES FOR THE FEET-FIRST SURFACE DIVE

Techniques	Illustration	Major and/or Common Performance Errors
A. Tread water, allowing feet to go directly under body. Extend arms sideward from the body and parallel to surface, palms down.	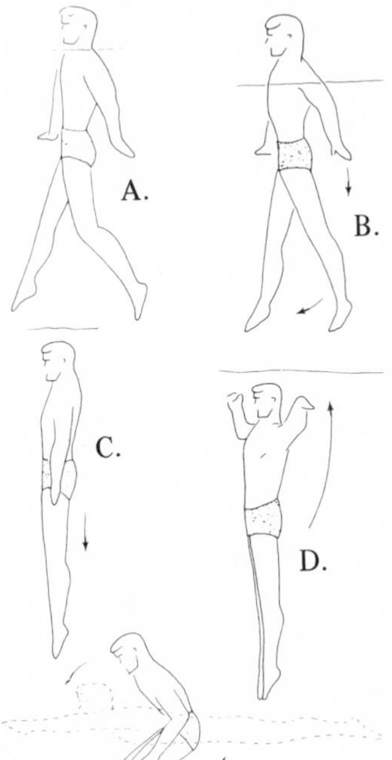	A. Failing to extend arms sideward, with palms down.
B. Press downward to the thighs at the same time a vigorous kick is given (causing chest to rise well out of the water).		B. Failing to press and kick efficiently enough to raise chest out of water.
C. Allow weight above surface to begin to force body downward.		C. Moving arms sideward or upward.
D. After head submerges, force extended arms (palms upward) toward the surface. To obtain additional depth, fin with the hands while they are overhead.		D. Forcing hands upward too soon (thus causing them to come out of the water). Thrusting arms upward (rather than pulling with arms extended).
E. When desired depth is reached, tuck body and then extend both arms and legs. Swim underwater to desired locale.		E. Failing to tuck chin when assuming horizontal position.

CHART 4:21
PERFORMANCE TECHNIQUES FOR THE TUCK SURFACE DIVE

Techniques	Illustration	Major and/or Common Performance Errors
A. Gain momentum (usually by performing one or two breast-strokes).	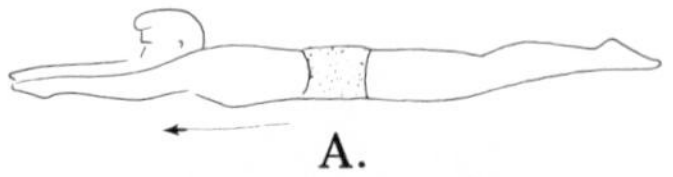	A. Failing to achieve momentum.
B. Bring chin to chest, bend body to right angle at hips, tuck arms to chest.	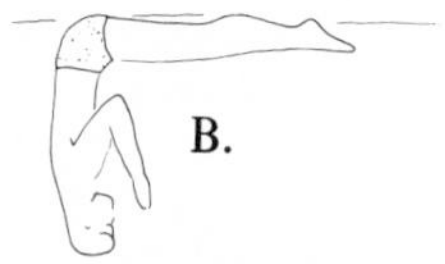	B. Failing to lower the head and bend enough at the hips.
C. Bend at knees and at hips to place body in tight tuck.	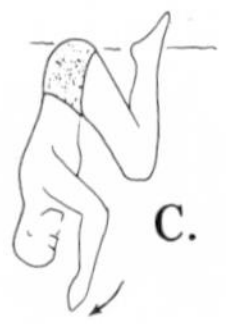	C. Failing to assume a tight tuck position.
D. Extend legs vigorously by pushing toes upward. Arms extended downward. Legs straight and together; toes pointed.	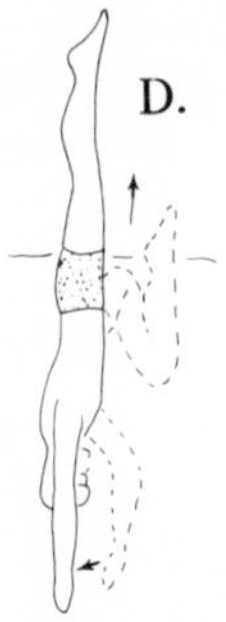	D. Failing to keep legs straight, together, and toes pointed after extension. Throwing feet backward (arching back) instead of upward.
E. Let weight of the legs cause body to sink. Use breaststroke pull to attain greater depth if needed.	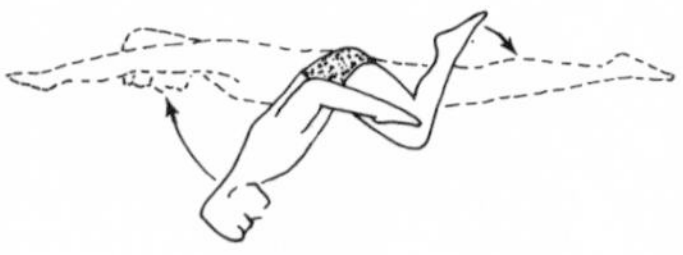	E. Failing to let weight of legs force body down. Failing to use arm movements to attain desired depth.
F. When desired depth is reached, tuck body or arch back to get it to horizontal position. Swim underwater to desired locale.	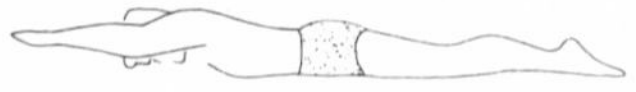	F. Failing to lower the chin toward the chest when assuming the horizontal position.

PERFORMANCE TECHNIQUES FOR THE PIKE SURFACE DIVE

Techniques	Illustration	Major and/or Common Performance Errors
A. Achieve momentum with breaststroke movements.	 A.	A. Failing to achieve momentum.
B. Pull arms all the way back to the thighs.	 B.	B. Failing to pull arms clear back to the thighs.
C. Bend the body at right angles at the hips.	 C.	C. Putting body at more or less than a right angle. Failing to keep legs straight.

D. Pull the extended arms (palms facing head) downward toward the head.
    Raise legs upward without knee bend, but with toes pointed.
	
	D.
		D. Failing to use arms to obtain leverage so as to raise the legs.
		    Failing to keep legs straight or toes pointed.

E. Use weight of legs to cause body to sink.
    Use breaststroke pull to attain greater depth.
	
	E.
		E. Failing to permit legs to force body down.
		    Failing to use arm movements to attain desired depth.

F. When desired depth is reached, tuck body or arch back to get it to horizontal position. Swim underwater to desired locale.	 F.	F. Failing to lower the chin toward the chest when assuming the horizontal position.

Teaching the Surface Dives

There are no special techniques for teaching any of the surface dives. For the pike and tuck dives, forward momentum before the body is bent at the waist is most important. An easy way to begin to learn the dives is to have the swimmers push off the wall and attempt the dive before they lose their momentum.

UNDERWATER SWIMMING

Like the surface dives, underwater swimming is more popular with the younger set than with the older swimmers. However, it is possible that swimmers of any age may have to locate some submerged object at some time — or pass an ARC or YMCA course. Moreover, possession of the skill is essential for participation in such activities as skin diving, spear fishing, and scuba diving. Thus, instruction should be given in underwater swimming. This skill is good for confidence-building and for increasing the breathing capacity. Swimmers must remember that they will travel further underwater if they glide as long as possible between strokes and if they have their feet on a slightly higher plane than their head.

Performing Underwater Swimming

There is no really defined form for underwater swimming; whatever works best is recommended. Underwater swimming is begun by the swimmer taking two or three deep breaths, thus getting rid of some of the carbon dioxide that is normally present in the inspired air. An instructor must never permit swimmers to take more than five deep breaths before swimming under water. An excessive amount may cause the swimmer to "black out" while underwater without being aware of it.

The stroke itself (see Chart 4:23) is usually a modified breaststroke.

CHART 4:23
PERFORMANCE TECHNIQUES FOR UNDERWATER SWIMMING

Techniques	Illustration	Major and/or Common Performance Errors
A. Extend arms forward, then pull and push them completely back to the thighs. Tuck chin toward chest. Keep feet at slightly higher level than head. (Some swimmers prefer to have a continuous, wide, slow flutter kick while the arm movement is being done.)	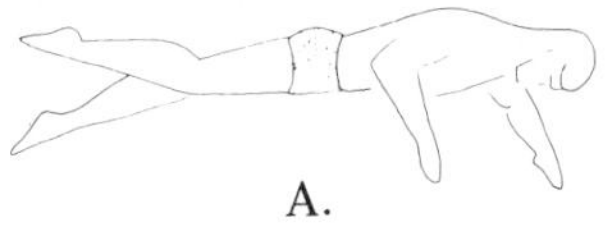 A.	A. Failing to keep head low, chin tucked.
B. Glide. (Some swimmers prefer to deliver a short series of flutter kicks during the glide, or to continue the wide, slow flutter kick).	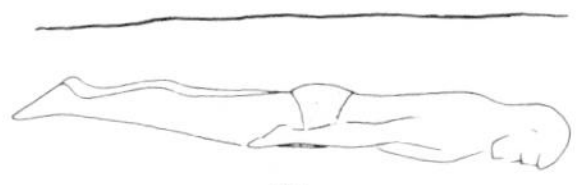 B.	B. Failing to glide.
C. Gently recover arms to forward extended position. (Some swimmers prefer to deliver a breaststroke or scissors kick as the arms are recovering, or to continue the wide, slow flutter kick.)	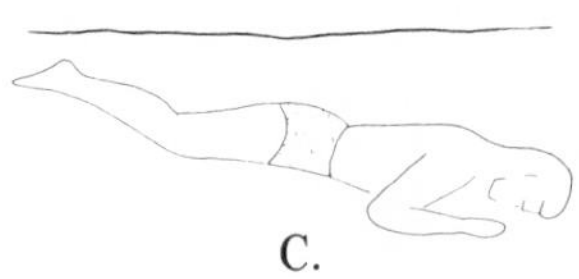 C.	C. Recovering the arms too vigorously (thus retarding momentum).
D. Glide with arms extended. (Some swimmers may prefer to continue the wide, slow flutter kick.)	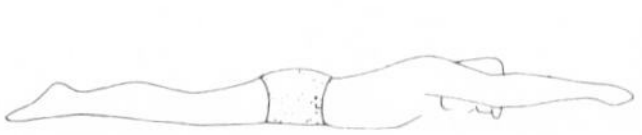 D.	D. Failing to glide.

Teaching the Underwater Swim

The usual procedure to teach this skill is to have the swimmer duck underwater close to the pool side, and then push off from the side with arms extended. As the glide speed slackens, he pulls and pushes vigorously with his arms and glides again. When that speed disappears, he recovers his arms and glides. This procedure may be done several different times until the most satisfactory kick and timing have been determined. However, two cautions must be observed when this skill is being taught: (1) no more than two or three pulls at one submersion should be allowed; and (2) no more than three or four individual trials in any one day should be allowed.

DIVING FROM BOARD

Again, diving from either the low or high board is of most interest to the younger swimmers. If adults do not want to dive, we customarily do not press the issue. However, if at all possible, we try to encourage all younger swimmers to dive, because experience shows that this is a skill that is socially desirable. Diving from the board is discussed in great detail in Chapter 5; especially, see pages 109-110 for comments dealing with the instruction of novice divers.

CLOTHING INFLATION

General Comments

Excellent sources for material on clothing inflation are found in the books by Torney, Silvia, and Lanoue. There is material on clothing inflation in other sources (Boy Scouts and the Red Cross) which also may prove helpful. All swimmers need to know at least the basic skills of clothing inflation, because the popularity of such aquatic sports as fishing and boating mean that a sizeable segment of our population is around the water when fully clothed. Authorities disagree as to whether or not the clothes should be removed if a person is thrown in the water, although there is general agreement that shoes should be removed. Our experience has been that good swimmers are skilled enough to remove their clothes, while poorer swimmers (primarily because they cannot tread water very well) have a difficult time. For this reason, all swimmers should first practice drownproofing with clothes on, and then practice the other skills mentioned below.

Performing Clothing Inflation

Upon entering the water the swimmer should begin drownproofing. This enables him to keep his head and to avoid the panic which is so prevalent in cases such as this. After achieving some stability (both of mind and body) the swimmer then decides what article(s) of clothing to inflate. We recommend swimmers be taught the skills shown in Chart 4:24, in the order presented.

PERFORMANCE TECHNIQUES FOR THE INFLATION OF CLOTHING

Techniques	Illustration	Major and/or Common Performance Errors
SHIRT A. After drownproofing a bit to reduce panic, blow air inside shirt. Button top button, open the shirt between second and third buttons and blow air inside. B. When sufficient air has entered, rebutton shirt and float face down (as in drownproofing). NOTE: T-shirts are virtually impossible to inflate, and some short-sleeved blouses are unsatisfactory. The swimmer may have to hold the collar tight if a button is missing.	 A. B.	A. Failing to lean forward when blowing into the shirt. B. Assuming a backleaning position (causing air to escape between buttons).

REMOVE SHOES
 	
C. Tuck shirttails in or tie them in front of waist.
    Float face downward, slowly untie knots in one shoe.
    Remove it, repeat with other shoe.
    NOTE: Some experts favor removing shoes first. We think it is better to attain some degree of calmness and buoyancy before attempting this.
	
	C.
		C. Failing to tuck or tie shirttails (causing air to escape around the waist).
		    Failing to keep face down in water.

PANTS
 	
D. After reinflating the shirt if needed, unfasten pants at the waist.
    Slide them down to the knees.
 	
E. If breath is needed, take one before removing one pant leg.
    Remove other pant leg.
    NOTE: Some experts favor removing one pant leg, then tying a knot in it before removing the other pant leg.
 	
F. Using air trapped in the shirt to float in a vertical position, zip or button pants at waist.
	
	D.
	E.
	
	F.
		D. Removing pants with hurried motions (causing pant legs to cling to body).
		
		E. Letting both pant legs drop to ankles, thus "tying up" legs.
		    Pulling one pant leg inside out while removing it.
		
		F. Failing to remain in upright position.

G. Tie overhand knot at end of each pant leg.

H. Spread pants (fly-side down) at water's surface.

I. Inflate by one of these methods:

    1. Holding waistband open. "Push" air into pants.
      Repeat until they are inflated.

OR

    2. Holding waistband open, submerge, blow air into pants. Repeat until they are inflated.

OR

    3. Holding pants behind head, sling them over and downward. Repeat if needed.

J. Keeping waistband below water's surface, put one leg (or one arm) through crotch.

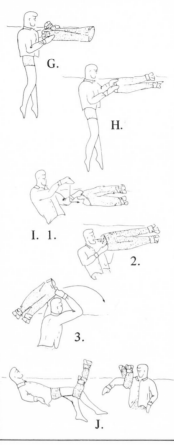

AIR PILLOW

K. Using inflated pants, float on back, slowly unbutton shirt or blouse.

L. Slowly remove one sleeve.
    Tie a single overhand knot just above the slit near the cuff.

M. Slowly remove other sleeve.
    Tie knot above slit.

N. Spread shirt or blouse out (back side up); gather all edges underneath.

O. Submerge, blow air into pillow.

P. Hang on, letting pillow act as the support.

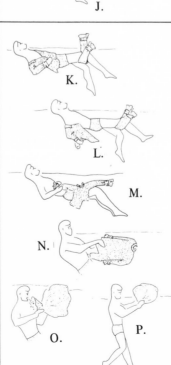

G. Tying the knot too high or too low on the leg.

H. Failing to have fly down.

I.

    1. Failing to have hand above the water when starting to "push" air.
      Not keeping waistband below water.

    2. Not keeping waistband below surface of water.

    3. Not keeping waistband open so as to catch the air.

J. Putting too much weight on pants, thus squeezing air through the cloth.

K. Failing to use inflated pants.
    Failing to move slowly.

L. Failing to tie knot just above the slit.
    Failing to move slowly.

M. Failing to tie knot just above slit.
    Failing to move slowly.

N. Failing to grasp all edges.

O. Failing to keep loose edges of shirt underwater.
    Failing to submerge in order to blow up into the pillow.

P. Applying too much body weight, thus causing air to escape.

Chart 4:24 – Performance Techniques for the Inflation of Clothing (continued)

AIR CHEST OR BELT

Q. If shift or skirt is worn, float on back.

Grasp hemline, raise it 1-2 feet above water.

R. Trap air as hemline is returned to water surface.

Repeat two or three times if necessary.

Float.

NOTE: If shift is worn, be sure collar is closed or else air will escape.

OR

S. If shirt is worn, remove it.
1. Using inflated pants, float on back, slowly unbutton shirt or blouse.
2. Slowly remove one sleeve.
Tie a single overhand knot just above the slit near the cuff.
3. Slowly remove other sleeve.
· Tie knot above slit.
4. Put shirt on "backside-front," buttoning behind neck.
5. Grasp the shirttails, and raise them 1-2 feet above the water.
Trap air as the tails are lowered to the water.
Repeat two or three times if necessary.
6. Tie the tails behind back or tuck into undergarments.
Float.

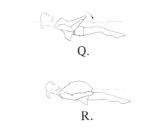
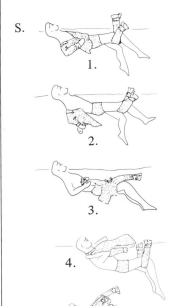

Q. Failing to raise hemline of skirt out of water.

R. Failing to keep hemline below water surface (thus permitting air to escape).

S.
1. Failing to use inflated pants.
Failing to move slowly.
2. Failing to tie knot just above the slit.
Failing to move slowly.

3. Failing to tie knot just above slit.
Failing to move slowly.
4. Having shirt inside out (pockets on inside).

5. Failing to get sufficient air into shirt.

6. Failing to tuck or tie shirt-tails.

Teaching the Skills of Clothing Inflation

When teaching clothing inflation, plan to take a whole period of class time (at least 35 minutes) so that students practice what they see demonstrated. Emphasize that clothes brought from home should be clean; even so, there will be enough thread, etc. from them to cause increased filtration work. While the students are practicing the above skills, do not let them touch the sides or pool bottom. When all have inflated both pieces of clothing, have them attempt to force all of the air out by climbing on top of the clothes. The students will actually see the folly of trying to use clothes as rafts, and quickly ascertain that they must not climb on them. Finally, have students swim a distance with their clothes on. They will also discover that the crawl or trudgen strokes (arm recovery over water) are less desirable than the sidestroke, elementary backstroke, breaststroke, or inverted breaststroke (arm recovery underwater).

CLASS ASSIGNMENTS

1. Locate a friend who cannot swim at least one of the strokes or skills presented in this chapter. Using our suggestions, teach the stroke or skill to your friend. In a short written report, summarize your success or failure to accomplish the task.

2. Talk to a teacher of intermediate swimmers. In a written report, indicate:

   a. Would he or she agree to the standards and skills proposed in this chapter? Explain any deviation.
   b. What are the hardest strokes or skills to teach this group, according to the instructor?
   c. How many sessions does it usually take to teach this course?

3. Talk to a teacher of advanced swimmers. In a written report, indicate the answers to the questions given above in Assignment 2.

4. Using the analysis sheets at the end of this chapter, evaluate the sidestroke, overarm sidestroke, breaststroke, butterfly stroke, back crawl stroke, single trudgen stroke, double trudgen stroke, trudgen crawl stroke, and inverted breaststroke of a swimmer.

BEHAVIORAL OBJECTIVES

Virtually all aquatic instructors will teach either intermediate or advanced swimmers. Thus, you should know the material in this chapter.

1. Be able to explain in writing a logical teaching progression (part, or progressive-part method) for the sidestroke, breaststroke, butterfly stroke, single trudgen stroke. Unless you are an experienced teacher (as determined by your instructor) the progressions must be those given in this text. Experienced instructors must base their progressions on those principles given in Chapter 3.

2. Be able to successfully demonstrate the strokes and skills given below. A successful demonstration is one with no major and/or common errors, as noted in the respective charts.

   a. Sidestroke (each side)
   b. Overarm sidestroke
   c. Breaststroke
   d. Butterfly stroke
   e. Back crawl stroke
   f. Single trudgen stroke
   g. Double trudgen stroke
   h. Trudgen crawl stroke

   i. Inverted breaststroke (plus variation)
   j. Open turns (crawl, back, breast)
   k. Surface dives (tuck, pike, feet-first)
   l. Underwater swim (30 feet)
   m. Clothes inflation (pants, shirt)
   n. 200-yard medley swim
      (girls - - - - 5:30 or better)
      (boys - - - - 4:15 or better)

BIBLIOGRAPHY

American National Red Cross. *Swimming and Water Safety.* Washington: The American National Red Cross, 1968, Chapters 5, 6, 7, 8, 9. See also *Charts on Nine Styles of Swimming* by same organization.

Armbruster, David A., Robert Allen and Bruce Harlan. *Swimming and Diving,* 3rd edition. St. Louis: The C. V. Mosby Company, 1958.

Lanoue, Fred R. *Drownproofing.* Englewood Cliffs, N.J.: Prentice Hall, Inc., 1963.

Silvia, Charles E. *Life Saving and Water Safety Instruction,* 3rd edition. New York: The Association Press, 1958.

Torney, John A., Jr. *Swimming.* New York: McGraw-Hill, 1950.

U. S. Navy. *Swimming.* Annapolis, Maryland: United States Naval Institute, 1944.

PERFORMANCE ANALYSIS SHEET FOR THE SIDESTROKE*

DIRECTIONS: Check √ all items that apply to the performance of this skill. Add other noted errors in the spaces provided.

NAME _____
(of performer)

NAME _____
(of analyzer)

Illustrations of correct techniques	Analysis of Performance

BODY POSITION

____ The form *is* acceptable.
____ The form is *not* acceptable because:
    ____ Arms and legs not fully extended.
    ____ Legs not together.
    ____ Body not stretched and straight.
    ____ Body turned toward stomach-down position.
    ____ Body turned toward back-down position.
    ____ Head not turned toward the upper shoulder to facilitate breathing.
    ____ (Other)_____ _____

LEGS

____ The form *is* acceptable.
____ The form is *not* acceptable because:
    ____ Legs separated vertically; resulting in a breast-stroke kick.
    ____ Inverted scissors kick used.
    ____ Legs do not bend enough at knees during recovery.
    ____ Knees brought too far in front of stomach during recovery.
    ____ Legs recovered too vigorously.
    ____ Legs not straightened before the squeeze.
    ____ Too little effort during squeeze.
    ____ Ankles not extended to point toes during late part of squeeze.
    ____ Legs pass each other at end of squeeze.
    ____ (Other)_____

ARMS

____ The form *is* acceptable.

____ The form is *not* acceptable because:

    ____ Pull of the leading (lower) arm too short.

    ____ Pull of leading arm too deep.

    ____ Leading arm not recovered with finger tips leading.

    ____ Elbow of leading arm not brought to ribs before recovery of that arm.

    ____ Trailing (upper) arm does not pull to thigh.

    ____ (Other)_____

    _____

COORDINATION AND BREATHING

____ The form *is* acceptable.

____ The form is *not* acceptable because:

    ____ Both arms pull toward feet at same time.

    ____ Leading arm begins pull immediately after recovery.

    ____ Leading arm pulls at same time kick is delivered.

    ____ Kick delivered before leading arm ready to recover.

    ____ Exhalation is at a time other than during leg kick or during glide.

    ____ Inhalation does not follow immediately after exhalation.

    ____ The duration of the glide is too brief.

    ____ (Other)_____

    _____

*Method by Barbara J. Sanborn

PERFORMANCE ANALYSIS SHEET FOR THE OVERARM SIDESTROKE*

DIRECTIONS: Check √ all items that apply to the performance of this skill. Add other noted errors in the space provided.

NAME_____
(of performer)

NAME_____
(of analyzer)

Illustrations of Correct Techniques	Analysis of Performance

BODY POSITION

_____ The form *is* acceptable.
_____ The form is *not* acceptable because:
    _____ Arms and legs not fully extended.
    _____ Legs not together.
    _____ Body not stretched and straight.
    _____ Body turned toward stomach-down position.
    _____ Body turned toward back-down position.
    _____ Head not turned toward the upper shoulder to facilitate breathing.
    _____ (Other)_____

LEGS

_____ The form *is* acceptable.
_____ The form is *not* acceptable because:
    _____ Legs separated vertically, resulting in a breast-stroke kick.
    _____ Inverted scissors kick used.
    _____ Legs do not bend enough at knees during recovery.
    _____ Knees brought too far in front of stomach during recovery.
    _____ Legs recovered too vigorously.
    _____ Legs not straightened before the squeeze.
    _____ Too little effort expended during the squeeze.
    _____ Ankles not extended to point toes during late part of squeeze.
    _____ Legs pass each other at end of squeeze.
    _____ (Other)_____

ARMS

_____ The form *is* acceptable.

_____ The form is *not* acceptable because:

    _____ Pull of the leading (lower) arm too short.

    _____ Pull of leading arm too deep.

    _____ Leading arm not recovered with finger tips leading.

    _____ Elbow of leading arm not brought to ribs before recovery of that arm.

    _____ Trailing (upper) arm not recovered overwater.

    _____ Trailing arm pounded into the water on recovery.

    _____ Trailing arm reaches too far forward on recovery.

    _____ Trailing arm does not pull through to thigh.

    _____ (Other)_____

_____

COORDINATION AND BREATHING

_____ The form *is* acceptable.

_____ The form is *not* acceptable because:

    _____ Both arms pull toward the feet at the same time.

    _____ Leading arm begins to pull immediately after recovery.

    _____ Leading arm pulls at the same time the kick is delivered.

    _____ Kick delivered before the leading arm is ready to recover.

    _____ Exhalation is at a time other than during leg kick or during glide.

    _____ Inhalation does not follow immediately after exhalation.

    _____ Duration of the glide too brief.

    _____ (Other)_____

_____

*Method by Barbara J. Sanborn

PERFORMANCE ANALYSIS SHEET FOR THE BREASTSTROKE*

DIRECTIONS: Check √ all items that apply to the performance of this skill. Add other noted errors in the spaces provided.

NAME _____
(of performer)

NAME _____
(of analyzer)

Illustrations of Correct Techniques	Analysis of Performance

BODY POSITION

_____ The form *is* acceptable.
_____ The form is *not* acceptable because:
    _____ Body not straight and stretched.
    _____ Legs not extended and together.
    _____ Ears not between extended arms.
    _____ (Other)_____

LEGS

_____ The form for whip kick *is* acceptable.
_____ The form for whip kick is *not* acceptable because:
    _____ Knees outside the heels during recovery of legs.
    _____ Toes not pointed backward during recovery of legs.
    _____ Legs recovered too quickly and vigorously.
    _____ Legs not straightened before backward press.
    _____ Too little effort applied to backward press.
    _____ Toes of one foot turned inward during the press.
    _____ (Other)_____

_____ The form for wedge kick *is* acceptable.
_____ The form for wedge kick is *not* acceptable because:
    _____ Heels inside the knees during recovery of legs.
    _____ Toes not pointed backward during recovery of legs.
    _____ Legs recovered too quickly and vigorously.
    _____ Legs not straightened before backward press.
    _____ Too little effort applied to backward press.
    _____ Toes of one foot turned inward during the press.
    _____ (Other)_____

ARMS

_____ The form *is* acceptable.
_____ The form is *not* acceptable because:
　　　_____ Arms pressed backward too far (___ to ribs; ___
　　　　　to thighs).
　　　_____ Arms pulled too vigorously.
　　　_____ Hands not brought in front of the chest before
　　　　　extension forward.
　　　_____ Arm pull too much under body.
　　　_____ Elbows not bent for leverage.
　　　_____ (Other)_____

_____

COORDINATION AND BREATHING

_____ The form *is* acceptable.
_____ The form is *not* acceptable because:
　　　_____ Arm pull begins immediately at end of recovery
　　　　　of arms.
　　　_____ Leg recovery begins immediately at end of leg
　　　　　kick.
　　　_____ Leg kick and arm pull occur at the same time.
　　　_____ One kick delivered to each pull of arms and one
　　　　　kick to each recovery of arms.
　　　_____ Duration of the glide is too brief.
　　　_____ Exhalation does not occur at end of glide.
　　　_____ Inhalation does not occur during early part of
　　　　　arm pull.
　　　_____ (Other)_____

_____

*Method by Barbara J. Sanborn

PERFORMANCE ANALYSIS SHEET FOR THE BUTTERFLY STROKE*

DIRECTIONS: Check √ all items that apply to the performance of this skill. Add other noted errors in the spaces provided.

NAME_____
(of performer)

NAME_____
(of analyzer)

Illustrations of Correct Techniques	Analysis of Performance

BODY POSITION

_____ The form *is* acceptable.
_____ The form is *not* acceptable because:
    _____ Body inclines toward vertical.
    _____ Legs too low.
    _____ Head too high.
    _____ Arms and legs not extended at the end of arm recovery.
    _____ (Other)_____
    _____

LEGS

_____ The form *is* acceptable.
_____ The form is *not* acceptable because:
    _____ Kick is a flutter kick.
    _____ Legs bend too little at knees.
    _____ Legs bend too much at knees.
    _____ Feet come above water surface.
    _____ Legs are not together.
    _____ Leg kick lacks vigor.
    _____ Ankles are not extended to point toes backward.
    _____ Upward and downward movement of the hips too great.
    _____ (Other) _____
    _____

ARMS

____ The form *is* acceptable.

____ The form is *not* acceptable because:

____ Pull not started with the hands forward from shoulders.

____ Arms press downward too far.

____ Arms press downward too strongly.

____ Arms do not bend during pull-push.

____ Arm pull ends at shoulders rather than at thighs.

____ Arms are not recovered over water.

____ Arms thrust forward rather than swung from shoulders.

____ Hands do not enter water before elbows enter.

____ Head not lowered before arm entry.

____ (Other)_____

_____

COORDINATION AND BREATHING

____ The form *is* acceptable.

____ The form is *not* acceptable because:

____ A leg kick and arm pull do not occur at the same time.

____ A leg kick and arm recovery do not occur at the same time.

____ Spine is stiff; body does not undulate.

____ Exhalation does not occur during glide or during early part of arm pull.

____ Inhalation does not occur as arms are pulled and pushed.

____ Head raised too high for breathing.

____ (Other)_____

_____

*Method by Barbara J. Sanborn

PERFORMANCE ANALYSIS SHEET FOR THE BACK CRAWL STROKE*

DIRECTIONS: Check √ all items that apply to the performance of this skill. Add other noted errors in the spaces provided.

NAME _____
(of performer)

NAME _____
(of analyzer)

Illustrations of Correct Techniques	Analysis of Performance

BODY POSITION

____ The form *is* acceptable.
____ The form is *not* acceptable because:
____ Body not straight.
____ Body position not horizontal.
____ Hips too low.
____ Head raised too high.
____ Head inclined backward.
____ Body lunges from side to side.
____ (Other)_____

KICK

____ The form *is* acceptable.
____ The form is *not* acceptable because:
____ Toes not pointed.
____ Knees bend too much.
____ Feet come above the surface.
____ Feet too low in the water.
____ Kick too narrow.
____ Kick too wide.
____ Legs too stiff.
____ Trudgen kick used.
____ (Other)_____

94

ARMS

_____ The form *is* acceptable.

_____ The form is *not* acceptable because:

  _____ Arm pull is too deep.

  _____ Elbow leads the hand during pull.

  _____ Arm pull too jerky and vigorous; is not a steady press.

  _____ Arm does not pull through to thigh.

  _____ An arm push does not follow arm pull.

  _____ Arm is thrust forward on recovery rather than swung from the shoulder.

  _____ On recovery, elbow enters water before hand enters.

  _____ On recovery, hand crosses the center line of body before entering water.

  _____ (Other)_____

  _____

COORDINATION AND BREATHING

_____ The form *is* acceptable.

_____ The form is *not* acceptable because:

  _____ Too many kicks delivered to each arm stroke.

  _____ Too few kicks delivered to each arm stroke.

  _____ Legs and arms perform independently of each other.

  _____ Breathing not easy and rhythmic.

  _____ (Other)_____

  _____

*Method by Barbara J. Sanborn

PERFORMANCE ANALYSIS SHEET FOR THE SINGLE TRUDGEN STROKE*

DIRECTIONS: Check √ all items that apply to the performance of this skill. Add other noted errors in the spaces provided.

NAME _____
(of performer)

NAME _____
(of analyzer)

Illustrations of Correct Techniques	Analysis of Performance

BODY POSITION DURING GLIDE

_____ The form *is* acceptable.
_____ The form is *not* acceptable because:
    _____ Arms and legs not fully extended.
    _____ Legs not together.
    _____ Body not stretched and straight.
    _____ Body turned toward face-down position.
    _____ Head not turned toward the upper shoulder to facilitate breathing.
    _____ Head above the surface at all times.
    _____ (Other)_____

LEGS

_____ The form *is* acceptable.
_____ The form is *not* acceptable because:
    _____ Inverted scissors kick is used.
    _____ Legs do not bend enough at knees during recovery.
    _____ Knees brought too far in front of stomach during recovery.
    _____ Legs recover too vigorously.
    _____ Legs not straightened before the squeeze.
    _____ Too little effort applied during squeeze.
    _____ Ankles not extended to point toes during late part of squeeze.
    _____ Legs pass each other at end of squeeze.
    _____ (Other)_____

ARMS

_____ The form *is* acceptable.
_____ The form is *not* acceptable because:
    _____ Pull-through of one arm shorter than pull-through of other.
    _____ Recovery of one arm shorter than recovery of other.
    _____ Arms not recovered over water.
    _____ On recovery, arms thrust forward rather than swung forward from shoulders.
    _____ Hand does not enter water in front of shoulder of that arm.
    _____ (Other) _____

_____

COORDINATION AND BREATHING

_____ The form *is* acceptable.
_____ The form is *not* acceptable because:
    _____ Body does not roll onto the stomach after glide on the side.
    _____ Kick delivered at the same time that arm on the breathing side recovered.
    _____ Pull of leading arm begun immediately at end of recovery of that arm.
    _____ Head lifted rather than turned to the side.
    _____ Exhalation at a time other than during leg kick or during glide.
    _____ Inhalation does not follow immediately after exhalation.
    _____ Duration of the glide too brief.
    _____ (Other)_____

_____

*Method by Barbara J. Sanborn

PERFORMANCE ANALYSIS SHEET FOR THE DOUBLE TRUDGEN STROKE*

DIRECTIONS: Check √ all items that apply to the performance of this skill. Add other noted errors in the spaces provided.

NAME _____
(of performer)

NAME _____
(of analyzer)

Illustrations of Correct Techniques	Analysis of Performance

BODY POSITION

____ The form *is* acceptable.
____ The form is *not* acceptable because:
    ____ Body not straight and stretched.
    ____ Face above water at all times.
    ____ Body not in horizontal position.
    ____ (Other)_____

KICK

____ The form for narrow scissors kick *is* acceptable.
____ The form for narrow scissors kick is *not* acceptable because:
    ____ Inverted scissors kick used.
    ____ Legs do not bend enough at knees during recovery.
    ____ Knees brought too far in front of stomach during recovery.
    ____ Legs recovered too vigorously.
    ____ Legs not straightened before the squeeze.
    ____ Ankles not extended to point toes during late part of squeeze.
    ____ (Other)_____

____ The form for breaststroke kick *is* acceptable.
____ The form for breaststroke kick is *not* acceptable because:
    ____ Toes not pointed backward during recovery of the legs.
    ____ Legs recovered too vigorously.
    ____ Legs not straightened before backward press.
    ____ Too little effort applied to backward press.
    ____ (Other)_____

98

ARMS

_____ The form *is* acceptable.

_____ The form is *not* acceptable because:

    _____ Each arm begins pull immediately at end of recovery.

    _____ Pull-through of one arm is shorter than pull-through of other.

    _____ Recovery of one arm is shorter than recovery of other.

    _____ Arms are not recovered over water.

    _____ On recovery, arms are thrust forward rather than swung forward from the shoulder.

    _____ Hand does not enter the water in front of shoulder of that arm.

    _____ (Other)_____

_____

COORDINATION AND BREATHING

_____ The form *is* acceptable.

_____ The form is *not* acceptable because:

    _____ Rate of stroking too rapid.

    _____ Duration of glide after each arm pull too brief.

    _____ A kick does not accompany each arm pull.

    _____ Head lifted rather than turned sideward for breathing.

    _____ Hips not rolled enough to permit a scissors kick as the body is turned onto each side.

    _____ (Other)_____

_____

*Method by Barbara J. Sanborn

PERFORMANCE ANALYSIS SHEET FOR THE TRUDGEN CRAWL STROKE*

DIRECTIONS: Check √ all items that apply to the performance of this skill. Add other noted errors in the spaces provided.

NAME _____
(of performer)

NAME _____
(of analyzer)

Illustrations of Correct Techniques	Analysis of Performance

BODY POSITION DURING GLIDE

____ The form *is* acceptable.
____ The form is *not* acceptable because:
    ____ Legs and arms not fully extended.
    ____ Legs not together.
    ____ Body not stretched and straight.
    ____ Body turned toward face-down position.
    ____ Head not turned toward upper shoulder to facilitate breathing.
    ____ (Other) _____

KICK

____ The form for trudgen kick *is* acceptable.
____ The form for trudgen kick is *not* acceptable because:
    ____ Inverted scissors kick used.
    ____ Legs do not bend enough at knees during scissors kick recovery.
    ____ Knees brought too far in front of stomach during scissors kick recovery.
    ____ Legs recovered too vigorously.
    ____ Legs not straightened before scissors kick squeeze.
    ____ Too little effort applied during squeeze.
    ____ Ankles not extended to point toes during late part of scissors squeeze.
    ____ (Other) _____

____ The form for flutter kick *is* acceptable.
____ The form for flutter kick is *not* acceptable because:
    ____ Toes not pointed backward.
    ____ Knees bend too much.
    ____ Width of the kick too narrow.
    ____ Width of the kick too wide.
    ____ Number of kicks too few.
    ____ Number of kicks too many.
    ____ No flutter kick used.
    ____ (Other) _____

ARMS

_____ The form *is* acceptable.
_____ The form is *not* acceptable because:
      _____ Arms do not pull through to thighs.
      _____ Pull-through of one arm shorter than pull-through of other.
      _____ Recovery of one arm shorter than recovery of other.
      _____ Arms are not recovered over water.
      _____ On recovery, arms thrust forward rather than swung forward from shoulders.
      _____ Hand does not enter the water in front of shoulder of that arm.
      _____ (Other)_____

_____

COORDINATION AND BREATHING

_____ The form *is* acceptable.
_____ The form is *not* acceptable because:
      _____ One scissors kick not coordinated with pull of one arm.
      _____ Flutter kicks not coordinated with pull of one arm.
      _____ Face held above surface at all times.
      _____ Head lifted rather than turned to one side for breathing.
      _____ Duration of the glide in on-side position too brief.
      _____ (Other)_____

_____

*Method by Barbara J. Sanborn

PERFORMANCE ANALYSIS SHEET FOR THE INVERTED BREASTSTROKE*

DIRECTIONS: Check √ all items that apply to the performance of this skill. Add other noted errors in the spaces provided.

NAME _____
       (of performer)

NAME _____
       (of analyzer)

Illustrations of Correct Techniques	Analysis of Performance

BODY POSITION

____ The form *is* acceptable.
____ The form is *not* acceptable because:
    ____ Ears not in the water.
    ____ Eyes not looking upward.
    ____ Body not straight ___ Hips sag ___ Knees bent ___ Toes not pointed.
    ____ After arm pull, arms not extended along sides.
    ____ After leg kick, arms not extended forward beyond shoulders.
    ____ (Other)_____

LEGS

____ The form for whip kick *is* acceptable.
____ The form for whip kick is *not* acceptable because:
    ____ Knees come above surface during recovery.
    ____ Toes not pointed backward during recovery.
    ____ Thighs drop downward as legs extend.
    ____ Feet not turned outward during press.
    ____ Kick not vigorous enough.
    ____ (Other)_____

____ The form for wedge kick *is* acceptable.
____ The form for wedge kick is *not* acceptable because:
    ____ Knees come above the surface during recovery.
    ____ Knees not spread enough during recovery.
    ____ Thighs drop downward as legs extend.
    ____ Toes not pointed outward during the leg press.
    ____ Kick not vigorous enough.
    ____ Legs not straight as they are squeezed together.
    ____ (Other)_____

ARMS

_____ The form *is* acceptable.
_____ The form is *not* acceptable because:
    _____ Arms recovered too forcefully.
    _____ Arms recovered above surface.
    _____ Arms not recovered close to body.
    _____ Elbows not lowered as arms recover.
    _____ Arms not fully extended after recovery.
    _____ Arms not fully extended after pull.
    _____ Arms not extended straight forward (in line of progress) from shoulders after recovery.
    _____ (Other) _____

COORDINATION AND BREATHING

_____ The form *is* acceptable.
_____ The form is *not* acceptable because:
    _____ Kick occurs before hands recover to shoulders.
    _____ Arms begin the pull immediately at end of recovery.
    _____ Arms begin recovery immediately at end of arm pull.
    _____ Leg kick and arm pull occur at the same time.
    _____ Inhalation occurs during leg kick.
    _____ Inhalation occurs during arm pull.
    _____ Inhalation does not occur immediately after exhalation.
    _____ (Other) _____

*Method by Barbara J. Sanborn

103

CHAPTER 5

Performing and Teaching Springboard Diving Skills

What Must the Diving Teacher or Coach Be Prepared to Do?
Qualities a Beginning Diver Should Have
Fundamentals of Springboard Diving
Teaching the Novice Diver
Forward and Reverse Dive Components
The Forward Dive in Layout Position
The Forward Dive in Pike Position
The Forward Dive in Layout Position, with One-half Twist
The Reverse Dive in Layout Position
Backward and Inward Dive Components
The Back Dive in Layout Position
The Inward Dive in Pike Position
The Scoring of Diving Competition

The importance of springboard diving is to be measured in terms of its benefits to the individual. It enables him to prove to himself that he can master a challenge, that he has courage, and that he can coordinate nerve and muscle in the acquisition of a desired skill. It develops grace and control of muscle and balance. It equips him with a means to enjoyment of leisure. And it opens to him the satisfaction and thrill of engaging in competition.

WHAT MUST THE DIVING TEACHER OR COACH BE PREPARED TO DO?

As a beginning instructor, you will need to know how to instruct the novice who asks you to teach him to dive. He may inquire because he has certain tests which he must pass or simply because he wants to learn. In the latter case, his interests are likely to be limited to a forward dive, a back dive, and perhaps a reverse or inward dive. You must be prepared to tell him what to do and it is desirable, though not absolutely essential, that you be able to demonstrate what he is to do.

As coach of one of the great many park and recreation department, voluntary organization or community club teams, you will need to be able to give sound basic instruction in techniques to this unskilled candidate for membership on your team. In the beginning, you will not have extensive knowledge concerning springboard diving, but you must be able to equip the novice with a sound basis for later acquisition of additional and more difficult dives, and you must be able to refer him to textbooks which will provide the detailed descriptions he requires as his abilities improve.

Only six of the more than sixty recognized dives are described in this chapter. These six descriptions will suffice to set a pattern for teaching, but you will have need to refer to other sources in order to present additional skills to learners and in order to better prepare your divers for competition.

QUALITIES A BEGINNING DIVER SHOULD HAVE

Learning will progress faster when the novice possesses certain qualities. Objectives are likely to be unattainable when these qualities are lacking. The novice must have a definite desire to learn, a willingness to attempt, confidence in his instructor, a satisfactory degree of neuromuscular control and sense of timing, and courage to continue despite discomfort resulting from incorrect contact with the water. He must be reasonably persistent and must be attentive to instructions. He must be able to think through what he will attempt to do and to relate himself to the performance. His sensitivity to balance, derived from the semicircular canals of the ear, should be reasonably good in order that he may be aware of the interaction of his body and movement in space. He should have flexibility adequate to enable him to stretch, reach, and twist in a fluid manner and without undue effort.

FUNDAMENTALS OF SPRINGBOARD DIVING

Certain basic knowledge is essential to success in mastering the art of springboard diving. The learner must know and correctly apply principles pertaining to the springboard, to the control and manipulation of body parts while moving in space, and to the relationship of thought and action.

In addition, in order to know how a dive in part or in total should be performed, it will be helpful to refer to the rules which have been established to govern competitive diving. These have been written by a joint committee representing collegiate-scholastic and amateur athletic organizations and appear in rule books published by the National Collegiate Athletic Bureau and the United States Amateur Athletic Union. Of course, not all divers will have aspirations to perform in competition, but the techniques described by the rules are helpful in establishing what should be practiced in order to learn the correct methods of executing each dive.

Diving competition has caused expert divers and coaches to refine existing techniques and to create new dives. Basic techniques are likely to remain unaltered; but some changes in the rules will be made from time to time and it will be helpful, therefore, for you to always have at hand a current copy of the rule book published by one of the two organizations mentioned above.

Dive Groups

The diver may leave the board while he is facing forward or backward, he may dive forward or backward, and he may incorporate a twist in the dive. Hence, dives are classified into five groups (Chart 5:1).

CHART 5:1
THE FIVE GROUPS OF DIVES

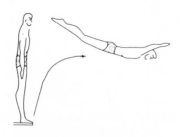

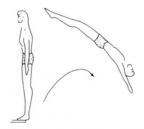

A. Forward dive
(Facing the water on take-off and diving forward.)

B. Back dive
(Facing the board on take-off and diving backward.)

Chart 5:1 The Five Groups of Dives (continued)

C. Reverse dive

(Facing the water on take-off and diving backward.)

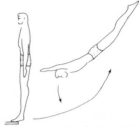

D. Inward dive

(Facing the board on take-off and diving forward.)

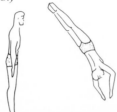

E. Twist dive

(Including a twist in any one of the four preceding types of dive.)
Example: a forward dive with one-half twist.

Dive Positions

In performing a dive within any one of the five groups, the diver may be in (a) layout (straight) position; (b) pike (jackknife) position; or (c) tuck position. Chart 5:2 shows these positions. Some twist dives may be performed in (d) free position in which a combination of tuck, pike, or layout is used (Chart 5:2).

CHART 5:2
THE FOUR DIVE POSITIONS

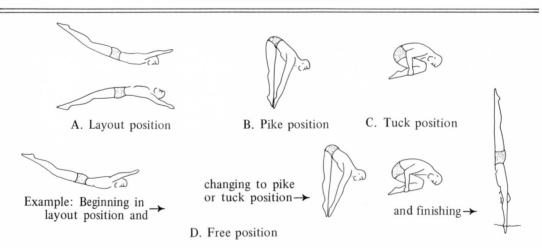

A. Layout position

B. Pike position

C. Tuck position

Example: Beginning in layout position and →

changing to pike or tuck position →

and finishing →

D. Free position

Action of the Board

The board is a springing device that is used by the diver to propel himself into the air for subsequent entry, either feet- or head-first into the water. Although termed a "board" because of its original construction of solid or laminated wood, it also may be constructed of metal or fiberglass. It is anchored upon a support at its shore-end base and at about its mid-point rests upon a fulcrum which, when moved, increases or decreases the flexibility of the board. The diving end projects over the water; the common heights of the board over the water surface are one meter (39.37 inches) for the low board and three meters (118.11 inches) for the high board.

When the impact of weight depresses the board downward, it must return to its original point of rest and beyond, casting the weight upward and outward. The learner has two tasks: first, to sense and adjust to the depression and lift of the board so that he and the board are one; and second, he must accommodate to the condition that the plane of the board while it is depressed is not horizontal and the lift propels outward as well as upward. Chart 5:3-A illustrates how the amount of depression of the board may alter the angle at which the diver is propelled from the board unless he adjusts by increasing his lean backward to compensate for any greater depression of the board downward.

Varying weights depress the board to greater or lesser degree. For each diver, there is an amount of board flexibility which is best and he should adjust the movable fulcrum to obtain it. The farther the fulcrum is moved out, the lesser is the flexibility and the faster is the board action; the farther the fulcrum is moved inward, the greater is the flexibility and the slower the board action. Chart 5:3-B shows that when the fulcrum is moved outward the amount of flexibility is as the heavy diver wants it to be but is unsuitable for the light diver, and when the fulcrum is moved inward, the amount of flexibility is too great for the heavy diver but is satisfactory for the light diver.

CHART 5:3
THE EFFECTS OF BODY WEIGHT AND FULCRUM POSITION UPON BOARD ACTION

A. The relationship of Body Weight to the Amount of Depression of the Board	B. The Relationship of Fulcrum Position to the Amount of Flexibility of the Board

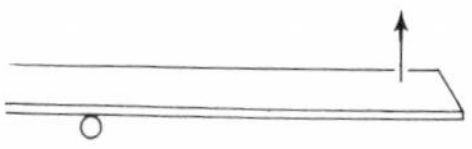

The position of the board when it is at rest.

The farther the fulcrum is moved outward, the less is the flexibility.

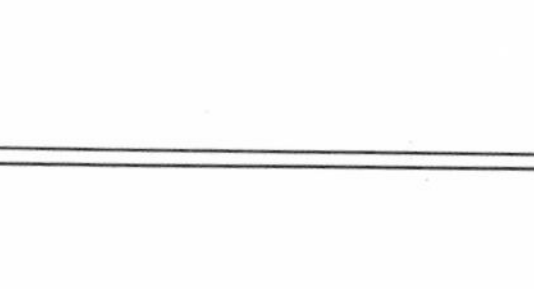

The position of the board when it has been depressed by a light diver.

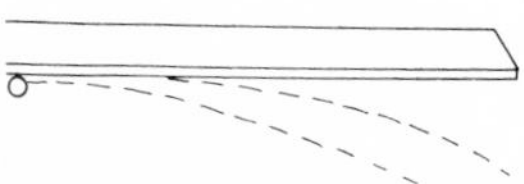

The less the fulcrum is moved outward, the greater is the flexibility.

The position of the board when it has been depressed by a heavy diver.

Coordination of the Arms and Legs During Take-off from the Board

In the performance of a dive, arms and legs do not act separately. They must act together in a coordinated movement or series of movements. For example, when the diver's arms are swinging upward during take-off from the board, his hips, knees, and ankles are extending at the same time.

Line of Upward Flight

During the early rise from the board, the line of lift is in a straight body line with the top of the head leading the rise. Then the leading point may be transferred to the chest and hips as in a back dive in layout position, or to the hips as in a forward dive in pike position (Chart 5:4).

CHART 5:4
EXAMPLES OF LEADING POINTS DURING UPWARD FLIGHT

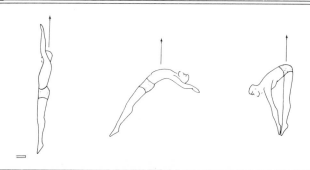

Line of Fall

The line of fall should be nearly vertical, or such as to insure water-entry within 6 feet of the end of the board.

Center of Balance

As a diver moves in the air, his total weight will have a center of balance at some point. That center will not be the same in all dives. In the performance of dives in layout or pike position, the hips are the center of balance as is the hub of a wheel or the fulcrum of a teeter-totter. In tuck position dives, the center of the compact mass is approximately at the lower ribs (Chart 5:5).

Arms, head, and legs are used to help to maintain balance. Poor control over the positions or actions of these parts will disturb balance (e.g., having one arm in a different position than the other, bending the knees, raising or lowering the head). Deliberate changes in the position of any of these parts will permit desired changes in position to be effected (e.g., lowering one arm helps in the performance of a twist, and bringing the legs into tuck position makes somersaulting easier).

CHART 5:5
CENTER OF BALANCE AND RATE OF ROTATION

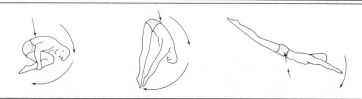

108

TEACHING THE NOVICE DIVER

The teacher is the catalyst that causes desired results. He must know what to teach and how to teach effectively. He must understand the feelings of the learner. He must know the capabilities and the limitations of the learner. He must know the mechanics related to the skill, the teaching aids which may be employed to advantage, the appropriate progressions to use, and the performance faults that are common to the novice:

Safety Precautions

Not only does the instructor need to be certain that he has not made himself vulnerable to liability but also he has the moral obligation to do all that should be done to protect the diver.

Safety in equipment and facilities. The diving board must be of proper construction, without flaw resulting from use, securely anchored and without sharp edges or protruding screws or bolts. The board should be placed at least 7 feet from the nearest wall and 15 feet from an adjacent board. The water should be clear and at least 12 feet in depth. When possible, the diving area should be separated from the swimming area. Printed notices relevant to use of diving equipment, and warnings pertinent to use at the diver's risk, should be posted prominently.

Safety in instruction. The instructor must give clear and complete safety instructions and must stringently enforce safety regulations. Repetition of instructions from time to time is advisable but, above all, it is important that the instructor be able to establish that each learner has been present at some time when instructions were given in order to avoid a charge of negligence. The instructor must be present during the entire class time. He must not compel a diver to do against his will something that he is afraid to do.

TABLE 5:1
EXAMPLES OF SAFE PROCEDURES WHEN USING THE TRAMPOLINE OR DIVING BOARD

Safe Procedures Pertaining to the Learner's Use of the Trampoline and the Tumbling Belt.	Safe Procedures Pertaining to the Learner's Use of the Diving Board.
The learner practices on a trampoline with a padded frame and avoids practicing on a trampoline with an unpadded frame.	The learner keeps his hands extended in front of his head after he has entered the water head-first.
He mounts the trampoline by stepping from the frame to the bed.	He has his knees slightly flexed when he contacts bottom on any feet-first dive.
He dismounts by stepping from the frame to the floor.	He abstains from diving when a swimmer is in the area.
He practices in his bare feet.	He takes care not to follow too closely after a preceding diver.
He kills his bounce on the trampoline by flexing his knees (especially when he is landing off balance).	He "bounces" the board only once rather than two or more times in succession.
He practices only when an instructor is present and when the instructor has provided capable spotters (usually four).	He stops practice before becoming overtired.
He learns how to spot for others.	He bends at his hips, knees, and ankles on contact with the board in order to kill the bounce when landing off balance or when not leaving the board in a dive.
He uses a safety belt when learning new skills.	

Health Precautions

Sudden entry into the water affects and effects pressures within the body. Air may be compressed, and water may intrude into sinus cavities and eustachian tube, especially when the diving entry is feet-first. Discomfort is a mild effect, but when water is contaminated or when the diver has a mouth or nose infection which may be carried into sinus or inner ear areas, the effect is likely to be serious. Water may penetrate from the outer ear to the inner ear if the eardrum is ruptured; hence, no one with a ruptured drum should dive.

Additional precautions are helpful to anyone who practices the more complex dives to an appreciable extent, and they are especially important to the diver with a physical problem (e.g., susceptibility to sinus infection). These precautions include sealing the nostrils with waterproof adhesive tape or wearing a firm nose clip when dives involving feet-first entry are practiced, and inserting lamb's wool in the outer ear to protect the drums. The diver should not practice when he has an infection, and he must avoid diving in contaminated water.

Use of Teaching Aids

Devices and methods which implement effective teaching may be categorized as kinesthetic, visual, auditory, and drill aids. The following table indicates some of them.

TABLE 5:2
TEACHING AIDS

Types of Teaching Aid	Instructor Actions That are Examples of the Use of Each Type of Teaching Aid
The kinesthetic type of teaching aid.	The instructor has the learner use a tumbling belt, twisting belt, or trampoline. He manipulates the learner's arms. He walks on the deck beside the learner, in front of him (for the learner to mimic the actions he sees), or behind him (with his hands on the learner's hips), in order to impart technique and rhythm. He places his hands behind the learner's hips in order to guide the learner, who places his hands overhead and leans off-balance in the back dive.
The visual type of teaching aid.	The instructor shows motion pictures, loop films, film strips, or utilizes television instant-replay. He uses diagrams, which may be predrawn or may be drawn on the blackboard in the presence of the learner. He uses photographs, figure drawings, and still-pictures-in-series. He has the learner view himself in a mirror during deck practice. He has expert divers give demonstrations or he gives demonstrations himself.
The auditory type of teaching aid.	The instructor shows motion pictures with accompanying comment or description on a sound track. He plays his taped comments in conjunction with television instant-replay of the learner's performance. He makes comments before and after the learner's dive attempt. He gives sound signals while the learner is in flight.
The drill type of teaching aid.	The instructor has the learner walk and spring on the deck in order to learn the approach and hurdle. He has the learner perform headfirst and feetfirst entries from the deck, with emphasis on a straight body line and pointed toes. He has the learner spring upward from the board and make a one-half or full pivot before entering the water feetfirst. He has the learner bounce the board *lightly* to sense the rhythm. He has the learner wear a short-sleeved sweat shirt for the learning of new dives. He has the learner dive over a lightweight stick or bamboo pole that is held approximately 2 feet outward from the end of the board and at a height of approximately 6 feet above the surface of the water, in order to teach the learner not to spring too far outward.

The Order in Which Dives Should Be Taught

There is no absolute order in which dives should be presented to the learner. Decision will be based upon such factors as the total number of dives to be taught, the elements common to two or more dives, the preferences and aversions of the learner, the ability of the instructor to demonstrate, the previous experience of the learner, and the sex of the learner. Following is a table showing possible order for the presentation of the more common dives, based upon different criteria.

TABLE 5:3
ORDER OF TEACHING THE MORE COMMON DIVES

Dive	The Authors' Suggestion	Possible Order By Learner Preference	Possible Order By Similar Facing Position	Possible Order By Similar Dive Position
Forward, layout	1	1	1	1
Forward, pike	2	2	2	5
Back, layout	3	6	6	3
Forward, one-half twist, layout	4	3	3	2
Forward single or one-and-one-half somersault, tuck	5	4	4	7
Inward, pike	6	5	7	6
Reverse, layout	7	7	5	4

FORWARD AND REVERSE DIVE COMPONENTS

A dissection of each dive reveals that it is composed of distinct but interrelated parts. It is important that these elements be seen as occurring in series and with effects transmitted from one to the next in order as when the first in a row of dominoes is pushed against the next in line. Error in the execution of one dive-part tends to produce error in the next part.

When a forward dive or a reverse dive is performed with a running approach, the components are: the starting position, the approach, the hurdle, the take-off, the flight, and the entry.

If the diver elects to perform these dives from a standing position at the diving end of the board, the parts are: the starting position, the take-off, the flight, and the entry.

CHART 5:6
RUNNING FORWARD AND REVERSE DIVE COMPONENTS

| Starting Position | Approach | Hurdle | Take-off | Flight | Entry |

Starting Position

The starting position is, as the name implies, the position taken by the diver before beginning the execution of the dive. This part of the total dive is important because this is the time when both muscle and mind are placed in states of balance and readiness.

Running dives. The starting position for forward and reverse dives, with running approach and hurdle, is a standing position at the shore end of the board and facing the water. The body position resembles the military position of attention, with weight somewhat forward on the balls of the feet rather than on the heels. The mental position should be one of alertness, confidence, and with mind fixed upon the mechanics of the dive to be performed.

Standing dives. The starting position for standing forward and reverse dives is the same as the position for running dives with the exceptions that the position is taken at the diving end of the board rather than at the shore end and that the arms may be extended overhead.

Approach

The running approach for forward dives and for reverse dives is, actually, more correctly described as a walk rather than as a run. Movement that is faster than a rapid walk imparts excessive forward body-motion and restricts the attainment of appropriate height in the hurdle and take-off. The approach is comprised of three or more steps and should be performed in a manner that is both graceful and forceful. Muscular control, but not effort, should be evident. Arm swing in conjunction with leg action should be free and natural. The head should be erect and its movement during the run (walk) should be in a straight line and not a side-to-side action induced by an improperly balanced approach.

Hurdle

The hurdle for running forward and reverse dives is a leap from one foot, followed by a landing on both feet simultaneously on the end of the board. The final step of the running approach places the foot of one leg in position for a subsequent extension of knee, ankle, and toes of that leg in an upward and forward spring from the board. Simultaneously, the knee of the other leg is raised to hip level or higher, with the foot in vertical line below the knee. While the diver is in the air, both legs are brought together, straight and with toes pointed toward the board. The toes are raised prior to impact of the balls of the feet upon the board.

The actions of the arms and legs are synchronized. As the spring off one foot is effected, the arms swing forward and upward. They move sideward, backward, and downward as the body drops to the board preparatory to take-off.

As the diver alights on the end of the board, contact is made with the balls of his feet. As the board is depressed by the impact of the weight upon it, the ankles and knees are flexed somewhat in order to eliminate jarring and to place the diver in readiness to spring upward as the board whips upward.

The hurdle affects the take-off and the flight; height of the hurdle will have some effect upon the degree of depression of the board and subsequent height of take-off; excessive length of hurdle is likely to result in excessive forward movement (outward from the board) on the take-off. The distance of the hurdle should be approximately equal to the height of the hurdle, height will be determined by the maximum lift the diver is able to obtain when springing, in an erect position, from one leg.

Take-off

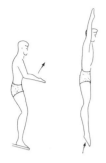

The take-off is an important part of the dive because the nature of it and the height obtained from it determine, to a large degree, the quality and appearance of the dive. In intricate dives, as in multiple somersaults and in twist dives, the height imparted by the take-off must be adequate to provide the time for the component movements to be completed prior to entry into the water.

Running dives. At the completion of the hurdle, the board is at its lowest point of depression and the diver's arms are at the lowest point of the downward arm swing. As the board springs upward, casting the diver with it, the diver must coordinate the forward and upward lift of his arms with the extension of his knees, ankles, and toes in timing with the rise of the board. His actions must be neither too early nor too late and must appear to be flowing rather than with explosive effort; he must use the board rather than fight it.

The teacher of diving must emphasize three additional specific points with reference to take-off. First, the diver must practice the take-off from standing position in order to sense the force and timing of the board's action and to adjust his body actions to that force and timing. A single bounce of the board serves this purpose (repeated as an individual action and with the reassumption of the starting position between each two bounces); continuous bouncing of the board is hazardous and should be prohibited emphatically.

Second, the bounce and take-off may be followed, in practice, by entry into the water or by return to the board feet-first, and in the latter case the diver must be taught to recontact the board with knees slightly flexed in order to "kill" the action of the board and permit the diver to regain a balanced standing position.

Third, since all boards differ to a greater or lesser degree, any diver should adjust to the board and to fulcrum positions before committing himself to the dives he will perform for pleasure or in competition, take-off trials may tell him that the performance of certain dives on that particular board will be especially difficult.

Standing dives. After assuming the starting position for standing forward and reverse dives, the diver usually will lower his arms to his sides. To execute the take-off, he extends his ankles and rises to his toes as he raises his arms forward, upward, and backward. He bends at the hips, knees, and ankles as the arms continue to circle backward and downward; these combined actions place him in a position to spring upward as he brings his arms forward and upward and extends his hips, knees, and ankles to place his body in a straight position as he rises upward.

The diver must take care that, in an endeavor to depress the board to obtain greater lift and height, he does not lift one or both feet above the board (crow hop) and pound them down upon the board prior to take-off.

Flight

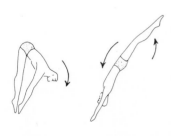

Forward   Reverse
dive   dive

The nature of the approach, hurdle, and take-off receive scant attention from the casual observer and only limited attention from the competitive-diving judge. Primarily, it is the dive itself (what happens while the diver is in the air and how he enters the water) that commands the attention of untrained observer and judge alike.

Running dives. If the approach, hurdle, and take-off have been without appreciable error, the quality of dive execution will depend upon the degree of mastery of techniques (as described for specific dives later in this chapter) and upon the fluid and controlled manner of performance.

Standing dives. Subject to absence of appreciable error in starting position and take-off, the quality of execution of standing dives will depend upon the same factors as those indicated for a running dive.

Entry for all dives is made with the body fully controlled until submersion is complete, with legs straight and together and with toes pointed, with the head in erect position, and with the arms extended in advance of the head (head-first entry) or along the sides (feet-first entry).

The point of completion of the dive is not the water surface; it should be the pool bottom. Moreover, a smooth water surface cannot be distinguished by the diver when he is performing the more complex dives and, therefore, the surface should be made more easily discernible by splashing or by creation of air bubbles (from submerged air hose or dry ice) which rise and burst at the surface.

Entry

Timing of the entry is important. The entry is the final, and often the strongest, impression that the observer has of the dive. If splash is created or if the legs bend at the knees when contact is made with the water, favorable impression of what has gone before is impaired and appraisal may be affected to a disproportionate degree.

Entry should be accomplished in longitudinal alignment with the board and within six feet of the end of the board. The line of entry should be approximately vertical but, because the motion of the dive is somewhat outward from the board, the head will enter slightly outward from a vertical alignment with the feet; the farther the take-off and flight carries the diver outward from the board, the greater the divergence from vertical needs to be.

A dive is "short" when the diver's body fails to approach the vertical position (Chart 5:7). A dive is "long" when his body progresses beyond the normal angle of entry (Chart 5:8). A twist may be short or long as the diver's body fails to reach or carries beyond the correct line of entry, or when the diver completes too little or too much twist.

CHART 5:7
SHORT FORWARD AND REVERSE DIVES

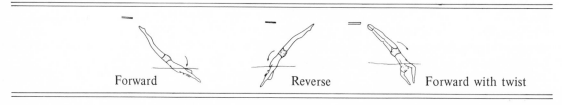

Forward   Reverse   Forward with twist

CHART 5:8
LONG FORWARD AND REVERSE DIVES

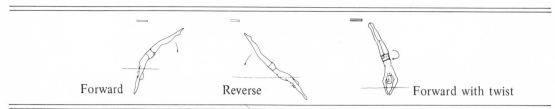

Forward   Reverse   Forward with twist

THE FORWARD DIVE IN LAYOUT POSITION

The novice who is learning to dive from the springboard probably will begin with a dive from standing position. Learning of the approach and hurdle will be postponed until the standing dive has been mastered.

Performance Techniques for the Forward Dive in Layout Position

The diver will have acquired previously (Chapter 3) the techniques for performance of the plunge dive from the deck, and these can be adapted to the dive from the springboard. From standing position, the plain dive is less complex and is easier to perform than is either the "swan" or the "jackknife" and, consequently is likely to be the first taught (Chart 5:9).

CHART 5:9
FORWARD DIVES

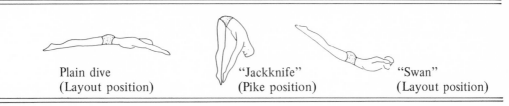

Plain dive
(Layout position)

"Jackknife"
(Pike position)

"Swan"
(Layout position)

When the learner has mastered the performance of the plain front dive, the instructor and learner will decide whether the next dive to be taught and learned will be the forward dive (layout), or forward dive (pike), or back dive.

When one or more forward dives from standing position have been learned, the next likely objective will be the mastery of the techniques of approach and hurdle and the performance of each of those dives following an approach and hurdle.

CHART 5:10
PERFORMANCE TECHNIQUES FOR THE FORWARD DIVE IN LAYOUT POSITION

Techniques	Illustration	Performance Errors	Illustration
A. Take off from the board in a line of flight upward and slightly outward from end of board.		*Standing dive:* A. The swing of the arms is not used to implement leg-spring of the take-off (a). The feet are lifted above the board (crow hop) during the first part of take-off (b).	a. b.
		Running dive: The approach steps are too long, too fast. The approach is a rapid run rather than walk (c). Forward body-lean is excessive (c).	c.
		During the approach and hurdle, the head is inclined downward with eyes looking straight at end of the board rather than being held erect with eyes looking down the nose (d).	d.
		In contacting the board following the hurdle, the knees bend excessively, body weight does not depress the board and, after a brief pause, the dive is made as from a standing position (e).	e.

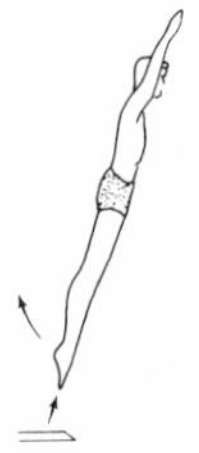

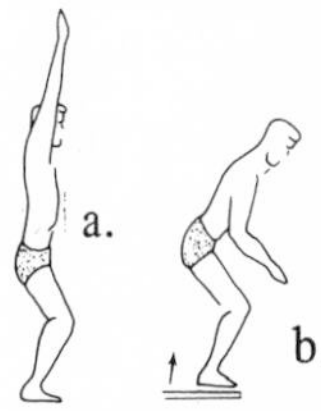

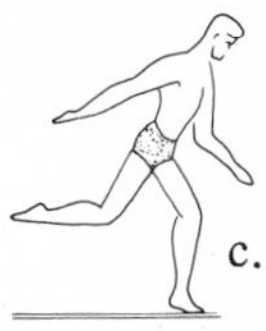

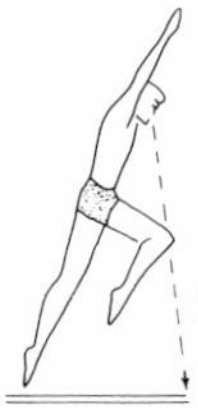

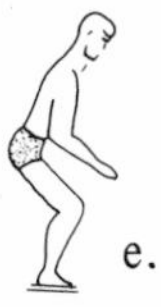

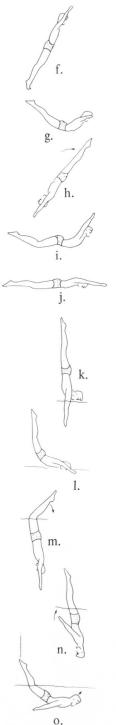

Standing and running dives:
Prior to take-off, the feet are pounded down on the board.
The diver does not wait for and utilize lift of the board.

B. On take-off, the body has excessive forward lean (f) (h).
The back is arched in order to raise heels upward (g) (i).
In flight, the feet are raised too rapidly or too much (h).
In flight, the feet are not raised to sufficient height.
The body is too rigid; smooth adjustment is difficult.
The hips are placed in partial pike position (i).
The head is too low; chin is depressed toward chest (j).
At entry, the head is held in raised position and impact is taken on face (k).
The back is arched prior to entry and impact is taken on face and chest (l).
The knees flop over on entry (m).
The arms are not maintained in an extended position on entry (n).
The point of aim for completion of the dive is the water surface rather than below.
The diver arches his back and endeavors to surface as soon as his head enters the water (o).

B. Make the hips the pivot point as feet are permitted to continue to rise upward over the board and to a position overhead.

Cause the head and upper part of body to rise more slowly than legs, until head is in a vertical position below the hips and feet, as the hips are lifted or permitted to rise upward.

Raise the arms upward in front of the body and directly overhead as the body rises; move the arms to sideward extension when approaching the peak of upward flight; hold them in sideward position until shortly before entry, and then bring them together in advance of the head and with arms pressed against the ears.

During the upward rise, hold the head in normal (erect) position; at the peak of the rise and during most of downward flight, raise head slightly; shortly before entry, return head to normal position.

C. Because direction of motion of the body in flight is somewhat outward from the board, effect entry into the water before the body reaches a true vertical alignment.

Teaching Progression for the Forward Dive in Layout Position

Before undertaking the teaching of the forward dive in layout position, you must first make certain that the diver has had essential basic preparation. The plunge dive from the deck must be reviewed, emphasizing the use of arms and legs to effect the spring, and with attention to the correct position in flight and at entry. The diver should be taught the coordination of arm and board actions as he takes a single gentle spring at the end of the board and returns to the board feetfirst, and he should be taught to spring upward from the board and enter the water feetfirst.

As progress is made from the simple to the more complex and by means of logical connected steps in sequence (Chart 5:11), you should anticipate the probable errors in learner performance, give the positive technique instruction that will make the occurrence of errors less likely, and instruct the learner to eliminate them when they do occur. Appropriate kinesthetic, visual, auditory, and drill aids (Table 5:2) should be used to speed learning. As the learner makes his first dive attempts from the board, you should anticipate that the board action may throw the diver's legs upward and over and cause him to somersault.

CHART 5:11
TEACHING PROGRESSION FOR THE FORWARD DIVE IN LAYOUT POSITION

Step 1	Step 2	Step 3
Teach the plain front dive from standing position on the board.	Teach the "swan" (forward, layout) dive from standing position on the board.	Teach the approach and hurdle by use of drills on the deck.

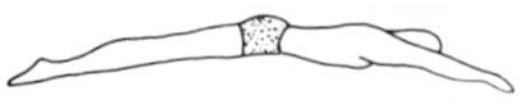

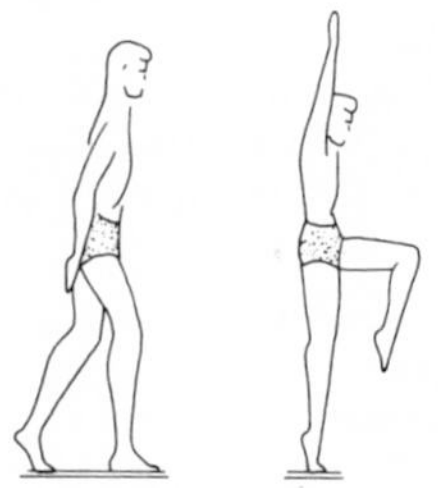

Step 4	Step 5	Step 6
Teach the hurdle on the board, followed by a take-off and feetfirst entry.	Teach the three-or-more step approach, hurdle, take-off, and feetfirst water entry.	Teach the forward dive in layout position, complete with starting position, approach, hurdle, take-off, flight, and entry.

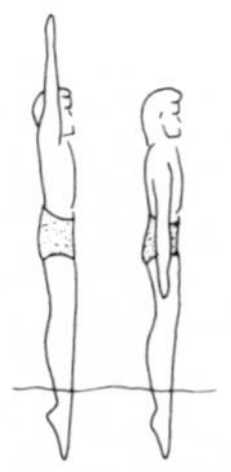

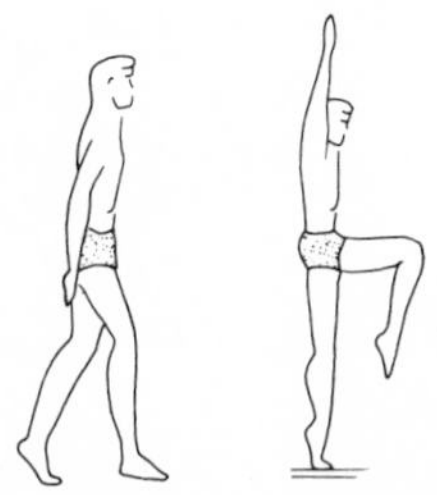

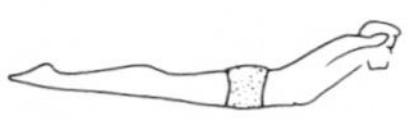

THE FORWARD DIVE IN PIKE POSITION

Because several different dives are performed in the pike position, mastery of the forward dive with pike facilitates learning of the dives that are related by position.

Performance Techniques for the Forward Dive in Pike Position

In the execution of a plain forward dive, bending at the hips in order to adjust balance and entry is a common learner action. Many instructors suggest that, for this reason, the forward dive in pike position should be taught before the forward dive in layout position and after teaching a plain front dive. In the final analysis, the instructor should experiment by teaching the plain front dive and the layout dive to some learners, and the plain dive and pike dive to others, and then arrive at his own decision relative to the order in which he prefers to introduce these dives to his students. Chart 5:12 presents the performance techniques that should be emphasized when teaching the forward dive in pike position.

CHART 5:12
PERFORMANCE TECHNIQUES FOR THE FORWARD DIVE IN PIKE POSITION

Techniques	Illustration	Performance Errors	Illustration
A. Take off from the board with body straight as it rises almost directly upward from the board; extend the arms and point them upward in an extension of body line.		*Standing dive:* A. The swing of the arms is not used to aid leg spring on take-off. The dive is performed with arms overhead (a). The feet are lifted from board (crow hop) during the spring before take-off (b).	 a.  b.
		Running dive: The approach steps are too long, too fast (c). During the approach and hurdle, the head is inclined downward with eyes looking straight at end of the board (d). In contacting the board after the hurdle, the knees bend excessively (e).	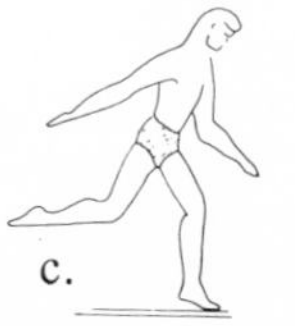 c.  d.
		Standing and running dives: Prior to take-off, the feet are pounded down on the board. The diver does not utilize lift of the board. On take-off, body has excessive forward lean (f).	 e. 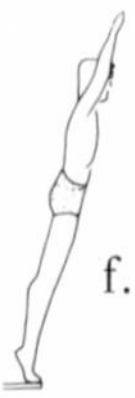 f.

B. As body nears the peak of the upward flight, permit the hips to continue to rise, bend at the hips, and bring fingers slightly forward and then downward to toes or to grasp legs at the calves or ankles as the legs are brought forward to meet the hands.

Keep the legs straight and without bend at the knees.

C. At the beginning of downward fall, straighten hips and lift legs upward without knee bend until almost directly above the body.

Extend the arms to point downward and place head between extended arms.

Because the direction of motion of the body in flight is somewhat outward from the end of the board, effect entry before the body reaches true vertical alignment.

B. The pike position is assumed immediately after take-off (g).

The feet are brought up to hands rather than hands down to feet (h).

The hands are brought vertically downward rather than slightly forward and downward.

The knees are flexed to enable the hands to reach for the feet; the ankles are flexed and toes are extended (i).

The back is humped in order to attain a pike position (j).

The body is too rigid (thus, smooth adjustment is difficult).

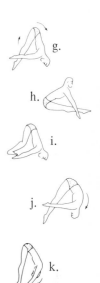

C. The chin is depressed toward chest (k). The pike position is held too long (thus, impact is taken on the back) (l).

At entry, the head is held in raised position and impact is taken on the face (m).

The back is arched prior to entry and impact is taken on face and chest (n).

The knees bend (flop over) on entry (o).

On entry, the arms are not maintained in extended position (p).

The point of aim for completion of the dive is at the water surface rather than below.

The diver arches his back, extends his wrists, elevates his arms and begins to surface as soon as his head enters the water (q).

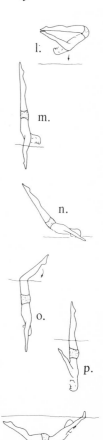

Teaching Progression for the Forward Dive in Pike Position

In order to be sure that the proper foundation is laid, you should have the learners review the plunge dive from the deck, teach (or review) the coordination of arm and board actions in a single gentle spring with return to the board feet-first, and teach (or review) the coordination of arm and board actions in a single vigorous spring from a standing position on the board and with entry into the water feetfirst. The next steps in teaching should be as shown in Chart 5:13.

CHART 5:13
TEACHING PROGRESSION FOR THE FORWARD DIVE IN PIKE POSITION

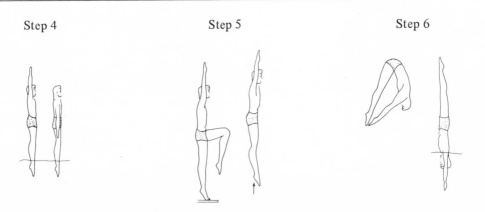

Step 1	Step 2	Step 3
Teach or review the plain front dive from standing position on the board.	Teach the jackknife (forward, pike) dive from standing position on the board.	Teach (or review) the approach and hurdle by use of drills on the deck.

Step 4	Step 5	Step 6
Teach (or review) the hurdle on the board, followed by a take-off and feetfirst water entry.	Teach (or review) the three-or-more step approach, hurdle, take-off and feetfirst water entry.	Teach the complete forward dive in pike position, using appropriate teaching aids.

THE FORWARD DIVE IN LAYOUT POSITION, WITH ONE-HALF TWIST

The incorporation of a twist into a dive presents yet one more challenge to the learner who desires to acquire all-around competence in this area of skill. Moreover, twist dives comprise one of the five categories of dive in competition, and, therefore, the diver who aspires to compete with others must become able to perform at least one of the several dives in the twist category.

Performance Techniques for the Forward Dive in Layout Position, with One-half Twist

Because the element of twist is added to the performance-requirement of a forward, reverse, back or inward dive, execution of the dive with twist is a bit more complicated than is execution of the same dive without twist.

Basically, the mechanics appropriate to the twist dive will conform to those applying to the dive of which the twist is a part. In the performance of the forward dive in layout position, with one-half twist, the mechanics for take-off and early flight (attaining height, raising heels upward, pivoting at the hips) are essentially the same as those for the forward dive in layout position, and the mechanics for late flight and entry (straight body, entry at slight angle) are essentially the same as those applying to the back dive.

CHART 5:14
PERFORMANCE TECHNIQUES FOR THE FORWARD DIVE, LAYOUT POSITION, WITH ONE-HALF TWIST

Techniques	Illustration	Performance Errors	Illustration
A,B. Perform the take-off in the same manner as for forward dive in layout position (Chart 5:10).		A,B. Commission of errors common to learners of the forward dive in layout position (Chart 5:10). Commission of errors common to learners of the back dive in layout position (Chart 5:21).	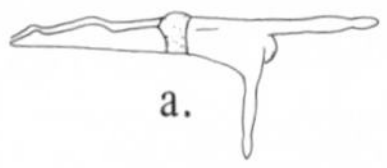 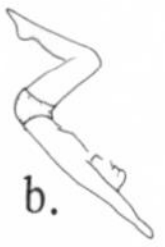
C. Lower one arm to point sideward from the shoulder and turn the head to look down that arm and toward the hand. Press the shoulder of the other arm backward and toward the neck.	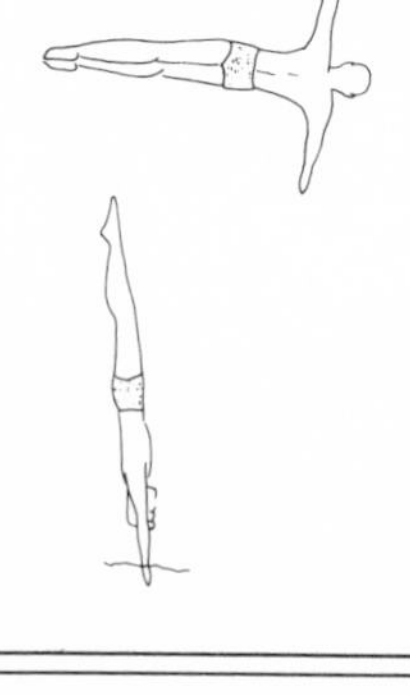	C. The head is inclined forward and downward; the eyes look *under* the extended arm (a). The extended arm is pointed forward in front of the body. The hips flex, a pike position is assumed (thus, the body somersaults (b)).	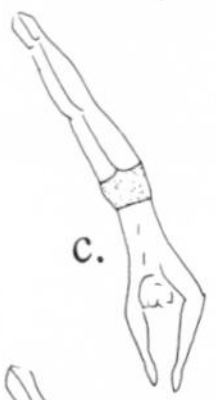 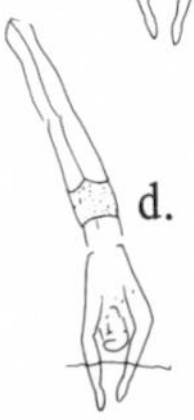
D,E. At the conclusion of the half-twist, bring both arms together in advance of the head as for a back dive entry (Chart 5:21).		D,E. The amount of twist is too little (¼ twist) (c), or too great (¾ twist) (d). The hips and legs are carried over too strongly in the twist (e).	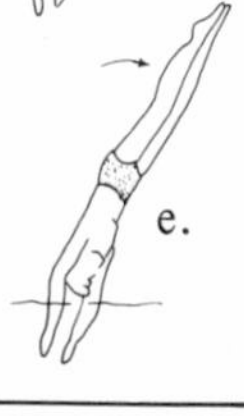

Before giving instruction in the forward dive with one-half twist, you should teach (or review) the standing forward dive in layout position, teach (or review) the running forward dive in layout position, and teach (or review) the back dive in layout position. Chart 5:15 shows the progression that follows completion of these preliminary steps.

CHART 5:15
TEACHING PROGRESSION FOR THE FORWARD DIVE, LAYOUT POSITION, WITH ONE-HALF TWIST

Step 1	Step 2	Step 3

Teach the arm and body action of the one-half twist, as a deck drill.	Teach the standing forward dive with one-half twist, from the deck; first, with fall-in, then with spring.	Teach the standing forward dive with one-half twist from the diving board.

Step 4

Teach the running dive with one-half twist from the diving board, using appropriate aids to teaching. Of these, the tumbling belt, demonstration, and showing of slow-motion pictures are likely to be most helpful.

THE REVERSE DIVE IN LAYOUT POSITION

The novice diver is likely to be more reluctant to attempt the reverse dive than he is to learn a dive in any other group. In performing the reverse dive, he is not able to see the diving board until after he has committed himself to action which brings his head in the direction of the board. Consequently, he tends to protect himself by obtaining more carry outward from the board than is necessary.

Performance Techniques for the Reverse Dive in Layout Position

It is to be noted that the movement of the body must be somewhat forward and away from the board, while the direction of body rotation is backward and toward the board. The greater the amount of motion outward from the board, the more difficult it will be to effect the required amount of reverse rotation. Entry into the water should be effected after the body has passed slightly beyond the point of true vertical alignment. Chart 5:16 gives a description of the dive and indicates additional errors the learner may commit in the performance of it.

CHART 5:16
PERFORMANCE TECHNIQUES FOR THE REVERSE DIVE IN LAYOUT POSITION

Techniques	Illustration	Performance Errors	Illustration
A. During upward flight, raise the arms not only overhead but also beyond and behind the body line, and press the shoulders back to accent this arm action. Elevate the chest, arch the back moderately, and press the head back behind the body line as the hips are raised and pressed forward and upward. Continue the movement of the arms in a flowing action to place them in a position of extension sideward from the body.	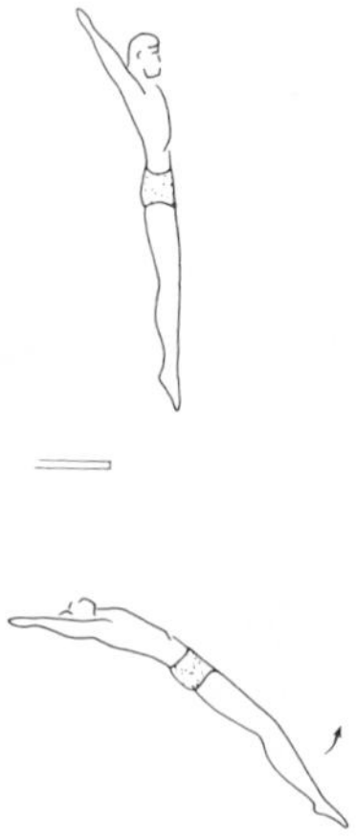	*Standing dive:* A. Commission of errors common to learners of the standing forward dive (Chart 5:10). Commission of errors common to learners of the standing back dive (Chart 5:21). *Running dive:* Commission of errors common to learners of the running forward dive (Chart 5:10). *Standing and running dives:* Body carry-out from the end of the board is excessive, height is insufficient (a). Chest and hip elevation is not emphasized (b).	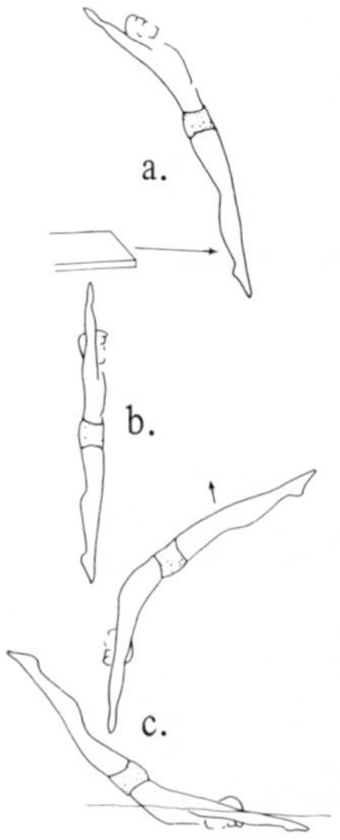 a. b. c.
B,C. Shortly after the peak of the dive is reached, look for the water.	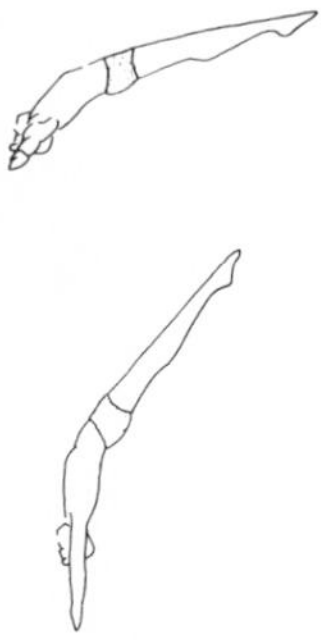	B,C. In flight, the legs are raised excessively; the dive is long (c). In flight, the legs are not raised high enough; the dive is short (d). The knees bend in flight (e). The hips bend in flight (f). The chin is drawn toward the chest (g).	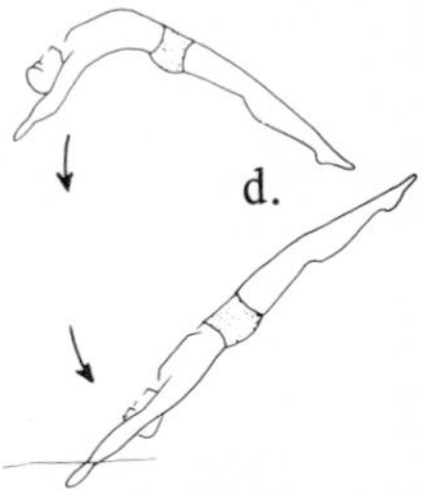 d. e. f.
D,E. At time of entry, have head in normal (erect) position, the body straight and the arms extended in advance of the head.	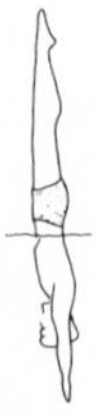	D,E. The stretch of the arms is uneven and the head is drawn to one side of the center line (thus, the body tends to twist).	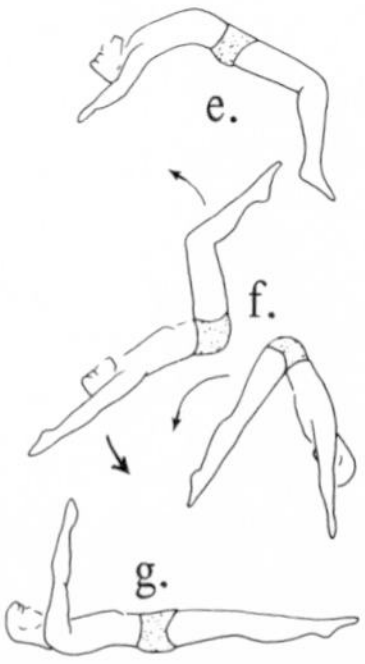 g.

Teaching Progression for the Reverse Dive in Layout Position

Instruction in performance of the dive should be preceded, first, by teaching (or reviewing) a take-off from standing position while facing outward at the end of the board, reaching for height on the early flight and entering the water feetfirst. The next action should be to teach (or review) the same take-off and entry following a running approach and hurdle. Then the back dive should be taught or reviewed. Chart 5:17 shows the steps that follow the preceding three-stage review.

CHART 5:17
TEACHING PROGRESSION FOR THE REVERSE DIVE IN LAYOUT POSITION

Step 1   Step 2

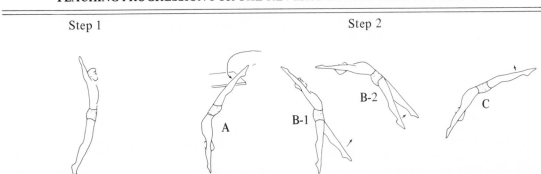

Teach the arm and upper body actions of the reverse dive as a deck drill.

Teach the reverse dive from standing position on the board. Optional preliminary steps, in teaching take-off and early flight, are: (A) Making initial entry at the side of the board rather than off the end of the board, and (B-1) raising first one leg and then raising the second leg (B-2) into position beside the first leg. Entry is aided by upward momentum of feet (C).

Step 3

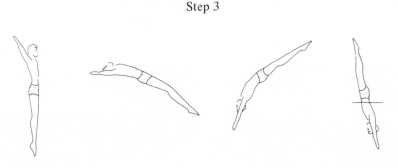

Teach the running reverse dive.

BACKWARD AND INWARD DIVE COMPONENTS

The components of backward and inward dives are the starting position, the take-off, the flight, and the entry. A major distinguishing characteristic of these dives is that the starting position is a stance taken at the diving end of the board and facing the shore end of the board. In general, the same techniques of take-off, flight, and entry apply to these dives as have been described for the forward and reverse dives from standing position.

Starting Position

To assume the starting position for back dives and inward dives, the diver walks to the diving end of the board and places one foot at the end of the board. He pivots on that foot to turn his back to the water, turning in the direction of the pivot foot. As he pivots, he raises his arms to point directly forward from his shoulders and places the other foot in position on the end of the board. Although he may then extend his arms upward overhead, the almost universal practice is to slowly lower the arms to the sides (Chart 5:18).

CHART 5:18
THE ASSUMPTION OF THE STARTING POSITION FOR BACK AND INWARD DIVES

Take-off

To execute the take-off, the diver extends his ankles and rises to his toes as he raises his arms forward, upward, and backward. He bends at the hips, knees, and ankles as his arms continue to circle backward and downward; these combined actions place him in position to spring upward as he brings his arms forward and upward and extends his hips, knees, and ankles to place his body in a straight position (Chart 5:19).

CHART 5:19
THE TAKE-OFF FOR BACK AND INWARD DIVES

Crow hopping is the lifting of one or both feet from the board after executing a press-down of the board and the subsequent pounding or pressing of the feet down on the board. It is a practice which the instructor must endeavor to prevent the learner from acquiring as a habit. Not only is it a telltale sign of inexpert performance, but also its use in competition will require the diving judges to subtract points from the evaluation that the execution of the dive merited otherwise.

Flight

Because the back and inward dives are performed without the advantage that the hurdle contributes to other dives through the greater depression of the board and stronger lift of the diver, the backward and inward dives must be completed within somewhat less time and somewhat less height. Temptation to hurry the performance will be great, and if the diver succumbs to that urge, the quality of flight will suffer accordingly.

Entry

The techniques of entry for back and inward dives are essentially the same as have been indicated for forward and reverse dives. Differences between back and inward dive entries are presented later in this chapter in conjunction with descriptions of the two types of dives.

Chart 5:20 shows entries which may result from technique errors in take-off and flight.

CHART 5:20
LONG AND SHORT BACK AND INWARD DIVES

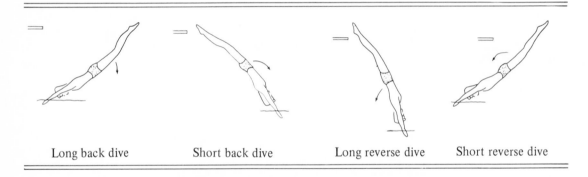

Long back dive Short back dive Long reverse dive Short reverse dive

THE BACK DIVE IN LAYOUT POSITION

The back dive, in addition to being one required of the competitive diver, is one that most novices want to learn. It involves some degree of daring and yet performance techniques are relatively simple.

Performance Techniques for the Back Dive in Layout Position

Such difficulty as may be attached to learning of the back dive is due primarily to the back-down position of the diver and, consequently, to his inability to see the water during most of the time consumed in the performance of the dive. Performance is sure to be faulty when the learner loses confidence during the dive and fails to do as he has been told; the learner must have his mind set to follow exactly the directions given by the instructor. Chart 5:21 shows techniques for performing the dive and indicates performance errors which may occur.

PERFORMANCE TECHNIQUES FOR THE BACK DIVE IN LAYOUT POSITION

Techniques	Illustration	Performance Errors

A. At take-off, have the body in a straight line and extend arms overhead.
 	
   In a continuing flowing movement, drift the arms from overhead position to a position sideward and slightly backward, and extend them sideward from the body.
 	
   Elevate the chest to lead the rise.
 	
   Press the hips upward and press the shoulders backward. Assume a slight arch in the back.
		A. The backward lean on take-off is excessive (a); entry is back-first (b) or stomach-first (c).
		
		   The back arch assumed is too great; the learner tends to somersault.
		
		   The body does not stretch for height on take-off. Time to complete the dive is too limited.
		
		   The chest and hips do not press upward as arms are placed in position sideward from shoulders; there is little force to cause the body to invert to head-down position.

B. Permit the hips to continue to rise and become the pivot point until the straight legs rise into a position overhead.		B. The upward press of hips is too great (thus, the entry is long) (c).
		
		   The knees bend during flight (d).
		
		   The hips bend during flight (e).

C. During the early part of the downward flight, tilt the head backward to permit sight of the water.		C. The arms are not precisely level and identical in position, the head is turned to one side (thus, the body tends to twist (f)).
D. Before entry is made, bring the arms from sideward position to a position of full extension in advance of the head, and return the head to normal (erect) position.		D. The chin is pressed to the chest, the upper back is bowed, and arms are raised upward as confidence is lost (thus, entry is back-first (g)).

Teaching Progression for the Back Dive in Layout Position

   Practice of the back dive from the deck is unwise because a dive which is "long" (the diver's legs go over too far) may direct the diver into the wall. Although space is rather inadequate to accommodate both learner and teacher, instruction should take place on the diving board. Chart 5:22 shows an effective teaching progression.

Step 1

Step 2

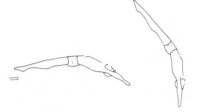

Teach the back dive arm action (limited) on the deck.

Teach a fall-in back dive from the board, starting with learner's arms stretched overhead and with the instructor controlling the dive attempt by placing his hands behind the learner's hips, restraining the learner as he leans and falls backward, removing the restraining hands when the learner has looked at the water and his hands are pointing toward the water.

Step 3

Step 4

Step 5

Teach a fall-in dive, started with learner's arms stretched overhead and completed without instructor's assistance.

Teach the back dive with learner's arms stretched overhead and with gentle spring from the board.

Teach the back dive, starting with learner's arms at his sides and following with correct arm and leg action and conventional take-off.

THE INWARD DIVE IN PIKE POSITION

The learner who would become a competitive diver must learn one or more of the dives that comprise the inward dive group in order to comply with requirements stipulated for competition. Other novices will have need to master the performance of the inward dive in the interest of attaining a versatile competence. Chart 5:23 presents the performance techniques for the dive.

Performance Techniques for the Inward Dive in Pike Position

Three points should be noted concerning the inward dive. First, the movement of the diver is outward from the board but the direction of rotation is inward toward the board. Second, the dive is performed from standing position and less height is attained in take-off than is possible in running dives. Third, the dominant thought of the learner will be to avoid contact with the diving board during flight and, consequently, he will tend to overcompensate by springing too far backward and not enough upward.

CHART 5:23
PERFORMANCE TECHNIQUES FOR THE INWARD DIVE IN PIKE POSITION

Techniques	Illustration	Performance Errors	Illustration
A. Permit the downward slope of the depressed board to direct the body slightly outward and, in conjunction with limited spring backward, to cause the body to be outward from the board during flight.	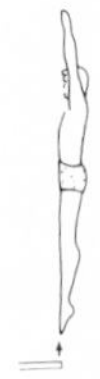	A. Backward lean of the body is too great; forward rotation cannot be accomplished (a). The spring is too much backward; not enough upward; forward rotation cannot be accomplished (b).	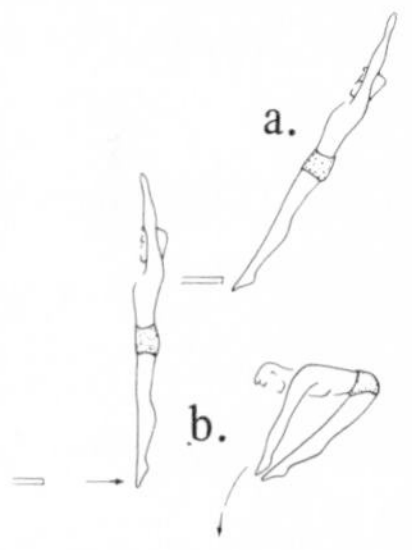 a. b.
B. During take-off and upward flight, bring arms forward and downward to reach for the ankles or calves as the body bends into pike position at the hips.		B. The hip lift is not accented; inversion to head-down position is difficult. The feet are brought upward to the arms rather than the arms to the feet; forward rotation is prevented (c).	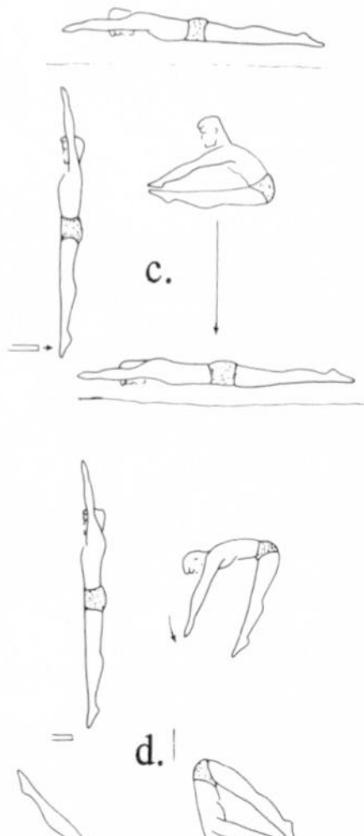 c.
C. As the body approaches the peak of the rise, straighten the legs to a position overhead, extend the body, and place the head between extended arms.	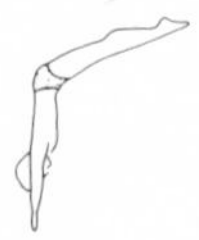	C,D. The hip lift and the outward-downward-inward arm action are over-emphasized; the body tends to somersault (d).	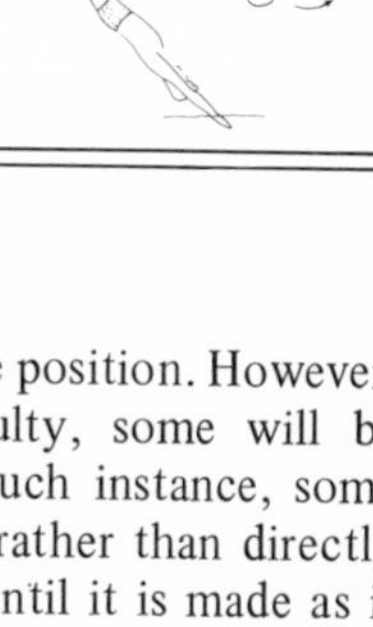 d.
D. Effect entry after the body has passed the point of true vertical alignment.	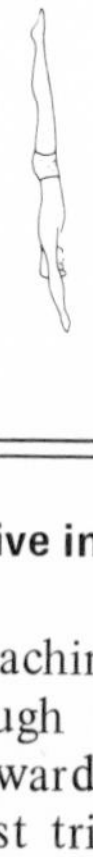		

Teaching Progression for the Inward Dive in Pike Position

Chart 5:24 presents an effective teaching progression for the inward dive in pike position. However, although learners will progress through the first three steps with little difficulty, some will be apprehensive about diving inward toward the board as indicated in Step 4. In such instance, some instructors suggest that entries on first trials should be at the side of the board rather than directly outward from the diving end. As confidence is gained, the diver adjusts his entry until it is made as it should be.

CHART 5:24
TEACHING PROGRESSION FOR THE INWARD DIVE IN PIKE POSITION

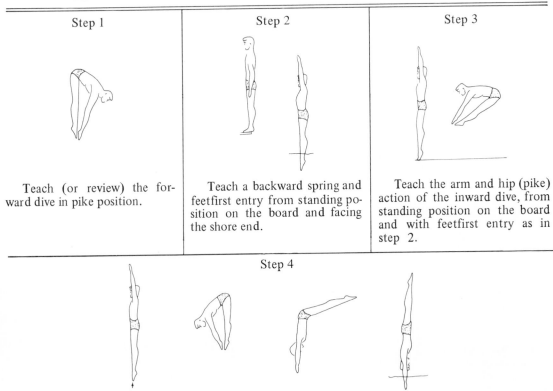

Step 1	Step 2	Step 3
Teach (or review) the forward dive in pike position.	Teach a backward spring and feetfirst entry from standing position on the board and facing the shore end.	Teach the arm and hip (pike) action of the inward dive, from standing position on the board and with feetfirst entry as in step 2.

Step 4

Teach the complete inward dive. Use the teaching aids that are appropriate and available (Table 5:2).

THE SCORING OF DIVING COMPETITION

It is helpful to the novice to know the value attached to each dive and to have experience in appraising the performances of others. In order to judge properly, he must know what makes a dive good and what makes a dive bad, and thus he acquires knowledge which he utilizes in improving his own diving performances. Moreover, the observations and comments of other novices, as they become competent in observing and diagnosing can be quite helpful to the learner.

You are reminded that the bases for the appraisal of dive performance quality are stated in the official A.A.U. and N.C.A.A. rule books. Table 5:4 indicates some of these.

TABLE 5:4
CRITERIA FOR JUDGING DIVES

Dive Component and Position	Criteria as Officially Stated to Assist Diving Judges*
Starting position.	No undue delay. The starting position is assumed when the contestant is ready to take his first step.
Standing.	Body straight. Head erect. Feet together. Arms straight against the sides. Fingers together. The dive begins when arms leave the side of the body.

Approach.	Smooth, straight, forceful. Not less than three steps.
Hurdle.	Alighting on both feet simultaneously.
Take-off.	From both feet simultaneously. Forceful and reasonably high.
Standing.	Diver must not rock the board. Must not lift feet from board.
Flight.	
Straight (Layout).	Without bend at knees or hips. Feet together. Toes pointed. In forward dive layout and inward dive layout, arms sideways in line with shoulders. Just before entry, arms brought rapidly together and extended beyond head.
Pike.	Bend at hips without bend at knees. As compact as possible. Toes pointed.
Tuck.	As compact as possible. Toes pointed. Without knees spread.
Free.	Combination of layout, pike or tuck.
Twist.	May be performed at any time during the dive except in forward dive ½-twist pike, back dive ½-twist pike and inward dive ½-twist pike, in which the pike must be performed first. Free position may be used only as listed in tables.
Somersault.	Turn must commence as soon as the contestant leaves the board (except in flying somersault).
Entry.	Vertical or nearly so. Body straight. Toes pointed.
Head-first.	Arms stretched beyond the head in line of the body. Hands close together.
Feet-first.	Arms close to body, without elbow bend.

*National Collegiate Athletic Association, *Official Collegiate-Scholastic Swimming Guide,* 1970, pp. 28-29. Used by permission.

Values Assigned to Dives

Interscholastic, intercollegiate, AAU, and Olympic Committee diving experts, as members of the Joint Diving Committee, have compiled a diving table in which each recognized dive has been assigned a current degree of difficulty; for example, 1.0, 1.6, 2.2, 2.9. This assigned value is used as a multiplier of the sum of the judges' awards.

Table 5:5 provides examples of dive values (degree of difficulty) which will be helpful in class work, but it is to be kept in mind that the Joint Diving Committee periodically reviews the diving tables and may alter the degrees of difficulty listed therein. The competitive diver must consult the official rule book governing the competition he is entering in order to obtain official, current values for dives.

TABLE 5:5
EXCERPTS FROM OFFICIAL SPRINGBOARD DIVING TABLES*

Dive Number	Dive	Dive Group	1-meter dive			3-meter dive		
			Tuck	Pike	Layout	Tuck	Pike	Layout
101	Forward Dive		1.2	1.2	1.4	1.3	1.3	1.6
102	Frd Somersault	FORWARD	1.4	1.5	1.7	1.7	1.7	1.8
201	Back Dive		1.6	1.6	1.6	1.7	1.7	1.7
202	Bk Somersault	BACKWARD	1.5	1.6	1.7	1.5	1.7	1.6
301	Reverse Dive	REVERSE	1.7	1.7	1.7	1.7	1.9	1.9
401	Inward Dive	INWARD	1.2	1.3	1.7	1.2	1.3	1.6
511	Forward Dive ½ Twist	TWISTING	---	1.7	1.8	---	1.8	1.9

*National Collegiate Athletic Association, *Official Collegiate-Scholastic Swimming Guide,* 1970, p. 32. Used by permission.

Awards for Dive Performance

In diving competition, a diver must, in accordance with the official governing rules, perform a specified number of required dives (a dive or dives he must do; in dual meets it is usually one drawn by lot, in championship meets the usual requirement is one dive from each of the five groups) and a stated number of optional dives (dives he prefers to do; in dual meets he usually must do one from each of the five groups, in championship meets he must do a total of five or six optional dives with at least one dive from each of the five groups).

As the competing divers perform the dives they have submitted on their entry blanks, each judge observes each dive and awards to it a value ranging between 0 and 10. When there are three judges, the ratings given by the three are added together to give a total award; when there are five judges, the highest and lowest scores of the five are cancelled and the remaining three are totalled. This sum of awards for the one dive performed by the diver is multiplied by the degree of difficulty for the dive (the multiplier previously mentioned) and the total point award for the one dive by the one diver is obtained. At the conclusion of the competition, the total point awards earned for each of the several dives are added to obtain the sum of points earned by the diver in that competition. The final placing of the divers is determined by ranking them by sum of points earned.

Computation of final scores and final placing achieved by class members in intra-class competition will, on appropriate occasions, be done by the instructor and not by the learners; it is advisable that the learners have an understanding of the methods by which scores are determined in diving competition.

Chart 5:25 presents an example of the scoring of one competitor's dives in dual meet competition.

CHART 5:25
AN EXAMPLE OF A SHEET FOR SCORING DIVING

NAME *Merill Newton* CLUB *Swanson High* DIVING ORDER *1*

Visiting team *Pullman*

	Mealy	Carlson	Hoff	Holstrom	Sawhill	Judge's Total	Degree of Diff.	Running Totals
			Judge's Awards					
201 Required Dive Back Dive Layout	5	3	7	4	6	15	x 1.6	24.0
102 Optional Dives 1. Frd Somersault Tuck	6	4	7	5	8	18	x 1.4	25.2
202 2. Bk Somersault Pike	7	6½	5	6½	4	18	x 1.6	28.8
301 3. Reverse Pike	6	4	5	7	6	17	x 1.7	28.9
401 4. Inward Pike	7	6	6	6	5	18	x 1.3	23.4
5112 5. Frd 1 Twist Layout	3	3	3	2	4	9	x 2.0	18.0

Scoring By _____ Frank Sheldon

FINAL SCORE _____ *148.3*

Checked By _____ Thad Carpenter

PLACE _____

Referee's Acceptance _____ Ted Schall

132

WRITTEN ASSIGNMENTS

1. Show the similarities and differences in two dives by comparing: the back dive and reverse dive or the forward dive (pike) and inward dive (pike).

2. Prepare a 30-minute lesson plan for the presentation of one dive. Include objectives, materials, and equipment needed, safety precautions, aids which will be used, methods for group organization and control, information to be given and leading questions, and the time schedule for the period.

3. Prepare a report on the use of visual aids in teaching diving.

4. Select a list of one required (inward dive) and five optional dives as you would to enter a high school dual meet diving competition. Enter the position and the correct degree of difficulty for each dive. Assign imaginary scores awarded by five imaginary judges to each of your dives, compute the total of awards for each dive and the sum of points you are awarded for the performance of the one required and five optional dives.

5. Using the analysis sheets at the end of this chapter, evaluate a diver's performance on these dives: forward dive, layout position; forward dive, pike position; forward dive, layout position with ½ twist; reverse dive, layout position; back dive, layout position; inward dive, pike position.

BEHAVIORAL OBJECTIVES

The examination on this chapter will be both written (short answer questions) and practical. You may be asked to reply to any or all of the questions below.

1. Discuss the attributes a learning diver should have (as presented in this chapter).
2. Diagram four dive groups (not including twist group).
3. Diagram the layout, pike, and tuck dive positions.
4. Discuss at least one aspect of safety precautions to be taken by the diving instructor.
5. Discuss at least two teaching aids that may be used when instructing divers.
6. Name, in order of occurrence, the parts of a running springboard dive.
7. Discuss diving entries, including what may affect them, the meaning of "long" and "short," and the appearance of the body immediately prior to entry.
8. Indicate four performance errors of which a learner may be guilty for any one dive described in this chapter.
9. Give a description of correct performance of any one dive described in this chapter.
10. Outline (describe/diagram) the teaching progression for any one dive described in this chapter.
11. Explain how points are earned by a diver in competition.
12. Define crow hopping, fulcrum, degree of difficulty.
13. From the springboard, perform any two dives (each from a separate group) illustrated in this chapter. Each must be judged by the instructor and two students and must receive an average award of 5.0 or higher.

BIBLIOGRAPHY

Amateur Athletic Union. *Official Handbook: Swimming, Diving, Water Polo.* New York: Amateur Athletic Union, 1969.

American Association for Health, Physical Education and Recreation. *DGWS Handbook: Aquatics Guide.* Washington: American Association for Health, Physical Education and Recreation, 1968.

American National Red Cross. *Swimming and Water Safety.* First Edition 1968, Chap. 8.

Armbruster, David A. and Bruce Harlan. *Swimming and Diving.* St. Louis: C.V. Mosby Company, 1964.

Fairbanks, Ann Ross. *Teaching Springboard Diving.* Englewood Cliffs, New Jersey: Prentice-Hall, Inc., 1963.

Moriarty, Phil. *Springboard Diving.* New York: The Ronald Press, 1959.

National Collegiate Athletic Association. *Official Collegiate and Scholastic Swimming Guide.* Phoenix, Arizona: Collegiate Athletics Publishing Service, 1970.

PERFORMANCE ANALYSIS SHEET FOR THE
RUNNING FORWARD DIVE IN LAYOUT POSITION*

DIRECTIONS: Check √ all items that apply to the performance of this skill. Add other noted errors in the spaces provided.

NAME _____
(of performer)

NAME _____
(of analyzer)

Illustrations of Correct Techniques	Analysis of Performance

STARTING POSITION

_____ The form *is* acceptable.
_____ The form is *not* acceptable for the following reasons:
    _____ Backward lean
    _____ Knees locked, body tense
    _____ Forward lean
    _____ (Other) _____

APPROACH

_____ The form *is* acceptable.
_____ The form is *not* acceptable for the following reasons:
    _____ Arm swing not free
    _____ Forward lean
    _____ Steps too long
    _____ Head not erect
    _____ Run (walk) is too rapid
    _____ (Other) _____

HURDLE

_____ The form *is* acceptable.
_____ The form is *not* acceptable for the following reasons:
    _____ Too long
    _____ Forward lean
    _____ Not high enough
    _____ Landing flat-footed
    _____ Knees bend on contact with board
    _____ (Other) _____

TAKE-OFF

____ The form *is* acceptable.
____ The form is *not* acceptable for the following reasons:
    ____ Too much lean forward
    ____ Arm and leg actions not synchronized
    ____ Actions of body and board not synchronized
    ____ Feet leave board too soon
    ____ Feet do not rise backward and upward
    ____ Arm circle is reversed
    ____ (Other)_____

FLIGHT

____ The form *is* acceptable.
____ The form is *not* acceptable for the following reasons:
    ____ Not enough height
    ____ Feet raised too much
    ____ Partial pike is assumed
    ____ Legs bend at knees
    ____ Feet not raised enough
    ____ Too much back arch
    ____ Arms do not flow into position sideward
    ____ (Other)_____

ENTRY

____ The form *is* acceptable.
____ The form is *not* acceptable for the following reasons:
    ____ Too long
    ____ Too far out from the board
    ____ Body not straight
    ____ Too short
    ____ Ears not between arms
    ____ Legs flop over
    ____ Dive is shallow
    ____ Arms pull to sides
    ____ (Other)_____

*Method by Barbara J. Sanborn

PERFORMANCE ANALYSIS SHEET FOR THE
RUNNING FORWARD DIVE IN PIKE POSITION*

DIRECTIONS: Check √ all items that apply to the performance of this skill. Add other noted errors in the spaces provided.

NAME _____
(of performer)

NAME _____
(of analyzer)

Illustrations of Correct Techniques	Analysis of Performance

STARTING POSITION

_____ The form *is* acceptable.
_____ The form is *not* acceptable for the following reasons:
_____ Forward lean
_____ Backward lean
_____ Body tense
_____ (Other)_____

APPROACH

_____ The form *is* acceptable.
_____ The form is *not* acceptable for the following reasons:
_____ Forward lean
_____ Arm swing not free
_____ Steps too long
_____ Head not erect
_____ Run (walk) is too rapid
_____ (Other)_____

HURDLE

_____ The form *is* acceptable.
_____ The form is *not* acceptable for the following reasons:
_____ Too long
_____ Forward lean
_____ Not high enough
_____ Arm action not synchronized with leg action
_____ Landing flat-footed
_____ Knees bend on contact with board
_____ (Other_____

TAKE-OFF

____ The form *is* acceptable.
____ The form is *not* acceptable for the following reasons:
    ____ Forward lean; take-off is outward
    ____ Arm circle is reversed
    ____ Arm and leg actions not synchronized
    ____ Body and board actions not synchronized
    ____ Feet leave board too soon
    ____ Head is faced downward
    ____ (Other) _____

FLIGHT

____ The form *is* acceptable.
____ The form is *not* acceptable for the following reasons:
    ____ Not enough height
    ____ Pike is partial
    ____ Legs not straight
    ____ Pike held too long
    ____ Pike held too briefly
    ____ Pike assumed too soon
    ____ Feet brought up to hands
    ____ Toes not pointed; ankles not extended
    ____ Legs bend at knees
    ____ (Other) _____

ENTRY

____ The form *is* acceptable.
____ The form is *not* acceptable for the following reasons:
    ____ Too short
    ____ Too far out
    ____ Ears not between arms
    ____ Too long
    ____ Body not straight
    ____ Legs flop over
    ____ Dive is shallow
    ____ Arms pulled to sides
    ____ (Other) _____

*Method by Barbara J. Sanborn

PERFORMANCE ANALYSIS SHEET FOR THE
FORWARD DIVE, LAYOUT POSITION, WITH ONE-HALF TWIST*

DIRECTIONS: Check √ all, items that apply to the performance of this skill. **Add** other noted errors in the spaces provided.

NAME_____
(of performer)

NAME_____
(of analyzer)

Illustrations of Correct Techniques	Analysis of Performance

STARTING POSITION

_____ The form *is* acceptable.
_____ The form is *not* acceptable for the following reasons:
    _____ Forward lean
    _____ Backward lean
    _____ Body tense
    _____ (Other)_____

APPROACH

_____ The form *is* acceptable.
_____ The form is *not* acceptable for the following reasons:
    _____ Forward lean
    _____ Arm swing not free
    _____ Steps too long
    _____ Head not erect
    _____ Run (walk) is too rapid
    _____ (Other)_____

HURDLE

_____ The form *is* acceptable.
_____ The form is *not* acceptable for the following reasons:
    _____ Too long
    _____ Forward lean
    _____ Not high enough
    _____ Landing flat-footed
    _____ Knees bend on contact with board
    _____ (Other)_____

TAKE-OFF

_____ The form *is* acceptable.
_____ The form is *not* acceptable for the following reasons:
    _____ Forward lean; take-off is outward
    _____ Arm circle is reversed
    _____ Arm and leg actions not synchronized
    _____ Feet leave the board too soon
    _____ Spring precedes board lift
    _____ Feet do not rise backward and upward
    _____ Head is faced downward
    _____ (Other)_____

_____

FLIGHT

_____ The form *is* acceptable.
_____ The form is *not* acceptable for the following reasons:
    _____ Not enough height
    _____ Feet raised too much
    _____ Partial pike is assumed
    _____ Too little twist (¼)
    _____ Feet not raised enough
    _____ Legs bend at knees
    _____ Too much back arch
    _____ Too much twist (¾)
    _____ Head looks under arm
    _____ Hips and legs carry over beyond vertical
    _____ (Other) _____

_____

ENTRY

_____ The form *is* acceptable.
_____ The form is *not* acceptable for the following reasons:
    _____ Too short
    _____ Too far out
    _____ Ears not between arms
    _____ Too long
    _____ Body not straight
    _____ Legs flop over
    _____ Dive is shallow
    _____ Arms pulled to sides
    _____ (Other)_____

_____

*Method by Barbara J. Sanborn

PERFORMANCE ANALYSIS SHEET FOR THE REVERSE DIVE IN LAYOUT POSITION*

DIRECTIONS: Check √ all items that apply to the performance of this skill. Add other noted errors in the spaces provided.

NAME_____
(of performer)

NAME_____
(of analyzer)

Illustrations of Correct Techniques	Analysis of Performance

STARTING POSITION

_____ The form *is* acceptable.
_____ The form is *not* acceptable for the following reasons:
　_____ Forward lean
　_____ Backward lean
　_____ Body tense
　_____ (Other)_____

APPROACH

_____ The form *is* acceptable.
_____ The form is *not* acceptable for the following reasons:
　_____ Forward lean
　_____ Arm swing not free
　_____ Steps too long
　_____ Run (walk) is too rapid
　_____ Head not erect
　_____ (Other)_____

HURDLE

_____ The form *is* acceptable.
_____ The form is *not* acceptable for the following reasons:
　_____ Too long
　_____ Forward lean
　_____ Arm action not synchronized with leg action
　_____ Not high enough
　_____ Landing flat-footed
　_____ Knees bend on contact with board
　_____ (Other) _____

140

TAKE-OFF

_____ The form *is* acceptable.
_____ The form is *not* acceptable for the following reasons:
     _____ Forward lean; take-off is outward
     _____ Chest and hip elevation not emphasized
     _____ Arm and leg actions not synchronized
     _____ Body and board actions not synchronized
     _____ Not high enough
     _____ (Other)_____
          _____

FLIGHT

_____ The form *is* acceptable.
_____ The form is *not* acceptable for the following reasons:
     _____ Chest and hip elevation not emphasized
     _____ Pike is assumed
     _____ Chin drawn to chest
     _____ Knees bend
     _____ Body tends to twist
     _____ (Other)_____
          _____

ENTRY

_____ The form *is* acceptable.
_____ The form is *not* acceptable for the following reasons:
     _____ Too short
     _____ Too far out
     _____ Ears not between arms
     _____ Too long
     _____ Body not straight
     _____ Legs jackknife at hips
     _____ Dive is shallow
     _____ Arms pulled to sides
     _____ (Other)_____
          _____

*Method by Barbara J. Sanborn

PERFORMANCE ANALYSIS SHEET FOR THE BACK DIVE IN LAYOUT POSITION*

DIRECTIONS: Check √ all items that apply to the performance of this skill. Add other noted errors in the spaces provided.

NAME_____
(of performer)

NAME_____
(of analyzer)

Illustrations of Correct Techniques	Analysis of Performance

STARTING POSITION

_____ The form *is* acceptable.
_____ The form is *not* acceptable for the following reasons:
  _____ Arms not used for balance during pivot
  _____ Body bends forward at hips; body not erect
  _____ Pivot on the one foot is not smooth
  _____ Arm actions are too fast and uneven
  _____ (Other)_____

TAKE-OFF

_____ The form *is* acceptable.
_____ The form is *not* acceptable for the following reasons:
  _____ Leg and arm actions not synchronized
  _____ Body and board actions not synchronized
  _____ Feet lifted and returned to board before take-off
  _____ Backward lean is too great
  _____ Not enough height
  _____ Spring is outward
  _____ (Other)_____

FLIGHT

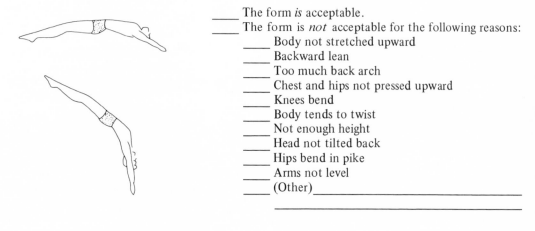

____ The form *is* acceptable.
____ The form is *not* acceptable for the following reasons:
     ____ Body not stretched upward
     ____ Backward lean
     ____ Too much back arch
     ____ Chest and hips not pressed upward
     ____ Knees bend
     ____ Body tends to twist
     ____ Not enough height
     ____ Head not tilted back
     ____ Hips bend in pike
     ____ Arms not level
     ____ (Other)_____
     _____

ENTRY

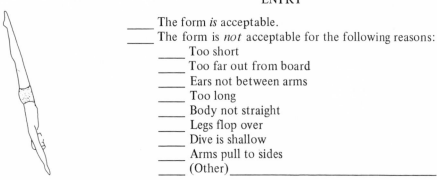

____ The form *is* acceptable.
____ The form is *not* acceptable for the following reasons:
     ____ Too short
     ____ Too far out from board
     ____ Ears not between arms
     ____ Too long
     ____ Body not straight
     ____ Legs flop over
     ____ Dive is shallow
     ____ Arms pull to sides
     ____ (Other)_____
     _____

*Method by Barbara J. Sanborn

PERFORMANCE ANALYSIS SHEET FOR THE INWARD DIVE IN PIKE POSITION*

DIRECTIONS: Check √ all items that apply to the performance of this skill. Add other noted errors in the spaces provided.

NAME _____
(of performer)

NAME _____
(of analyzer)

Illustrations of Correct Techniques	Analysis of Performance

STARTING POSITION

_____ The form *is* acceptable.
_____ The form is *not* acceptable for the following reasons:
    _____ Arms not used for balance during pivot
    _____ Body bends forward at hips; body not erect
    _____ Pivot on one foot is not smooth
    _____ Arm actions too fast and uneven
    _____ (Other)_____
    _____

TAKE-OFF

_____ The form *is* acceptable.
_____ The form is *not* acceptable for the following reasons:
    _____ Leg and arm actions not synchronized
    _____ Actions of the body and board not synchronized
    _____ Feet lifted and returned to board before take-off
    _____ Backward lean
    _____ Backward spring
    _____ (Other)_____
    _____

FLIGHT

_____ The form *is* acceptable.
_____ The form is *not* acceptable for the following reasons:
     _____ Too much backward lean
     _____ Not enough height
     _____ Feet brought to hands
     _____ Pike held too long
     _____ Legs not straight
     _____ Too much backward spring
     _____ Hip lift not accented
     _____ Pike is too soon
     _____ Pike held too briefly
     _____ Toes not pointed
     _____ (Other)_____

_____

ENTRY

_____ The form *is* acceptable.
_____ The form is *not* acceptable for the following reasons:
     _____ Too short
     _____ Too far out from board
     _____ Ears not between arms
     _____ Too long
     _____ Body not straight
     _____ Legs flop over
     _____ Dive is shallow
     _____ Arms pulled to sides
     _____ (Other)_____

_____

*Method by Barbara J. Sanborn.

145

CHAPTER 6

Performing and Teaching Lifesaving Skills

This chapter presents a compilation of material presented in the two standard lifesaving courses taught in the United States, the American Red Cross and the YMCA Programs. All skills required for either course are covered, plus certain others felt by the writers to have special application to lifesavers. You will note that we require our students to perform any of the skills with a male partner of approximately equal size. The reason for this is obvious, when you consider that males are usually stronger and less buoyant—and thus represent the most difficult group of victims. A lifeguard who cannot rescue such a person is in great personal danger, and, for his or her own sake, should not be awarded a certificate.

Since the majority of the users of this text will already have completed a senior lifesaving course, the description of lifesaving techniques will be relatively brief, but yet enough to remind you of the correct form. Complete descriptions of all techniques are given in the publications by the ARC, Silvia, and Lanoue, and represent the final word in relation to a specific course.

BASIC THOUGHTS BEFORE TEACHING A LIFESAVING CLASS

A certain amount of thinking must be done before teaching any class, and lifesaving is no exception. The first problem facing an instructor is the acceptance of students into his class. It is obvious that all certified lifesavers need to be strong swimmers. But, in the beginning of every class, there are weak swimmers who vow that they will be able to swim much better in a short time. True—but will they be enough better? It is much better to reject, or later fail, the weak swimmers than it is to pass them. They conceivably may guard where a situation they cannot handle would arise. For this reason, there are some instructors who will not permit a girl in their class unless she is an exceptionally strong swimmer—in fact, much better than the average male in the class. These instructors feel that this is for the girl's own good; they say that a lifesaving certificate given to a weak swimmer could be a death certificate. We agree that a weak swimmer has no place in a lifesaving class, but feel that female lifeguards are wise enough not to work at locations where the elements (tides, currents, etc.) would add to the danger.

146

In relation to weak swimmers, it is noteworthy that the ARC has a requirement that before starting the senior lifesaving course, the person should be able to swim one-quarter mile without stopping. Many prospective lifesavers consider this requirement too stringent, claiming that they are just "temporarily" out of shape. It is true that after a good lifesaving class all persons could swim the one-quarter mile with little or no trouble—but would they retain their physical condition? It is the feeling of the writers that anyone who cannot swim this distance on the first day of lifesaving class is not yet ready for the class.

On the other hand, it must be admitted that this class could represent the first aquatic course in some time and that the student could swim the distance after a few practice sessions. It certainly is obvious that, if permitted to remain, the student would learn a great deal and make himself much more safe in the water. If there are not too many in he class, the best solution to this problem might be as follows; let all enrollees remain, but give the one-quarter mile test within a week after the first session. Anyone who fails must then leave the class.

It is to be noted that in lifesaving classes, not much stress is placed on performing the strokes with correct form. If a student uses a scissors kick while performing the breaststroke in the tired swimmer's carry, nothing is said. In lifesaving, the emphasis is on strength of movement and ability to complete the task. However, do not let students perform an incorrect stroke without telling them so. The number of lifesavers who do not know the correct form for certain strokes (the breaststroke, especially) is legion. As an instructor of an advanced swimmer or instructor-trainer course, you will quickly find that possession of a senior lifesaving certificate does not mean that the student swims all strokes correctly, or even strongly.

Most lifesaving classes are composed of both boys and girls. This may lead to some social problems, but not if the instructor takes preventive action first. Sometimes the girls (or their mothers!) complain that a certain boy is using his hands more than necessary during the class. The best way to forestall any problems in this area is to tell the whole class at the beginning that at the first sign of any misconduct the person responsible will be asked to leave. This usually prevents all problems, if not, make good your promise.

As the course continues, there will be more skill on the part of the students—and more struggling by the victims. This can be dangerous, so it is wise to establish some sort of a warning system when one of the partners wants to cease the struggle. Usually, a pinch system is agreed upon; that is, when pinched twice in rapid succession by a partner, separate immediately.

GENERAL APPROACHES TO TEACHING SKILLS IN A LIFESAVING CLASS

Teaching lifesaving skills is really no different than teaching other aquatic skills. The instructor should first explain the skill to be learned and then demonstrate it both on land and in the water. The procedures whereby partners practice on land and repeat the practice in the water is recommended by most authorities. However, Silvia (1965, p. 23) claims that whatever can be done on land can better be done in the water. It is obvious that the practice of skills must occur under the watchful eye of the instructor in order that they be correctly learned. Each session should provide for a review of skills previously learned, preferably in some new situation. There are several suggestions throughout this chapter which illustrate different situations for practice; use them to add variety to your instruction.

The skills should be practiced with logical combinations. For example, in one session it is better to learn approach stroking, underwater approach, the chin pull, and the cross-chest carry than it would be to learn the front surface approach, the rear approach, and the underwater approach. By practicing in logical combinations the student derives two benefits. He sees how these separate skills go together to form an effective means of rescue, and he reaches better physical condition as a result of more swimming.

There is no substitute for *much swimming* in the lifesaving course. It should be a vigorous course from the start. The early classes should begin with swimming lengths, featuring those strokes and adaptations that are part of the lifesaving course. In the middle and later stages of the course, carrying or towing the partner will increase endurance because of the extra weight to be moved. We have found that swimming lengths in one big circle (faster swimmers to the inside, slower ones nearer the edge) is better than swimming in assigned lanes. There is no excuse for stopping when a large circle is used. Occasionally, pulling lengths or kicking them is good practice, for it adds variety and forces swimmers to work on all parts of their strokes. In the early parts of the course, much stress should be put on approach stroking at a fast speed. If the group is young or in especially poor physical condition, then one or two days of slow swimming would be acceptable, but why let students swim slowly when they will not be doing so in a real situation? Persons learn by practicing correctly, therefore, fast approach stroking is the thing to stress. It is possible to set certain time standards (or norms) for your pool in approach stroking, carrying, or almost any other phase of the course. This is an incentive for students and may be used for grading purposes if desired. For example, all lifesavers should be able to swim 100 yards of approach stroking (using acceptable form) in less than 2 minutes. In the later stages of the course, approach stroking is less important as a conditioning device when compared to towing a struggling victim.

Pop quizzes (short, unannounced exams) are a legitimate part of the course. You know from experience that it is easier to teach something if students have studied beforehand. Why not see to it that your students have studied by telling them the material for the next session and then occasionally seeing if they have studied? This has obvious uses in grading, but there really is a more utilitarian use—that of having them prepared. If you are going to give pop quizzes, it is only fair to tell the students what the next part of the class will be on.

It should be noted that the Red Cross, Silvia, and the Council for National Cooperation in Aquatics have outlined a daily lesson plan for teaching the lifesaving course (see Bibliography). These plans have been developed by experienced instructors. It is recommended that you follow them until you have gained experience in teaching lifesaving—and even then, you may not want to deviate from these tested plans.

Another decision to make before starting the course is whether or not you will enter the water yourself for testing purposes. Some instructors say "No" because they cannot see all they want to for testing purposes, or else they just cannot stand the physical rigors of the testing situation. Other instructors say "Yes" because this is the only way for the instructor to make certain that the victim struggles enough to make it a good examination. However, bringing in some outside victims will provide victims who truly struggle and will enable the instructor to watch and to evaluate.

WHAT ARE THE ESSENTIALS OF LIFESAVING SKILLS?

According to the revised Red Cross program, the senior lifesaving course can be divided into ten categories, as shown. (While the titles and sequence vary, the YMCA course is substantially the same.)

1. Personal Safety and Self-rescue
2. Reaching and Equipment Rescue
3. Swimming Skills for Lifesaving
4. Approaches
5. Swimming Assists and Carries
6. Defenses and Releases
7. Search and Rescue
8. Removing Victim from Water
9. Resuscitation
10. Small Craft Safety

The remainder of this chapter is divided into the ten categories. Unless specifically indicated, all skills shown are required in either the ARC or YMCA lifesaving course. In order to obtain a certificate, students in our regular lifesaving classes must pass the final skill and written examination required by either the Red Cross or YMCA. The specific examination is not given here; however, each consists of skills and knowledges discussed in this chapter. In addition, many students in our Senior Lifesaving Classes gain employment as lifeguards. For this reason, we make certain that these students possess the skills and knowledge needed by lifeguards (see Chapter 7).

Though not a part of the Red Cross or YMCA course, a few additional skills are presented in this chapter. We think they are of value to all persons and we teach them in our classes, but they are part of the examination only for certified aquatic workers. Specific behavioral objectives for this latter group will be found at the end of the chapter.

PERSONAL SAFETY AND SELF-RESCUE SKILLS

Skills related to personal safety are not taught very often by the lifesaving instructor because they appear to be common sense. "Why waste valuable class time?" goes the argument. The fact of the matter is that these skills are necessary for the lifesaver, and while they can be learned quickly, they must be practiced in order that all will know. Chapter 3 of the present text describes the skills of survival floating, floating on the back, the elementary backstroke, and the use of the lifejacket. It also describes treading water, swimming, and release of cramps; the ARC lifesaving course prescribes that these latter three skills be done while wearing clothes. Methods of clothing inflation are presented in Chapter 4.

With the exception of the use of the lifejacket (ARC only), all of the personal safety skills mentioned above are required in both the YMCA and ARC course in lifesaving.

REACHING AND EQUIPMENT RESCUE

There is a saying in lifesaving courses that the preferred sequence of rescue is *"Reach* first, *throw* if you can, and then *go* if you must." This point must be continually stressed to students, because the glamorous part of lifesaving is the plunging in and effecting a personal rescue. It is also the most dangerous. Therefore, reaching for a victim or throwing something to him are much more desirable forms of rescue. Although not usually stressed at this point in a lifesaving course, the teaching of the principle of "keep your eyes on the victim" must begin at this time.

Performing the Reaching and Equipment Rescues

Reaching assists are the most desirable forms of rescue, even though they may seem less heroic. The use of literally any piece of equipment should be stressed—a towel, stick, board, piece of clothing, arms. Chart 6:1 discusses the reaching and wading assists.

CHART 6:1
PERFORMANCE TECHNIQUES FOR REACHING ASSISTS*

Techniques	Illustration	Major and/or Common Performance Errors
A. Keep center of gravity low and behind edge of dock, deck or shore.	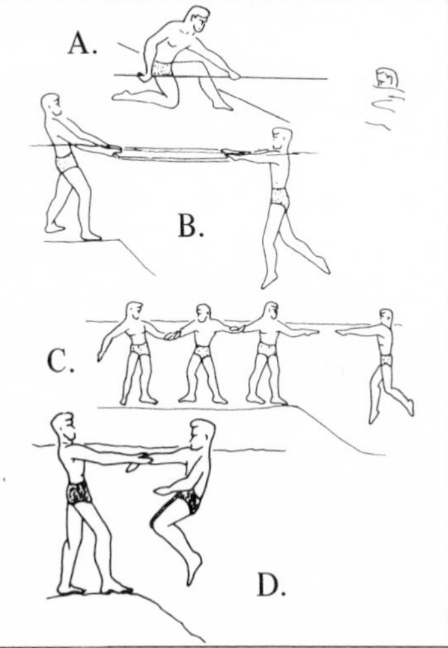	A. Placing center of gravity too high.
B. Keep weight back as far as possible.		B. Placing weight on forward foot.
C. Rescuers face opposite directions as they grasp each other's forearms. Spread legs; keep body leaning in direction of safety.		C. Failing to spread legs and plant feet firmly (thus, being pulled off balance). Failing to have body leaning back toward safety.
D. Wade to shoulder depth. Grasp victim's wrist.		D. Wading too far (thus being pulled off balance). Letting victim grasp rescuer's wrist. Failing to lean backward.

*Unless indicated otherwise, all skills depicted in the charts in this chapter are required in both the senior ARC and YMCA courses. Because requirements change from time to time and vary from junior to senior courses, consultation with the latest publications of the organization is recommended.

Throwing a ring buoy accurately, whether or not it has an attached line, is difficult for most lifesavers. Chart 6:2 shows how the ring buoy should be used.

CHART 6:2
PERFORMANCE TECHNIQUES FOR THROWING THE RING BUOY

Techniques	Illustration (Right-handed thrower)	Major and/or Common Performance Errors
A. Keep hand virtually flat so that rope can easily leave the hand.	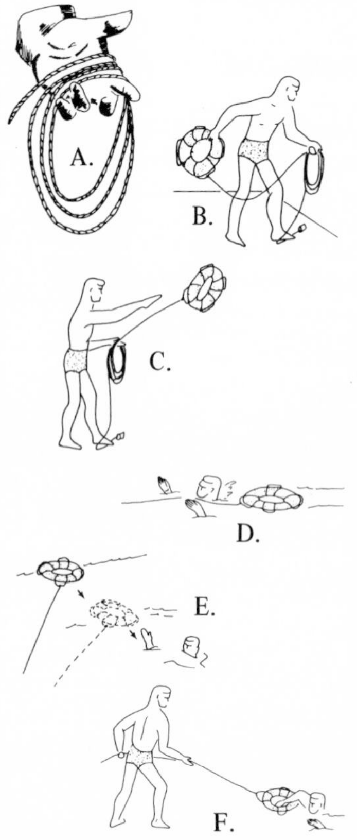	A. Grasping rope tightly.
B. Foot opposite throwing arm is forward. Grasp buoy in throwing hand, hold rope in other. Step on end of rope with foot opposite throwing arm. Use underhand throw (unless deck railing interferes).		B. Reversing foot position. Failing to step on rope end (thus permitting entire rope to be drawn into water).
C. Release buoy at eye level. Follow through with throwing arm.		C. Releasing buoy too soon (resulting in low throw) or too high (resulting in too short a throw).
D. Aim so that buoy hits behind the victim.		D. Throwing in front of victim; throwing downstream or downwind from victim.
E. Throw up-current, let buoy drift down to victim.		E. Throwing downcurrent (thus, causing buoy to be carried out of reach).
F. Tell victim to put one arm through hole in center. Slowly reel line in, keeping weight on rear foot.		F. Jerking the line, causing the victim to lose grasp.

The proper technique for advancing a free-floating support into position for a rescue depends on the equipment and the swimmer. It is recommended that the rescuer either push or pull the support with him until he comes close to (but not next to) the victim. The victim is told to grab one end of the support but not to climb onto it. Continuous talking to the victim will tend to reassure him and cause him to cooperate. During the return, the rescuer will usually use the breaststroke kick or a scissors kick. During the tow, the rescuer must watch the victim to make certain that all is well.

The shoulder loop and torpedo buoy are usually employed in beach situations. If an assistant is not available, then these assists become free-floating devices and are used as described earlier. If an aide is available, then his task is to play out the line slowly until the rescuer has neared the victim. When the contact is made, the aide pulls in the line slowly.

Both clothing and surfboards are very effective in helping victims. Chart 6:3 depicts desirable techniques for each.

CHART 6:3
PERFORMANCE TECHNIQUES FOR THE USE OF CLOTHING
AND SURFBOARDS AS FREE-FLOATING SUPPORTS

Techniques	Illustration	Major and/or Common Performance Errors
A. Place inflated clothing under legs (or arm) of victim. If two rescuers available, one supports victim while other inflates clothes.		A. Forcing air out of the clothing by putting all of victim's weight upon the inflated article.
B. Grasp forearms of victim; use surfboard as support.		B. Failing to grasp victim securely.

C. Use a surfboard to bring victim ashore.
  1. Turn board upside down. Get victim on side of board opposite rescuer. Grasp victim's forearm with one hand, the far side of the board with the other.
  2. Roll board toward self, pulling victim on top of it.
  3. Turn victim so his legs are atop the board. Paddle to safety.
		C.
		  1. Failing to turn board upside down before grasping victim.
		
		  2. Failing to grasp the victim's forearm tightly enough.
		  3. Failing to place victim completely on top of the board.

Teaching the Reaching and Equipment Rescues

Essentially, teaching these skills is a matter of explanation, supervised practice, and for some items, continual daily practice. We hope that most lifesavers will "reach" or "throw" before they "go," yet in most lifesaving courses about 2% of the time is spent on the latter forms of rescue. It is no wonder that students forget that they are to reach, then throw—because after the first two sessions, these skills are not usually practiced! The best way to ingrain these desirable forms of rescue into the minds of lifesavers is to have a daily practice session on at least one of the skills. At first, the instructor will have to direct this practice, but soon the students will do it as a part of the daily warmup. It is agreed that the other skills are the most dangerous and thus should receive the most effort of the class, but it seems unequal and unsound when so little time is spent on what is stressed as the preferred method of rescue.

Teaching about reaching, wading, and free-floating rescues is best done with a partner. After explanation and demonstration, the class is formed into two groups with the members of one group acting as the victim. All possible situations should be practiced, but not just one or two times at the beginning. The instructor can have a number of warm-up situations available for posting on the board. After the shower, the students read what is to be done and they and their partners proceed. Sample warm-ups are:

1. Partner is 4 feet from side in water 8 feet deep. Jump in, grab gutter with one hand, and extend leg to victim. Pull him to safety.
2. Partner is directly under low board. Standing on the side deck (as close to him as possible), throw the ring buoy to him.
3. Partner is in middle of pool. Grab the nearest loose kickboard and use it to rescue him.

It is recommended that a complete series of situations be put on one mimeographed sheet. The instructor then merely has to post one sheet, circle the skill or skills to be done that day and then students will know what to do. When the sheet becomes too water-wrinkled, post a fresh one.

151

In learning to throw the ring buoy, it is best to start with a short underhand throw (10 feet) and limited follow-through. Girls especially have difficulty in learning to throw this piece of equipment. After gaining accuracy, practice throwing to a partner who moves farther away each day. Because most pools or beaches have only two to three buoys at the most, it is difficult for everyone to get adequate practice. The instructor can designate one couple to practice five throws each before a class and another to practice five throws after the class. Thus, four students per day will practice throwing the buoy, which will permit everyone to practice at least two or four times after initial instruction. Students just cannot get too much practice on this skill. When an uneven number of students are in class, it is possible for the odd person to practice throwing the buoy while the others are practicing tows, releases, etc. No matter how it is done, ring throwing must be practiced—or else the lifesaver will forget that this is one other thing he should do before entering the water.

SWIMMING SKILLS FOR LIFESAVING

These skills represent the basic foundation for the lifesaving course; as such, they must be taught early and well. They are items that can be used as warm-up efforts throughout the course.

Performing the Lifesaving Swimming Skills

Entry into the water is accomplished in one of two ways, the feetfirst jump or a shallow dive. Since the cardinal rule is to keep the eyes on the victim, the jump is usually preferred. But because the jump has one serious disadvantage (it takes longer to reach the victim because there is no forward momentum) both entry forms should be learned. Chart 6:4 discusses both these forms of entry.

Approach stroking is merely a means of reaching the victim by swimming. It can be done with either the crawl or breast strokes as long as two essentials are met—keeping eye contact with the victim and arriving as fast as possible without being exhausted. The crawl stroke, with head up, is usually considered the best stroke for this purpose because it is faster and not as tiring to the rescuer. Keeping the head up while swimming this stroke does not call for drastic alteration of the stroke; the feet usually will kick deeper in the water because of the arching of the back, but this is of no great consequence. The breaststroke is usually the second-preferred stroke; it suffers from the handicap of being a slower stroke, but for swimmers with a poor flutter kick it could be faster.

The quick reverse is a skill that is taught only in lifesaving class. The consequences of doing it poorly are grave, because the victim will surely grasp the rescuer if he can. The correct procedure is shown in Chart 6:5.

CHART 6:4
PERFORMANCE TECHNIQUES FOR THE LIFESAVING
JUMP AND SHALLOW DIVE ENTRIES

Techniques	Illustration	Major and/or Common Performance Errors
JUMP A. Leap outward with head and hips forward of legs; legs spread, arms well away from body; eyes on victim.	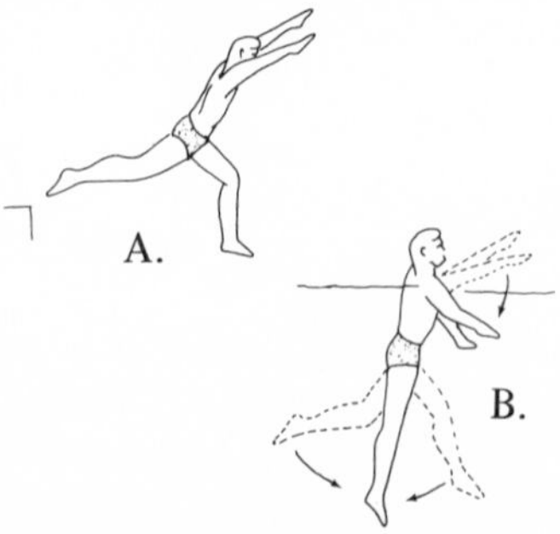 A. B.	A. Entering water in erect position, without any forward lean.
B. Upon contact with water, squeeze legs and then press down with arms. Keep head above water; keep eyes on victim.		B. Permitting head to go underwater (thus, losing sight of victim).

SHALLOW WATER DIVE

C. Lean off-balance forward.
   Keep eyes on victim as long as possible.

D. Thrust arms forward vigorously; lower the head at last possible moment; enter water at slight angle downward.

E. Come to surface as soon as possible.
   Begin approach stroking.

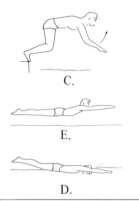

C. Failing to keep eyes on victim.

D. Failing to watch victim as long as possible.
   Entering water at a steep angle.

E. Remaining under water longer than necessary.

CHART 6:5
PERFORMANCE TECHNIQUES FOR THE FRONT AND REAR APPROACHES

Techniques	Illustration	Major and/or Common Performance Errors

FRONT APPROACH
 	
A. Approach within 3 feet of victim.
   Stop forward momentum.
	A.	A. Getting too close (thus, permitting victim to grab rescuer).
		   Failing to stop (thus, drifting into victim).
		   Stopping too far away (thus, having to swim closer).

B. Shift body weight by leaning back, tucking legs ahead of hips.
   Extend legs into position for scissors or breaststroke kicks.
   Extend one arm backward, ready for pulling.
	B.	B. Making contact before legs and arm are ready to propel rescuer toward safety.

REAR APPROACH
 	
C. Approach within 2 feet of victim.
   Stop forward momentum.
	C.	C. Getting too close.
		   Failing to stop (thus, drifting into victim).
		   Stopping too far away (thus, having to swim closer).

D. Shift body weight by leaning back.
   Prepare legs to deliver scissors or breaststroke kicks.
   Prepare one arm to pull toward safety.
	D.	D. Making contact before legs and arm are ready to propel rescuer toward safety.

When towing a victim, a variation of the side stroke is frequently used. The usual scissors kick tends to become tangled in the legs of the victim during a cross-chest carry and for this reason the inverted kick must be taught. The shallow arm pull, formerly taught only in lifesaving, is now the accepted style for the side stroke (as noted in Chapter 4). Thus, no distinction need be made in the arm action.

The modification of the breaststroke which is necessary for lifesaving is nothing more than a "heads up, back arched" position. This virtually eliminates any appreciable glide but does provide visibility and stability for the tired swimmer carry, and, during approach stroking, helps the rescuer to keep his eyes on the victim.

Towing a victim will sometimes be done on the back; this calls for the strongest possible kick. It can be done several ways, as long as the rescuer is partially "sitting up" so that he can be looking at the victim at all times. This body position will naturally cause the body to bend at the hips and the kick to be deeper than usual.

Chart 6:6 depicts the modifications necessary in the sidestroke, breaststroke, and supine kicking.

CHART 6:6
LIFESAVING PERFORMANCE TECHNIQUES FOR THE
SIDESTROKE, BREASTSTROKE, AND SUPINE KICKING

Techniques	Illustration	Major and/or Common Performance Errors
SIDESTROKE A. Use the sidestroke shallow arm-pull and the inverted scissors kick.	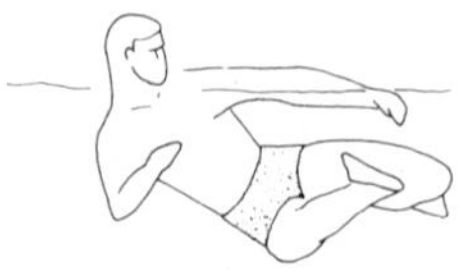 A.	A. Bringing top leg forward (as in the regular scissors kick).
BREASTSTROKE B. Arch back so that head is completely out of water at all times.	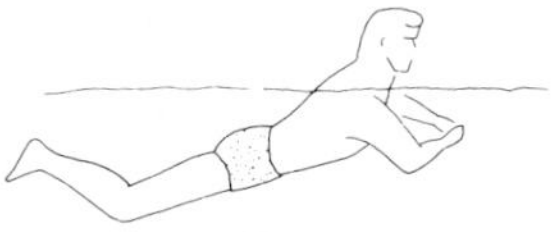 B.	B. Failing to have head up far enough to permit the eyes to always remain on victim.
SUPINE KICK C. Use either a scissors, whip or wedge kick. Have feet much deeper than usual. Keep eyes on victim.	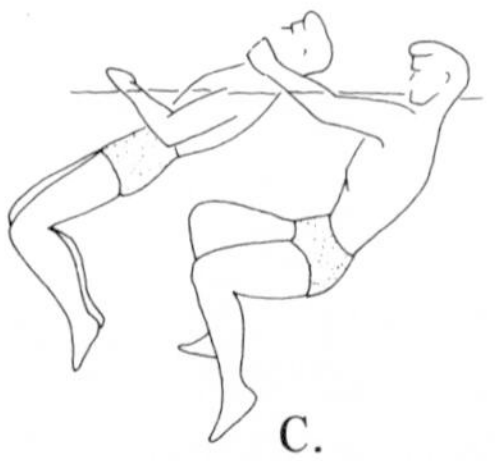 C.	C. Entangling feet with those of victim. Taking eyes off victim.

The swimming skills can be taught and practiced in the sequence presented in this section, that is: entry, approach stroking, quick reverse, towing. Once the first two skills are learned, they can be practiced. Then the third can be added, and so on. The main teaching procedure should be the usual pattern of explanation, demonstration, practice under supervision, and review.

One of the best ways to add meaning to this whole sequence of skills is to time students for various segments. For example, any lifesaver should be able to enter the water and approach stroke 60 feet within 30 seconds. Standards for your particular lake or pool can be set up or records can be kept (best time ever recorded, best average time by a particular class, best time for each sex, best time using breaststroke, etc.). The same type of procedure could be followed for the towing skill, either with or without a victim.

An excellent conditioning method (which also is a good drill because it features work on one skill at a time) is width swimming in deep water as follows:

1. Groups A & B on opposite sides in deep water, instructor in middle on shore (or diving board).

2. Instructor gives specific directions to each group: "Group A—feetfirst surface dive, swim under water to other side, Group B—breaststroke approach stroking," or "Group A—towing an imaginary victim with inverted scissors kick, Group B—pike surface dive and underwater swim."

3. Each group leaves its base at the same time and as they near each other, performs as directed.

4. Repeat, with appropriate variations, for 2 minutes at first, gradually doing up to 5 minutes. As group becomes strong, make them tread water at each side instead of grabbing pool or dock.

This drill may also illustrate poor teaching. As students become tired, they tend to do the surface dives or strokes with improper form or fail to swim underwater the required distance. Some instructors overlook these matters, concentrating instead on the conditioning aspects of the drill. If there are sound reasons why strokes or dives should be done in a particular manner, then it is poor teaching to let violations occur without telling the swimmer. Working the group to exhaustion is not the way to perfect skills.

APPROACHES

The two most important things to stress in this category are: 1) the approach is designed to put the rescuer in position for a chin pull. This means that the chin pull, while technically not a part of the approach, is for all practical purposes the final result in this category; and 2) the rear and front surface approaches must include a satisfactory reverse.

Performing the Approaches

The rear approach is preferred over all others, for the obvious reason that the rescuer cannot be easily grabbed by the victim. After approaching to within 2 feet of the victim, the rescuer reverses as described earlier (Chart 6:5-D). He then applies the chin pull, levels the victim, and carries him in this fashion until shifting to one of the regular carries. Chart 6:7 summarizes the rear approach, ending in the chin pull.

CHART 6:7
PERFORMANCE TECHNIQUES FOR THE REAR APPROACH, CHIN PULL, AND LEVEL

Techniques	Illustration	Major and/or Common Performance Errors
A. Approach within 2 feet of victim. Stop forward momentum. Shift body weight by leaning back. Prepare legs to deliver scissors or breaststroke kicks. Prepare one arm to pull toward safety.	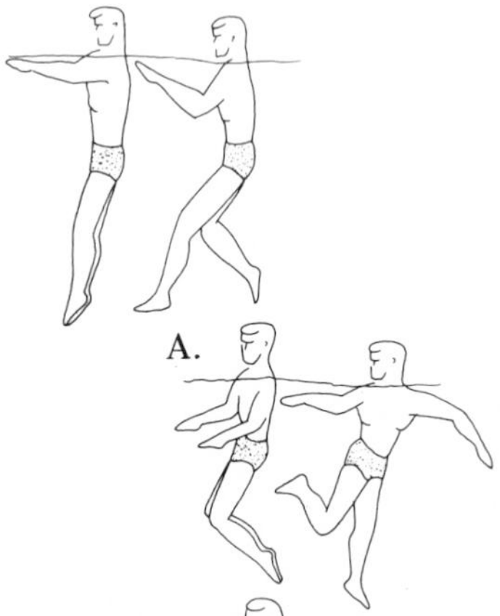 A.	A. Approaching too closely. Failing to stop (thus, drifting into victim). Stopping too far away.
B. Quickly put arm closest to victim over his shoulder.	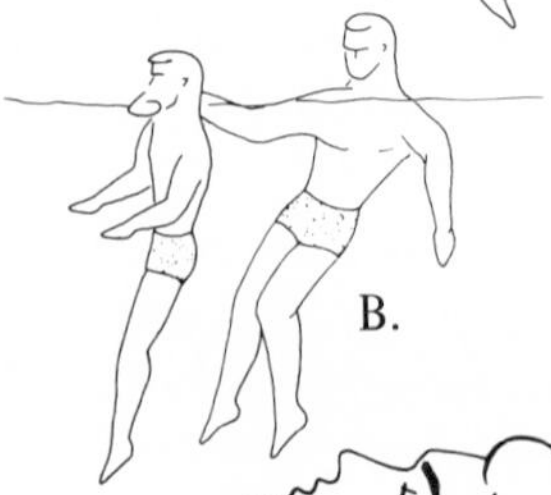 B.	B. Failing to move quickly.
C. Grasp chin with two fingers above point of chin, two fingers below.	 C.	C. Placing more than two fingers above point of chin (thus, rescuer's fingers in victim's mouth). Placing less than two fingers (thus, choking victim).
D. Deliver several vigorous and quick kicks. (Momentum will level body in water).	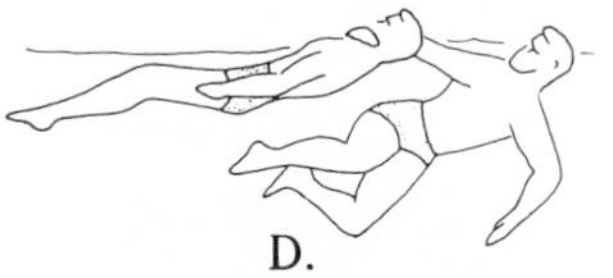 D.	D. Failing to achieve momentum.
E. Shift to a regular carry after victim is leveled.	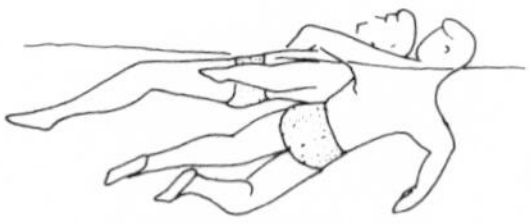 E.	E. Continuing to carry victim with chin pull. Failing to continue kicking while shifting to carry.

The front surface approach, in its regular version, is used when the victim is semiconscious and barely staying afloat in the water. Assuming that his arms are thrust forward at the surface, the rescuer swims to within 3 feet of the victim, reverses, and grasps him. As the leveling kicks are delivered, the victim is rolled on his back, the chin pull is applied, and an appropriate carry is performed. Chart 6:8 describes these maneuvers in greater detail.

A variation of the front surface approach makes it much easier to perform the task of rolling the victim on his back. The rescuer goes to one side of the victim and grasps the underside of the victim's wrist (right hand of rescuer to right wrist of victim or left to left). Rolling the rescuer's arm over will roll the victim onto his back. Chart 6:8 also shows this variation.

156

PERFORMANCE TECHNIQUES FOR THE FRONT APPROACH

Techniques	Illustration	Major and/or Common Performance Errors
REGULAR A. Grasp victim's wrist with own same hand (right on right, left on left) with knuckles of own hand facing upward and thumb to outside.	A.	A. Grasping wrong wrist.
B. Deliver several kicks, pulling victim to floating position on stomach.	B.	B. Failing to achieve a level position.
C. Move victim's wrist and arm across between self and victim. Rotate own arm to turn thumb downward and then outward to roll victim onto his back.	C.	C. Failing to move arm diagonally enough (thus, victim will not roll over).
D. After victim rolls on back, apply chin pull and appropriate carry.	D.	D. Releasing grip on victim's wrist before chin pull is applied.
VARIATION* E. Grasp victim's wrist with own same hand (right to right or left to left) with back of own hand facing downward and thumb to inside.	E.	E. Grasping top of wrist. Grasping wrong wrist.
F. Deliver several kicks. Level the victim.	F.	F. Failing to achieve level position.
G. Move victim's wrist and arm across between self and victim. Rotate own arm to turn thumb upward, outward, and then downward to roll victim onto his back.	G.	G. Not moving arm diagonally enough (thus victim will not roll over).
H. After victim rolls on back, apply chin pull and appropriate carry.	H.	H. Releasing grip on victim's wrist before chin pull is applied.

*Neither ARC nor YMCA.

Lanoue (1963, pp. 50-1) presents another variation of the front surface approach which certainly bears attention by lifeguards. He maintains that making any physical contact with a victim, even if he is barely conscious, is undesirable and dangerous. Therefore, Lanoue advocates that until the victim is almost exhausted, it is better to circle him and not attempt any type of hold or carry. If the rescuer can urge the swimmer to safety, so much the better. Lanoue says that in a surprisingly large number of cases, the victim will swim to safety and thus eliminate the need for any physical contact. If the victim cannot swim to safety, the rescuer should wait until the victim is nearly exhausted before using either the front surface approach or the rear approach. Since the victim is so exhausted, the danger of a prolonged physical struggle with the victim is greatly lessened.

Our general rule is: A struggling swimmer, with obvious vigor remaining, should not be approached (or contacted) from the front. In such cases, use the rear approach if you are able. If not, use the underwater approach. The victim whose strength is weak or spent probably will have his hands at the surface. He does not have strength remaining to cause trouble, so there is no need for the underwater approach. If his hands are convenient for contact, use the front surface approach.

The underwater approach is used when the victim is actively struggling to stay afloat. The primary goal is to come up behind the victim; in order to do this, you usually have to turn him around. After approach stroking, the rescuer surface dives. (It might be preferable for the feetfirst surface dive to be done, because there is less chance of moving forward while doing the dive and running the risk of letting the feet be grabbed by the victim.) From a position below the feet, the rescuer swims up to the victim, grabs him at the knees, and turns him around. While the victim is thus facing away, the rescuer slides the hands up the victim until his head breaks water. The rescuer quickly goes into the chin pull and levels the victim. Chart 6:9 describes the underwater approach.

CHART 6:9
PERFORMANCE TECHNIQUES FOR THE FRONT UNDERWATER APPROACH

Techniques	Illustration	Major and/or Common Performance Errors
A. Make surface dive 6-10 feet from the victim. Go to a depth below the victim's feet.	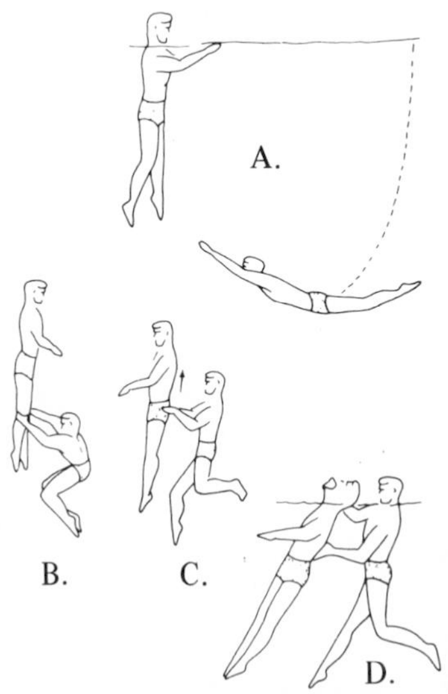 A.	A. Diving closer than 6 feet or farther than 10 feet from victim. Failing to dive deeply enough.
B. Grasp victim at knees. Turn him around by pushing on one leg and pulling on the other.		B. Failing to notice direction of victim's knees (he might have turned around trying to find rescuer).
C. Maintain contact (tickle) with victim while rising to the surface.		C. Permitting victim to turn around and face rescuer. Lifting victim up toward the surface. Pulling down on victim while rising.
D. Upon reaching surface, go immediately into chin pull, level, and appropriate carry.	B. C. D.	D. Permitting victim to sink or turn around.

Recovering a submerged victim calls for a search of the bottom; regardless of whether the headfirst or feetfirst surface dive is done, the rescuer must scan or feel the bottom. If the water is murky, then the rescuer must come close enough to the bottom so that his hand would touch any body. The task is simpler, of course, for the trained scuba diver—the air tanks let the searcher remain underwater and the face mask makes his vision much better.

Once the victim is located, the rescuer swims to a position behind him and, grabbing the upper arm, he either pulls or pushes him to the surface. If the chin pull can be done while the victim is coming to the surface, so much the better. If the bottom is firm, it is desirable for the rescuer to push off from it, but a muddy or unknown bottom presents so many dangers that the rescuer should swim up.

Teaching the Approaches

For all the skills mentioned in this section, partner drills in shallow and then deep water are recommended. As long as the rescuer is doing the skill correctly, the victim acts in a passive role for the first six to ten practices. However, if the rescuer is not doing everything right, then the victim should react. The instructor should insist on a reaction by the victim when something is wrong; this will make both learners more aware of the correct procedure.

In the standard front surface approach, the turning-over of the victim is not easy. Some "victims" help out by initiating the roll themselves. This is not desirable; the rescuer should practice until he has mastered the diagonal pull and can turn over a resisting victim.

When practicing the underwater approach, there are at least four drills which should be used. In each of them, have all the rescuers approach the victims in a wave formation timed so that they will all surface dive at the same time. *Without telling the rescuers,* have the victims do as Chart 6:10 suggests.

CHART 6:10
DRILLS FOR PRACTICING THE FRONT UNDERWATER APPROACH

Techniques	Illustration	Reason For The Drill
A. Victim tries to grab legs of rescuer just after he begins the head-first surface dive. If successful, the victim hangs on tightly.	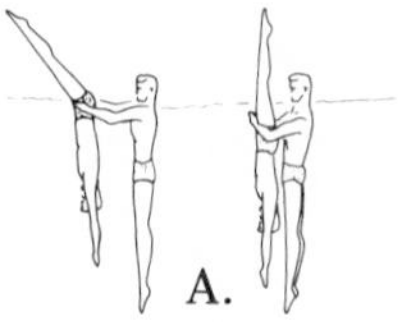 A.	A. Make rescuer aware of the dangers of surface diving too close to the victim.
B. Victim turns around just after rescuer surface dives. If rescuer does not notice, he will turn the victim back around and be greeted by a front head hold as he breaks the surface.	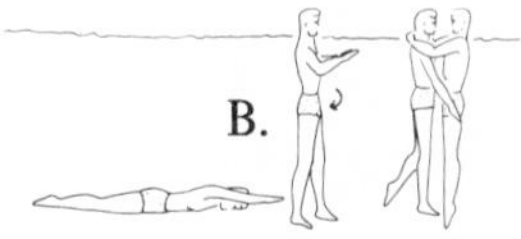 B.	B. Make rescuer realize that the victim might turn around in an attempt to locate the rescuer.
C. After victim has been turned around, he tries to turn back as rescuer rises to surface. If successful, rescuer will be greeted by front head hold.	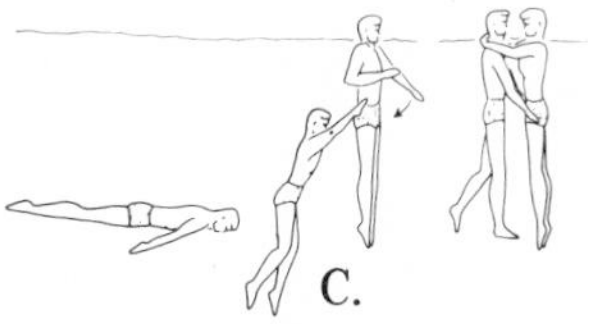 C.	C. Emphasize to the rescuer the importance of maintaining contact and using force if necessary to stay behind the victim.
D. Victim does feetfirst surface dive just after rescuer has done so. Victim tries to grab the rescuer while both are under water.	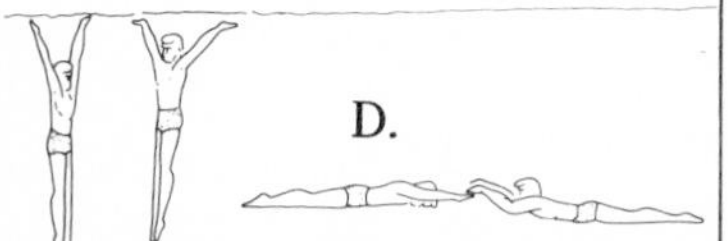 D.	D. Have rescuer realize that this possibility exists, and that any way he can get behind the victim is acceptable.

It is possible to combine the recovering of a submerged victim with underwater swimming. Have both the victim and the rescuer submerge, with the rescuer closing his eyes. After a quick count to five, the rescuer opens his eyes, locates the victim, swims behind, and brings the victim to the surface. The victim should be in different places for each practice—near the surface, over in a corner of the pool, near a dock piling, etc. Older lifesavers and/or better swimmers can take longer to hide, but the count of five at first is sufficient for both parties to get practice.

SWIMMING ASSISTS AND CARRIES

Even though a rescuer has to enter the water to assist a victim, he still should try to avoid the more glamorous holds and carries. The less physical contact he has with the victim, the safer he is. Even more important, if the victim can get to safety without being towed or carried, he has learned a valuable lesson—that if he would not panic, he could probably avoid the dangerous and embarrassing predicament next time.

Performing the Swimming Assists

One frequently overlooked method of assisting a swimmer to safety is pushing (or shoving). Frequently, a swimmer is within six feet from the pool edge or shallow water. It really doesn't make much sense to use the tired swimmer carry, the chin pull, etc. for such a distance if an easier and equally safe method can be used. The pushing (or shoving) technique is done exactly as its name implies—the rescuer places his hands on the hips (or upper body, or arm) of the victim and pushes him toward safety. The pushing technique is especially effective in pools where there is a solid bottom for the rescuer to push-off from, and a definite pool edge for the victim to grab. Neither the ARC nor YMCA prescribe this assist.

The easiest method of helping a swimmer who is in deep water consists of placing the rescuer's hand under the upper arm or shoulder and then swimming with the victim. In the shoulder support the rescuer is at the side of the victim while the victim is supported under the arm. Essentially the same support occurs when the rescuer is towing the victim while both are on their backs. A third method is perhaps more dangerous because it permits the victim to grasp the wrist of the rescuer, and he could begin to climb up the arm if he so desired. All these techniques are shown in Chart 6:11.

CHART 6:11
PERFORMANCE TECHNIQUES FOR THE SWIMMING ASSISTS

Techniques	Illustrations	Major and/or Common Performance Errors
SHOULDER ASSIST A. Swim to side of victim, place near hand under the victim's near shoulder or upper arm.	 A.	A. Failing to achieve sufficient momentum (thus, inducing panic in victim). Lifting victim above surface.
SHOULDER TOW B. Both rescuer and victim are in back-down position. Place one arm under shoulder or on upper arm of victim and use legs to propel him toward safety.	 B.	B. Swimming at side of, rather than ahead of the victim.
ARM ASSIST C. Extend arm for victim to grab. Use inverted kick for propulsion as victim pulled to safety.	 C.	C. Failing to achieve sufficient momentum (thus, inducing panic in victim). Failing to keep hand ready to place against victim's chest if he decides to climb toward rescuer.

The tired swimmer carry is really a pushing movement, and thus can be classified as a swimming assist. As Chart 6:12 shows, the rescuer approaches the victim from the front and begins a continual stream of encouraging words as soon as possible. Interspersing these comments ("Let me help you a bit," "This won't take very long," etc.) with directions ("Put your hands on my shoulders," "Look at the sky," "Keep your arms straight," etc.) the rescuer swims smoothly into the victim and makes contact. The rescuer usually must make a wide turn in order to head for safety. It is easier to swim if the victim's legs are split on either side of the rescuer's body; but for the beginning lifesaver, this is not advisable because it can lead to a body scissors if the victim becomes panicky.

Lanoue (1963, pp. 47-50) presents arguments that the traditional tired swimmer carry is not a very effective way of performing the task. In the traditional method, the temptation is great for the victim to press down on the rescuer's shoulders, because this is the only solid thing that he can contact. Lanoue points out that in rough water, where breathing is difficult unless the rescuer and victim both hold their heads high, a terrific physical strain is placed on the rescuer. He further says that if the victim should get water in his mouth, his natural reaction is going to be to hug the rescuer tightly. Therefore, Lanoue advocates a position where the rescuer pushes the victim but does not allow the victim to make contact except with his feet. Chart 6:12 also depicts Lanoue's variation of the tired swimmer carry.

CHART 6:12
PERFORMANCE TECHNIQUES FOR THE TIRED SWIMMER CARRY

Techniques	Illustration	Major and/or Common Performance Errors
TRADITIONAL A. Approach victim and begin reassuring talk to him.	 A.	A. Failing to talk before making contact with victim.
B. Tell victim to put his head back, place his hands on rescuer's shoulders; look at sky; put both legs to one side of rescuer; keep arms straight.	 B.	B. Permitting victim to sit in water, or raise head, or lay head back too far, or bend his arms.
C. Continue to swim (breaststroke) and talk.	 C.	C. Swimming a stroke that causes victim's hands to slip from rescuer's shoulders. (e.g., crawl stroke, sidestroke.) Surging ahead with a powerful stroke, and then dropping back so as to cause loss of contact.
D. Change direction of victim by grasping one elbow, continue stroking with other hand.	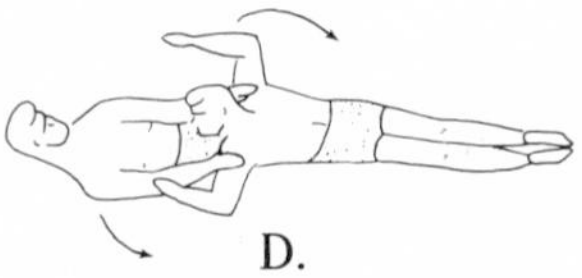 D.	D. Turning in wrong direction. Turning too sharply (thus, causing loss of momentum).

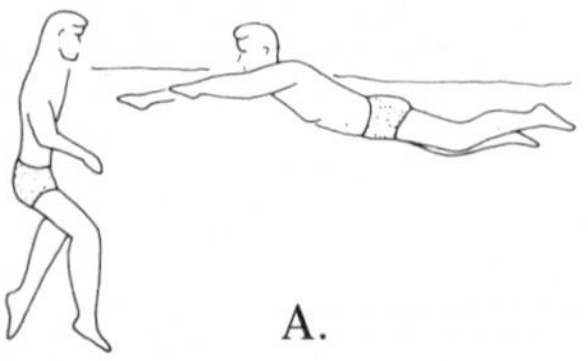

Chart 6:12 – Performance Techniques for the Tired Swimmer Carry (continued)

VARIATION (LANOUE)*

E. Approach victim and begin reassuring talk to him.

F. Tell victim to put head back, arms at side, thrust chest toward sky, look at sky.

G. Grasp victim's ankles; kick two or three times to gain momentum. (If distance is short, continue kicking until safety is reached.)

H. Place victim's toes inside waistband of suit, bend knees slightly (OR place toes in shoulder straps).
   Keep eyes on victim.

I. Use drownproofing technique for travelling a distance.

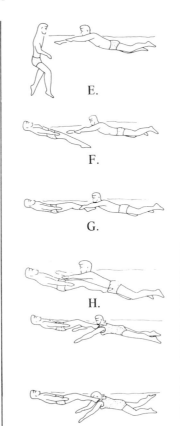

E.

F.

G.

H.

I.

E. Failing to talk before making contact with victim.

F. Permitting victim to sit in water, or raise head, or lay head back too far, or bend his arms.

G. Failing to gain momentum.

H. Failing to place toes securely to prevent loss of contact.
   Failing to keep eyes on victim.

I. Submerging excessively (inducing panic in victim because he thinks he is sinking).

*Neither ARC nor YMCA.

Teaching Swimming Assists

Since the first responsibility of the instructor is to teach the skills advocated by his organization (ARC, YMCA, etc.), this means that the traditional methods of assisting the tired swimmer must be taught. However, it is our opinion that the shoving method and Lanoue's technique for the tired swimmer carry should be practiced, if only to make lifesavers aware that there are several ways to achieve a particular objective. It is recommended that if time permits, the students be given an opportunity to swim a distance (say, 300 yards) and see which of the tired swimmer methods is less tiring. Lanoue says that ". . . under average conditions, the rescuer, who is exhausted at a few hundred yards with standard techniques, will be quite comfortable after half a mile using this different technique." (Lanoue, 1963, p. 49). Is he right? If the distance to be covered is great, it is important for the lifesaver to know.

There are many drills which can be used to aid learners in perfecting the tired swimmer carry. Some of these are summarized in Chart 6:13. In addition, each instructor probably will develop his own.

CHART 6:13
DRILLS FOR PRACTICING THE TIRED SWIMMER CARRY

Techniques*	Illustration	Reason For The Drill
A. In deep water, two students face one another and place their hands on each other's shoulders. At the signal each tries to force the other's head underwater.	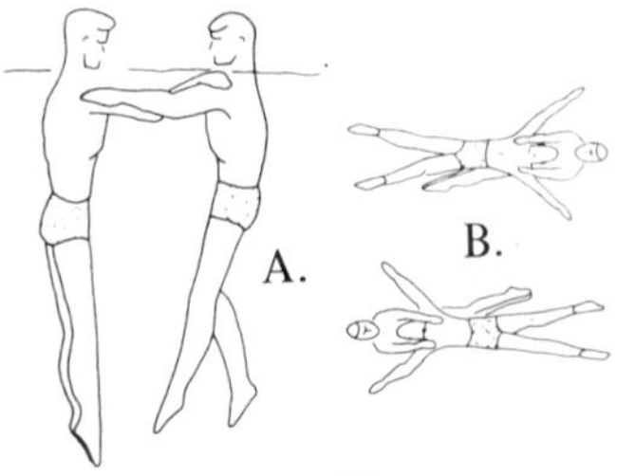	A. Develops kicking power and endurance.
B. Swim 100-200 yards in non-stop circle formation, carrying a tired swimmer.		B. Develops ability to turn without losing contact.
C. Swim 50-100 yards in a non-stop circle formation, carrying a tired swimmer. Rescuer must talk almost all the time. If he stops talking for more than ten seconds, victim applies front head hold and body scissors. Rescuer must release himself and continue.	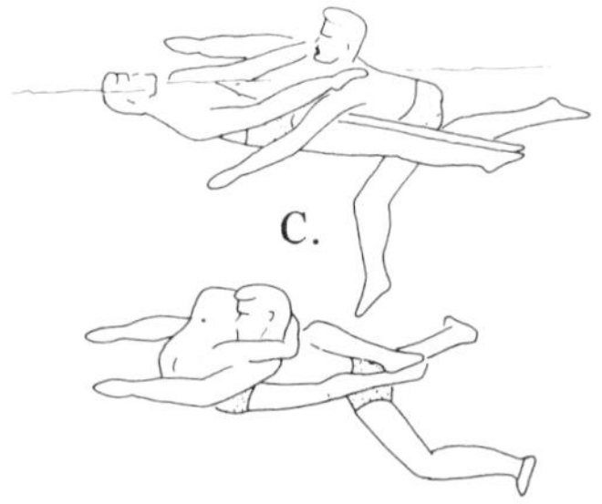	C. Develops habit of continual talking. Develops endurance.
D. Swim 100-200 yards (circle formation, nonstop). Victim presses down on rescuer's shoulders as rescuer swims and talks.	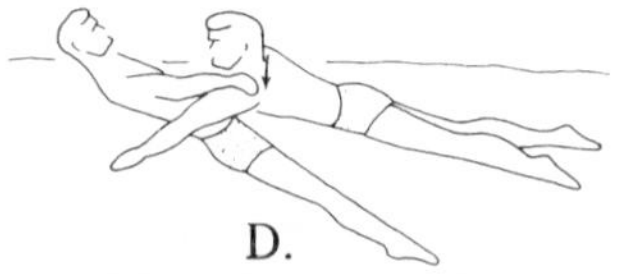	D. Develops endurance.

*All techniques can be made more difficult either by increasing distances, using nonfloaters, or using partners who weigh considerably more than the rescuers.

Comments about Tows and Carries

Once the victim has been placed into a control hold (usually the chin pull), he must be carried or towed to safety. The tired swimmer carry (given earlier) is one method of doing this, and is most desirable. However, it is not safe to use when the victim is extremely scared or when he is of much greater physical strength. Therefore, the purpose of the other carries or tows is to propel (under control and in safety) those victims to shore who are unable to be placed in the tired swimmer carry. For a struggling victim, the cross-chest carry with control hold is the most desirable. The head carry and the armpit carry are relatively safe, while the hair carry is limited to use with victims with sufficient hair.

The chin pull (or chin tilt), as described in most texts, consists of placing the cupped hand of the rescuer on the chin of the victim, and then towing him on his back with the rescuer's arm held fairly straight. Pressure is exerted on the chin so that the victim is supposedly under control (Chart 6:14A).

However, what happens if the victim tries to escape from this chin tilt? In half the cases he will succeed. If he tries to roll *away from* the cupped hand, he can be stopped by the rescuer (6:14B). But if he rolls *toward* the cupped hand, the rescuer cannot stop him (6:14C). Using the usual chin pull, there is no way to maintain contact if the victim violates the text and rolls toward the rescuer's hand.

An alternative method of the chin pull is to proceed as before, but for the rescuer to bend his arm so that the head of the victim can be clamped between the rescuer's upper and lower arm segments (6:14D). This hold prevents the victim from escaping. It is tiring for the rescuer to maintain for more than one or two minutes, but it does serve to make sure that the victim remains under control while leveling him.

PERFORMANCE TECHNIQUES FOR THE CHIN PULL

Techniques	Illustration	Major and/or Common Performance Errors
REGULAR A. Place two fingers above point of chin, two fingers below; arm straight. Swim on the side, with eyes on victim.	A.	A. Placing more than two fingers above point of chin (thus, rescuer's fingers in victim's mouth); placing less than two fingers (thus, choking victim).
B. If victim tries to escape by rolling *away* from rescuer's hand, he usually cannot.	B.	B. Failing to roll with the victim.
C. If victim tries to escape by rolling *toward* rescuer's hand, he probably will succeed.	C.	C. Failing to push away from victim immediately if he succeeds in turning.
VARIATION* D. Grasp victim's head as before, but clamp the back of his head into the angle formed by upper and lower arm segments of rescuer.	D.	D. Failing to clamp victim's head tightly.

*Neither ARC nor YMCA

The hair carry usually is advocated for use with a tired or unconscious victim. Chart 6:15 shows this carry.

The collar pull is simply what its name describes. The rescuer grabs the rear collar of the victim and tows him to safety. If the collar is buttoned, the insertion of fingers by the rescuer may cause panic in the victim. See Chart 6:15 for this carry also.

PERFORMANCE TECHNIQUES FOR THE HAIR CARRY AND COLLAR PULL

Techniques	Illustration	Major and/or Common Performance Errors

HAIR CARRY
 	
A. Take free hand and place it (fingers spread) on top of victim's head.
 	
B. Hand is moved forward until hairline is reached.
 	
C. Curl fingers to make a fist (include greatest possible amount of hair in grasp).
 	
D. Tow victim smoothly, being sure wrist is held down and arm is straight.
    Eyes kept on victim.
	
	A.
	
	B.
	
	C.
	
	D.
		A. Failing to place hand on the top of victim's head.
		
		B. Failing to move hand forward.
		
		C. Grabbing hair at front of victim's head (without performing techniques A and B).
		
		D. Failing to hold wrist down (thus, tilting victim's head forward and putting his mouth in the water).
		    Failing to hold arm straight (thus permitting victim to reach underneath himself and grab rescuer's legs).

COLLAR PULL* E. Grasp rear of victim's collar; tow as in hair carry.	E.	E. Inserting more fingers than necessary (thus causing choking).

*ARC only.

In the cross-chest carry, the weight of the victim is carried on the side of the rescuer. For this reason, it is the most tiring of the carries, but is valuable because it provides a strong degree of control. The free arm of the rescuer (that is, the arm not used for the chin pull) is placed diagonally across the chest of the victim with the hand forced firmly into the armpit. Some authorities advocate that the rescuer's arm be at about a 75° angle (16A) while others maintain that the arm should go diagonally across the victim from the shoulder to arm pit (16B). There is no doubt that the position in 6:16B affords greater control.

There is also a disagreement as to which hand should be used for the cross-chest carry. Some advocate using the same hand for both the chin tilt and the cross-chest carry, making the transition very quickly (6:16C). This does allow a moment or two of freedom for the victim, during which he may begin to struggle again. The more common practice is to retain the chin pull with one hand until the other arm is placed for the cross-chest carry (16D).

Lanoue (1963, pp. 52-54) has a variation of the cross-chest carry that deserves study by lifesavers. He maintains it would be better if the rescuer served as a buoyant raft upon which the victim could float, rather than have the victim as a weight on the hip. Chart 6:16 depicts both the traditional of the cross-chest carry and the Lanoue variation.

PERFORMANCE TECHNIQUES FOR THE CROSS-CHEST CARRY

Techniques	Illustration	Major and/or Common Performance Errors

REGULAR
 	
A. Place hip under the victim, one arm pressed tightly against victim's chest with the hand pressed against the victim's side near his waist.
 	
 OR
B. Place hip under the victim, one arm pressed tightly against victim's chest with the hand pressed against the victim's side at his armpit.
 	
C. Same hand may be used for both cross-chest carry and chin pull when changing from one to the other.
 	
 OR
D. When going from chin pull to cross-chest carry, hold chin pull until other hand has completed the cross-chest hold.
 	
LANOUE'S VARIATION*
 	
E. Float on back, directly under the victim. Victim's head should be just below rescuer's chin.
  Place one hand on victim's breastbone, clamping him securely.
  Use scissors or inverted breaststroke kick, plus the hand not holding victim, for propulsion.
	A.
	
	B.
	
	C.
	
	D.
	
	E.
		A. Failing to securely grasp the victim.
		  Failing to place hip tightly to victim's back.
		
		B. Failing to securely grasp the victim.
		  Failing to place the hip tightly to the victim's back.
		
		C. Failing to quickly reestablish control of the victim (thus permitting him to escape).
		
		D. Failing to have ability to swim equally well on either side.
		
		E. Failing to retain control of victim.
		  Entangling own legs with those of victim.

*Neither ARC nor YMCA.

The control carry (not to be confused with a control hold) is used when a victim is struggling so much that the rescuer is afraid he cannot maintain control. The victim cannot escape from this carry, assuming that the rescuer is of approximately equal strength. If the victim is rolling from side to side, the rescuer merely has to maintain the hold. It is often easier to roll over completely with the victim (thus putting him underwater briefly) than to try to resist. Chart 6:17 describes the control carry.

Two other carries, of more limited value, are also described in Chart 6:17. The armpit carry, described by the YMCA, is useful when short distances must be traveled. It is not a very restful stroke for the rescuer. The head carry is useful when a limited amount of control over the victim is needed.

PERFORMANCE TECHNIQUES FOR THE CONTROL CARRY, ARMPIT CARRY, AND HEAD CARRY

Techniques	Illustration	Major and/or Common Performance Errors

CONTROL CARRY*
 	
A. After the cross-chest carry is completed, use free hand to grasp wrist of other arm.
   Clamp victim tightly.
   Use scissors or breaststroke kick for propulsion.
	A.	A. Failing to provide momentum because of a weak kick.

ARMPIT CARRY* B. Swim to side of victim, place near hand under victim's near shoulder or upper arm.	B.	B. Failing to achieve sufficient momentum (thus inducing panic in victim). Lifting victim above surface.

HEAD CARRY*
 	
C. Place hands on each cheek of victim, palms in; fingers curled around victim's chin (middle finger on edge of jawbone), heels of hands close to ears and thumbs pressing in strong contact with forehead above eyebrows.
   Swim on the back, eyes on victim, using scissors or breaststroke kick.
	C.	C. Failing to tilt victim's head backward so his mouth is out of water.
		   Swimming in a near-vertical position.
		   Failing to achieve sufficient momentum with the kick.

*YMCA only.

Teaching the Skills of Towing and Carrying

It is wise to have some standards with which the students can compare themselves. It is fairly easy to establish these, using the following procedure:

1. Perform the skill (for example, a feetfirst entry, swim 60 feet, do the rear approach and then the cross-chest carry back to the starting point).
2. Record the times for at least fifteen students of each sex.
3. Judge the good and bad times arbitrarily; and
4. Use these standards until a greater sample has been tested.

As mentioned in other sections, it would be wise for you and your students to compare the different methods of performing the cross-chest carry. The degree of ease with which each carry can be done should be determined. If time permits, it would be enlightening for the students to see how far they could carry their partner with each method. It is conceivable that sometime the lives of two people could depend on this knowledge.

There should be much work with struggling, not passive, victims. If a victim, especially a girl, does not struggle, the lifesaver might just as well tow a log. Require the victims to struggle and, if they do not, have them repeat the performance.

A teaching method useful for showing the value of the recommended chin pull (where rescuer clamps victim's head in the crook of his elbow) is to tell victims that if they get a chance they should roll out of the chin tilt at *any* time during the course. If the victim does not become aware of such a chance, you should call it to his attention. (The rescuer will certainly know!) By continual awareness of the danger of the usual chin pull, rescuers will soon become skilled in the use of the recommended method and thus be safer.

DEFENSES AND RELEASES

We hope the rescuer will not have to use his knowledge of defenses and releases. It should, however, be stressed to lifesavers that a person, no matter how weak he is on land, can be a "tiger" when struggling in the water. Letting the victim tire himself out before the rescuer makes physical contact is theoretically sound, but a lifesaver might find himself grabbed or held by a victim, and thus knowledge in this area is essential.

Performing Defenses and Releases

Blocking, with one or two hands, is used to keep away from close contact with the victim and does not end in a control hold. As shown in Chart 6:18, the technique involves putting one hand (or two) on the chest of the victim. It is possible to use one foot (6:18B) as a blocking device, but this prevents the rescuer from using a kick to back away if needed. The YMCA technique indicates that the rescuer can stay at the surface or go under water to block, while the ARC method is to go underneath (6:18C). Each has advantages: staying at the surface enables the rescuer to breathe and to see clearly what the victim is doing, while going below removes the victim's temptation to continue grabbing for the rescuer.

The block and carry is a natural extension of the block. If the distance to safety is short, then the rescuer can let the victim maintain the hold on the arm and tow him to safety (Chart 6:18D). This technique has much to recommend it if the distance is short and the victim is smaller than the rescuer; it has obvious drawbacks if these conditions are not met.

CHART 6:18
PERFORMANCE TECHNIQUES FOR THE BLOCK, AND BLOCK AND CARRY

Techniques	Illustration	Major and/or Common Performance Errors
BLOCK A. Place fully extended arm at the base of the victim's throat and hold the victim away.	A.	A. Permitting victim to approach too closely. Failing to keep blocking arm fully extended.
B. Place one foot against chest of victim and hold him off.	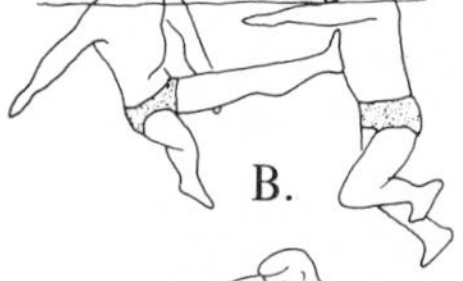 B.	B. Kicking the victim, rather than placing foot on his chest.
C. Using extended arm, go under water to hold victim off.	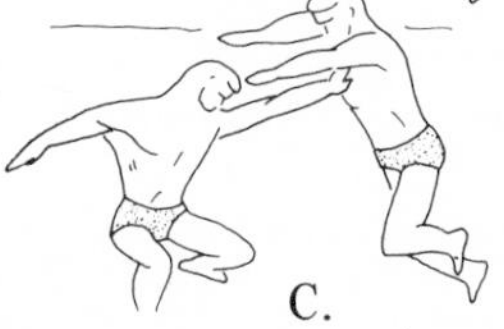 C.	C. Failing to keep blocking arm fully extended.

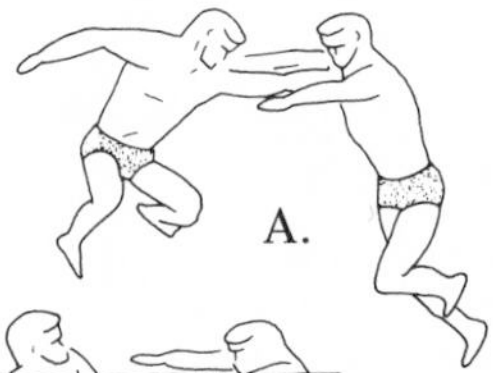

BLOCK AND CARRY*

D. Swim toward safety as victim retains grip on one arm.	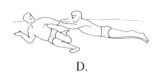 D.	D. Permitting victim to "climb the arm," forcing the rescuer underwater. Failing to keep blocking arm fully extended.

*YMCA only.

The block and turn, and the front parry are techniques used to free the rescuer from the victim's grasp and place him in a control position. Both are shown in Chart 6:19.

CHART 6:19
PERFORMANCE TECHNIQUES FOR THE BLOCK AND TURN, AND FRONT PARRY

Techniques	Illustration	Major and/or Common Performance Errors
BLOCK AND TURN* A. Reach with free hand to just above closest elbow; fork grip (thumb to inside) used to grip victim.		A. Grasping victim's arm below elbow. Failing to grasp victim with proper fork grip.
B. Lift up on victim's arm and push it across to opposite side; arm that has been seized is forced down and thus freed from grasp of victim.		B. Failing to lift victim's arm up before pushing it to opposite side.
C. Maintain grip until chin pull is secured with other hand.		C. Releasing grip on victim's upper arm before chin pull is applied.
FRONT PARRY** D. Use both hands to contact victim's arms near armpits. Lift victim slightly, at the same time chin is tucked.		D. Failing to tuck chin (thus giving victim opportunity to grab rescuer's head).
E. Maintain grip on one of victim's arms. Go behind the victim, and apply chin pull.		E. Failing to maintain grip on one of victim's arms.

*ARC only
**YMCA only.

The pushaway release from a front head hold is advocated by both ARC and YMCA. The rescuer deliberately sinks underwater and pushes on the victim's hips. If the rescuer's thumbs are forced into the abdomen and the heels of the hand pushed vigorously against the victim's hips, it will be found that the victim will release the hold quite readily. The use of the thumbs is not mentioned by either the ARC or YMCA, but we have found it most effective. Chart 6:20 depicts this release.

It is possible that the victim will apply a scissors grip with his legs around the waist of the rescuer along with the front head hold. There is no accepted method for releasing this grip; whatever works is acceptable. See Chart 6:20 also.

CHART 6:20
PERFORMANCE TECHNIQUES FOR THE RELEASE FROM FRONT HEAD HOLD

Techniques	Illustration	Major and/or Common Performance Errors

HEAD HOLD (PUSHAWAY) RELEASE
 	
A. Deliberately sink and place hands on the victim's hips.
 	
B. Pull head down and forward (tuck chin).
    Push vigorously against victim's hips.
 	
C. Maintain control of victim.
    Roll victim over.
 	
D. Come to surface and apply chin pull.
 	
HEAD HOLD AND BODY SCISSORS RELEASE*
 	
E. Reach behind victim's head, grasp hair at forehead.
    Place other hand on forehead of victim.
 	
F. Push vigorously with both hands, breaking victim's hold.
 	
G. Sink underwater, thus reducing chance the victim will grab for rescuer's head.
    Break the scissors grip by any prying method.
    Use appropriate approach, level, and carry.
	
	A.
	B.
	C.
	D.
	E.
	G.
	F.
		A. Attempting to remain on surface of water.
		
		B. Failing to tuck the chin.
		
		C. Losing contact with victim, either before or after rolling him over.
		
		D. Failing to apply chin pull before victim regains his hold.
		
		E. Failing to securely place hands on the victim.
		
		F. Failing to push vigorously enough.
		
		G. Failing to submerge.
		    Permitting victim to regain the head hold.

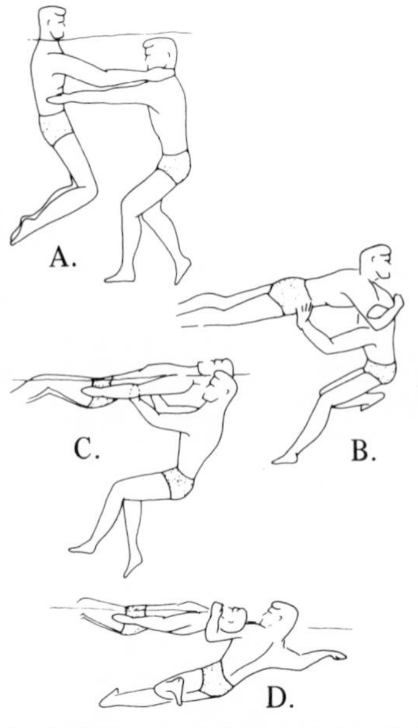

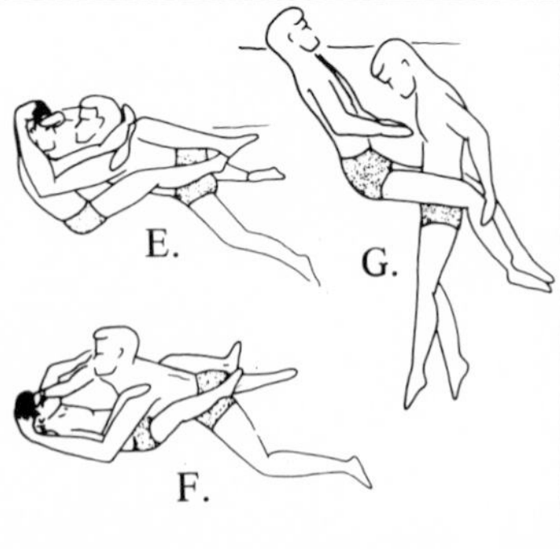

*YMCA only.

Releasing a double grip on one arm is done differently by the two groups. The YMCA would like its lifesavers to pull the victim close, and turn him around by pressure on the chin. The ARC advocates using one foot. Each method is shown in Chart 6:21.

PERFORMANCE TECHNIQUES FOR THE RELEASE FROM DOUBLE GRIP ON ONE ARM

Techniques	Illustration	Major and/or Common Performance Errors

YMCA METHOD
 	
A. Pull victim toward self, at same time reaching with free hand across shoulder and clear around back of head.
 	
B. Grasp victim's chin and twist head.
 	
C. Kick (to raise self up) and apply downward force on shoulder.
    Pull arm being held by victim back, thus forcing him to let go.
 	
D. When grip is released, continue chin pull.
    Level victim.
    Apply appropriate carry.
		A. Failing to pull victim close enough to get free arm around head.
		
		B. Failing to get tight grip on chin.
		
		C. Failing to push victim underwater.
		    Failure to pull arm back with sufficient force.
		
		D. Failing to maintain chin pull until appropriate carry position is attained.

RED CROSS METHOD
 	
E. Reach across with free hand and grasp top wrist of victim. At same time, press down on other wrist, forcing victim underwater.
 	
F. Bring foot (same side of body as free hand) up and over victim's shoulder.
    Place it on chest of victim.
 	
G. Straighten the leg as victim releases grip.
    Maintain grip on victim's wrist.
 	
H. Kick to gain momentum, turn victim around and apply chin pull.
		E. Failing to grasp correct wrist.
		    Failing to force victim underwater.
		
		F. Failing to bring foot outside the shoulder.
		
		G. Kicking the victim (rather than pushing him away).
		    Losing contact with victim.
		
		H. Failing to obtain sufficient momentum.
		    Failing to turn victim around before he applies another hold.

Releasing the rear head hold likewise can be done two ways, after the initial bite of air is taken. The YMCA recommends that one arm is forced between the stomach of the victim and the back of the rescuer. The other arm is thrust vigorously across the stomach of the rescuer, thus enabling the rescuer to pivot rather quickly. The ARC technique permits the rescuer to use the leverage of the victim's arms to effect the rear head hold release. Both those releases are explained in Chart 6:22.

PERFORMANCE TECHNIQUES FOR THE REAR HEAD HOLD RELEASE

Techniques	Illustration	Major and/or Common Performance Errors
YMCA METHOD A. Grab a bite of air. Tuck chin in and turn it to one side. B. Drop one shoulder. Force this arm (elbow-first) between self and victim. Thrust free arm vigorously across own chest. C. Twist around to face victim. D. Use pushaway release, ending in chin pull.	A. B. C. D.	A. Failing to grab bite of air and/or tuck chin. B. Forcing the arm hand-first, rather than elbow-first. C. Failing to use free arm for leverage for the twist. D. Attempting to remain on surface of water. Failing to tuck and turn the chin. Losing contact with victim, either before or after rolling him over.
RED CROSS METHOD E. Grab a bite of air. Tuck chin in and turn it to one side. F. Place one hand (thumb on top) over victim's lower hand. Place other hand (fork grip, thumb to inside) above elbow of victim's same arm. G. Twist victim's arm downward and inward. Duck head. H. Continue twisting, as victim is pulled forward. End with victim's arm in hammerlock. I. Retain grip on wrist until chin pull is applied.	E. F. G. H. I.	E. Failing to grab a bite of air and/or tuck chin. F. Failing to grasp proper hand of victim. Failure to grasp victim's elbow. G. Failing to apply sufficient pressure to force victim to release hold. H. Failing to continue pressure until hammerlock position attained. I. Failing to retain hammerlock means victim is free to try another hold.

Each of the two main certifying groups has a separate technique for dealing with two drowning victims who are grasping each other. The YMCA maintains that if the distance is short and it is feasible, the rescuer should put one of the victims into the head carry and tow them both to safety.

However, when this cannot be done the ARC presents a technique for separating them. (The question always arises—should the victims be separated? This cannot be answered in any text. It depends on the rescuer, the distance to safety, and similar factors. It is obvious that if they are separated, one has a much greater chance of reaching safety than the other. You could argue that if they were separated, the one might be able to reach safety by himself. Common sense would tell the rescuer that he should try to rescue the weaker of the two swimmers.) In the ARC technique, the rescuer swims up behind one victim, separates him from the other, and tows him to safety. Chart 6:23 describes both methods.

CHART 6:23
PERFORMANCE TECHNIQUES FOR RESCUING AND/OR
SEPARATING TWO DROWNING PERSONS

Techniques	Illustration	Major and/or Common Performance Errors
YMCA METHOD (Rescue both persons) A. Get behind one victim, grasp his chin or upper arm, tow both toward safety. RED CROSS METHOD (Separate the two, rescue one) B. Get behind one victim, place cupped hands over victim's chin. C. Press down on victim's shoulders; place one foot on chest of the other victim. NOTE: If one victim has grasped the other from behind, then rescuer must place his foot on the upper back of the other victim. D. Press to straighten leg, thus separating the victims. Continue with chin pull on the one victim.	 A. B. C. D.	A. Attempting to swim a great distance towing two victims. B. Failing to get secure hold on the chin. C. Failing to submerge the victims. Failing to securely place the foot in position. D. Kicking the second victim, rather than pressing against him with one foot.

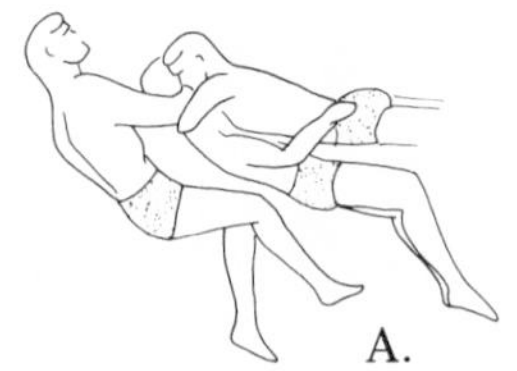

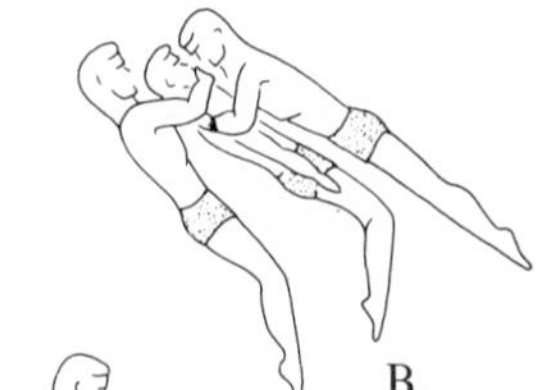

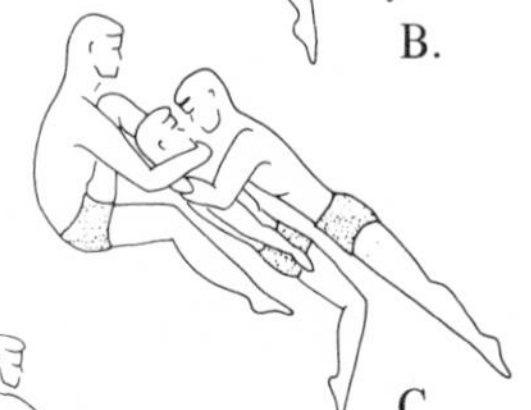

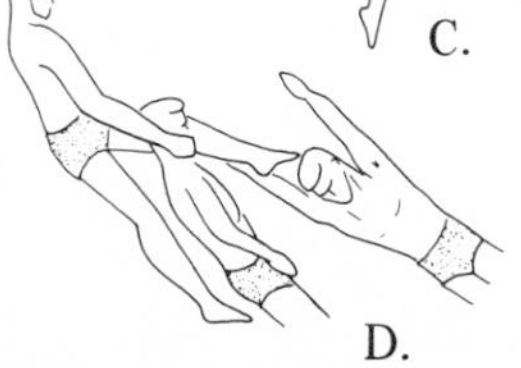

Teaching the defenses and releases

It is important to remind the students that a real victim probably has not read the textbook and that he probably will not react in precisely the same fashion as described here. The lifesaver's job will be to break the hold and maneuver until he gets into the control position. In order to perform this task successfully, lifesavers should have a number of practice sessions where the victim does not do quite as the book says. For example, the victim can grip one wrist and then suddenly go to the other one. Or he can apply certain holds at random; he can grab the rescuer's right wrist and after the rescuer is set to react to this, go to a front head hold.

Another way for the rescuer to develop the ability to react quickly is to have him swim into a situation about which he knows nothing. For example, have the victims about five feet apart, hanging onto the trough or treading water in a straight line. One rescuer starts to swim parallel to this group with his eyes *closed*. A designated victim (unknown to the rescuer) will grab the rescuer. When contact is made, the rescuer must open his eyes and react in an acceptable manner. A note: Reacting in an acceptable manner is not always as the textbook indicates. As an instructor, you must see that the lifesaver can properly do the skills required by the organization. But in "ad lib" situations virtually any way (barring injury to the victim) that the control hold can be reached is acceptable.

The instructor must continually stress that the holds used in the class are dangerous and that the students must be careful when they are practicing. Accidents will happen, but negligence on the part of the instructor will be difficult to disprove if a neck is injured or a shoulder dislocated.

SEARCH AND RESCUE

Even though scuba equipment is the preferred method of searching underwater, it is seldom that such gear could be used to rescue a victim who has disappeared but could be resuscitated. Thus, lifesavers must be able to employ less effective but quicker means of searching.

Performing searching and rescuing

The surface dive techniques have been presented in Chapter 4. Search drills are nothing more than formations or patterns whereby every square foot of the bottom is examined. There is no universal pattern for use in every instance, but a formation which covers all of the bottom must be employed. Chart 6:24 illustrates the basic principles of searching the bottom and diagrams the commonly-used formations.

CHART 6:24
PRINCIPLES AND FORMATIONS FOR SEARCHING THE BOTTOM

Techniques	Illustration	Major and/or Common Performance Errors
PRINCIPLES A. Rescuer(s) in line with object on shore (and with each other).		A. Failing to take a sighting (thus perhaps overlooking part of the bottom).
B. Rescuer(s) wade as far as possible. All dive together. Dive within 1 foot of bottom.		B. Failing to dive within 1 foot of the bottom.
C. Take preestablished number of strokes underwater. Come straight up.		C. Failing to take same number of strokes may cause some part to be overlooked.
D. Back up 3-4 feet, dive again and continue search.		D. Failing to back up for next dive may mean overlooking area just beyond previous dive.

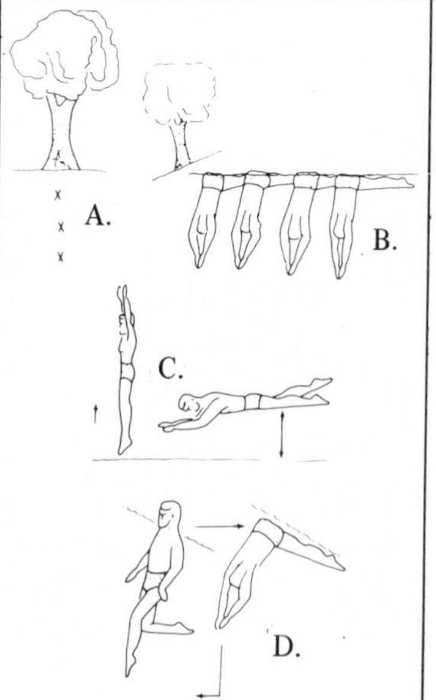

COMMON FORMATIONS

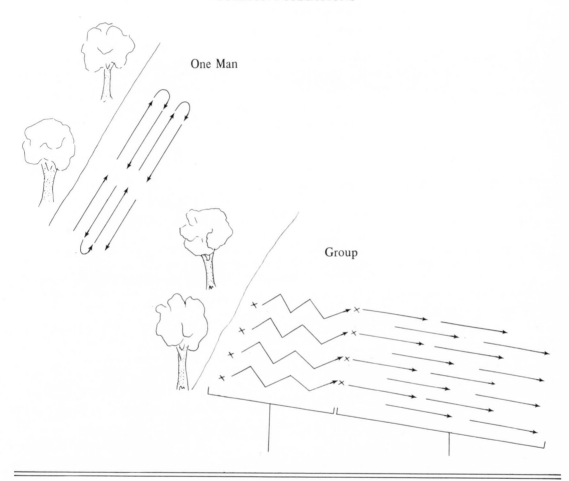

The use of mask, fins, and snorkel is a new addition to the ARC course. Instructors who are not familiar with these pieces of equipment should read pp. 71-75 of the *Lifesaving and Water Safety Courses: Instructor's Manual.* Each learner's mask and fins should be checked to insure proper fit before the class enters the water. He should be shown how to defog the face mask (by rubbing the inside with water or saliva), how to put it on (face is covered first, then the strap is stretched to the back of the head), and how to check for leaks. A mask that is filled with water can be emptied by letting it run out while the head is above the surface or, when under the water, by tilting the head and pressing the top side of the mask to the face while exhaling slowly through the nose. As the swimmer goes into deeper water, he may relieve pressure on the ears or face mask by exhaling slightly through the nose.

Backward walking with fins is recommended when on land, but it would be better never to wear fins out of the water. Once in the water, kicking with a long, wide, and slow flutter kick is recommended.

The snorkel mouthpiece is inserted so that it is gripped with the teeth. Keeping the snorkel vertical to the surface is desirable. Clearing it after surfacing involves a forceful exhalation through the mouth.

Basic principles of searching while using fins, mask, and snorkel are shown in Chart 6:25.

CHART 6:25
PERFORMANCE TECHNIQUES FOR SEARCHING WITH MASK, FINS, AND SNORKEL

Techniques	Illustration	Major and/or Common Performance Errors
A. When entering water with face mask, use the lifesaving jump or somersault from the deck. Hands must hold mask firmly to face.	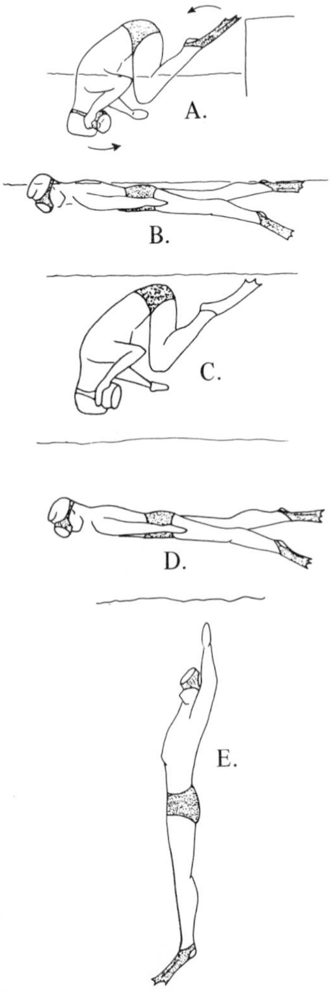 A.	A. Failing to use one or both hands to hold face mask in place.
B. Swimming at surface is similar to prone glide with arms at side.	B. C.	B. Moving too fast (thus causing segments of bottom to be overlooked).
C. Surface dive, using any type. Use hands to hold mask firmly to face.	D.	C. Failing to back up before surface diving (thus causing part of bottom to be unsearched).
D. Underwater searching is done with kick for propulsion.	E.	D. Failing to sweep eyes over area ahead of rescuer.
E. When surfacing, stop just before surface, look up, extend arms.		E. Failing to see if surface is clear before emerging.

Recovering objects is merely a matter of placing the object (e.g. brick) on the hip and pushing off the bottom. If a person is found, the rescuer swims to a point behind the victim's head, grasps him in a chin pull or head carry, or by the wrist, and swims to the surface. A pushoff from the bottom should not be attempted unless the bottom is known to be firm and clean.

Teaching Searching and Rescuing

Much practice is needed in these skills because most swimmers are not too familiar with this equipment. Because masks, fins, and snorkels are usually limited in number, we recommend that these skills be taught early in the course so that practice is not confined to one or two sessions. These skills should be part of the daily practice drills mentioned earlier.

176

REMOVING A VICTIM FROM THE WATER

Lifts and carries are more valuable than many lifesavers believe because they may need to be carried out quickly if resuscitation efforts are to commence in time. If the victim is conscious and uninjured, it is usually preferable to let him rest briefly in shallow water and leave under his own power, rather than use one of the techniques mentioned below.

Description of Skills and Techniques of Removing Victim from Water

The pool lift is a technique whereby one rescuer can lift the victim to the deck or boat to continue resuscitation. It is important to remove the victim as quickly as possible, without injuring him. Chart 6:26 shows the accepted form for the pool (or boat) lift. When a neck injury is suspected (as is often the case in a diving accident) the victim is not moved until some means of rigid support is available. This is also shown in Chart 6:26.

CHART 6:26
PERFORMANCE TECHNIQUES FOR REMOVING A VICTIM FROM THE WATER

Techniques	Illustration	Major and/or Common Performance Errors
POOL, DOCK, OR BOAT LIFT A. Place hands of victim one atop the other and cover them with one of rescuer's own hands. Maintain pressure on his hands while climbing out of the water.		A. Permitting hands of victim to slip back into the water.
B. Grasp wrists of victim, lift him straight up until waist is even with deck.	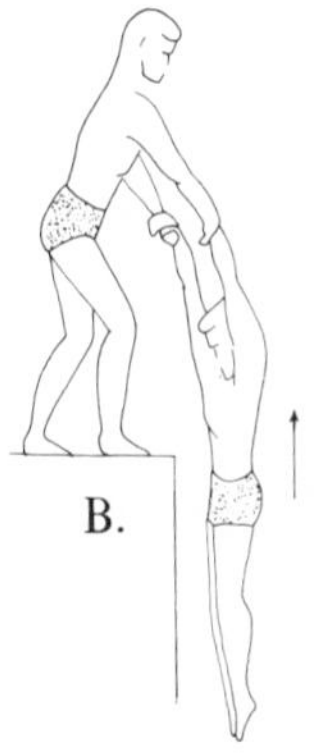	B. Failing to lift straight up will cause victim's stomach to be scraped.
C. Fold top half of victim's body over onto deck. (If victim is unconscious, cross one arm underneath his head as he is laid down. This avoids letting his head drop on the deck).	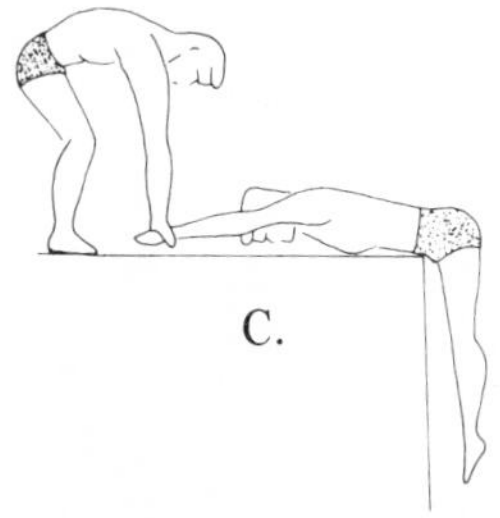	C. Failing to raise top half of victim's body out of the water. Failing to exercise caution when lowering upper half of body to the deck.
D. Hold top part of victim's body while pulling near leg of victim toward the deck.	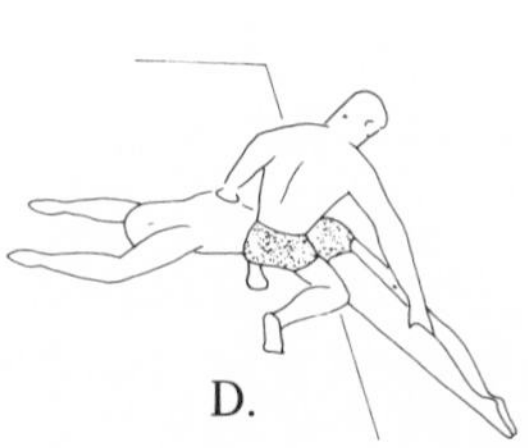	D. Permitting top half of body to slide back into the water.

Chart 6:26 — Performance Techniques for Removing a Victim from the Water (continued)

SUSPECTED NECK INJURY

E. Float long rigid object underneath victim.

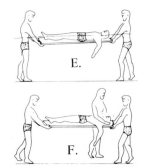

E. Failing to use great care in
placing the object under victim's
body.

F. One rescuer holds victim's
neck steady while victim is being
carried.

F. Failing to immobilize neck of
victim while he is being carried.

When the victim must be removed from a lake or river, there are three carries that are commonly used. The drag to the beach (although technically not a carry) is preferable because it is the quickest. The saddleback carry is used when a heavy victim must be carried a distance, while the fireman's carry is employed when the victim is of equal or less weight than the rescuer. Chart 6:27 depicts these methods.

CHART 6:27
PERFORMANCE TECHNIQUES FOR CARRYING A VICTIM FROM THE WATER

Techniques	Illustration	Major and/or Common Performance Errors
DRAG TO THE BEACH* A. Stand behind victim, clasp hands over his chest. 　Walk backward, dragging heels of victim on ground.	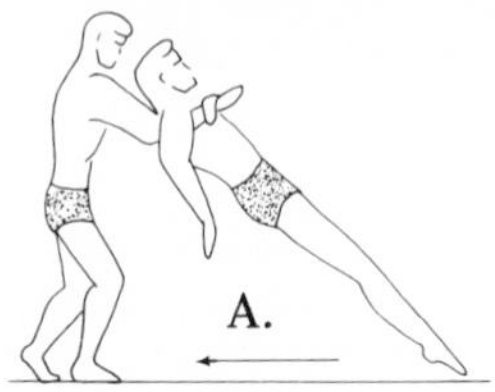 A.	A. Permitting seat or legs of victim to drag.
SADDLEBACK CARRY B. Face head of victim with hips at right angles to victim's body.	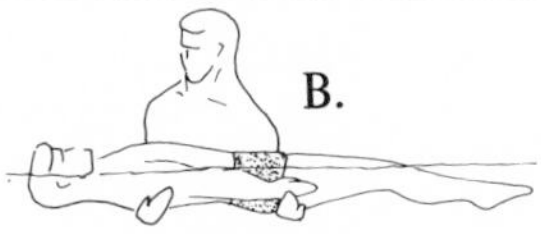 B.	B. Having stomach to victim's side, rather than hip.
C. Reach with outside hand, grasp underside of victim's far wrist.	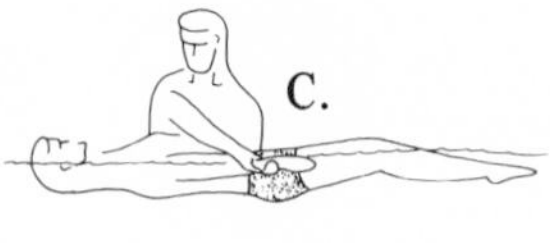 C.	C. Failing to reach with outside hand. 　Failing to grasp underside of wrist.
D. Lift victim's wrist around back of head; at same time turn so that back is toward victim's stomach.	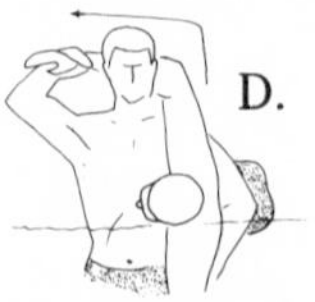 D.	D. Failing to face away from victim in order to turn back toward him.
E. Other hand slides across victim's back to support head. 　Release grip at wrist and encircle legs just above knees.	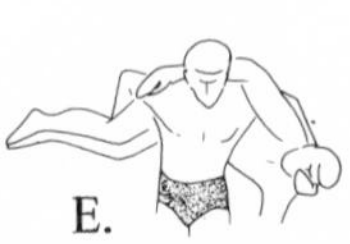 E.	E. Failing to keep victim's face out of water.

178

FIREMAN'S CARRY**

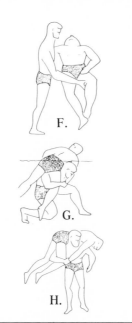

F. Face victim with one hand under his neck and the other over the near leg and under the far knee.

F. Failing to reach over the near leg before grasping the far leg.

Extending arm between victim's legs from below instead of from above.

G. Duck under water.
Roll victim onto near shoulder.

G. Failing to submerge completely under the water.

H. Stand.
Grasp near wrist of victim, securely holding victim to the rescuer's shoulders.

H. Failing to properly position victim before standing.

*ARC only.
**YMCA only.

Lowering the victim to the ground is not easy. If done too quickly, injury may result; if done too slowly, valuable time is taken. Chart 6:28 shows how the victim is lowered to the ground in the drag, the saddleback, and the fireman's carry.

CHART 6:28
PERFORMANCE TECHNIQUES FOR LOWERING A VICTIM TO THE GROUND

Techniques	Illustration	Major and/or Common Performance Errors
DRAG A. Lower victim to ground, stepping over his body with one foot. This places victim on stomach.		A. Failing to roll victim over as he is placed on the ground.
SADDLEBACK B. Kneel, slowly lean back. Victim is gently lowered to ground.		B. Permitting victim to drop to ground.

Chart 6:28 — Performance Techniques for Lowering a Victim to the Ground (continued)

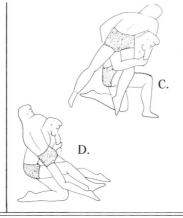

FIREMAN'S CARRY*	
C. Kneel on knee opposite the shoulder on which the victim is carried. Other leg is bent at right angles, foot securely placed on the ground.	C. Kneeling on wrong knee. Failing to place other leg in secure position.
D. Victim is placed in sitting position on knee of rescuer. Victim is lowered to ground by gently placing him on his back or side.	D. Failing to retain tight grip on victim. Failing to lower victim slowly.

*YMCA only.

Carrying a victim is obviously much easier when two or three rescuers are available. Chart 6:29 illustrates these techniques.

CHART 6:29
PERFORMANCE TECHNIQUES FOR THE TWO- AND THREE-MAN CARRIES

Techniques	Illustration	Major and/or Common Performance Errors
TWO-MAN CARRY* Carry A. Victim is carried feetfirst— one rescuer supporting the knees, the other supporting the upper back. Kneel to lower victim gently to the ground.	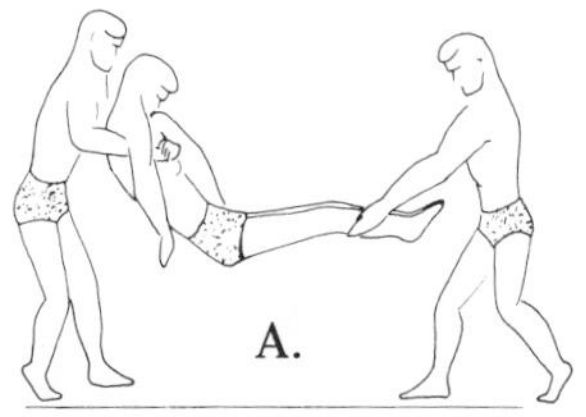 A.	A. Supporting victim under shoulders and/or the lower legs. Failing to place the victim on the ground gently.
THREE-MAN CARRY* B. One rescuer supports the legs as shown; the other two clasp each other's arms and support the victim at the abdomen and shoulders. Victim is lowered to ground by kneeling and gently placing him on the ground (chest first).	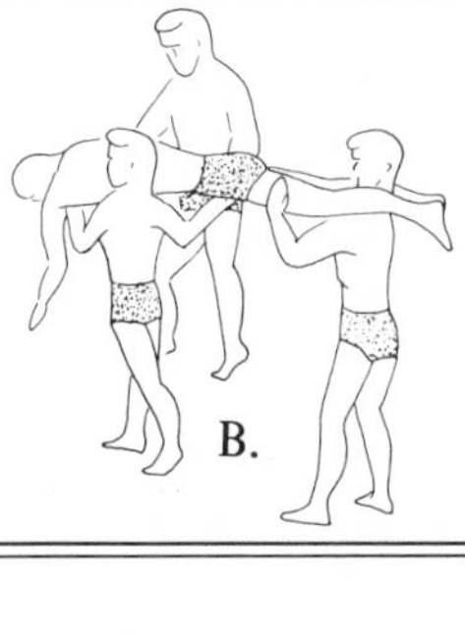 B.	B. Failing to securely grasp arms with fellow rescuer. Failing to place victim on the ground gently.

*YMCA only.

Teaching the Skills of Removing Victim from Water

There are no special teaching devices to use in this area. It is recommended that a lift or carry and let-down be made a part of the daily practice.

RESUSCITATION AND CARE OF VICTIM

The techniques of mouth-to-mouth resuscitation have been presented earlier (Chapter 3). While all swimmers *should* master this technique, it *must* be mastered by lifeguards. The back pressure—arm lift and the back pressure—hip lift methods are presented below. Presentation of three different methods (and there are at least two more accepted ones) confuses lifeguards. Why not just learn the best one? The answer seems to be that there may be an occasion when the best method (mouth-to-mouth) cannot be done because of facial injuries. A more practical reason is that the YMCA requires the lifeguard to know at least three methods of resuscitation. At any rate, it should be clearly understood by lifeguards that mouth-to-mouth resuscitation is the emergency procedure recommended by all U.S. health groups. Deviation from this method may expose the rescuer to a legal charge of negligence. It goes without saying that if a mechanical resuscitator and a trained operator are available, they should be used instead.

The application of external heart massage by lifeguards is debatable. The ARC does not recommend it and while the YMCA manual describes it, it is not emphasized. Until the various national agencies (including medical and health agencies) advocate this technique, it is recommended that a lifesaver not use it.

Performing Resuscitation

The mouth-to-mouth method of resuscitation has been presented earlier (Chapter 3). The back pressure—arm lift (Nielsen) method of resuscitation is used when the mouth-to-mouth method cannot be used. It does not put as much oxygen into the blood as the mouth-to-mouth method, but it has been used successfully in hundreds of cases. The chest pressure—arm lift method should also be known by lifesavers, as it is conceivable that a victim (e.g. a pregnant woman) needs to be on the back. The official Red Cross directions for both back pressure—arm lift and mouth-to-mouth methods are given in Chart 6:30.

CHART 6:30
MANUAL METHODS OF ARTIFICIAL RESPIRATION*

CHEST PRESSURE—ARM LIFT

Place the victim in a face-up position and put something under his shoulders to raise them and allow the head to drop backward.

Kneel at the victim's head, grasp his wrists, cross them, and press them over the lower chest (Figure 1). This should cause air to flow out.

Immediately release this pressure and pull the arms outward and upward over his head and backward as far as possible (Figure 2). This should cause air to rush in.

Repeat this cycle about 12 times per minute, checking the mouth frequently for obstructions.

If a second rescuer is available, have him hold the victim's head so that the jaw is jutting out (Figure 3). The helper should be alert to detect the presence of any stomach contents in the mouth and keep the mouth as clean as possible at all times.

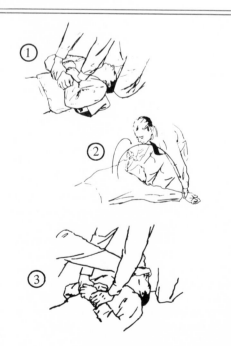

BACK PRESSURE–ARM LIFT

Place the victim face-down, bend his elbows and place his hands one upon the other, turn his head slightly to one side and extend it as far as possible, making sure that the chin is jutting out. Kneel at the head of the victim. Place your hands on the flat of the victim's back so that the palms lie just below an imaginary line running between the armpits (Figure 4).

Rock forward until the arms are approximately vertical and allow the weight of the upper part of your body to exert steady, even pressure downward upon the hands (Figure 5).

Immediately draw his arms upward and toward you, applying enough lift to feel resistance and tension at his shoulders (Figure 6). Then lower the arms to the ground. Repeat this cycle about 12 times per minute, checking the mouth frequently for obstruction.

If a second rescuer is available, have him hold the victim's head so that the jaw continues to jut out (Figure 7). The helper should be alert to detect any stomach contents in the mouth and keep the mouth as clean as possible at all times.

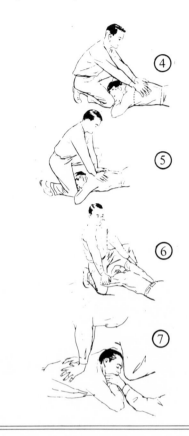

*Adapted from ARC, *Saving A Life by Artificial Respiration.* Poster 1002, Revised October, 1959. Used by permission.

After a victim has been revived, the lifesaver's job is not finished. The victim should be kept quiet until he is breathing regularly. Warm him with blankets, coats, and similar articles; be especially watchful for signs of shock (pallor, more rapid pulse, nausea, vomiting, irregular breathing, cold and clammy skin). Although this may be difficult to enforce at times, the lifesaver should try to ensure that the victim rests for at least 30 minutes before getting to his feet.

Teaching the Techniques of Resuscitation

An excellent source of information on this topic is Chapter 11 in Silvia's book, *Lifesaving and Water Safety Today.* This chapter contains an interesting history of this area, the medical background of resuscitation, and explanations and illustrations of all currently recommended techniques and mechanical apparatus. Also, Chapter 8 in *Lifeguard Training* is desirable reading.

The most important fact to emphasize to students is that resuscitation must be started as soon as possible and continued as long as possible. It is desirable that resuscitation be started while the victim is being transported to shore. It is apparent that in a swimming rescue the victim has to be taken to safety as quickly as possible—and this usually means the shore or deck. But students fail to realize that it is more important to begin resuscitative measures immediately than to return to shore. Recovery statistics, such as those presented in Table 6:1 below, should be given to students so they may see the need for immediate resuscitative efforts.

TABLE 6:1
RECOVERY STATISTICS*

After breathing has stopped and artificial respiration is begun the *chances of recovery* are (averages only as individuals differ):

1 minute after breathing has stopped	98 out of 100
2 minutes after breathing has stopped	92 out of 100
3 minutes after breathing has stopped	72 out of 100
4 minutes after breathing has stopped	50 out of 100
5 minutes after breathing has stopped	25 out of 100
6 minutes after breathing has stopped	11 out of 100
7 minutes after breathing has stopped	8 out of 100
8 minutes after breathing has stopped	5 out of 100
9 minutes after breathing has stopped	2 out of 100
10 minutes after breathing has stopped	1 out of 100
11 minutes after breathing has stopped	1 out of 1000
12 minutes after breathing has stopped	1 out of 10,000

In connection with the above, the American Red Cross stresses the fact that artificial respiration will have to be applied for three or four hours before signs of recovery are apparent in severe cases of electrical shock. In cases of drowning, signs of recovery should appear within approximately 25 minutes.

*From *Railroad Newsletter,* date unknown.

Showing the movie *Rescue Breathing* (available from most ARC or state health department offices) is an excellent way to initiate teaching about resuscitation. Arousing interest beforehand should be done by asking the questions, "How would you like to be drugged so you couldn't breathe?" "What would be a good way of determining which methods of resuscitation were successful?" Such questions always create interest and the movie cited actually shows drugged "victims" and dramatically illustrates the superiority of mouth-to-mouth resuscitation over the Nielsen method.

The ARC recommends that students do not actually practice mouth-to-mouth resuscitation. We feel that from a hygenic standpoint this admonition makes sense, but not from the standpoint of the training a lifeguard should receive. The use of ResusciAnne (available through most ARC offices, state health departments, and university physical education departments) is recommended. This lifelike dummy enables each person to actually practice mouth-to-mouth resuscitation in an acceptable hygenic manner. Even without ResusciAnne, the use of Kleenex or a handkerchief over the "victim's" lips will prevent actual contact, yet allow practice. Plastic mouthpieces are also available. In our view, every lifeguard should have his own "Resuscitube"; this is available in drug stores.

Regardless of how it is done, lifeguards should practice mouth-to-mouth resuscitation. It is too important to be left to a movie and/or a lecture. Usually, lifesaving students practice resuscitation only once or twice. Considering the potential usefulness, this should be done at least several times during the course.

SMALL CRAFT SAFETY

Many lifesaving courses are taught without the use of rowboat or canoe. If at least one of these craft is available, then it should be used. If there truly is no craft, then it is still possible to show the movie "Oars and Paddles" (available from the ARC). The movie should be followed with at least an explanation of the following material and then a rescreening of the film.

183

Chart 6:31 depicts the techniques to be followed when entering, changing positions, or leaving a small craft. It also shows the preferred manner for sculling.

CHART 6:31
PERFORMANCE TECHNIQUES FOR SKILLS RELATED TO SMALL CRAFT*

Techniques	Illustration	Major and/or Common Performance Errors
ENTERING A. Grasp gunwales (sides) as first step is made in center of craft. Knees bent, center of gravity low.	A.	A. Failing to step in center of craft.
B. Assist another person by extending a hand while seated.	B.	B. Failing to assist another person.
C. Assist another person to enter a canoe by bracing the craft with a paddle (or holding dock).	C.	C. Failing to either brace the craft or hold it onto the dock.
LEAVING D. Leave a craft by reversing the above procedures.	D. See A, B, C, above.	D. See A, B, C above.
CHANGING POSITIONS E. Grasp gunwales; keep center of gravity low.	E.	E. Failing to keep center of gravity low.
SCULLING F. Hold oar at 45° to water, submerged to throat and flat to water's surface; wrist is straight and arm bent.	F.	F. Failing to achieve proper angle of oar.
G. Drop wrist, causing blade to push against water as it moves sideward.	G.	G. Failing to exert pushing force against water.
H. Raise the wrist, causing same edge of blade to push against water as it moves back to original position.	H.	H. Failing to exert pushing force against water.
HAND PADDLING I. Sitting in bottom, use hand as paddle.	I.	I. Leaning too far to the side while paddling.

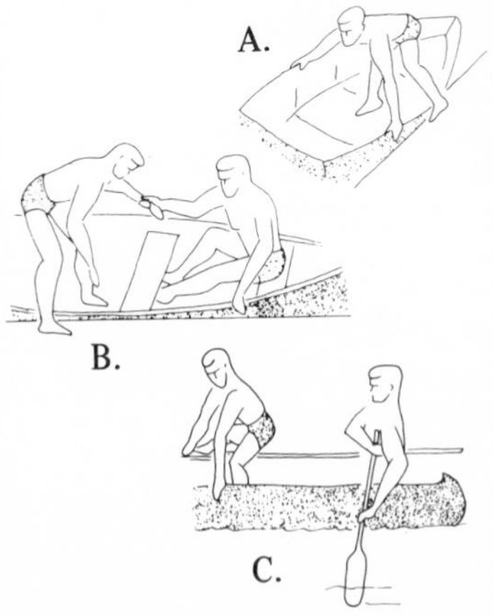

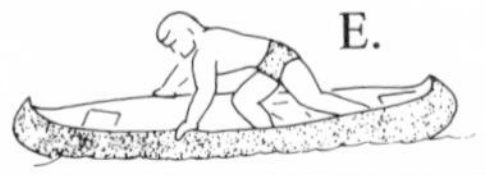

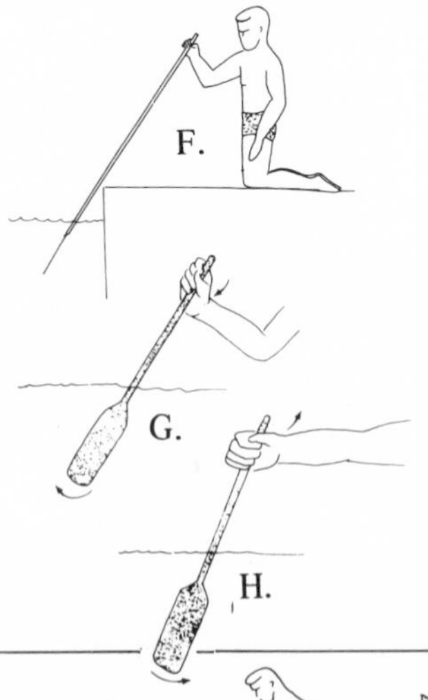

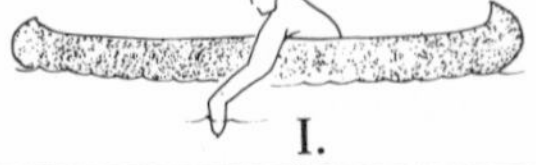

*ARC only.

Entering and leaving a craft while it is in deep water is much more difficult than it sounds. The lifesaver needs to return to the craft after making his rescue. Chart 6:32 shows these methods.

CHART 6:32
PERFORMANCE TECHNIQUES FOR LEAVING AND ENTERING A CRAFT IN DEEP WATER*

Techniques	Illustration	Major and/or Common Performance Errors
LEAVING BOAT OR CANOE A. Put one hand on gunwale; leap over. Retain grip to prevent craft from being pushed away.	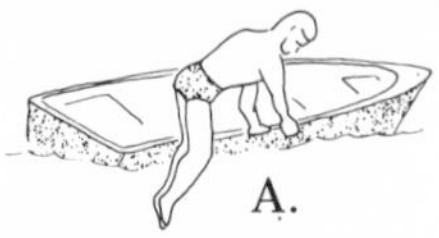 A.	A. Failing to retain grip on gunwale.
ENTERING BOAT OR CANOE B. Climb over stern of boat; if motor interferes, enter at corner of stern.	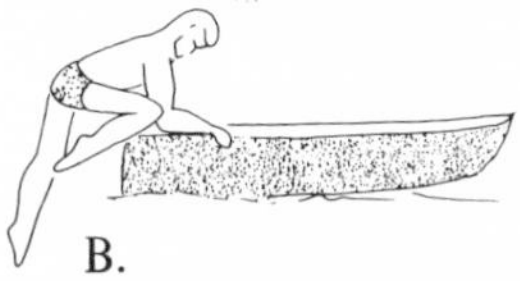 B.	B. Failing to enter boat without tipping it.
C. In canoe, depress gunwale with stomach; grasp far gunwale.	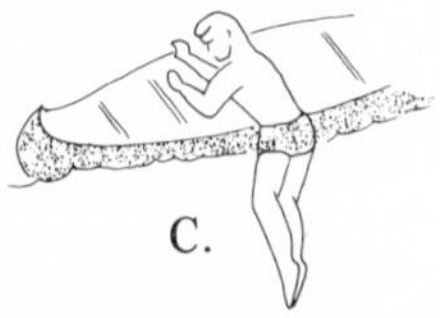 C.	C. Depressing gunwale so much that water enters the canoe.
D. Put as much weight on far hand as possible; lift legs and slide inside.	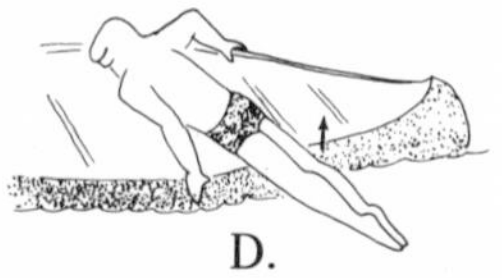 D.	D. Failing to shift weight to far hand.
ENTERING SWAMPED BOAT OR CANOE E. Depress one gunwale no more than necessary; slide in on stomach.	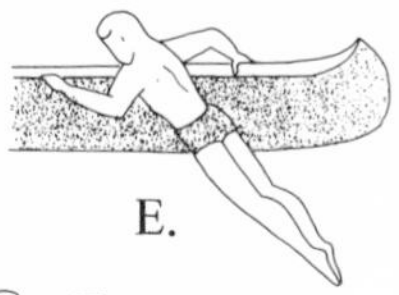 E.	E. Depressing gunwale so much that canoe tips.
F. Roll over; sit in middle and paddle with hands.	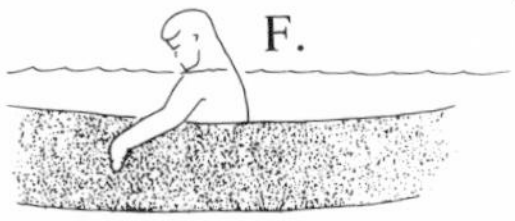 F.	F. Failing to sit in middle while paddling.

*ARC only.

A capsize routine involves deliberately swamping a boat or canoe and then maneuvering it to safety. Once the craft is swamped, the swimmer enters it, sits in the bottom, and hand-paddles it to safety. Lifesavers (as well as all persons) should realize that a boat or canoe seldom sinks to the bottom. Thus, they should attempt to maintain contact with the craft and use it as a raft.

Lifesavers should know that the essential principle of rescuing a victim with a boat or canoe is the same as in a swimming rescue—keep the eyes on the victim. This means rowing the boat stern first if there is only a short way to go or frequent glances over the shoulder if rowing bow first. The rescuer may extend an oar, or paddle to the victim, or stand and throw a ring buoy. Once a victim has been brought to the craft, the steps outlined in Chart 6:33 are followed.

PROCEDURES TO FOLLOW ONCE VICTIM REACHES BOAT OR CANOE*

Techniques	Illustration	Major and/or Common Performance Errors
BOAT RESCUE A. If needed, begin resuscitation immediately. B. If possible, get victim into boat for resuscitation. Injuries may prevent this. C. If victim has strength, let him hang onto transom and be pulled to safety. D. Or, lift victim into boat using pool lift. E. Keep victim warm. Check for shock. **CANOE RESCUE** F. If needed, begin resuscitation immediately. If possible, get victim into canoe (using pool lift). G. Victim enters canoe by grasping gunwale and climbing; rescuer must sit and lean to other side.	A. B. C. D. F. See A, B, above. G.	A. Failing to begin resuscitation immediately. B. Failing to determine if victim is injured. C. Rowing too vigorously (thus, causing victim to lose his grasp). D. Failing to brace self to prevent falling or being pulled into water. E. Failing to observe first aid precautions. F. Failing to begin resuscitation immediately. G. Failing to counter-balance victim's weight by leaning to other side of canoe.

*ARC only.

Use of the surfboard to rescue a victim has been presented earlier in the chapter (Chart 6:3).

Teaching the Skills and Techniques of Small Craft Safety

There is no substitute for actual experience with small craft, yet sometimes they are just not available. As stated earlier, showing a film and assigning text readings is always possible. The bibliography indicates other aids for the students.

WRITTEN ASSIGNMENTS

1. Observe a local lifesaving class in action and talk to the instructor.
   a. Are all students skilled and strong enough to become good lifeguards?
   b. What seems to be their weakest skills?
   c. How many "dropouts" have there been?

2. Have a friend (who has no lifesaving experience) grab you with various holds. Can you release them? (Be certain that you have arranged a pinch system beforehand.)

3. Talk to local lifeguards. Make a table showing answers to these questions:

   How many lifeguards were interviewed? _____
   How many rescues had they made? _____
      How many were reaching rescues? _____
      How many were throwing rescues? _____
      How many were boat or canoe rescues? _____
      How many were swimming rescues? _____
      How many rescues were in pools?_____Lakes?_____Ocean?_____
      How many rescues demanded application of releases? _____Holds?_____
        Carries of more than 10 feet?_____

BEHAVIORAL OBJECTIVES

Virtually all aquatic instructors will teach lifesaving classes and they should know the material in this chapter.

1. In writing, accurately reflect the authors' thoughts in regard to these items that should be considered before teaching a lifesaving class:
   a. Inclusion of swimmers who are unable to swim 440 yards in the class.
   b. Inclusion of girls in the class.
   c. Emphasis on form in the various strokes.
   d. Possible solution to the problem of "wandering hands."
   e. Value of a "pinch" system of communication.

2. In writing, accurately reflect the thoughts of the authors in regard to these techniques used in teaching the class:
   a. The use of approaches, holds, releases, and tows as logical teaching assignments.
   b. One method of conditioning the class (other than solo swimming of a certain distance).
   c. The value of quizzes.
   d. One reason why the instructor should enter the water for testing purposes.
   e. One reason why the instructor should not enter the water for testing purposes.

3. Perform any or all of the following skill tests, meeting the standards shown.

Test	Skill	Conditions	Standards
A	1. Throw ring buoy.	Victim 25 feet away.	1. Throw buoy or line within reach of victim two out of three times.
B	2. Approach from rear.	Male victim of equal weight; deep water.	2. Correct form as described in text.
	3. Reverse.		3. As #2 above.
	4. Chin pull (trad.)		4. As #2 above.

Test	Skill	Conditions	Standards
C	5. Approach swim from front.	Struggling male victim of equal weight; deep water.	5. As #2 above.
	6. Surface dive (any type).		6. As #2 above.
	7. Underwater approach.		7. As #2 above.
	8. Chin pull (variation).		8. As #2 above.
D	9. Tired swimmer s carry (variation).	Partner of same sex; carry 100 feet (including one turn); end in deep water.	9. As #2 above.
	10. Pool lift.		10. As #2 above.
E	11. Release rear head-hold.	Struggling male victim of equal size; deep water.	11. As #2 above.
	12. Shove to safety.	8 feet from safety.	12. Victim reaches safety with one push.
F	13. Release double grip on one wrist.	Struggling male victim of equal size, deep water.	13. As #2 above.
	14. Control carry.	Carry 50 feet.	14. As #2 above.
G	15. Back press—arm lift resuscitation.	Partner of same sex, on deck or beach.	15. As #2 above.
H	16. Chest pressure—arm lift resuscitation.	Partner of same sex; on deck or beach.	16. As #2 above.

BIBLIOGRAPHY

American National Red Cross. *Basic Canoeing.* Washington: ARC, 1963 and 1965.

American National Red Cross. *Basic Rowing.* Washington: ARC, 1964.

American National Red Cross. *Life Saving and Water Safety.* Washington: ARC, 1956.

American National Red Cross. *Life Saving and Water Safety Courses: Instructor's Manual.* Washington: ARC, 1968.

Boy Scouts of America. *Aquatic Program.* New Brunswick, N. J.: Boy Scouts of America, 1965.

Council for National Cooperation in Aquatics. *Lifeguard Training: Principles and Administration.* New York: Association Press, 1968.

Lanoue, Fred R. *Drownproofing.* Englewood Cliffs, N. Y.: Prentice Hall, Inc. 1963.

Silvia, Charles E. *Lifesaving and Water Safety Today.* New York: Association Press, 1965.

CHAPTER 7

The Skills and Knowledges Needed by Lifeguards

What Must an Efficient Lifeguard Know and Do?
What Are the Characteristics of a Good Lifeguard?
What Are the Technical Skills Needed by a Lifeguard?
What Are the Knowledges Needed by a Lifeguard?
What Are the Actions of a Good Lifeguard?
What Are the Main Faults of Lifeguards?

Lifeguarding is the application of certain skills and techniques necessary to prevent and/or handle aquatic accidents. Despite the glamour shown on television, lifeguarding is a monotonous, tiring job. A knowledge of lifesaving skills is essential, but equal in importance is the knowledge of how to prevent accidents.

WHAT MUST AN EFFICIENT LIFEGUARD KNOW AND DO?

A capable lifeguard possesses skills, knowledge, and attitudes that enable him to act promptly and correctly. This chapter is divided into broad categories which describe the good lifeguard, what skills and knowledges he needs, and what specific actions he should (and should not) take. How did we arrive at these categories? Primarily through our experience in employing dozens of lifeguards. We know what we want, and it is logical that pool managers everywhere place great importance on the majority of the points raised here.

You may have had previous experience in lifeguarding, and thus might think that this chapter is not written for you. Perhaps so—but can you accurately predict what we consider to be the desirable attributes of a good lifeguard? The points included in our discussion of the skills needed by a guard might seem easy to predict, but our category includes more than just the physical ability needed to make a water rescue. Again, most of the knowledges needed by guards are not covered in the usual lifesaving class. Finally, what specific actions distinguish the good guard from the poor one? (There may even be one or two actions in the "poor" category that describe you!)

WHAT ARE THE CHARACTERISTICS OF A GOOD LIFEGUARD?

The lifeguard usually is pictured as possessing all the qualities of a modern-day hero. While no two guards possess the same qualities to the same extent, there are several personal qualities that all good guards possess to a certain minimum degree. Table 7:1 presents eight different characteristics, all of which are found in the good lifeguard.

189

TABLE 7:1
PERSONAL CHARACTERISTICS OF A GOOD LIFEGUARD

Attribute	Discussion of This Attribute
Emotional Maturity.	Emotional maturity implies the ability to remain alert, for the responsibility of the guard is great. Temptations and boredom are equally great. Even though lifeguards may have vastly different ages, their emotional maturity must be equal to that of a conscientious citizen who knows he has a responsible and potentially dangerous position. Emotional maturity can be developed; it does not automatically come with the lifesaving certificate.
Attitude Favoring Continual Readiness to Act.	The ability to react quickly and correctly is so obviously a desirable characteristic that it does not require elaboration. This correct action can only be expected from lifeguards who are emotionally mature and well-trained.
	The attitude that prompt and correct response comes only after *repeated practice* is an essential characteristic of a good lifeguard. This action can only be expected from lifeguards who do as doctors, nurses, firemen, and policemen do—review their skills on a regular basis. Good lifeguards, then, are persons who periodically practice emergency procedures in order that proper actions can be taken quickly.
Physical Strength.	The physical strength of a lifeguard, after he or she has passed the lifesaving course, is seldom thought of by persons who guard at pools. But considering the consequences of trying to rescue a much stronger person, the lifesaving certificate may become a death certificate. Even though a water rescue is carried out as a last resort, adequate physical strength is another essential characteristic for a good lifeguard.
Technical Skill and Knowledge.	These are discussed at length in later sections of this chapter. See especially Tables 7:2 and 7:4.
Dependability.	The importance of this characteristic is too obvious to need amplification here. An undependable guard just cannot be tolerated.
Judgment and Tact.	Enforcement of rules demands a technique, not just a loud voice. The problem here is to be tactful, and this is much easier said than done. Younger guards tend to be dogmatic; that is, if a rule is broken, the swimmer is "kicked out" of the pool for a time. Experience will soon tell you that sometimes it is better to have flexible punishments for rule violations, because every instance is unlike another. Tactfulness comes through experience, and experience leads to maturity. Veteran guards usually have few pool problems and they seldom ask a swimmer to leave. This does *not* imply that pool regulations are not to be enforced; it emphasizes that their enforcement should be tempered with judgment and tact.
Attitude of Accepting Responsibilities to Others.	The lifeguard must not only realize his responsibilities to different groups, but must adopt the attitude that these responsibilities cannot be cast off while guarding.
	The guard has a responsibility to the swimmers he is protecting; they expect him to know how to guard and how to rescue. If a guard feels incapable of adequately protecting a given group, it is far better to play safe and obtain help than to be sorry after an unpleasant incident occurs. A teenager guarding when the lake is filled with male showoffs, or a guard working when he is ill, represent situations fraught with danger. To permit these and similar situations is to evade responsibility.

The guard also has a responsibility to his employer. The employer expects that an alert and capable person is on duty, that the pool or swimming area is safely secured in the evening, that equipment is maintained. In short, the guard must accept the responsibilities for himself that he would wish an employee to have.

To fellow employees the guard has the responsibility for doing his share of the work, reporting for work on time, helping on special occasions, etc. The "golden rule" is likewise applicable here.

WHAT ARE THE TECHNICAL SKILLS NEEDED BY A LIFEGUARD?

The best way to summarize most of the technical skills needed by a lifeguard would be to outline Chapter 6 (Performing and Teaching Lifesaving Skills) and then add comments on common injuries occurring in and around the water. First aid was not covered earlier because technically it is not a part of a standard lifesaving course. It should be obvious that a guard's job does not end when the victim has been removed from the water. For both legal and practical reasons we strongly urge that every lifeguard be properly certified in first aid, preferably by the Red Cross. (A question of legal liability, discussed at length in Chapter 8, arises when a lifeguard does not give the proper first aid treatment.) It is beyond the scope of this chapter or text to present even a cursory first-aid course; however, a section of Table 7:2 does present basic information on the most common injuries found in and around the water. It is impossible to say which specific lifesaving skills are the most important, because there are so many different lifeguarding situations. Even so, Table 7:2 indicates the skills that are probably the most important.

TABLE 7:2
TECHNICAL SKILLS NEEDED BY A GOOD LIFEGUARD

Category	Possibly the Most Important Skills in This Category		
Reaching Assists.	Use of pole or towel.		
Rescue with Equipment.	Throwing ring buoy or torpedo buoy.		
Water Rescue.	Push to safety, tired-swimmer assist, control carry, cross chest carry, searching bottom.		
Boat Rescue.	Rowing stern first.		
First Aid.	*Injury*	*Symptom*	*Treatment*
	*Suffocation.	Stoppage of breathing; blueness of face.	Mouth-to-mouth resuscitation (or mouth-to-nose).
	Cuts.	Profuse bleeding.	Stop by direct pressure on wound, or pressure point.
	*Shock.	Dizziness; fainting; paleness; sweating.	Keep warm; place head lower than feet.
	Broken bone.	Extreme localized pain.	If possible do not move; splint if necessary.
	*Concussion.	Unconsciousness; headache, bleeding from ears.	If possible, do not move; if movement essential, use stretcher; keep warm.
	Sunburn.	Red skin, painful in affected areas.	Shield exposed area from sun; apply lotion or cream.

Table 7:2—Technical Skills Needed by a Good Lifeguard (continued)

*Heat Stroke.	Flushed face, sallow skin, rapid pulse.	Cool body by sponging with cool water.
*Heart Failure.	Unconsciousness; nonbreathing.	Artificial respiration; keep warm.
Epileptic Seizure.	Thrashing of limbs; unconsciousness.	Keep victim from harming himself; have him rest in reclining position until seizure is over.
*Neck and Back Injury.	Unconsciousness or semiconsciousness; extreme pain in back and head region.	Don't move if possible; keep head and neck level with back; place rigid support in the water under the victim, and then remove him; keep warm.
Embolism; Gas Poisoning (scuba divers).	Unconsciousness; pain, twitching.	Serious scuba accidents require immediate medical attention and use of decompression tank. Other than getting victim to these resources, there is not much a lifeguard can do to help.

*Immediate attention by a physician is required.

Although Chapter 8 discusses pool equipment, mention is made here of the first-aid kit which should be available at every aquatic site. Table 7:3 lists the supplies it should contain. You will find out quickly that continual replenishment of the kit is necessary, as some items have a way of disappearing.

**TABLE 7:3
ITEMS FOR FIRST-AID KIT***

Cotton-tipped applicators.	Aromatic spirits of ammonia (ampules and inhalants).
Sterile gauze squares (2″ x 2″, 3″ x 3″, 4″ x 4″).	Tweezers.
Antiseptic solution.	Scissors.
Compresses on adhesive strips (preferably waterproof bandaids).	Paper drinking cups.
Adhesive tape (assorted widths).	Surgical needle (for removal of splinters).
Gauze roller bandages (assorted widths).	Soap.
Burn dressings.	Eye drops.
Burn treatment (creams, etc.).	Blankets.
Triangular bandages.	Stretcher.
Safety pins.	Splints.

*Adapted from *Lifeguard Training*, 1968, pp. 138-39. Used by permission of CNCA and Association Press.

WHAT ARE THE KNOWLEDGES NEEDED BY A LIFEGUARD?

It is commonly assumed that once the guard has attained the lifesaving certificate, he is prepared (for at least three years) to be a well-qualified guard. Not so! Mere possession of the certificate implies little or much knowledge of guarding, depending upon the person. The lifeguard must have knowledge of the rules, regulations, and danger areas of the aquatic site he is guarding, knowledge of when to use the whistle, knowledge of the legal implications of his job. Additionally, knowledge concerning application of first aid (discussed above) is required. Table 7:4 summarizes this information.

TABLE 7:4
KNOWLEDGES NEEDED BY A GOOD LIFEGUARD

Attribute	Examples of This Attribute	
Knowledge of Rules and Regulations He Must Enforce.	Rules vary for each situation, but the common ones are presented here. Refer also to Table 9:15.	
	Lake	*Pool*
	Swim within marked areas. No horseplay. Obey signs and guards. Swim only when a guard is present. Swim close to a partner. Parents should watch children. Boats, paddleboards, inner tubes are not allowed in swim area. A whistle means danger—pay attention to it! Do not talk to lifeguards except for safety reasons. Do not swim if you have open wounds or bandages.	No horseplay or running. Obey signs and guards. Swim only when a guard is present. Take a thorough shower before swimming. Do not swim if you have open wounds or bandages. A whistle means danger—pay attention to it! Do not talk to lifeguards except for safety reasons.
Knowledge of the Danger Areas of Aquatic Site.	Underneath dock. Far side of, or underneath, the diving raft. Semideep (6-9 feet) water area in front of diving board. Slippery docks.	Area in front of diving board. Around ladders in deep end. Semideep water (where bottom slopes sharply). Shallow water (diving accidents). Area between diving board and closest side (diving accidents). Slippery decks.
Knowledge of When to Use the Whistle.	Selective, not continual, use of the whistle, comes with maturity. While it is imperative that swimmers be informed when they are violating the rules, they cannot be "whistled at" frequently. Sometimes it is wise to call everyone's attention to a rule or violation, and the use of a whistle for this purpose is acceptable. But if the group assumes that this whistle is just another "Don't run on the deck" warning, the majority will not even listen. At certain times, you might want the undivided attention of everyone—and the whistle is the quickest, surest, and easiest way to get it.	

Table 7:4—Knowledges Needed by a Good Lifeguard (continued)

Knowledge of Negligence.	A major discussion of the legal implications of pool administration will be found in Chapter 8. However, lifeguards should understand that they may be personally liable for their own negligence. Negligence may be defined as "failure to exercise the care required by law." Lifeguards may be negligent for any action that they perform (an act of commission) or an action they neglect to perform (act of omission). Examples of either position range from performing resuscitation in a grossly improper manner to leaving a pool or beach unguarded during a regularly scheduled work period. A lifeguard must realize that he is hired to competently perform his task, and that if he fails to do so, not only may a life be lost or serious injury occur, but he also may be subjected to a court decision which could involve a large sum of money.
Knowledge of Proper First-Aid Procedures.	See Table 7:2 for a bare outline of first-aid procedures. Better yet, become properly trained by taking a standard first aid course.

WHAT ARE THE ACTIONS OF A GOOD LIFEGUARD?

Lifeguarding consists of more than sitting on a tower watching people frolic in the water. It is a serious, responsible job, and a demanding one. It takes at least one season of experience for a person to become competent as a guard, because some things cannot be learned from a book or from limited practical experience.

Table 7:5 attempts to describe the actions of a good lifeguard. We hope this is a portrayal of you—or the lifeguards at the local swimming site.

TABLE 7:5
ACTIONS OF A GOOD LIFEGUARD

Attribute	Discussion of This Attribute
Constant Vigilance.	The first technique that guards must master is the habit of sweeping their eyes constantly over the surface of the water. Many guards devote most of their attention to the deep water, or to one to two swimmers. The ideal guard would have a head which is incapable of stopping for more than ten seconds at any one position. This trait may be learned—and is learned quickly by those guards who realize that accidents can happen to swimmers of all ages, in all depths of water, and to both sexes. In short, the job calls for radarlike scanning of the area.
	A second technique that must be mastered is concerned with "selective listening"—the technique of distinguishing between shouts of joy and shouts for help. In most pools, the word "help" is heard each day. Seldom is it meant in such a way that a guard would react. Swimmers (especially younger ones) simply will not cease yelling and shouting, and they pay little attention to the words they use. If the eyes have been scanning the surface, it is easy to tell when the noise is one that demands a response.

It is amazing to find guards who cannot talk to swimmers without taking their eyes off the pool. Of course, the rules say that the guard should never talk to swimmers while on duty, but this simply cannot be done. Sometimes conversations must be carried on about matters at hand and yet the guard must not take his eyes from the pool. While it is considered rude not to look at our target during a social conversation, it is negligent to do so while guarding.

Rapid Response When An Accident Occurs.

The importance of this attribute is obvious. This is the reason why the lifeguard is employed.

Prompt and Accurate Reporting of Accidents.

Accidents will happen, but sometimes the aftermath is more tragic than the incident. This can occur when the details of the accident are not accurately written down and can result in legal decisions which are not justified by the facts. The administrators of all pools and beaches should have a standard accident form. No attempt should be made to conceal facts which may appear to harm the pool or the lifeguard; reporting all details and listing all witnesses is all that need be done. An accident form which is suitable for all situations is presented in Table 7:6. Negligence in filling out such reports has cost some lifeguards their jobs.

Proper Conduct.

Lifeguards should serve as examples to the swimmers. It is surprising the number of guards who require swimmers to shower, while they themselves delight in entering the water unshowered. Enforcement of rules is very important; the task is much harder when swimmers know the guard does not follow them. "Do as I do" is a much better motto than "Do as I say." Walking on the pool deck in street shoes, eating and/or smoking in the pool enclosure, pushing people in the water are all common actions of lifeguards which are not tolerated from the swimmers. If the rules are necessary for one group, they should be followed by the other.

Careful Maintenance of Equipment.

Maintenance of equipment is part of a lifeguard's job. First-aid kits are continually short of bandaids; lifelines are always becoming twisted and unusable; filtration materials have a way of being lost; resuscitators disappear or will not work properly. The courts and your employer expect the equipment to be available and in good working order; your reputation will rise or fall as a result of your ability to use the equipment.

Miscellaneous Actions.

In most situations, the rules governing guard's conduct while on duty are few, but specific. Wearing a distinctive uniform and carrying a whistle are universally recommended. Some guards assigned to wading pools or shallow water will carry a towel; this is useful either for a reaching assist or to wipe oneself dry after swimmers have playfully splashed everyone within range. Remaining in assigned positions would certainly be expected of a lifeguard. The person who has set the guard location is convinced that there is a reason for the placement and it would be illogical not to be in that position. Roving guards are sometimes used in shallow-water situations, but, generally speaking, the fixed site is preferable.

TABLE 7:6
A SAMPLE FORM FOR REPORTING ACCIDENTS*

Date_____

Complete three copies of this report (two sent to the headquarters or employers, one kept with the pool records). Every injury, no matter how trivial, must be noted. Forms must be completed immediately after an accident.

1. Victim's name_____ Age_____

2. Address_____ Phone No._____

3. Place where accident occurred_____

4. Accident occurred on: Date_____ Day_____ Hour_____

5. Describe the accident_____

_____

_____

6. Was injured disobeying any rule or regulation in force at the time of the accident?_____Was the in-

   jured negligent?_____If so, in what way?_____

   _____

7. Supervisor in charge of activity:_____

8. Probable nature of injury:_____

9. Nature of injury determined by_____

10. Total number of persons present at the time of accident_____

11. Names of those who saw accident_____ _____

    _____ _____ _____

12. What was done for injured?_____

    _____

13. Was family notified?_____

14. Remarks_____

    _____

Report submitted by: Report received by:

_____   _____
                                          Date:

*Adapted from *Lifeguard Training: Principles and Administration.* New York: Association Press, 1968. p. 22. Used by permission.

WHAT ARE THE MAIN FAULTS OF LIFEGUARDS?

A seemingly endless list of faults of lifeguards could be made merely by taking the negative aspects of the tables in this chapter. However, our experience has shown that the faults can be summarized into three main categories, as described in Table 7:7 below.

TABLE 7:7
MAIN FAULTS OF LIFEGUARDS

Category	Discussion of this Category
Inattention to all Swimmers.	Lifeguarding soon loses its glamour—and it is at this point that adults start complaining about the lack of protection their children are receiving. Nothing creates ill will among parents as quickly as the belief that lifeguards do not watch everyone in all parts of the area. *Any* action that takes the attention of the guard from the swimmers is noted by the spectators. Especially conducive to poor public relations is the sight of the guard eating while on duty. Even though the stomach cramp seems to be grossly overplayed, it certainly does not give the general public any feeling of confidence to observe a guard eating while on duty.
Overattention to Swimmers of the Opposite Sex.	While a certain amount of interest in the opposite sex is normal, it should take place outside of working hours. The guard's main duty is to the entire group, not just a particular segment.
Deterioration of Rescue Skills.	The maintenance and improvement of lifesaving skills is of vital importance. However, there are many guards who do not realize that lifesaving certificates expire; a guard with an expired certificate is a clear indication of negligence on someone's part. Even worse than the expired certificate is that these guards cannot perform the skills they once could. Experience in guarding is necessary, but considering the potential hazards, the maintenance of skills is absolutely essential.

WRITTEN ASSIGNMENTS

1. Observe a recreational swim period at a local pool. Evaluate the lifeguard (or guards) as to their mastery of the five recommended techniques of lifeguarding. What about their interest in the opposite sex? Any sign of negligence?

2. Talk to an experienced lifeguard.
   a. When did he take his first lifesaving training?
   b. How many years has he guarded?
   c. When was the last time he reviewed (actually getting in the water and practicing) any lifesaving skills?
   d. What particular lifesaving skills has he used in an actual rescue?
   e. Does the guard think he could rescue a 200-pound man from the pool? From a lake?
   f. How long is he in one spot without relief?

3. Based on your understanding of material in both Chapter 6 and Chapter 7, what would you do if these situations came up while you were lifeguarding?
   a. Two people are drowning at the same time?
   b. A canoe tipped over outside the bathing area, and the occupants are drowning?
   c. A person is missing as darkness falls at the beach. There are no floodlights.
   d. A power failure shuts off pool lights during a crowded family swim period.
   e. A 200-pound ex-boxer encourages his son to take the family dog for a swim in your pool.

BEHAVIORAL OBJECTIVES

The objectives of this chapter will be evaluated by writing short answers to any or all of the following questions and could call for you to do any or all of the tasks below.

1. Rate yourself (excellent to poor) on each of the personal characteristics of good lifeguards.

2. Rate yourself (excellent to poor) on each of the technical skills possessed by a good lifeguard.

3. Describe the symptoms and treatment for those injuries serious enough to warrant a doctor's immediate attention, as given in Table 7:2.

4. Discuss these knowledges needed by lifeguards: a) danger areas of a lake; b) danger areas of a pool; c) selective use of the whistle.

5. Describe the actions of a good lifeguard, basing your explanation on Table 7:5.

6. Describe the three main faults of a poor lifeguard, basing your explanation on Table 7:7.

BIBLIOGRAPHY

Canadian Lifeguard Manual. Toronto, Canada: The National Lifeguard Service, 550 Church Street, 1967 printing.

Instructors' Guide and Reference. Toronto, Canada: Canadian Red Cross Society, 95 Wellesley Street East, I.G.R. Reprint, 1966.

Lifeguard Training: Principles and Administration. New York: Association Press, 1968.

The New Science of Skin and Scuba Diving. New York: Association Press, Third Edition, 1968.

CHAPTER 8

Organization and Administration of Aquatic Programs

What is Involved in Program Organization and Administration?
Sponsors of Aquatic Programs
Planning the Program of Instruction
The Pool Facility
The Beach Facility
Pool and Beach Equipment
Pool and Beach Security
Liability Implications
Communication with the Public
The Qualifications and Duties of Staff Personnel

A positive relationship exists between superior quality of administration and outstanding operation. Good aquatic programs rarely occur by accident. They result from careful planning by persons with knowledge and appreciation of the importance, relevance, and implications of the many facets of conceiving, nurturing, and sustaining them.

WHAT IS INVOLVED IN PROGRAM ORGANIZATION AND ADMINISTRATION?

Whether he serves as organizer, administrator or worker, the person who is a part of the aquatic program should have some knowledge concerning each aspect of it. To this end, it is important that the aquatic worker know the types of jobs that are available, the program facets to be organized, the pool and beach facilities that may be encountered, the equipment that is desirable or essential, the procedures that should be used to improve security of the premises, the ways to avoid legal liability, the ways to improve public relations, and the duties and desired qualifications of staff personnel.

SPONSORS OF AQUATIC PROGRAMS

Sponsors of aquatic programs are many in number and varied in kind. Moreover, their motives range from altruism to profit-making. As a trained aquatic person, you may work for any one or more of these organizations or persons. Following are tables indicating some of the sponsors of nonprofit and profit-making programs.

TABLE 8:1
SPONSORS OF NONPROFIT PROGRAMS

Examples of Organizations Sponsoring Nonprofit Programs	Sites That May Be Used By Sponsors	Services That May Be Offered By Sponsors
Some of the organizations that do not intend to make money from the program offerings are:	*Organizations use various sites and facilities to conduct their programs. Among the possible places are:*	*Some of the program facets that each sponsor may offer are:*
Recreation Departments, including organizations at state, regional, county, city and community levels.	An indoor pool.	Instruction.
	An outdoor pool.	Recreation.
Schools, including public and private schools at all levels.	A portable pool.	Competition.
	A pool designed for handicapped persons.	Entertainment.
Institutions such as penitentiaries, hospitals, and centers for the retarded, the physically handicapped, and the blind.	Natural spots (i.e., open water areas for scuba, sailing, or skin diving).	Camp experiences.
		Clinics.
	Resorts.	Summertime youth fitness.
Voluntary agencies, including Boy Scouts, Girl Scouts, YMCA, YWCA, Camp Fire Girls and Red Cross.	Parks.	Rehabilitation or therapy.
	Summer camps.	Certification in lifesaving and water safety, boating, sailing, canoeing, and scuba.
Church Youth organizations, including CYO and YMHA.		
Fraternal organizations and Service Clubs, including Elks, Lions, Kiwanis, and Chambers of Commerce.		
Multiple-interest sports clubs, including athletic, tennis, and golf and country clubs.		
Single-interest sports clubs, including scuba, power-boating, water skiing, and spear fishing clubs.		
Community clubs, including those with pool facility only and those with facilities for several sports.		
Incidental sponsors, including hotels, motels, resorts, condominiums, and apartment-recreation complexes.		
Joint sponsors, including a park department with the Red Cross, a newspaper and the Red Cross, and a school and a park department.		

TABLE 8:2
SPONSORS OF PROFIT-MAKING PROGRAMS

Examples of Organizations Sponsoring Profit-Making Programs	Sites That May Be Used By the Sponsor	Services That May Be Offered By the Sponsor
Some of the organizations that offer services in order to make a profit are:	*Places at which each organization may offer its services are:*	*Some of the services that may be offered by each organization are:*
Athletic clubs, sports clubs, and community clubs, at which the employee may be hired at a base rate with permission to use the facilities at certain times and to retain all earnings to supplement his base pay.	A club pool or a club beach.	Instruction, recreation, entertainment, competition, and certification.
Motels, hotels and resorts, at which the owner may rent the facilities to an instructor at a flat rate or for a percentage of the instructor's gross earnings.	A pool or a beach.	Instruction, recreation, and entertainment.
Swim schools giving instruction in swimming, diving, water ballet, water skiing, boating, sailing or scuba diving, and at which the owner may hire instructors who are paid at an hourly rate or who may rebate to the owner a percentage of the fees paid by the persons enrolled.	A pool at the home of the school director. A swim school pool. A private beach or pool. A public beach or pool.	Individual or group instruction. Single lesson or series of lessons. Aquatic certification. Recreation rentals of facilities at an hourly rate or according to the number in the renting group.
Multi-activity recreation complexes, at which tennis, golf, skating, bowling, and other activities are combined in one overall operation, and at which instruction is provided for a fee.	A pool or beach owned by the operators of the business enterprise.	Instruction, recreation, entertainment, and rentals of the facility.

Program Facets

As a part of each sponsored program, one or several services and attractions may be offered. Each is an undertaking that is a program in itself, requiring careful organization and administration. You should possess sufficient knowledge to permit you to install appropriate ones at the site where you work. Following is a table indicating some of the facets which you should be prepared to incorporate within the overall program.

TABLE 8:3
COMPONENTS OF AN AQUATIC PROGRAM

Program Components	Examples of Subparts Within Each Major Part
Instruction.	Instruction may be offered as a free service or upon the payment of a fee. It may be offered at ability levels (e.g., beginner). It may be given in various activities. It may be given to learners at various age levels. It may serve special needs (e.g., prior to induction into military service, aquatic certification, rehabilitation). It may be given under various conditions (e.g., with the teacher-pupil ratio ranging from 1-1 to 1-100). It may be given by various methods (e.g., conventional teacher-pupil, one parent assistant for each child).
Recreation.	Recreation may be made available without charge or for a fee. It may be as open sessions (e.g., open to all ages, open to both sexes). It may be a family session, including all family members. It may be a restricted session (e.g., to one sex; one age-group; mother-daughter or father-son; housewives; businessmen; faculty; staff; polo players; or handicapped persons).
Competition.	Competition may involve both practice sessions and meets. It may be intraorganizational, interorganizational or open. It may involve various activities (e.g., swimming, diving, synchronized swimming, lifesaving, spear fishing, sailing). It may be offered for various levels of ability (e.g., novices, tiny tots, experts, handicapped persons).
Testing.	The purpose of testing may be to provide a basis for assigning grades to school students. It may be to qualify individuals for a higher level of instruction. It may be to provide a basis for the issuing of achievement cards or certificates. It may be to certify persons as qualified instructors. It may be to measure one's own teaching effectiveness. It may be to discover deficiencies and abilities of new enrollees for instruction. It may be to motivate the learner to greater achievement.
Outdoor Recreation Experiences.	Outdoor recreation experiences will be related primarily to camping programs that emphasize outdoor living, nature study, and recreation and competition in water-oriented activities. They may be related to a public or private camp or beach, or may be a part of a subsidized program for disadvantaged youngsters. They may be related to trips taken by, or outings of, single-interest clubs (e.g., boating, surfing, rafting, spear fishing, kayaking). They may relate to weekend or two-week aquatic schools.
Motivational devices.	Motivational devices may be games, stunts, or contests that are used to generate interest. They may be long-term goals (e.g., a fifty-mile swim) or a stunt-for-the-day (e.g., swim with hands tied, bail out a canoe, do a twist dive). They may be boards on which individual and group records are kept up-to-date.
Entertainment.	Entertainment may be in the nature of demonstrations or exhibitions given by members of your own group or by performers from outside your organization. Its purpose may be to educate as well as entertain. It may be a swim show or like project that requires weeks of planning and preparation by the show chairman and by the chairmen of the various committees (e.g., lighting, sound, choreography, communications, schedules, personnel, scenery, finance, properties, publicity, programs, tickets, cleanup).

Clinics.	Clinics may be designed to upgrade teaching, coaching, officiating, or performing skills.
	They may be designed to serve parents, students, organization members, or the general public.
	They help in the exchange of ideas and innovations.
	Each clinic requires the preparation of an agendum and arrangements for needed equipment and use of facilities.
Research.	Most research is done by professionally trained researchers (graduate students, college teachers and coaches, and personnel in recreation departments, hospitals, medical schools, health departments).
	But much research can be done by untrained persons who merely ask such questions as "Why is this done in this way? Is there a better way?" and then try to find the answers for themselves.

The Obligation to Serve Varied Interests

If you are blessed with adequate aquatic facilities, it is not enough that you do one or two things extremely well. Within reasonable limitations, you must do something for each segment of the public you serve. You must cater to all ages, all interests, and all abilities. In a school, you must serve students, faculty and staff, and perhaps alumni and public; you must provide something for the atypical, the beginner, and the expert. At a community beach or pool, you should provide something for preschool children, teen-agers, working men and women, and the senior citizens. You should, in any program in which you are working, identify the interests of all persons who might be served by your program and then endeavor to offer something to satisfy each of those interests.

Why must you do all this? The answers are simple. First, swimming pools cost much money, and the taxpayers or public-spirited citizens who donated money deserve to use them. These citizens are not all nonswimmers, or children, or competitors. Each should have a chance to use the facilities. Second, it costs very little more to use a pool sixteen hours a day than to use it four hours—and the chances are that increased use will increase income. Thirdly and most important, the tremendous rise in aquatic sports participation (fishing, water skiing, scuba diving, etc.) means that all citizens need to become familiar with swimming skills.

PLANNING THE PROGRAM OF INSTRUCTION

The teaching of aquatic skills is a major part of the total aquatic program. There are many persons who must be taught to swim and, once each has learned, he is likely to want to progress through each of the levels that follow the first. Many of these will want, also, instruction in lifesaving, diving, synchronized swimming, and other facets of the total program. A successful organization and administration of the program of instruction requires that attention be given to a number of important details. Some of them are discussed in Table 8:4.

TABLE 8:4
SUGGESTIONS CONCERNING THE PROGRAM OF INSTRUCTION

Classification of Suggestion	Some Suggestions to Guide the Pool Manager in Decisions Pertaining to the Program of Instruction
Pertaining to scheduling for instruction.	Plan an instructional program that includes a wide variety of activity offerings. In all activities, schedule more beginning classes than advanced classes; for example, schedule more beginning than advanced swimming classes, more junior than senior lifesaving classes.

Table 8:4–Suggestions Concerning the Program of Instruction (continued)

Schedule more than one class in the pool at the same time. Scheduling classes for different ability levels will make better use of water space (e.g., beginning swimmers in shallow water, intermediate swimmers at mid-pool, and advanced swimmers or lifesavers in deep water), and will help those parents with children in more than one level. Most diving boards are noisy; therefore, a concurrent diving class may make instruction in swimming classes difficult. Recreation swimming and/or team practice should not be permitted at the same time that swimming instruction is being given in a pool, but little difficulty results when this is done at a beach site.

Determine the number of class sessions to comprise a complete series of lessons. The number may range between eight and twenty, with the most common figure being ten. The number in school programs is likely to be ten or twenty in schools operating under the quarter system and fifteen to thirty in those on the semester system. Many non-school programs for youngsters are arranged to adjust to the semester system of the schools.

Arrange for two to four make-up sessions for each series of lessons to accommodate those who are forced to miss one or more lessons.

Limit the number of hours assigned to instruction. Maintain a program that is balanced to include all facets.

Schedule fewer classes during the fall, winter, and spring than are scheduled during the summer months. People are more swimming-minded during the summer and are likely to have fewer conflicting interests.

Schedule the learners to come to a class once or twice a week during the fall, winter, and spring. Schedule each class to meet five days a week during the summer.

Study the calendar and avoid scheduling classes to meet on days when conflicts are probable. It is folly, for example, to schedule classes to meet on the Fourth of July.

Plan for a free-play period of from five to fifteen minutes between classes. The learners will be less likely to want to play during class time and the instructor may have an opportunity to relax for a brief time. If the number of swimmers involved is not too great, the short period between classes may be a free-play time for both those who were in the preceding class and those who will be in the following class. During this time, the teaching aides should assist the lifeguards by watching over the swimmers.

When you have planned the schedule to your satisfaction, submit it to your superior for his suggestions and approval. He may know of things that you have not considered, and he may anticipate problems that you have not foreseen.

When the schedule has been approved, publicize it widely. This may be done by means of brochures, bulletins, news letters, posters, news articles, announcements flashed on the screen of the local theater, and radio and television announcements.

Pertaining to en-rollment for instruction.

Establish a plan whereby enrollment is by preregistration. This will make it easier for you to limit the number enrolled and will permit you to schedule additional sections if the demand is greater than you have anticipated.

Decide whether you will give preference to those who have taken a class in your pool previously or will enroll all students on a first come, first served basis. We suggest that you adopt the second method but with these exceptions: members of the organization for which you teach should be given a preferred status, and any advanced swimmer who volunteers to help you in the instructing of beginners should be given enrollment preference for the class in which he wants to receive instruction.

Set minimum age limits for enrollment in order to avoid problems. For example, a parent who wants his child to learn to swim as soon as possible may insist that you enroll a four-year-old in a class with seven-year-olds. The one child may require more attention than is required by all of the remaining members of the class.

Set a minimum height for enrollment if the class is to be taught in a pool. That height should ensure that the child will be able to stand in the water with his head above the surface. We recommend a minimum of 36 inches from the floor to the learner's shoulders unless it is your plan to admit any pupil who is accompanied in the water by a parent.

Consider the factors that affect class size. The number of teaching aides available to assist is one factor, and the ability level required by the type of class is another. For example, a limit of four or five is ideal for a class of beginners, a limit of ten is desirable, and a limit of twenty is imperfect but, with competent teaching aides, is acceptable. Expert swimmers require less individual attention and, consequently, a larger number may be enrolled in an advanced class.

Establish the qualifications for acceptance at each level of instruction and confirm that each enrollee has these qualifications. For example, to be accepted into an intermediate class the applicant must have met these standards: vertical float for thirty seconds, breathing and bobbing for one minute, drownproofing for two minutes (and the remainder of the items shown in Table 3:1).

If a fee is to be charged for instruction, establish one that is reasonable and realistic. The fee per pupil for a series of ten lessons may vary from no charge (e.g., in a Park Department tax-supported program), to a charge of $5-$10 in a program that is supported by public subscription and memberships (as a Y.M.C.A. program), or to $15-$25 in a program that must be self-sustaining or profit-making.

It is poor economy to enroll pupils who pay by the lesson and are frequently absent from classes. Usually, persons who pay in advance are ones who plan to attend all sessions. Prepayment enables the teacher or manager to know precisely what the dollar income will be from a series of lessons.

If fees are charged, set a policy that no refunds will be made. Otherwise, you will find it very difficult to decide which excuse justifies a refund and which excuse does not. A better procedure is to schedule make-up sessions for those who do miss regular sessions, or permit the missed sessions to be made up in a later series of classes.

Pertaining to planning for instruction.

Endeavor to obtain an ideal ratio of one teacher to five pupils.

Obtain teaching aides to help in attaining the five-to-one ratio. Be certain, however, that they are competent.

Obtain helpers (who may be unskilled, or in fact, nonswimmers) to record test results and perform similar tasks.

Assign only highly competent and certified personnel, either male or female, to be instructors.

Insist that classes show organization and control. Pupils must not be permitted to engage in horseplay; they must not be neglected or allowed to become separated from the group.

Permit each instructor to use the teaching methods he has found to be effective. But insist that all instructors emphasize and require the same standards in form and techniques.

Place sensible limits on the intensity of learner activity. Require a physician's approval for participation in such activities as scuba diving and team training.

Although spectators may be a distraction, the motivational benefits gained by permitting parents and friends to observe the sessions will outweigh the disadvantages.

Present to each learner some card or certificate of accomplishment. You may use standard Y.M.C.A., Red Cross or Park Department cards, or you may construct your own.

Plan your testing and the items on your achievement card so that every person enrolled will have proof that he has succeeded (i.e., "passed") in at least some items.

THE POOL FACILITY

Facilities are related in three ways to the program and to the work you do. First, they set the limits within which you can plan and conduct programs: for example, total water area is a factor in determining the number of swimmers to be accommodated; inadequate water depth will rule out springboard diving and water polo; cold water temperatures at an outdoor site may require adjustments in the length of instructional periods; and currents and drop-offs will limit program offerings and demand more extensive supervision. Secondly, excellence or deficiency in facility will relate to your concern for safety and security. Finally, certain accepted principles will relate to objectives and operation; total community use should be involved, facilities should be used to near capacity, programs should provide some services to all segments of the population of the organization or community, and programming should conform to accepted standards and practices.

Pool Standards

You should be reasonably familiar with accepted standards that apply to pool facilities. This is not because you will be constructing a pool, but because you must be sure that the facilities are appropriate for the program facets you plan to incorporate. Table 8:5 indicates the most pertinent standards.

TABLE 8:5
PERTINENT STANDARDS FOR SWIMMING POOLS

Pool Item	Examples of Standards Applying to the Pool Items
Decks and floors.	Decks and floors in the showers and in the toweling room should be nonslip.
Storage space.	Storage space should be easily accessible and adequate for all categories of equipment.
Humidity (indoor).	Humidity control should be sufficient to prevent condensation. It should not be above 60 percent. Some air movement or some venting to the outside should be provided.
Acoustics (indoor).	Acoustical material or baffles should be provided on the ceiling and on at least two walls.
Lighting.	White lighting should measure from 50 (minimum) to 125 (desirable) foot-candles at deck level. Television filming may require more than 50 foot-candles.
Air temperature (indoor).	Air temperature should be greater than water temperature but not greater by more than five degrees at a height of 4 feet above the surface of the water.
Water temperature.	Water temperatures for meets should be from seventy-two to seventy-five degrees; for instruction and recreation, seventy-five to eighty degrees; for beginners and therapy, seventy-eight to eighty-three degrees.
Water clarity.	Clearness should be such that the body of a swimmer in the deepest spot in the pool is clearly visible from the deck.
Water purity.	Readings for chlorine and pH should meet health department requirements. Water samples should meet quantitative (number of bacteria) and qualitative (no coliform bacteria) requirements of the health department.
Water depth.	Generally accepted standards for water depth are:

	For Preschool and Elementary School and for Handicapped Persons		For Preadolescent and Adolescent Ages		For College and Adult Ages	
Without Diving:	Minimum	Desirable	Minimum	Desirable	Minimum	Desirable
Shallow	2 feet	2 feet	3 feet	3 feet	4 feet	4 feet
Deep	4 feet	4½ feet	3 feet	4½ feet	4 feet	5 feet

With diving:											
Under 1-m board					9	feet	12	feet	9	feet	12	feet
Under 3-m board					9	feet	12	feet	9	feet	12	feet
Under 5-m board									12½ feet		14	feet
Water area:											
Width	16	feet	30	feet	25	feet	42	feet	36	feet	45	feet
Length	36	feet	75	feet	60	feet	75	feet	45	feet	75	feet

THE BEACH FACILITY

The nature of the waterfront area may range from simple to complex and quality may vary from poor to excellent. It will be your task to analyze the conditions which confront you and to organize and administer programs in accordance with the characteristics of the site.

The area should be delimited in accordance with the availability of qualified personnel to patrol it. Conversely, personnel should be supplied in number adequate to guarantee effective supervision.

Beach Standards

The clarity of the water should be such that the body of a swimmer is visible in depths of up to 15 feet. The bottom should be even and without drop-offs or holes, and it should have a slope of from 6 to 12 feet in 100 feet of horizontal distance. The bottom should be sand or gravel and without mud, marine weeds, barnacles, or submerged objects. Depths and boundaries must be indicated clearly. Restraining lines, booms, cribbing, or solid walls should be provided to designate areas.

The Waterfront Plan

The beach layout should be the result of careful planning which is designed to ensure maximum safety and efficiency. Ideally, the layout will provide a complex of floats, docks, and restraining lines. that are arranged in a pattern to define specific areas for different ability levels and for several aquatic activities.

Important considerations are that certain activities (boating, water skiing, sailing, scuba diving) should be located at the ends of the complex to insure that danger to swimmers is reduced to a minimum. Boats must not be permitted to intrude into areas for diving, lifesaving, swimming, and skin and scuba diving; swimmers must be forbidden to intrude into boating or diving areas; skin and scuba diving areas must be marked by buoys to signify the presence of divers below the surface. The water skiing course must be defined clearly and skiers must be required to start in a perpendicular direction from the shore. Separate open water areas may be designated for water skiers and fishermen, or arrangements may be made for both to use the same areas but at different hours during the day.

POOL AND BEACH EQUIPMENT

Individual items of equipment may be classified within several categories. You should be cognizant of these categories and know of the various items in order that you may be prepared to request those which will improve the quality of your program. It is to be noted, of course, that the use of any one item may not be restricted to one category; the same item may have application within other categories as well.

Whether an item is essential or desirable is relative to the conditions prevailing in each situation. The same item may be classified as essential in a sophisticated program, and merely as desirable in a simple one; in the latter case, you may find it necessary to improvise or make do. (For example, kickboards placed in the overflow trough may substitute for a polo goal, a megaphone for a public address system, flashlights for a communication system during swim shows.) Consequently, our designation of items as essential or desirable serves only as a somewhat guide and is subject to modification in accordance with the nature of each situation.

TABLE 8:6
EQUIPMENT CATEGORIES AND EQUIPMENT ITEMS

Category and Importance of Equipment Item	Examples of Essential and Desirable Items of Equipment
Instruction: Essential;	Instruction program items that are judged to be essential are restraining lines and lines for demarcation of areas; kickboards for swimming classes; a rubber brick for lifesaving classes; swim fins and snorkels for skin diving classes; a canoe for canoeing classes; polo balls and goals for water polo classes; and scuba equipment for scuba classes (renting scuba equipment may be better than purchasing it).
Desirable.	Instruction program items that are judged to be desirable are diving boards with adjustable fulcrums; charts and diagrams; motion pictures and loop films; slide projectors, motion picture projectors and screen; a television instant-replay camera; and bulletin boards and chalk boards.
Recreation: Essential;	The pool itself is the only essential need for a recreation program. Moreover, many items provided for the instruction and competition programs may be used in the recreation program.
Desirable.	Recreation program items that are judged to be desirable include water basketball goals; basketballs and volleyballs; diving pucks and rings; record player or tape player and records or tapes.
Competition: Essential;	A listing of the essential items for a competition program includes floating lane lines (they may be cork and rope) and a fixed or portable scoreboard. Stopwatches; clip boards; diving flash cards and a diving-score computer; polo caps; and paper forms for officials' use.
Desirable.	A listing of the desirable items for a competition program includes: starting stands; a starting gun and shells; ticket booths; accommodations for representatives of press, radio and television; a table for the scorer; service lines for telephone and television: A public address system with convenient service outlets for microphones; a phonograph recording or tape of the national anthem of the home team and visiting teams; A typewriter and a duplicating machine; Bunting or similar material for decorations; an American flag; Presswood boards and holders for the identification of swimmers in lanes, letter and number stencils; brush and paint; A pacing clock and a record board; Racing trunks, suits and warm-up apparel; Weight-lifting and isometric exercise equipment.
Special events: Essential;	A listing of essential items for shows, demonstrations, exhibitions, and clinics includes portable chalk boards, seating accommodations, movie, slide and opaque projectors. Paint brushes, carpenter tools, and easels.
Desirable.	A listing of desirable items for special events includes an air thermometer and air conditioning. Communication lines and underwater communication or signaling device. Scenery and lights (may be spot, black, or color disk). Costumes and properties.

Safety:
Essential;

A listing of items essential for safety includes throwing lines; ring buoys with lines attached; reaching poles, and shepherd's crooks with blunt ends.

Whistles, megaphones, or bull horns; guard chairs or stands; face masks.

Posted regulations; posted depths; warning signs; boundary markers and restraining lines to define safe areas.

Boats and oars; paddle boards; diamond or torpedo buoys with lines attached; and surf boats (at ocean beaches).

Auxiliary lighting for use in power failure.

A cot and blankets, a stretcher and a 10- or 12-unit first-aid kit.

Desirable.

Suggestions for desirable safety items include mechanical and mouth-to-mouth resuscitation devices.

Security:
Essential;

A listing of items that are essential for security includes sturdy locks on gates and doors, with the keys numbered and issued to only a trustworthy few persons.

Bars on accessible windows, on trapdoors to the room, and over air vents; locks on storage areas where a person may hide until after closing time.

Fencing around the outdoor pool area.

Desirable.

A listing of items judged to be desirable for security includes outdoor flood lighting of the grounds.

An alarm system to warn of trespassers at times when the facility is not in operation.

Services:
Essential;

A listing of essential items in the service category includes toilets and toilet tissue; showers; wall clocks; wash basins; paper towels; and benches.

Desirable.

A listing of desirable items in the service category includes a toweling room for swimmers; a drying room for equipment; a storage room for swimmer equipment (e.g., fins, masks).

Key boards, lockers and keys; and storage baskets.

A weighing scale, hair dryers, hair oil, and nose clips.

Suits and trunks, swimming caps and towels.

Sanitation and
Maintenance:
Essential;

A listing of essential items within the sanitation and maintenance category includes a vacuum (suction) cleaner, a wall brush, and built-in or manual skimmers.

Scrub brushes, mops, brooms, buckets, and squeegees.

Bleaching chemicals and disinfecting agents.

Chemicals to add to the pool water, and a water-testing kit.

Materials for repair and upkeep (e.g., tile pieces, grouting, adhesive, paint and brushes.

An ammonia bottle and gas mask (for emergency use if chlorine-gas leakage is suspected between the chlorine tank and point of injection of gas into water line.

A thermometer to indicate water temperatures.

Desirable.

A listing of desirable items pertaining to sanitation and maintenance includes a shower between the sun deck and the indoor pool, garden hoses and nozzles.

A pool cover (for an outdoor pool).

Administration:
Essential;

A listing of items essential for administration includes file cabinets, a desk, chairs, a telephone, and a wall clock.

Locker keys, a key board, and a safe.

Identification pins or wrist tags if clothing and personal effects are checked while the swimmer is in the pool.

Table 8:6–Equipment Categories and Equipment Items (continued)

	Paper forms (e.g., for recording attendance or pool test results, for sanitation and maintenance records, for personnel work-time records, and for conducting competitions).
Desirable.	A listing of items desirable for administration includes a desk lamp, private locker, shower, and dressing space.
	A dictation machine or tape recorder; this item is desirable also for recording coaching comments and clinic talks and for presenting a swim show.

Principles Pertaining to Equipment

If it is your responsibility to purchase equipment and if you are responsible for the issue of equipment, there are governing principles by which you should abide. Table 8:7 summarizes the more important of them.

TABLE 8:7
PRINCIPLES OF EQUIPMENT PURCHASE AND EQUIPMENT ISSUE

Action Category	Important Principles	Reasons for the Application of the Principles
Purchase of equipment.	Buy early.	A purchased item that is not as specified can be returned to the dealer for replacement and the replacement can be received before the need of it is acute.
	Buy standard equipment.	Uniformity in an item is maintained when additional numbers of the same item must be ordered.
	Buy official equipment.	Rules of the governing organizations (e.g., A.A.U.) specify the requirements for items for use in competition (e.g., trunks, diving boards, starting stands).
	Buy quality equipment.	Buying equipment that is cheap in price but low in quality is long-range false economy.
	Buy within the ability to pay.	The interest on charge accounts erodes purchasing power. The need to meet current debts restricts the making of further purchases.
	Buy according to need.	The purchase of an over-supply of certain items creates a problem of storage and it ties up a portion of the available money in the budget. Keeping an up-to-date inventory helps to prevent over-buying.
	Take wise precautions before ordering.	A choice of inferior products is avoided when samples are inspected and subjected to tests. Misfits are avoided when care is taken to obtain correct measurements for personal equipment. Money is saved when advantage is taken of discounts given for paying cash or for ordering early.
	Buy according to policies of the sponsoring organization.	You protect yourself and your organization when you obtain proper authorization for purchases, make orders in written form, inspect all deliveries for correct number and compliance with specifications, and keep a codified record of all purchases.

Issue of equipment.	Identify equipment items.	Losses may be reduced or eliminated by marking and numbering each article as belonging to your organization.
	Assign responsibility for issue.	Alert watchdogs are created by making trustworthy persons responsible for equipment issue.
	Require user responsibility.	Return of and proper care of an issued item is far more likely when a money deposit, signature, or identification card is required.
	Be selective in the issue of equipment.	Equipment in need of repair will have a shorter life than will equipment maintained in good condition. A charge of negligence may be brought if items are issued that are dangerous to the user or to others, or are too advanced for the user's abilities, or if issue is unwise because the pool is crowded.

POOL AND BEACH SECURITY

Security at the pool and beach has two facets; appropriate actions must be taken during the hours that the facility is in operation and precautions must be observed during the hours when the facility is closed to use. Although determined effort is essential to prevent violation of regulations at either the pool or the beach, greater effort is required at the waterfront because the site is accessible by land and by water and only a constant patrol can give reasonable guarantee against violation. At both sites and in all aspects, security must be implemented by the conscientious efforts and alertness of employees.

TABLE 8:8
SECURITY CONSIDERATIONS

Time of Need for Security	Examples of Actions that should be taken to Improve Security
During operation.	Cashiers must be sure that swimmers purchase tickets when admission is charged, and must deny admission to rowdies and drunks. Attendants must insist upon proper identification when no admission charge is made.
	Matrons and locker room attendants must be alert to control locker and shower room behavior.
	All employees must be vigilant to prevent abuse or misuse of facilities or equipment, and must circulate in all areas to discourage the defacing of walls and damage to fixtures.
	Unauthorized persons must be prevented from entering the locker room or any other sensitive area. Loitering must be discouraged or prohibited.
	Lockers and baskets must be kept locked.
	Arrangements must be made to check the swimmers' valuable possessions.
	At the close of the day, the cashier's receipts must be stored in a good quality safe if they cannot be removed from the premises.
	At the close of the day's operation, equipment must be stored in a safe and secure place.
During non-operation.	At the end of the day, employees must not fail to perform duties.
	All windows must be closed and locked.
	Storerooms and rest rooms must be checked for persons in hiding.
	Doors must be locked and tried from the outside to confirm that they are secured. Night lights must be left burning inside and outside.
	A POOL CLOSED sign should be posted to protect the pool or beach operator if a trespasser injures himself and brings suit.
	Supervision should be provided by a night watchman or roving patrol.

Vandalism and Theft

Vandalism is most likely to occur during hours when the facility is closed. For various reasons, maladjusted persons are impelled to destroy, and a single visit by one or more such persons can leave the premises in a shambles. They may break windows, splash paint or ink on walls, scatter materials from filing cabinets, throw eggs or overripe fruit about, smash light globes, wrench plumbing fixtures from the walls, destroy equipment, throw objects into the pool, cut raft anchor ropes, smash holes in boats or canoes, or merely use the premises for a beer party which is livened by breaking the empty bottles. You must take every reasonable security precaution in order to discourage or prevent such incursions.

Theft may occur during the night or during the day. A concession stand or a food and drink storage area is an attractive target. Money in a safe, till, or vending machine is an enticement; only a minimal amount of money should be kept on the premises, and the safe door and till should be left open at any time that they are empty. Portable equipment may be stolen for use elsewhere, competitive swimmers may steal towels or similar items as trophies. Employees must anticipate these possibilities and be alert constantly to prevent these losses. Attendants must be vigilant to see that clothing is placed in locked lockers, that valuables are kept under lock, and that forgotten articles are placed in lost-and-found.

Additional Precautions

Further actions to improve security include the provision of fencing around the area, the installation of an alarm system to warn of intruders, and floodlights that may be turned on to illuminate the grounds when the presence of trespassers is suspected.

LIABILITY IMPLICATIONS

With the passing years, interpretations of law have tended to favor the injured party more and more. Suits to recover for injury have become more prevalent, a higher percentage have been won by the complaining person, and awards to him have been higher. Schools and similar public organizations that have enjoyed a privileged immunity have lost much of this protection. The moral obligation to provide maximum protection to facility users remains, but in addition and because of changes in attitude toward liability, it has become extremely important that every employee at beach or pool be constantly vigilant and exercise every precaution to avoid any action or lack of action which contributes to the injury of any other person.

Legal Terms

In order to better understand and discharge your responsibilities, you should be familiar with the meaning of the most common words and phrases pertaining to liability. Following is a table in which a few of them are explained.

TABLE 8:9
SOME LEGAL TERMS PERTAINING TO LIABILITY

Term Related to Liability	Definitions of the Related Terms
Liability.	Liability means responsibility, especially when negligence is a factor in injury occurrence.
Plaintiff.	The plaintiff is the person who has been injured and who brings suit.
Defendant.	The defendant is the person or organization whom the plaintiff charges was responsible for the occurrence of the injury.
Action for Tort.	An action for tort is a legal action brought by a plaintiff to obtain compensation.

212

Negligence.	Being guilty of negligence means that the defendant (you) acted improperly or failed to act properly. To establish negligence, a causal relationship between the defendant's action and the plaintiff's injury must be established.
Contributory Negligence.	Contributory negligence means that the actions of the plaintiff were a partial cause of the injury (e.g., a drunken person injured by diving in shallow water, a boy injured when continuing to scuffle after being warned by the lifeguard). Proof of it may minimize or eliminate the defendant's responsibility.
Trespass.	Trespass means unauthorized entry upon premises when such entry is prohibited. Except as related to small children, trespass weakens the plaintiff's case but does not necessarily invalidate it.
Attractive Nuisance.	An attractive nuisance is a thing or condition to which others may be attracted (e.g., a pool without fencing around it or with gate left unlocked).
Assumption of Risk.	Assumption of risk means that the element of risk is obvious to and accepted by the injured person (e.g., the use of a diving board, or playing water polo).
Respondent Superior Doctrine.	The respondent superior doctrine holds that the employer is responsible for the negligent acts of the employee.
Governmental Function.	A governmental function is one which a government agency is charged by the government to perform (e.g., duties of a fireman, school teacher, or public beach employee). It relates primarily to necessary nonprofit services to the public.
Proprietary Function.	A proprietary function is one that is profit-motivated (e.g., a commercially operated pool or amusement park). A municipal pool at which income from admission exceeds operation and depreciation costs may be interpreted as falling within the classification of proprietary function.
In Loco Parentis.	*In loco parentis* means that for a certain time and at a certain place, an agent temporarily assumes the parent's rights and responsibilities (e.g., at a summer camp).
Vis Major.	*Vis major* pertains to uncontrollable events; an "act of God" (e.g., destruction of a pool building by earthquake).

Negligence

With rare exceptions, the plaintiff must prove negligence on the part of the defendant if the plaintiff is to be successful in his action to obtain compensation for injury he has sustained. Negligent action, either as an improper act committed or as a proper act omitted, must be avoided by every employee. Table 8:10 shows the more common bases for actions for tort, and indicates the things that you should do and the things you should not do.

TABLE 8:10
BASES FOR LIABILITY SUITS

Categories of Basis for Suit	Examples of Specific Bases for Liability Suits
Failure to provide safe facilities.	The facility has slippery decks, inadequate lighting, steps and handrails which do not comply with government codes.
Failure to provide safe equipment.	The facility has a diving board with flaw, ladder handrails with sharp edges, a dock with protruding nails.
Failure to provide safety equipment.	The area lacks ring buoys, life boats, restraining lines.
Failure to supervise.	No lifeguard is on duty, an insufficient number of guards is provided, an instructor or guard leaves the area unattended.

Table 8:10—Bases for Liability Suits (continued)

Failure to post.	The management has permitted a lack or an insufficiency of signs indicating water depths, beach boundaries, age limitations on certain areas and on certain equipment, parents' responsibility for small children, boating regulations, and warnings pertaining to hazardous facilities and equipment.
Failure to comply with laws.	The management has permitted conditions of impure water and unsanitary facilities to exist. It has permitted ineffective laundering and disinfecting of towels and suits.
Failure to provide security.	Doors, gates, or windows have been left unlocked. A fence around an outdoor facility is lacking.
Failure of an employee to properly perform his duties.	An employee may be judged as failing to properly perform his duties if he is guilty of such improper actions as talking to persons while he is on guard duty; Leaving his post of duty; Engaging in unapproved activities (e.g., playing football or horseshoes on the beach).
Improper action.	Doing more than necessary when giving assistance. Giving instruction which is too advanced for a learner's level of ability. Forcing a learner to do something he objects to doing. Giving medication or treatment beyond approved first-aid practices, or giving incorrect first aid treatment. Handling an injured person roughly. Permitting activities that are dangerous to others (e.g., water polo play in a crowded pool). Issuing equipment that is dangerous to the user (e.g., scuba equipment to uninstructed novices).
Lack of action.	An employee may be judged as failing to properly perform his duties if he is guilty of such lack of action as: Failure to comply with employer's instructions; Failure to apply first-aid treatment; Failure to comply with parents' stated wishes; Failure to advise an injured person to obtain follow-up treatment; Failure to act promptly in effecting a rescue; Failure to restrict swimmers from the diving area; failure to restrict boats from the swimming area; Failure to enforce regulations and to eject violators; Failure to give safety instruction to class members; Failure to inspect the facility and equipment periodically; Failure to foresee the possibility of accident; Failure to exclude the introduction of dangerous objects; Failure to remove glass and tin cans from the beach.
Failure to administer properly.	A charge of failing to administer properly may result from employing or assigning unqualified personnel (e.g., appointing a lifeguard without lifesaving certification, assigning a young locker-room attendant to temporary lifeguard duty). Knowingly permitting dangerous conditions to exist (e.g., failing to correct a hazardous condition which has been reported by an employee or by a citizen).

Additional Actions You Should Take

For your own protection and for the protection of your employer there are things which you should do. You should post by the telephone the telephone numbers for hospital, doctor, ambulance, fire department, police department, and your employer. You should make out a detailed report on each accident and include the names and statements of witnesses. You should maintain and retain complete attendance records for all instruction classes and file dated copies of lesson plans in order that you may establish that an injured person was present when safety instruction related to the cause of accident was given by you to the class.

COMMUNICATION WITH THE PUBLIC

You will communicate with the public in three major ways: through interpretation, publicity, and public relations. The general purpose of each of the three is to influence people to believe as you want them to believe; differences between them lie in the specific purpose to be achieved and the methods employed.

Your relations with your public reveal your competence and justify the costs related to the operation of the facilities and program. Mere minimum performance of your functions may get you by as a transient employee. Ingenuity and extra effort earn you the praises of those who sponsor the program and of those who enjoy it and will establish you as a person to be recommended for a more attractive position.

TABLE 8:11
METHODS OF COMMUNICATION WITH THE PUBLIC

Methods of Communication	Purpose of the Method	Examples of Techniques which may be Used to Achieve the Purpose
Interpretation.	The purpose of interpretation is to report to employer, taxpayer, or other sponsor concerning his investment.	The aquatic program is interpreted by periodic or occasional written or oral reports, talks, speeches, articles, brochures, and demonstrations presenting objectives, philosophy, projections, needs, problems, costs, and accomplishments.
Publicity.	The purpose of publicity is to generate and sustain public interest in specific happenings; to persuade people to buy admission tickets.	Publicity is obtained by timely and continuous presentation of information concerning sponsored events by means of newspapers, television, radio, placards, posters, announcements, television and radio on-the-spot reporting, and post-event summaries.
Public relations.	The purpose of public relations is to earn and keep the goodwill of the public served, to create a favorable image and to induce people to approve, support, and participate.	Good public relations are created by conducting a well-planned, challenging program; By constantly improving the program; By attracting persons not yet participating; By posting and distributing schedules of activities; By speaking before groups, appearing on television and submitting news articles; By being courteous to the participating public; By being tactful when dealing with complaints; By involving members of the community in planning and carrying out the program; By giving recognition to those who achieve; By treating every user as a guest; By maintaining the facility in sparkling-clean condition; By maintaining working conditions that result in cheerful, courteous employees.

THE QUALIFICATIONS AND DUTIES OF STAFF PERSONNEL

When the quality of an aquatic program is judged, a prime consideration is the degree to which all employees work together in harmony and in a complementary manner. Each must have an appreciation of the overall objectives of the program and be dedicated to the realization of them. Each employee must, with reference to the employees above him in rank, have respect for those persons, readily accept direction from them, and be able to receive constructive criticism without resentment. The degree of harmony which prevails depends not only upon the competence of the administrator but also upon the willingness of the employees to strive diligently to make the administrator's planning effective.

The Role of the Administrator

The term "administrator" is a relative one; it may denote the person who is in charge of the total program, it may mean the head lifeguard from whom other guards take direction, or it may apply to the matron whose realm is the women's locker room. In short, any employee whose responsibilities include the direction of another employee is an administrator to a degree. Whatever the level of responsibility in the interaction of leader and follower, there are certain ingredients which make for harmonious and productive relationships.

TABLE 8:12
QUALITIES OF THE EFFECTIVE ADMINISTRATOR

Qualities of the Good Administrator	Examples of Indication that an Effective Administrator is in Charge
He communicates with those to whom he gives orders.	The employee feels free to ask, without fear and without embarrassment, for explanation or additional direction.
He states clearly what he wants done. He does not expect an employee to read his mind.	He feels free to suggest alternatives and to express disagreement or complaint.
He delegates tasks and responsibilities.	The work load is evenly distributed. The administrator is freed from less important tasks. The identity and importance of the employee is enhanced.
He inspires members of his staff.	Each employee is motivated to want to give his maximum effort and to take pride in total staff achievement.
He gives deserved compliments to members of his staff.	Each employee's hunger for approval is fed. (In general, the quality of employee work is in direct ratio to praise and acknowledgment given.)
He is sensitive to the reactions of each employee to his environment.	The administrator is aware that if the employee regards his work as dull, he will be lethargic and disinterested. Pleasant surroundings and satisfying working conditions result in greater employee effort. Demonstration of interest in the problems and aspirations of his employees will beget loyalty and admiration.

Desirable Qualities Applicable to All Employees

There are several qualities which are common to all employee positions. For example, every employee should be honest, dependable, industrious, and punctual. Each should be competent in his assigned task, committed to performing at his best, and able to accept responsibility. Each should be tactful, firm, patient, cheerful, courteous, friendly, helpful, sympathetic, and enthusiastic. And finally, each employee should show commendable grooming, speech, manners, habits, and conduct.

216

Duties Common to All Employees

Each employee will have assigned duties for which he is primarily responsible but a number of duties must be indicated as a partial responsibility to all staff members. This may be specifically stated as:

1. Each should know all or some of the tasks related to operation of the water purification system.
2. Each should work to create a favorable impression in dealing with the public.
3. Each should exercise concern for security.
4. Each should be safety-conscious and should take care to avoid negligence.
5. Each should help to maintain the premises in clean and sanitary condition.
6. Each should be active in the general maintenance of services.
7. Each should contribute to the care and protection of facility and equipment.
8. Each should aid in the control of the behavior of those who use the facility.

Qualifications and Duties Specific to Each Employee Position

In addition to qualities which are highly desirable attributes common to all employees, other qualities apply specifically to employees in certain positions.

It would be helpful if we could stipulate certain qualities as essential and others as desirable but the requirements for a high-salaried position in an extensive program will differ considerably from those stated for the same title within a limited undertaking. Obviously, the sponsor of the simple program is in no position to compete in the procurement of the most highly competent personnel; he must adjust qualifications and duties to the best level that his available dollar will obtain for him.

You must keep in mind, therefore, that although there are specific qualities which each employee *must* possess in accordance with his position (e.g., the lifeguard must be competent in performance of lifesaving techniques), other qualities can be indicated only as they *should* be possessed because no one formula will apply to all types of situations (e.g., the swimming teacher should be a certified water safety instructor, but an instructor without certification may be better than none).

The tables which appear below do not show such compromises. They represent composites of job analyses of positions in programs which operate in accordance with high standards. These are qualifications which you should plan to meet and duties which you should prepare yourself to perform.

TABLE 8:13
THE QUALIFICATIONS AND DUTIES OF THE POOL OR BEACH MANAGER*

Commonly-stated Requirements	Examples of Duties the Manager may be Required to Perform
Maturity; be at least 21 years of age.	A manager may be expected to teach aquatic activities and coach teams for competition.
Water safety instructor and first aid certification.	To conduct meets, shows, exhibitions, and clinics.
Competence in organizing a program, in leading and supervising others, and in preparing a budget.	To recruit and hire personnel and assign duties to them; to train and rate personnel; to conduct in-service training programs and to hear personnel grievances.
The ability to be articulate in writing and in speaking.	To instruct all employees concerning liability; to make periodic inspections of the facility and report needed repairs. To construct program schedules, activity schedules, and personnel work schedules; to evaluate and improve the program; to create and maintain good public relations; and to generate publicity.

217

Table 8:13—The Qualifications and Duties of the Pool or Beach Manager* (continued)

College training (this quality is desirable but usually is not mandatory).

A minimum height of five feet and six inches, and a minimum weight of 150 pounds. (The assumption is that large size suggests command and obedience. However, an alert and able lightweight person who is five feet and four inches in height may be a better manager than a massive person who lacks tact, judgment, and knowledge.)

To oversee overall facility maintenance; to make pool tests; and to establish procedures to be followed when an accident occurs.

To perform or oversee the operation of the water recirculation and purification system.

To oversee tasks related to equipment (care, repair, issue, inventory, storage, purchase and discard) and to submit requisitions for the purchase of equipment and supplies.

To establish governing policies and to enforce state, county, and municipal laws and regulations.

To maintain records related to operation (of water test results, accidents, personnel-hours worked, finances and attendance); to supervise the bookkeeping and the disposition of receipts; to deal with complaints and problems involving the public.

To serve as pool or beach lifeguard.

---

*The qualifications and duties that pertain to the manager also apply to the assistant manager. The manager will delegate many of his duties to his assistant. The assistant manager will be the acting manager when the manager is absent.

TABLE 8:14
THE QUALIFICATIONS AND DUTIES* OF THE SWIMMING COACH

Commonly Stated Requirements	Examples of Duties the Coach may be Required to Perform
Maturity beyond that of team members and sufficient to guarantee good judgment.	A swimming coach may be expected: to organize practice sessions, instruct candidates for team positions, select team personnel, and determine strategies to be employed.
Knowledge of physiology, physics, and the techniques of strokes, dives, and games.	To set, by counsel and by example, high standards of conduct for team members.
Teaching and leadership abilities.	To motivate parents and other persons to assist in the program.
Dedication to a sound philosophy of competition.	To inspire team candidates to greatest improvement and maximum effort and to create team pride and spirit.
Knowledge of the strategies pertaining to swimming, diving, and game competitions.	To organize and administer competitive events, and to conduct clinics for coaches, competitors, parents, public, and officials.
An ability to adapt to prevailing conditions (time, space, numbers).	

---

*(The duties may be performed by the manager, assistant manager, head lifeguard, assistant guard or by a person who holds no other employee position.)

TABLE 8:15
THE QUALIFICATIONS AND DUTIES OF THE MATRON

Commonly Stated Requirements	Examples of Duties the Matron may be Expected to Perform
Maturity. It is preferable but not mandatory that she be married or a widow. An ability to direct and supervise others. A good personality and disposition. First aid certification.	A matron may be expected: to supervise the women's hair dryers and enforce all regulations. To supervise the issue of locks, keys, baskets, towels, caps, and suits. To inventory equipment and keep attendance and other records. To instruct and supervise female employees under her jurisdiction. To counsel, warn or impose penalty on female swimmers directed or brought to her from pool or beach. To apply or assist in the application of first aid treatment. To assist in the preparations for shows, demonstrations, pageants, and clinics.

TABLE 8:16
THE QUALIFICATIONS AND DUTIES OF THE HEAD LIFEGUARD*

Commonly Stated Requirements	Examples of Duties the Lifeguard may be Required to Perform
Must be at least 17 years of age. Lifesaving and first aid certification. If he is to be assigned to teaching he must have water safety instructor certification. An ability to direct others. An ability to deal with the public. Good judgment. Keen awareness of his responsibility for the lives and general welfare of others. Prior experience as an assistant lifeguard, as a head lifeguard, or as a guard in a situation in which guards were not classified as head or assistant.	A lifeguard may be expected: To report promptly in proper uniform. If unable to report, he must notify the manager in time sufficient to permit obtaining a substitute. To teach classes in various aquatic activities. To coach swimming, diving, and water polo teams. To direct, or assist in the direction of, water shows, exhibitions, demonstrations, and clinics. To instruct, delegate duties to, and supervise assistant guards. To perform or oversee performance of facility maintenance (mopping, sweeping, hosing, and disinfecting). To supervise the pool or beach. To enforce regulations pertaining to showers, conduct, food and drink, street shoes on the deck, the wearing of jewelry, proper use and return of equipment, boisterous actions, and to warn or eject those who fail to comply with rules. To make water tests. To make periodic inspections of equipment and the facility and report unsatisfactory conditions, to suggest equipment needs, and to assist in the operation of the water recirculation and purification system. To guard lives, and to see that at the end of the day all equipment is in place and appropriate security precautions are taken.

*For the most part, the qualifications and duties of the assistant lifeguard are the same as for the head lifeguard. He may be somewhat younger, less experienced, and less able in leadership. He must be competent in the techniques of lifesaving, first aid and resuscitation. He may, without certification, assist a qualified instructor, but if he teaches alone he must have his own certification as a qualified instructor.

TABLE 8:17
THE QUALIFICATIONS AND DUTIES OF THE CASHIER

Commonly Stated Requirements	Examples of Duties the Cashier may be Required to Perform
Reasonable maturity. She (or he) must not be intimidated by adults, must be able to command respect and enforce policies and rules.	A cashier may be expected: To answer the telephone; to sell admission tickets. To check valuables; to maintain a lost-and-found service. To keep account books and prepare money for deposit.
Be trustworthy and able to handle money transactions without error.	To help with cleaning and maintenance of services. To make judgments on persons to be admitted and to deny admission to some.
Have a pleasant voice and personality.	If qualified as a water safety instructor, perhaps to teach classes during part of the day.

TABLE 8:18
THE QUALIFICATIONS AND DUTIES OF THE ATTENDANT

Commonly Stated Requirements	Examples of Duties an Attendant may be Expected to Perform
17 years of age or older. A locker-room attendant may be younger than 17, but not without increased surveillance by manager, matron, and head lifeguard.	An attendant may be expected: To obtain identification, to prevent unauthorized persons from entering the locker room, and to discourage loitering and prevent boisterous play. To issue locks, keys, baskets, suits, towels, equipment, and see that equipment is returned.
Lifesaving certification if on standby for guard duty.	To check valuables and maintain a lost-and-found service. To keep attendance and laundry records.
Water safety instructor certification if he is teaching alone rather than assisting a qualified instructor.	As locker room attendant, he may be expected: to keep the area clean; mop and disinfect locker room and toilets; flush toilets and replenish toilet tissue; clean mirrors and wash basins; and assist the public in the use of lockers or baskets. To enforce regulations (e.g., mandatory shower). To assist in total area cleanliness and assist in maintenance tasks.

Relative Salaries of Employees

Salaries paid to employees are not static. They may fluctuate in accordance with prevailing economic conditions. They are affected by the ratio of supply and demand and by minimum wage standards. They vary in terms of title of the position. They are influenced by the qualifications required and duties to be performed. However, an indication of relative salary levels may be obtained by placing the employee classifications on a 100-point scale; if, for example, the salary of the manager is $600 (100-point level), the salary of the matron will be approximately $480 (80-point level), the assistant manager will earn $552 (92-point level); the lifeguard and head lifeguard will earn amounts ranging from $360 to $480 (60- to 80-point level); the head attendant will earn from $270 to $360 (45- to 60-point level); the cashier will earn from $270 to $300 (45- to 50- point level); and the basket-room boy and locker-room attendant will earn from $180 to $240 (30- to 40-point level).

Procedures for Hiring Personnel

When definite effort is made to obtain the best persons to fill aquatic positions, certain steps are followed by the employer. You should know of these steps in order that you may be better prepared to go about applying for a position you desire and, second, in order that you, as an administrator at a later date, may be familiar with customary recruiting procedures.

TABLE 8:19
STEPS TO BE TAKEN WHEN HIRING PERSONNEL

Steps to be Taken	Suggestions Pertaining to the Steps to be Taken when Hiring Personnel
Prepare job descriptions.	State the required qualifications (e.g., age, certification, education, experience).
Advertise the open position.	Describe the position. State the duties to be performed. State the length of employment, the hours each day, and the salary paid.
Construct an application form.	Obtain information concerning name, sex, age, birth date, height, weight, address, telephone number of the applicant. Inquire concerning lifesaving, first-aid, and teaching certification, with indication of certifying authority and expiration dates of certification. Determine the applicant's previous experience and persons who may be contacted for references. Include space in which the applicant may enter additional information which he considers to be relevant.
Interview the applicants.	Review the applicant's application form prior to interviewing him in order to guide the discussion in fruitful directions and let the applicant know that he is receiving personal attention. Elicit additional information helpful to the applicant and to you. (Because final judgments often are based on the applicant's appearance, the applicant should take care to be well-groomed and alert.)
Administer tests.	Prepare and administer tests when testing is appropriate to a certain position (e.g., a water performance test for lifeguard).
Reassess the applicants and select those to be hired.	For each applicant, arrive at an evaluation based on information contained in the application form, on impressions gained from interview, and on scores earned in tests. Select the applicants that are best qualified for each position.
Notify the successful applicants.	Contact the selected ones and complete the hiring-in details. Instruct each new employee concerning his duties, and inform him where and when to report on the first day of work. File, for reference when personnel addition or replacement is necessary, the data concerning the better of the unsuccessful candidates.

WRITTEN ASSIGNMENTS

1. Survey your local community and submit a report indicating the available aquatic facilities and programs. Name the sponsor, give the type of site, and list the program facets offered.

2. Make inquiry to determine the titles, job descriptions, duties, and salaries pertaining to the aquatic program sponsored by your local Parks and Recreation Department.

3. Visit a local beach or pool and:
   a. evaluate the facilities
   b. evaluate the performances of employees

4. Study a local beach or pool operation and describe the details relating to the progress of the program participant while he is at the site (where he parks, where he is admitted and by whom, etc.).

5. Study a local site to determine the actions taken to obtain security.

6. Study a local site to determine if you can discover any conditions or actions which might be termed negligent.

7. Study a local site to determine what is done to enhance good public relations.

8. Study a local aquatic site and then show in chart form the duties performed by:

> The matron.
> The pool manager.
> The head lifeguard.
> The instructor-advisor for the presentation of a synchronized swimming water-show.
> A coach of swimming, diving, water polo or synchronized swimming.

BEHAVIORAL OBJECTIVES

The examination on this chapter will be written (short answer questions). You may be asked to reply to any or all of the questions stated below.

1. List at least four examples of possible sponsors of nonprofit aquatic programs, other than recreation departments and schools.

2. List at least two examples of possible sponsors of profit-making aquatic programs.

3. Define the term "program facets," as used in this text.

4. Explain why a pool operator has an obligation to serve varied interests.

5. Assume that you are in charge of an aquatic facility. Basing your answers on the information given in Table 8:4, outline your program of instruction. Give at least three specific suggestions for scheduling, three for enrollment, and three for planning the instruction.

6. List all the items which pertain to pool standards, being able to explain any two as completely as they are explained in the text.

7. Describe the ideal beach for swimming, using the standards mentioned in the text as the criteria.

8. Complete a chart which asks for at least two specific examples of items regarded as essential equipment for pools and beaches.

9. List and explain those principles of equipment purchase which have to do with:

> buying standard   buying with knowledge
> buying quality   buying according to
>   organization policy

10. Explain how equipment should be issued, according to the principles given in the text.

11. Explain how a pool or beach office could be protected from vandalism and theft, using the text as the source of ideas. Specifically mention at least three precautions to be taken during hours of operation and three precautions to be taken during hours of closure.

12. Define the following legal terms:

> Plaintiff   Attractive nuisance
> Action for tort   Assumption of risk
> Liability   *In loco parentis*
> Negligence   *Vis major*
> Contributory negligence

13. List and give one specific example of the nine bases for liability suits.

14. Explain the purpose, plus two specific examples of usable techniques, of the three methods of communication with the public.

15. Explain how personnel should be hired, using as the basis of the answer those steps noted in the text.

BIBLIOGRAPHY

The Athletic Institute and The American Association for Health, Physical Education and Recreation. *Planning Areas and Facilities for Health, Physical Education and Recreation.* Chicago: The Athletic Institute; Washington, D.C.: The American Association for Health, Physical Education, and Recreation, 1965.

"Court Decisions Affecting Municipal Swimming Pools," *Swimming Pool Age,* 31:8:68, August, 1957.

"Job Specifications for Lifeguards," *Swimming Pool Data and References Annual,* 31:171, 1964.

Klumb, John J. et al. *Construction Standards for California School Community Swimming Pools.* Sacramento: California State Department of Education, 1962.

Savastano, Orland L. and Harold Anderson. "How You Can Plan for an All-Around Aquatics Program," *Swimming Pool Age,* 42:9:26, September, 1968.

Terry, William L. *A Guide for Planning the School and College Swimming Pool and Natatorium.* New York: Bureau of Publications, Teachers College, Columbia University, 1959.

United States Dept. of Health, Education and Welfare. *Swimming Pools and Natural Bathing Places.* An Annotated Bibliography 1957-66. Public Health Service Pub. No. 1586. Wash: U.S. Govt. Printing Office.

CHAPTER 9

Swimming Pool Sanitation

Water is brought to, and maintained in, a pleasing and safe condition by the removal of physical matter and the control of plant life and bacteria. Physical matter is removed by skimming, flushing, and filtration. The growth of plants and bacteria is inhibited by the addition of chemicals. Contamination is prevented by the control of environment and swimmers. But these actions do not happen of themselves. Each must be performed by competent and dependable employees.

WHAT KNOWLEDGE CONCERNING SANITATION IS ESSENTIAL?

The persons who come to a beach or pool expect the water to appear inviting and to be harmless to health; they depend on employees there to ensure that this is so. If the employee is to meet this responsibility properly, there is knowledge that he must have; he must know the things to do, and he must know how and when to do them.

The employee will need to know what must be done at the beginning and at the ending of a season. He will need to know the components of a pool water recirculation and purification system, the function of each part, and how it is maintained in good working condition. He will need to know the standards which must be met and the tests that must be made. He will need knowledge of the regulations that must be enforced and of the duties that must be performed.

SANITATION STANDARDS

It is extremely important for you to be aware that all swimming places are subject to strict regulation. As an aquatic employee, it will be your responsibility to know those requirements that apply to the site where you work.

These standards are not the same from city to city or state to state. There may be differences between city, county, and state codes in the area where you are employed. Such differences are explained by the fact that one agency of government may set *minimum* standards which any one site *must meet* or be closed down, but some agencies require that standards higher than the specified minimum must be met. You should, therefore, be familiar with the standards set down by city, county, and state agencies in your area, as well as those indicated by the organization by which you are employed.

In this chapter, some of the standards most emphasized by departments of health are shown in order that you may know what may be expected of you. Specific knowledge of standards pertaining to your state may be obtained by consulting the publications of the Department of Health for the state in which you work or in which you expect to be employed (Appendix A).

THE POOL OPERATOR

Because incompetent operation of a swimming pool very possibly may endanger the health of the swimmers who use it, state departments of health are concerned that the facility shall be under the supervision of a qualified person, and several such departments emphasize this requirement in their publications.

For example, the printed materials of the Montana and Idaho State Health Departments include the statement, "Every swimming pool shall be operated under the close supervision of a trained operator. The Department of Health may require a certificate of competency obtained through attendance and successful completion of a swimming pool operator's training course as evidence of compliance with this section." The Kentucky State requirement not only includes the preceding statement but adds also, "Such operator shall be familiar with the equipment of the pool and shall be responsible for all the sanitary measures prescribed in this regulation to be observed." The Washington State Department of Health does not require completion of a training course but does stipulate that "All public and semipublic pools shall be maintained and operated by one or more persons familiar with the equipment and principles of swimming pool operation." The West Virginia materials include the statement that "A pool manager should have basic knowledge of the water-treatment processes at his pool, should know proper technique in the collection of water samples for bacteriological analysis, and be capable of performing the chemical tests necessary in pool control."

GENERAL CATEGORIES OF RESPONSIBILITY

In connection with your position as an aquatic worker, you are likely to be involved in seven categories of sanitation. A quick look at these categories, in Table 9:1, will provide a general introduction to more detailed treatment of them in the remainder of the chapter.

TABLE 9:1
GENERAL CATEGORIES OF EMPLOYEE RESPONSIBILITY FOR SANITATION

Categories of Responsibility.	Examples of Specific Employee Responsibilities Within Each General Category of Responsibility.
Preparation for the season.	All parts of the recirculation and purification system must be checked to verify that each is ready for operation. Requests must be made to have the utilities turned on.
Operation of the water recirculation and purification system.	Filters must be regulated and must be washed periodically. Gauges and meters must be observed. Pool sides and bottom must be cleaned. Chemical feeders must be set to ensure water purity and correct pH.

Table 9:1—General Caegories or Employee Responsibility for Sanitation (continued)

Solution of problems that arise.	Water cloudiness and discoloration must be corrected. Algae growth must be prevented. Pump, filter, and chemical feed malfunctions must be corrected.
Control of environment.	Tests must be made to determine purifying agent residual, pH, clarity, and air and water temperatures, and necessary adjustments must be effected.
Enforcement of regulations.	Regulations pertaining to swimmer and employee conduct and condition must be enforced.
Performance of duties.	Duties pertaining to the maintenance of a sanitary environment must be performed.
Preparation for the off-season.	Mechanical parts must be prepared for a period of nonuse. Equipment must be stored. Requests must be made to have the utilities disconnected.

PREPARATION FOR THE BEGINNING OF A SWIMMING SEASON

Some facilities remain in operation year round. Others are closed during a portion of the year and are opened for use during the more favorable months. In the latter case, it is likely that the pool operator, manager or aquatic director will be responsible for performing the tasks that are necessary to prepare the pool or beach for a resumption of operation. However, it is probable that some of the jobs will be delegated to lifeguards and other employees, and they must be able to carry out such assignments with competence. Table 9:2 indicates some of the things to be done.

TABLE 9:2
ACTIONS TO BE TAKEN TO READY THE FACILITY FOR OPERATION

The Order in Which Actions Should be Taken	Some Examples of Actions That Should Be Taken
Tasks that should be performed first.	Verify that all utilities have been connected (water, light, phone). Check all parts of the purification and recirculation systems to be sure that they are ready to be put into operation; make certain all connections are tight, no gaskets are worn, no air locks exist, and no rust or corrosion has caused a dangerous condition. Confirm that towels, suits, soap, toilet tissue, paper towels, and chemicals are adequate in supply. Be sure that all toilet, shower, fountain, and wash fixtures are operating properly. Wash with disinfectant. Make certain that an adequate supply of report forms, bottles for water samples and chemicals for the water-testing kit is on hand. Verify that there is an ample supply of mops, buckets, hoses, and disinfectants on hand. Clean away all accumulated dirt and sediment in the area. Remove all mold and plant growth. Replace fuses, light globes, reflectors, and similar items removed at the beginning of the closed season.
Actions that should be taken to begin recirculation and purification of the water.	Examine the top of each sand-and-gravel filter or the plastic cloths of the diatomaceous earth filter. Make certain that the chemical feed containers are filled. Be sure that the pump is filled with water before starting. Review the manufacturer's instructions for operation of the filtration and purification equipment. Apply diatom precoat. Turn on the water slowly to minimize the amount of rust and sediment loosened by the flow. Fill the sand-and-gravel filter from bottom to top before beginning normal filter flow. It is better to route the new water through the filter than to cause it to flow directly from the main into the pool.

Begin with the water pH at about 7.0 and add soda ash to raise the pH level to 7.2-7.6 by the time the pool is filled.

If chlorine is the purifying agent, start with a level of about 1.0 parts per million and maintain the level at about .4-.6 after the pool is filled.

Approximately ten turnovers of pool water volume will be required to bring the water to an acceptable degree of clarity, though seven may be enough.

Tasks that should be performed later.
Record the pH and residual chlorine readings that are taken and the clarity observations that are made. Record the amounts of chemicals used.

Take equipment from storage and install or station it in the proper places for use or issue.

See that warning signs, information posters, and regulations are posted.

On the beach, set out boundary signs and safety lines.

Make out sanitation duty assignments for pool personnel.

THE SWIMMING POOL WATER RECIRCULATION AND PURIFICATION SYSTEM

Swimming pool water is recirculated in order to strain it, add chemicals to it, filter it and heat it. The order of the arrangement of the components of the system will, in general, be similar in all pools but not identical, and some differences may be found between the plan in your pool and the plans shown in Charts 9:1 and 9:2. For example, it is certain that alum and soda will be injected into the flow line prior to routing of the water through sand-and-gravel filters, but chlorine may be added either before or after the water passes through the filters, and the pump may be located between pool outlet and filters or between filters and pool inlet. In the case of a diatomite filter system, the location of components will differ according to whether the filter is operated by pressure or by vacuum. It will be your task to identify the components and their locations in your pool.

Each component of the recirculation and purification system has an important part to play in the effort to maintain the pool water in a sparkling and hygienic condition. Table 9:3 shows the contribution of each part to the overall purpose of the system.

The details of operation, as you will apply them, must be as specified by the manufacturer of each unit. Models made by different manufacturers are not identical and the pertinent instructions may vary. For this reason we have been sparing in our quotations of figures lest they be misleading in some instances. Many State Departments of Health require that before installation of any part will be accepted, the manufacturer's directions for use and care must be provided. Your task is to insist that these instructions, for components at your pool, are provided to you.

TABLE 9:3
COMPONENTS OF A POOL WATER RECIRCULATION SYSTEM*

Component	Function of the Component of the Pool Water Recirculation System
Deck drains.	The function of this component is to route drip water and splash water to the recirculation system.
Overflow troughs.	The function of this component, when the pool water level is approximately ¼ inch *above* the top of the trough, is to provide reef action to smooth out rough water and to provide a skimming action at the water surface. The function, when the water level is *below* the top of the trough, is to receive splash and route it to the storm drains. The troughs also serve as a handhold for swimmers. Usually they surround the pool and are so designed that a swimmer cannot catch an arm or a foot in them or reach the bottom with his fingers when the water level is below the top level of the trough.
Skimmers.	The function of this component is to remove floating oils and waste and to serve in the place of overflow troughs.

	Skimmers are built into the pool wall and are automatically adjustable to pool water level. They must have a removable basket or screen and be equipped to prevent air locks in the suction line.
Wall brush.	The function of this component is to clean dirt and growth from the pool sides underwater. It is manually operated. Brushed material is drawn into the recirculation line by way of the outlets and is removed by the filters.
Suction cleaner.	The function of this component is to remove sediment and precipitated material from the pool bottom. It may be a portable pump and motor or it may be connected to the recirculation pump. When it is a part of the recirculation system, the recirculation pump provides suction by way of connections in the pool sides, for attachment of a suction hose, about 8 inches below the water surface. Water flow from the suction cleaner may be routed to the storm drain or to the recirculation line at a point ahead of the hair and lint strainer. It may be necessary to reduce the flow from the pool outlets during vacuuming in order to increase suction.
Pool bottom drains.	The function of this component is to route pool water to the recirculation system and to drain the water when the pool is to be emptied.
Surge tank. Balancing tank.	The function of this component is to prevent loss of heated and treated water by way of the overflow troughs and to the waste line because the pool water level is raised considerably by the entry of a number of swimmers into the pool; to maintain the water surface at a constant level by storing the volume of water displaced by swimmers entering the pool; to permit it to be returned to the recirculation line by pump action; and to facilitate the addition of makeup water. It should be equipped to measure, in terms of inches or gallons, the amount of new water added. The line for the addition of new water terminates at least six inches above the tank. The tank must have an overflow connection to sewer or sump. Chemicals, especially alum, may be added at this point in the recirculation system.
Hair and lint strainer.	The function of this component is to remove hair, lint, and coarse materials from the water during recirculation in order to prevent clogging of the pump and the filter. It is located in the recirculation line ahead of the pump and filters. It may be a sealed unit with a noncorrosive, removable, cylindrical strainer or it may be a screen at the point at which water enters the filter in a system with the pump located in the line following the filter.
Alum feeder.	The function of this component is to introduce alum into the recirculation line where it combines with soda to form a gelatinlike floc on the top surface of a sand-and-gravel filter. Alum is *not* added when the filter is diatomaceous earth.
Soda ash feeder.	The function of this component is to introduce soda ash into the recirculation line where it combines with alum to form a floc on the top surface of a sand-and-gravel filter. When the filter is diatomaceous earth, soda ash may be added to the line returning water to the pool inlets in order to maintain or raise pH.
Disinfectant feeder or purifying device.	The function of this component is to kill bacteria or to introduce chemicals that will kill bacteria. The purifying means may be chlorine, hypochlorite, bromine, iodine, ozone or ultraviolet ray. Chlorine is by far the most common means and may be used also to kill algae by superchlorination. The chemicals may be introduced prior to or after filtering of the water.

Pump.   The function of this component is to supply the power to force or draw water through the recirculation line, to supply suction for the suction cleaner, and to supply the power for backwashing.

Usually, the pump is powered to ensure from a six-hour to an eight-hour turnover and is powered to pump 12-15 gallons of water per minute per square foot of sand-and-gravel surface area.   A six-hour turnover means, for example, that the total number of gallons of water pumped during a time span of six hours is equal to the pool capacity in number of gallons.

Turnover must be related to the capacity of a sand-and-gravel filter; if water is forced through the filters too rapidly, channeling is likely and sediment is forced deep into the filter.

Valves.   The function of this component is to ensure control of the flow of water and of chemicals.

Examples of specific functions are to provide air escape at the filter, to shut off or redirect circulation flow at the hair and lint strainer to permit cleaning or inspection of the unit, to reduce water flow at pool outlets in order to increase suction cleaner efficiency, and to reverse the water flow through the filters and to route the flow to the waste drain.

Valves may operate automatically or may be operated manually.

Flow meter.   The function of this component is to indicate the flow of water during normal recirculation and to indicate the rate of water flow during backwashing of the filters.

When the filter type is sand-and-gravel, the flow meter usually is located after the pump and ahead of the filter and at some distance from the nearest valve or elbow.

When the filter type is diatomaceous earth, the flow meter usually is located on the filter outflow line rather than on the inflow line.

The recirculation system may be equipped with two flow meters.

Gauges.   The function of this component is to indicate water pressures at the inlets and outlets of filters; to warn of loss of head and of the need to backwash the filter; to register water temperatures in the water recirculation line; and to regulate the water heater.

Filter.   The function of this component is to remove from the water materials not trapped by the hair and lint strainer.

It may be the diatomaceous earth or sand-and-gravel type.

If the pool is equipped with a diatomaceous earth filter, the recirculation line may have a slurry tank as an additional component.

Slurry tank.   The function of this component is to mix diatomaceous earth with water before the earth is introduced to the water recirculation line.

Earth and water are stirred by an agitator in a vat or tank and this mixture, injected into the circulation flow, is carried to the filter.

Diatomaceous   There are two kinds of diatomaceous earth filters; the pressure type (in which
earth filter.   water is forced through a sealed unit) or the vacuum (in which the water is drawn, by suction, from an open vat).

The vacuum type is easier to maintain because the filtering unit is immediately accessible.

Diatomaceous earth is composed of the fossilized remains of microscopic water plants called diatoms. The chalklike substance is effective by itself and does not require the addition of a floc-forming chemical (alum) to complement its filtering action.

The filter unit is comprised of diatomaceous earth that has become attached, in the process of water flow-through, to removable synthetic filter cloths that cover filter elements (septa) in the form of tubes, plates, or discs. Most filter elements are made of monel metal or stainless steel. Water passes through the earth before penetrating the cloth and exiting through the element.

Operation must be in accordance with the manufacturer's specifications. The

Table 9:3—Components of a Pool Water Recirculation System* (continued)

	flow of water must not exceed three gallons per minute per square foot of filter surface. The filter is equipped with a line to the waste drain in order to permit backwashing.
Sand-and-gravel filter.	Coarse materials in the water are trapped by the sand and gravel. Fine materials are strained from the water by the floc formed on the top of the filter bed by the union of alum and soda ash. The filter type may be gravity (an open vat) or pressure (a sealed container). Flow of water must not exceed a rate of three gallons per minute per square foot of filter surface. Filter and pump must be operated night and day unless the pool is closed down for the season or because necessary water treatment actions must be taken.
Sight glass.	The function of this component is to make it possible for the operator to see the water and judge its clarity in order that he may know when a backwashing should be ended. It is installed on the discharge line from the filter. It must be removable for cleaning.
Water heater.	The function of this component is to heat the pool water while it is being recirculated and before its return to the pool.
Inlet(s).	The function of this component is to return the circulated water to the pool. Inlets are usually located in a position where, in conjunction with the pool drains, skimmers or troughs, they will produce the most effective circulation of water in the pool, and where swimmers in competition will not be hampered by currents.

*Refer to Charts 9:1 and 9:2 for possible location of each component.

NOTE: In the tables appearing in this chapter, a primary source has been the publications of all State Health Departments in general, and the publications by the Departments in Connecticut, Kansas, Montana, New York, North Dakota, Ohio, Oklahoma, Texas, West Virginia, and Wyoming in particular.

CHART 9:1
COMPONENTS OF A RECIRCULATION SYSTEM
EQUIPPED WITH PRESSURE PUMP AND SEALED SAND-AND-GRAVEL FILTERS

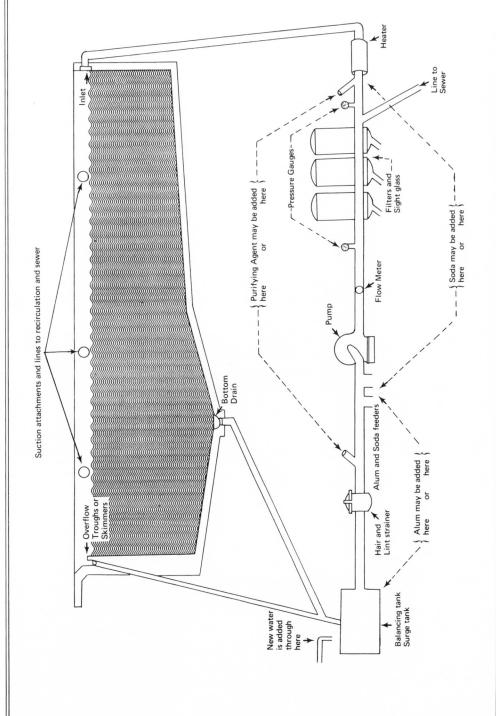

CHART 9:2
COMPONENTS OF A RECIRCULATION SYSTEM
EQUIPPED WITH SUCTION PUMP AND OPEN-VAT DIATOMACEOUS EARTH FILTER

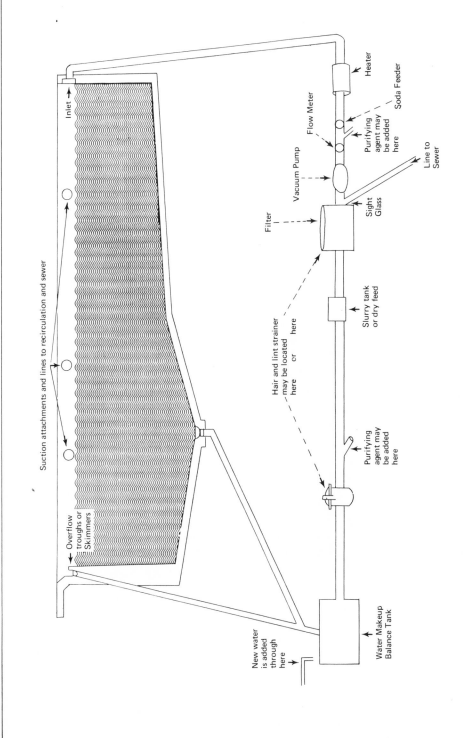

Suction attachments and lines to recirculation and sewer

Inlet

Overflow troughs or Skimmers

Heater

Soda Feeder

Flow Meter

Purifying agent may be added here

Vacuum Pump

Line to Sewer

Sight Glass

Filter

Hair and lint strainer may be located here or here

Slurry tank or dry feed

Purifying agent may be added here

New water is added through here

Water Makeup Balance Tank

THE CONTROL OF PLANT AND BACTERIA GROWTH

Chemicals are the primary means for the control of plant and bacteria growth. Health practices of swimmers in compliance with use regulations and the performance of sanitation duties by employees contribute greatly to successful control, but major reliance is upon the introduction of chemicals, in proper amounts and proportions, to the pool water.

The pH Symbol

The symbol p (potential) H (of hydrogen) represents acid-alkaline condition of the pool water. The figure which accompanies it (e.g., pH 6.8, pH 7.6, etc.) represents the degree or intensity of the condition. The standard scale ranges from 0.0 to 14.0, with each segment divided into tenths to permit more precise assessments of intensity. Water which is neither acid nor alkaline, and therefore neutral, is represented as 7.0. Figures from 0.0 to 6.9 reveal degrees of acidity and figures from 7.1 to 14.0 show degrees of alkalinity. Chart 9:3 portrays the pH scale. Reference also should be made to Table 9:7.

The condition of swimming pool water, in terms of being acid or alkaline, is affected by chemicals added to it. Addition of soda ash, hypochlorites, and fresh water (if alkaline) increases pH. Addition of alum, chlorine gas, body acids from bathers, bromine (slightly), sodium bisulphate, and fresh water (if acid) reduces pH. As pH increases, the same level of chlorine becomes less effective.

CHART 9:3
THE pH SCALE

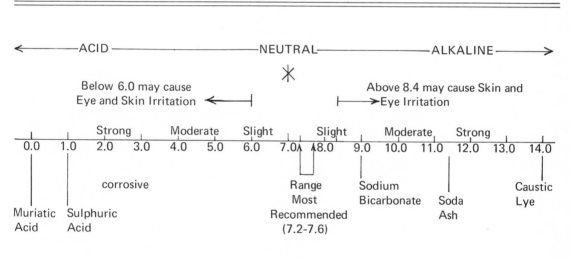

The Addition of Chemicals

The addition of chemicals to swimming pool water serves two major purposes: first, the formation of a gelatinlike floc on the surface of the sand-and-gravel filter in order to trap fine particles and suspended matter in the water; and second, germicidal action on living bacteria and inhibitive action on plant growth. In some situations a further purpose may be the removal of minerals that may cause discoloration of the water and impair filter action. Table 9:4 names some chemicals and their functions.

CHEMICALS MOST COMMONLY ADDED TO SWIMMING POOL WATER

The Chemical Added	The Function of the Chemical	Additional Pertinent Information Concerning the Chemical and its Use
Alum.	To unite with soda to form a floc on the top of the bed of a sand-and-gravel filter.	It is usually in the form of aluminum sulphate. The use of ammonia alum is inadvisable. It is usually introduced through a feeder or at the surge tank after backwashing a sand-and-gravel filter. Alum is *not* used with a diatomaceous earth filter.
Soda ash.	To unite with alum to form a floc on the top of the bed of a filter, and to increase the degree of alkalinity of pool water.	It is usually in the form of sodium carbonate. It is usually introduced through a chemical feeder. It may be added directly to the pool in powder or brick form.
Chlorine.	To kill bacteria and to kill algae.	Chlorine gas (liquid under pressure) is by far the most common means used to disinfect pool water and it is the method that has the widest acceptance by State Health Departments. It is usually introduced to the water by means of a chemical feeder (chlorinator), but it may be added directly into the pool in the form of liquid solution or cake. In the pool water, chlorine may be present both as *free available*, which is effective almost instantly, and as *combined available*, which may require an hour or more to perform its function. When ammonia from introduced chemicals or from urine is present in the water, the ammonia gas in the water tends to combine with the free chlorine to form *chloramines*. Chloramines alter the chlorine from free status to combined status; therefore, the addition of any ammonia-bearing compound is likely to make chlorine less effective. The chlorine in the water is reduced in amount by exposure to sunlight, wind or air, and by the splashing caused by swimmers and divers. Superchlorination (greatly increasing the amount of chlorine in the water) is one method used to kill algae.
Hypochlorites.	To kill bacteria.	This disinfectant may be introduced into the water in liquid solution form (sodium hypochlorite) or as a powder (calcium hypochlorite). The use of hypochlorite instead of liquid chlorine may cause a water discoloration that is difficult to eliminate.
Iodine.	To kill bacteria.	Iodine is used in conjunction with chlorine gas or with hypochlorites to separate iodine from potassium iodide. It is usually introduced by means of a chemical feeder. It does not contribute to the formation of chloramines. It may give a greenish tint to pool water when the amount in the water is above 2.0 parts per million.

Bromine.	To kill bacteria.	Bromine has an action similar to the action of chlorine.
		It is usually introduced by means of a feeder (brominator).
Copper sulphate.	To kill algae.	Copper sulphate may be introduced in the form of crystals or as a solution.
		(Refer also to Algae growth, Table 9:5).

SUGGESTIONS CONCERNING THE OPERATION AND MAINTENANCE OF RECIRCULATION SYSTEM COMPONENTS

The parts of the recirculation system require careful and continuing attention. Malfunction within one component can be disruptive to the entire process of recirculation and purification. Prevention is the most effective course of action and this means frequent inspection of all parts and diligent performance of all prescribed maintenance tasks.

Even though preventive measures are taken, problems will occasionally arise and appropriate steps must be taken to resolve them. Some problems are common to all areas of the States and Territories and some are likely to appear in certain sections of the country only.

Much of the task of observation can be assumed by unskilled employees but the important details of care should be performed by employees who have been instructed in the techniques relevant to the operation and maintenance of each component. Nevertheless, every employee should have at least a rudimentary knowledge concerning the tasks related to operation and maintenance of the system.

Table 9:5 indicates some of the pertinent tasks. However, the point must be emphasized that because conditions vary from area to area, all techniques performed must be as prescribed by the Health Department having jurisdiction in the section in which your pool is located or in accordance with the directions given by the organization that employs you, and must be as stipulated by the manufacturers of the individual components.

TABLE 9:5
OPERATION AND MAINTENANCE SUGGESTIONS

Recirculation system component or related aspect.	Possible Problems Related to the Component.	Some Suggestions For Solution of the Problem
The pump.	Failure to pump.	The solution is to look for the cause, which may be lack of priming, wrong direction of impeller rotation, or insufficient motor speed.
	Reduced pump capacity.	The solution is to look for the cause, which may be air leaks in the suction line, clogged or worn impellers, or clogged filter or hair and lint strainer.
	Excessive noise.	The solution is to look for the cause, which may be misalignment of shaft or a bent shaft, or improper proportioning of the suction and discharge lines.
The chlorinator.	Substandard performance.	The solution is to clean the parts of the apparatus with wood alcohol, detect and correct leaks, and install new gaskets.
	Leakage.	The solution is to locate the place of leakage, determine its cause, and take corrective measures.
		No investigation of suspected malfunction should be undertaken without first uncapping a bottle of ammonia; if chlorine gas is present in the room, a visible fog will form as gas and ammonia meet.
		A gas mask should be worn when repairs are made.

235

Table 9:5—Operation and Maintenance Suggestions (continued)

The filter: sand-and-gravel type.	Air bind.	The solution is to open the air release valve if it is closed or to restore it to working order if it is malfunctioning.
	Mud balls (pellets or deposits of filter sand and dirt held together by accumulated organic growth).	The solution is to backwash with increased regularity, feed an increased amount of chlorine to the water line ahead of the filter, or apply calcium hypochlorite to the filter surface.
	Clogging of filter surface with oil and grease.	The solution is to cover the filter surface, while the pump is stopped, with a lye solution (about one pound per square foot of filter surface), let it stand for several hours and then backwash to flush the solution away, or remove the top layer of filter sand, treat it with a lye solution, wash, and return the sand to the filter surface.
	Clogging of the surface by calcium and magnesium salts.	The solution is to treat the filter surface with a water softener.
	Channeling of the filter bed.	The solution is to look for the cause, which may be an excessive rate of water flow, clogging of the filter surface, or corrosion or clogging in the inflow line.
diatomaceous earth type.	Clogging by oil, grease, or organic matter.	The solution is to soak the elements in sodium hexametaphosphate (also sold under trade names as a remedy for this difficulty).
	Clogging by minerals (iron, magnesium, manganese).	The solution is to soak the elements in dilute hydrochloric (muriatic) acid or in sodium hexametaphosphate.
	Dirty plastic filter cloths.	The solution is to wash the filter cloths in a washing machine with detergent.
	Loss of filter coat.	The solution is to backwash the filter and add a new precoat of earth.
Pool water.	Brown color or organic color.	The solution is to determine the cause and take corrective measures. The cause may be an acid water condition; correction is by raising the pH (alkalinity). The cause may be plants contained in new (added) water; correction is by chlorination and filtration. The cause may be the presence of minerals (iron, manganese); correction is by the addition of oxalic acid together with a small amount of sodium bisulphite.
	Cloudy condition.	The solution is to determine the cause and take corrective measures. The cause may be that an excessive amount of alum is being used and some is passing into the pool and forming a floc in suspension; correction is by reducing the alum injection (when filter is sand type). The cause may be a pH that is too low; correction is by increasing the amount of soda added. The cause may be a ruptured filter cloth in a diatomaceous earth unit, permitting earth to pass into the pool; correction is by removing and replacing the cloth.

Algae growth, resulting in:		
	slippery surfaces,	The solution is to use the wall brush on the walls, and scrub decks, floors, and walkways with hypochlorite.
	clogging of filters,	The solution is to backwash the filters as clogging is indicated by loss of head.
	water discoloration, and reduction of clarity.	The solutions are to combat algae* growth by raising the chlorine residual to 4.0 or to as high as 10.0 and, after this superchlorination, reducing the residual by adding sodium thiosulphate, by placing copper sulphate crystals in a bag and dragging it through the water in the pool, or by injecting a copper sulphate solution into the recirculation line,** or by using commercial algicides.
		Measures to prevent algae growth include keeping the chlorine residual at 0.4 or above, perhaps raising it to 1.0 overnight, using hand skimmers to remove leaves and similar organic materials from the water, keeping the water temperature below 80 degrees, and painting the pool (non-tile) sides and bottom to seal rough surfaces.
Floors.	Slipperiness.	The solution is to scrub with a hypochlorite solution daily, or scrub the surfaces with a non-acid cleaning powder or dishwashing detergent.
Bathhouse.	Athlete's foot.	The solution is to mop with soap and hot water, apply chlorine, creosole or a copper sulphate solution, hose down the surface, scrub the surface with a lye solution, hose down the surface, and mop to dry it.

*Algae may be free-floating (usually green in color) or clinging (usually blue-green in color).

Two characteristics of algae are that they thrive in sunlight and heat, and may contribute to bacterial growth.

Warning signs that algae growth has begun are a sudden rise in the pH of the pool water, an increase in water turbidity, an increase in the amount of chlorine needed to maintain a desired chlorine residual, and small brown or black spots on the pool sides or bottom.

**Objections to the use of copper sulphate are that its effectiveness is limited when the water pH is high, it may unite with chemicals present in the natural waters in some areas and cause other complications; it may affect piping; it may tarnish metals and discolor swimmers' suits and hair when its proportion is in excess of 1.0 parts per million.

FILTER BACKWASHING

The function of the filter is to strain out foreign materials as pool water is circulated through it. The requirements of State Departments of Health, pertaining to the rate of water flow through the filters, are not identical in all States. Most specify that, for a sand-and-gravel filter, the rate shall not be more than 3 gallons per minute per square foot of filter surface and, for a diatomaceous earth filter, not greater than 2.5 gallons per minute per square foot of filter surface or within the range of 1½ to 3 gallons per minute per square foot of filter surface, depending on the type of unit.

After a length of time varying with the degree of control over the swimmers and other environmental conditions, materials will have accumulated to the extent of seriously impairing the passage of recirculated water. At this point action must be taken to wash away the accumulated materials. If the pool is equipped with a sand-and-gravel filter, that filter must be backwashed. If the pool is equipped with a diatomaceous earth filter, either the earth must be dislodged and permitted to recoat the elements or the earth must be washed away and diverted into a settling tank or waste drain.

Table 9:6 explains when and how, in general, backwashing should be performed. However, in each state, the specific instructions given by the State Department of Health must be followed. Stated simply, backwashing means reversing the direction of flow of water through the filter in order to cause the accumulated materials to be carried away from the filter surface.

TABLE 9:6
INFORMATION CONCERNING FILTER BACKWASHING

The Type of Filter in Use	The Basis for Decision to Backwash	Actions to be Performed in Order to Accomplish Washing of the Filter
The sand-and-gravel type:		*The steps to be followed when backwashing a sand-and-gravel filter are:* Open and close all valves slowly; Stop the water flow through the filter by closing the inlet and outlet valves; Open the valves on the waste line leading to the storm or sanitary sewer; Slowly open the wash-water valve until the proper rate is obtained; Continue to wash for from 5 to 10 minutes or until the water is clear in the sight glass on the waste line; Close the wash-water valve slowly; Open the inlet valve from the recirculation line; After air has been forced out of the filter, open the outlet valve to the recirculation line and resume normal recirculation. Add alum (not ammonium alum) to the recirculation flow ahead of the filter.
The flow of water is induced by pressure.	The need to wash the filter is indicated when the loss of head is 5-7 pounds per square inch.*	
The flow of water is induced by gravity.	The need to wash the filter is indicated when the loss of head* reaches 7-9 feet.	
		The rates of backwash for sand-and-gravel and for anthracite filters are: For a sand-and-gravel filter, usually not less than 15 gallons of water per minute per square foot of filter surface. Some states set the minimum at a 12-gallon rate. For an anthracite filter the stated minimums vary as much as 8, 9 or 12 gallons per minute per square foot of filter surface.
The diatomaceous earth type:		*The steps to be followed when backwashing a diatomaceous earth filter are:* Close the outlet valve; Close the inlet valve; Open the valve on the drain line; Open the backwash valve; Wash until the filter aid (earth) is removed. Return the filter to service as directed by the manufacturer's instructions.
The flow of water is induced by pressure.	The need to wash the filter is indicated when the loss of head* reaches 20-25 pounds per square inch (may be stated as 10-25 pounds).	
The flow of water is induced by vacuum.	The need to wash the filter is indicated when the vacuum gauge shows a reading of 15-20 inches of mercury.	The rate of backwash for a diatomaceous filter is 10-15 gallons of water per minute per square foot of filter surface. The diatomaceous earth may be separated from the filter cloths by backwashing (described above), by air-bump assist (compressed air), by spray wash (hosing down), or by agitation.

*Loss of head is the difference between the reading on the inflow pressure gauge and the reading on the outflow pressure gauge.

238

TESTS OF SWIMMING POOL WATER AND AREA CONDITIONS

It is imperative that tests be made often enough to ensure that the condition of the pool water and of the immediate environment are equal to or above specified minimum standards. Minor deviations must be discovered before they become major problems and frequent appraisal is the only way to guarantee early detection. State Departments of Health are quite explicit in saying that tests must be performed. Some emphasize that every pool must have a water testing kit; in any case, a testing kit will be available and directions for the use of it will be attached.

Table 9:7 indicates the tests which are the responsibility of the pool operator or manager, though he may delegate another employee to make them. An exception is the testing of water to determine the number (quantitative test—roughly, samples must show not more than 200 bacteria colonies per milliliter) and kind (qualitative test—samples must not show intestinal variety) of bacteria in the water. In this instance, the operator or designated employee, rather than someone from the Health Department, may obtain the water samples for delivery to the Health Department for analysis.

When using indicator equipment for pool water tests, periodically throughout the day or as your good judgment dictates, you *must* study and follow the directions for use; take care to use the exact amounts as stipulated; avoid contamination of the test sample; complete the test quickly; clean test tubes immediately after use; avoid interchange of equipment parts (do not put the dropper from one solution container into another, do not put the cap from one container on another container); avoid the use of the same test tube for different tests; avoid stirring the solution for one test with the dropper from another container and using a common implement to stir different solutions; and return the testing equipment to a storage place that is not exposed to sunlight or high or freezing temperatures.

TABLE 9:7
TESTS OF SWIMMING POOL WATER AND AREA CONDITIONS

Test to be Performed	Frequency of Test Performance	Method of Performing the Test
The test for chlorine residual.	The test is made from two to four times a day, and at least two times a day.	The need is to determine the degree to which the chlorine content of the water is free-available rather than combined-available. Readings can be misleading unless the test is performed immediately after the sample is taken because, otherwise, combined as well as free chlorine will be shown.
	The test is made only if chlorine is the means used to purify the pool water.	To make the test, fill two test tubes with sample water to the level indicated in the test kit directions and place them in the test rack (which may have either sliding or disk comparator colors). Use one test tube for color or optical compensation. To one tube, usually the right-hand one, add an amount of orthotolidine as directed. Move the comparator slide or turn the disk to bring a color into view that, when viewed through the left-hand tube, is most like the color of the right-hand sample. Take the reading for that color match.
The test for pH (alkalinity).	The test is made from two to four times a day, and at least once a day.	To make the test, fill two test tubes with samples of pool water to the level indicated by the directions in the test kit. Place them in the test rack of a test kit with sliding or disk comparator colors. Use one test tube for color or optical compensation. To the right-hand tube, add a small amount of sodium thiosulphate (to cancel chlorine influence). Mix by removing the tube from the rack and inverting it. Replace the tube in the rack, add an amount of phenol red or thymol blue as directed. Move the comparator slide or turn the disk to bring into view a color that, when viewed through the left-

The test for presence of bacteria.	Samples of pool water for the test are taken at least once, and perhaps twice, each week.	hand tube, is most like the color of the right-hand sample. Take the reading for that color match. Bottles to contain water samples may be obtained from the Health Department. One or two samples may be taken on each occasion. If two samples are taken, one should be taken from each end of the pool. The sample should be taken when there is a heavy swimmer-load in the pool. To obtain the water sample, remove the top from the sample bottle. Do not touch the inside of the lid. Do not rinse the bottle. Grasp the bottle near its bottom and, with the opening higher than the bottom, fill (but not to the brim) the bottle by a slow upward-sweeping arm action under the water surface. Keep the bottle moving ahead of the hand. Replace the lid immediately.
The test for water clarity.	The test is made as frequently as needed to confirm that standards are being met.	The test is made by verifying that the bottom of the pool at the deepest point is clearly visible. (Specific standards are described in Table 9:10). The best times for making the test are before opening the pool and after closing the pool on any day of use.
The tests for temperatures of air and water.	The tests are made two times daily.	To make the water test, submerge a water thermometer at points removed from the recirculation inlets. To make the air test, read an air thermometer at spectator level and at deck level.
The test for adequacy of lighting.	The test is made occasionally by observation, or is made by instrument before a time of special need (e.g., television).	The test is made by confirming that all areas of the pool bottom are clearly visible and that glare does not make vision difficult. (Specific standards are described in Table 9:12). The test is made by reading a light meter at various points about the pool area and at the water surface. Intensity may be measured in footcandles, watts or lumens (one watt is equal to twenty lumens). From 60 to 90 footcandles may be required for television.
The determination of swimmer load.	The determination is made daily.	The determination is made by referring to records of admission tickets sold, of locker locks or keys issued, or of suits and towels issued, and by making a count of swimmers in attendance at times during the day when their number is greatest.
The test for bromine (if bromine is the water purifier used).	The test is made from two to four times daily.	The chlorine test kit, also used with the addition of orthotolidine, may be used for color comparison. However, when the figures on the test kit indicate measures of chlorine, the figure is doubled to obtain the bromine reading. A residual of 1.0 parts per million is recommended as minimum. The usual range is between 1.0 and 2.0.
The test for iodine (if iodine is the water purifier used).	The test is made from two to four times daily.	The amount of iodine is determined amperometrically or may be determined with a color comparator in accordance with the manufacturer's instructions. The recommended range is between .1 and .5 parts per million. About 1.0, and especially above 2.0 there is risk of water discoloration. The higher the water pH reading (e.g., between 7.0 and 8.0) the more effective is the same amount of iodine.

STANDARDS REQUIRED OR RECOMMENDED
BY STATE DEPARTMENTS OF HEALTH

Although State Departments of Health vary in their stipulations pertaining to minimum standards, and although each aquatic worker must be guided by the Health Department in the State in which he works, a fuller understanding of the nature of acceptable conditions can be gained by observing the extremes within which requirements and recommendations are confined. Moreover, it is helpful to note the point between the extremes at which the greatest number of recommendations are in agreement.

Pool Water Standards

Most State Departments of Health indicate, to aquatic workers employed within their respective states, the water conditions that each requires or recommends. Tables 9:8, 9:9, 9:10, and 9:11 show some of them.

The quoted figures are indicative but not absolute. A figure given for chlorine residual, for example, may be conditional, depending on the level of pH. In the same manner, a pH figure in conjunction with a sand filter may not be the same as the figure in conjunction with a diatom filter. Figures for pH in Table 9:9 are based on the assumption that chlorine is the disinfecting agent.

TABLE 9:8
POOL WATER FREE CHLORINE REQUIREMENTS OF
STATE DEPARTMENTS OF HEALTH

	Required or Recommended Free Chlorine Figure or Range of Free Chlorine in Parts Per Million (ppm)											
	0.2 to 0.5	0.2 to 1.0	Not less than 0.25	0.25 to 1.0	At least 0.3	0.4	At least 0.4	0.4 to 0.6	0.4 to 1.0	0.4 to 1.5	At least 0.5	0.8 to 1.0
Number of States recommending or requiring	2	1	1	1	3	1	11	7	10	1	1	1

TABLE 9:9
POOL WATER pH REQUIREMENTS OF STATE DEPARTMENTS OF HEALTH

	Required or Recommended pH Figure or Range of pH														
	7.0 or more	7.0 to 7.6	7.0 to 8.0	7.0 to 8.4	Best at 7.2	At least 7.2	7.2 to 7.6	7.2 to 7.8	7.2 to 8.0	7.2 to 8.2	7.2 to 8.4	7.2 to 8.9	7.4 to 8.2	About 7.6	7.8 to 8.2
Number of States recommending or requiring	5	2	3	1	1	1	6	1	4	5	5	1	1	1	3

241

COMMON POOL WATER CLARITY REQUIREMENTS OF STATE DEPARTMENTS OF HEALTH

Requirement or recommendation

A black disk, six inches in diameter on a white field, when placed on the bottom of the pool, at the deepest point, is clearly visible from the sidewalks of the pool at all distances up to ten yards.

A disk two inches in diameter divided into quadrants of alternate colors of red and black is (shall be) clearly discernible through fifteen feet of water and the different colors readily distinguishable.

Area Standards

Desirable air and water temperatures for indoor pools are shown in Table 9:11. Acceptable lighting standards are presented in Table 9:12.

TABLE 9:11
INDOOR POOL TEMPERATURE STANDARDS OF STATE DEPARTMENTS OF HEALTH

Required or Recommended Temperature Figure or Range in Degrees Fahrenheit										The relationship of air temperature to water temp.			
Water temperatures													
A-bove 70	Not over 78	Not over 80	70 to 85	Not less than 74	74 to 84	75 to 82	75 to 85	76 to 78	76 to 80	3 degr. over	5 degr. over	Not more 8 over	Not less 2 under
Number of States recommending or requiring													
1	2	1	1	1	1	1	2	3	1	1	3	1	1

For practical reasons, day-to-day appraisal of the adequacy of lighting will be by the use of the middle two sections of Table 9:12, rather than in accordance with the first and fourth sections of the table.

TABLE 9:12
**EXAMPLES OF INDOOR POOL LIGHTING REQUIREMENTS
SPECIFIED BY VARIOUS STATE DEPARTMENTS OF HEALTH**

Required or recommended lighting standards

Underwater light: 0.5 watts per square foot of pool area.
Deck light: 0.6 watts per square foot of deck area.
When no underwater light, area and pool lighting combined shall provide not less than 2 watts per square foot of pool area, with 2 footcandles of illumination.

Lifeguard may see every part of the pool without being blinded by light.
All portions of the pool, including the bottom, may be readily seen without glare.
Sufficient to light all parts of the pool and water therein.
Light all areas of the bottom of the pool with no blind spots.

Adequate area lighting.
Adequate artificial lighting, including underwater lights.
Illuminate all parts of the pool, the water and the entire pool area.
Floor of the pool can be seen.
Pool and deck areas shall be well lighted by natural or artificial means.

242

Deck: 10 footcandles, 0.5-1.0 watts per square foot; underwater: 3.0-5.0 watts per square foot.
Thirty footcandles of deck lighting (for recreation swimming).
Fifteen footcandles at 30 inches above the walkway.
Underwater (indoor): 100 lamp lumens/square foot of pool surface.

User Load

Methods for the determination of maximum loads are presented in Table 9:13. In general, application of these methods is based on the assumption that, at any given time, one of three swimmers (deep water area) is on the deck and two of four or three of four nonswimmers (shallow water area) are on the deck.

Three pertinent points should be noted: first, pool depths (distinguishing nonswimmer and swimmer areas) will be altered as the pool water surface is raised or lowered; second, safe loads are related to the rate of pool turnover, the efficiency of the recirculation and purification systems and to the degree of swimmer compliance with regulations; and, third, the Health Department figures represent maximum limits—a smaller figure will mean less congestion and greater swimmer comfort.

TABLE 9:13
EXAMPLES OF MAXIMUM POOL LOAD STANDARDS REQUIRED OR RECOMMENDED BY VARIOUS STATE DEPARTMENTS OF HEALTH

300 square feet around each diving board reserved for diving; 24 square feet for each swimmer (water depth over 5 feet) *not including* the area reserved for diving; 10 square feet for each nonswimmer.

The area within radius of ten feet of the diving board reserved for diving (estimated 12 divers); 24 square feet per person in water depth over 5 feet; 10 square feet per person in water depth less than 5 feet.

Two or three persons within 15 feet of the end of each board; 30 square feet per person in water depth over 5 feet; 15 square feet per person in water depth less than 5 feet.

Three persons within a 10-foot radius of each diving board; 27 square feet per person in water depth over 5 feet; 10 square feet per person in water depth less than 5 feet.

24 square feet per person in water depth less than 5 feet.

One person for each 27 square feet of pool surface with water depth over 5½ feet; one person for each 10 square feet with depth under 5½ feet.

One person for each 27 square feet of pool surface with water depth over 5 feet; one person for each 10 square feet with water depth under 5 feet.

One person for each 24 square feet of pool surface.

One person for each 25 square feet of pool surface.

One person for each 40 square feet of pool surface.

One person for each 20 square feet of pool and deck surface combined.

One person for each 500 gallons of water in the pool(s); one person for each 500 gallons of water added (where disinfection not used).

POOL OPERATION REPORT REQUIREMENTS OF STATE DEPARTMENTS OF HEALTH

State Departments of Health require that records of operation be maintained and submitted, and they provide forms for this purpose. An example of such a form appears in Appendix B.

This responsibility of the pool operator is emphasized in the publications issued by the Departments. Some clarify this directive by stating some of the records that must be reported. In a few instances, the requirements are quite general; for example, records of tests and the operation of the place, and all operations influencing sanitation of the pool. In other instances, the requirements are quite specific; for example, interruptions in sterilizations and the reasons; the pool recirculation rate; the pressure gauge readings; algae control measures taken; walkway cleaned; and floors, toilet rooms, benches, and fixtures disinfected. Examples of the more common report requirements are presented in Table 9:14.

TABLE 9:14
SOME OF THE POOL OPERATION RECORDS REQUIRED OR RECOMMENDED
BY VARIOUS STATE DEPARTMENTS OF HEALTH

Record Category	Items to be recorded, with dates & times
Test findings.	Disinfectant residual. Alkalinity and/or pH. Results from samples taken and sent for bacteriological analysis. Clarity (turbidity). Temperatures of air and water.
Observations of Conditions.	Attendance (total load). Estimated peak load. Attendance figures for males, for females, for adults, and for children.
Operation.	The quantity (amounts) of chemicals added (used). Filters washed (backwashed). The amount of fresh (new) water added. The hours the pump has been in operation. The hours the filters have been in operation. Vacuum (suction) cleaner used. Pool bottom cleaned. Malfunctions of mechanical equipment. Rate-of-flow meter readings. Pool sides cleaned. Maintenance of equipment. Emptying pool. The hours the disinfecting device has been in operation. Injuries that have occurred (nature, cause, treatment). The amount of filter aid (diatomaceous earth) added. Personnel on duty (especially guards at time of peak load).

REGULATIONS PERTAINING TO POOL SANITATION

The importance of rules that are designed to make other sanitation procedures more effective is indicated by the fact that most State Departments of Health mention such regulations in printed materials prepared for pool employees and declare that these rules must be enforced. The nature of them is shown in Table 9:15.

Some reasons for swimmer exclusion that do not appear in Table 9:15 are: abrasions, blisters, cuts, open lesions, open wounds, rashes, sores; ear, nose, or throat infection; boils, impetigo, pimples, skin eruption; excessive sunburn, peeling; wearing adhesive tape, bunion pads or corn plasters; oil, grease or suntan lotion on the skin; coughs, fever; unclean suit or trunks, wool trunks; and being under the influence of liquor. Some individual pools require all persons with long hair, both male and female, to wear bathing caps.

Attitudes concerning footbaths range from requirement of them to ruling against their use. The consensus is that their potential for harm is greater than their potential for benefit.

244

TABLE 9:15
EXAMPLES OF REGULATIONS EMPHASIZED
BY VARIOUS STATE DEPARTMENTS OF HEALTH

Category of Regulation	Examples of Regulations Pertaining to Sanitation
Required swimmer actions.	The swimmer must take a shower in the nude, using soap, and rinse off soap suds. The swimmer must take a shower after using the toilet and before returning to the pool. Women and girls must wear bathing caps.
Reasons for swimmer exclusion.	Having a communicable or infectious disease. Having sore or inflamed eyes. Having a skin disease. Having a cold, or nasal or ear discharges. Wearing bandages. A lifeguard is not present.
Swimmer conduct restrictions.	Spitting, spouting water, or blowing nose is forbidden.
Restrictions on bringing articles into the pool area.	No gum or tobacco may be brought into the area. No food or drink may be brought into the area. No bottles or glass containers may be brought into the area. No animals may be brought into the area. No articles that may cause contamination may be brought to or thrown into the pool.
Regulations applying to employees.	Post the regulations applying to swimmers and divers. Permit no one on the deck in street shoes. Supply no brushes, combs, or towels for common use. Limit the time a bather may remain in the pool. Employ no assistant who has a communicable disease. Exclude any person who refuses to obey the regulations.

SANITATION DUTIES OF EMPLOYEES

It is imperative that all employees become involved in actions that contribute to good sanitation. When employees fail to perform their assigned tasks, an environment favorable to contamination is encouraged and the acquisition of disease is made possible. When employees are diligent in performing their duties, the pleasing appearance of the area and the tests of water conditions give evidence of that dedication.

Table 9:16 indicates some of the many possible tasks to be performed.

TABLE 9:16
SANITATION DUTIES OF BEACH AND POOL PERSONNEL

Category and Frequency of Duty	Examples of Specific Duties to be Performed by Employees at Beach or Pool
Common to both beach and pool:	
Constantly.	Enforce regulations (bottles, food, animals, etc.). Keep the area clean. Keep waste receptacles from becoming overfull. Keep windbreaks in good repair to limit foreign matter and impurities carried into the water by gusts and strong winds. See that showers are used and operated properly. Maintain the cleanliness of suits and towels issued to swimmers.

Table 9:16—Sanitation Duties of Beach and Pool Personnel (continued)

One or more times daily.	Estimate and record attendance. Clean and disinfect toilet rooms, shower rooms, dressing rooms. Clean and disinfect benches, seats, and fixtures. Inspect the area and make appropriate requests or recommendations.
As occasion requires.	Abide by restrictions on maximum swimmer load. Forbid swimming when the lifeguard is not present. Keep gates and doors locked when the facility is not in use. Take water samples for bacteriological analysis in containers containing sodium thiosulphate. Maintain records. Fill out report forms. Report detrimental conditions (water color, water cloudiness, algae growth, malfunctions, etc.), to superior.
Specific to the beach:	
Constantly.	Keep the area clean, Remove food particles, food and drink containers, fruit peels and cores, etc. Be alert for conditions such as water currents and wind direction that may bring contamination from sewer outfalls, septic tank effluents, refuse disposals, and discharges from boat toilets and bilges.
One or more times daily.	Note prevailing weather and water conditions.
As occasion requires.	Use copper sulphate or hypochlorites to combat algae growth if large scale flushing and fresh water addition is impractical.
Specific to the pool:	
Constantly.	Enforce pool regulations (showers, contagious diseases, etc.). Inspect swimmers as they enter onto the pool deck. Keep the spectator area clean (mop, rather than sweep). Keep toilet paper, paper towel, and soap dispensers filled. Maintain correct water and air temperatures. Maintain an inventory of the amounts of chemicals on hand. Appraise water clarity (by observation-judgment only until need for applying the specified test is apparent).
One or more times daily.	Clean the pool bottom with the suction cleaner. Clean the pool walkways (decks). (Do not splash water into the pool.) Clean toilets, urinals, wash basins, spit receptacles. Remove visible scum. Make tests for chlorine (2-4 times daily), pH (2-4 times daily), and air and water temperatures (daily).
As occasion requires.	Post the regulations governing use; keep them up to date. Backwash the filters when pressure gauge readings make it advisable. Use skimmer or overflow to clear the water surface. Remove hairpins from pool bottom (either from deck by use of magnet on a pole, or by hand while swimming underwater and waring a face mask). Clean pool sides by using wall brush. Repair grouting at joints and between tiles. Apply bleach to walkways.

CLOSING THE FACILITY AT END OF SEASON

When a pool or beach is closed down at the end of a season, each employee is tempted strongly to leave everything as it is and depart quickly without a backward glance. If he succumbs to this urge, he will regret his lack of foresight when the time comes to place the facility in operation again.

Table 9:17 shows a portion of the work to be done at end of season. The listing provides a beginning guide but does not represent a complete compilation of necessary actions. Each manager should construct two check lists, one for time of closing and one for time of reopening, that are applicable to the facility he operates. To the actions suggested in Table 9:17, he should add many other appropriate ones as they occur to him. For each action listed, space should be left in which he can write in the name of the person he assigns to perform the work and the time at which it is to be done.

Included in Table 9:17 are jobs that have no obvious relationship to sanitation but it is better that they be mentioned here than not at all. Also included are some jobs that do not apply in some sections of the nation. Some of the jobs must be performed only by an electrician, by an engineer, or by an employee who is skilled to do so. Each employee who assists must be instructed to attach an identifying label to each part removed (e.g., pump drain plug, pump switches, valves) and to see that the part is properly stored or is wired or tied to the item from which it is removed.

TABLE 9:17
ACTIONS TO BE TAKEN TO READY THE FACILITY FOR CLOSING

The Order in which Actions Should be Taken	Some Examples of Actions that should be Taken
Tasks that should be performed first.	Notify the test laboratory to discontinue sending bottles for water samples.
	Be sure that the air relief valve on the sand-and-gravel filter is open and operating. Leave it open.
	Open the manhole of the sand-and-gravel filter and inspect the top sand. Remove mudballs and other debris. Backwash with the manhole open and inspect the water action for even flow.
	Drain the sand-and-gravel filters completely. Leave cover off to permit filters to dry but cover the opening with screen. Leave drain lines open.
	Backwash the diatomaceous earth filter. Drain completely and leave drain line open. Remove the elements and wash with muriatic acid. Inspect the filter cloths and discard those that require replacement before the pool is reopened.
Tasks that should be performed next.	Drain all lines at the lowest point. Drain toilets and similar fixtures. Put kerosene in pipe traps and goosenecks. Confirm that all floor and deck drains are open and operating.
	If the pool is to stand empty, drain the water and leave drain lines open, place heavy screens over all drains and inlets to keep out rodents and trash, repair groutings to prevent seepage that may freeze and expand with thaw. Inspect the outlet grating, remove rust spots, and apply rust inhibitor.
	If the pool is not to be drained, set the water level at from 6 to 8 inches below the overflow level. Put in logs, poles, kegs, or barrels to counteract pressures from freezing and thawing (outdoor pool).
	Disassemble the chlorinator, drain it free of water, and clean and inspect all parts. Make necessary replacements of parts, identify all parts, store in dry place and protect with vaseline.
	Drain and disconnect other chemical feeders, leave lines open, and thoroughly wash off all chemicals.
	Open the pump casing and drain it thoroughly. Remove fuses from the motor switch, protect the starter against corrosion, grease the drain plug, and identify it with a tag. Have an electrician inspect the motor and wiring to determine repair or replacement needs. Inspect the impeller and shaft. Replace worn parts. Protect unpainted surfaces with rust inhibitor.
	Clean and inspect the hair strainer baskets and gaskets. Make necessary replacements, use rust inhibitor on unpainted surfaces.
	Disassemble valves, clean them thoroughly, use rust inhibitor, and identify by number the parts for reassembly when the pool is reopened. Parts may be stored in a pan of oil or in oiled paper.

Table 9:17—Actions to be Taken to Ready the Facility for Closing (continued)

Disassemble gauges and flow meter. Clean them thoroughly, use rust inhibitor, and replace parts as needed. Leave all openings open.

Brush all rust spots on piping, fixtures, and mechanical parts. Cover metal parts of recirculation system with vaseline. Paint marred or chipped spots on equipment and structures.

Clean the vacuum cleaner and replace parts as needed. Store it in a safe, dry place.

Store the water testing kit.

Remove remaining supply of chemicals which may deteriorate with the building unoccupied. Make a list of chemicals and all other items that must be ordered for delivery in ample time before the facility is reopened.

Inspect the groutings on inside and outside walls. Repair to protect them from damage due to freezing of seepage.
Confirm that roof drains are functioning properly.
Store or make nonfunctional any outdoor item that might be termed an attractive nuisance when left without supervision.
Store ring buoys, ropes, and similar items in a safe, dry place away from sun exposure. Be sure they are completely dry before storing.
Remove springboards from stands and store away from heat and moisture, position them to prevent warping, lying flat on pieces of 2″ x 4″ and with the same side up as would be the case when in use.
Pack suits and towels in rodent-proof containers and store in a dry place. Protect any woolen items against moths.

Tasks that should be performed last.

Place inverted barrels over outside drinking fountains.
Remove all outside light bulbs. Protect reflectors against weather and vandalism.
Bring in boundary signs, lifelines, and similar items for dry storage. Leave warning signs that the beach is closed.
See that boats and outside guard stands are transported and stored.

Apply rust inhibitor to gates, ladders, and other metal fixtures and equipment.
Clean up refuse and dirt. Leave the inside area spic and span. Remove all food, nesting materials, and other items that may attract and sustain rodents and insects.

Shut off the city water.
Discontinue gas and telephone services.
Discontinue electricity, remove fuses or open circuit breakers, unless it is necessary to continue service and leave one circuit breaker closed in order to keep the security alarm system operative.

Notify the police department of closure and that the premises will be unoccupied and unsupervised.

Assemble all records, reports and operating instructions and arrange for safe storage in order to have them on hand for reference when the facility is reopened.

Install storm shutters or board up windows. Lock all doors and windows. Secure all gates.

Submit to superiors a list of repairs, improvements, and supplies needed prior to reopening of the facility.

WRITTEN ASSIGNMENTS

1. Make up a time schedule of pool health and sanitation tasks that you may perform during one day of work at an indoor pool.

248

2. Observe a water testing process, describe how it was done, and state the readings obtained for residual chlorine and pH.

3. Observe a filter-washing process and describe how it was done.

4. Construct a diagram of the recirculation system in a particular pool. Show the location and the relationships of the parts.

5. Draw a facsimile of a pool operation report form and fill in hypothetical figures for one day of operation.

6. State what your actions would be if:
   a. Within hours, the pool water became increasingly green in color and the pH rose rapidly.
   b. Chlorine gas leakage was suspected.
   c. An electrical power failure made the pump inoperative for 36 hours.

BEHAVIORAL OBJECTIVES

The objectives of this chapter will be evaluated by writing short answers to any or all of the following questions and could call for you to do any or all of the tasks below.

1. State the function of the filter, gauges, sight glass, hair strainer, vacuum cleaner, and surge tank.

2. State the actions to be taken to ready a beach facility for closing at the end of season.

3. Illustrate a pH scale and indicate the desirable levels for pool water.

4. Give the pH, residual chlorine, and clarity standards required or recommended by the Department of Health in your State.

5. Explain how and when earth is added to a diatomaceous earth filter.

BIBLIOGRAPHY

American Public Health Association. *Suggested Ordinance and Regulations Covering Public Swimming Pools.* New York: American Public Health Association, 1964.

American Public Health Association. *Recommended Practice for Design, Equipment and Operation of Swimming Pools and Other Public Bathing Places.* New York: American Public Health Association, 1957.

State Health Associations. Publications (variously titled) of the Health Departments of the States and Territories of the United States (See Appendix A).

CHAPTER 10

Coaching the Swimming and Diving Team

What Must the Team Coach Know and Be Able to Do?
Types of Coaching Positions
Attributes a Coach Should Have
The First Season As Team Coach
Attributes a Swimmer or Diver Should Have
Training the Swimming and Diving Team
Coaching the Swimmer
Coaching the Diver
Coaching the Swimming and Diving Team
Administering a Swimming and Diving Meet
Officiating

You have noted in Chapter 8 that one of the several facets of the aquatic program is competition in swimming and diving. Consequently, knowledge pertaining to this aspect of the program is essential to full preparation for employment in the field of aquatics.

WHAT MUST THE TEAM COACH KNOW AND BE ABLE TO DO?

There is a great deal more to good coaching than merely instructing swimmers and divers in the acquisition of related performance techniques. The superior coach is a person who possesses many and diverse desirable attributes. He must know how to initiate a program in any one of a variety of possible coaching positions. He must be aware of the qualities which a good swimmer or diver should have. He must know the phases of a training season and how to condition a swimmer or diver effectively. He must know how to organize a swimming or diving practice session. He must be able to obtain help from other persons and be able to motivate the members of his teams. He must be able to administer competition and must know the officials that will be needed and the duties they perform.

Specific behavioral objectives are found at the end of this chapter.

TYPES OF COACHING POSITIONS

The degree of complexity of coaching assignments varies from the very simple to the highly complex; your responsibility may, for example, be to administer swimming races for a group of campers at summer camp, to coach a group of novice youngsters on a YMCA team, or to prepare a team for competition in a national championship meet. You may coach teams representing a school, church group, agency (as YMCA), parks and recreation department, community club, athletic club or aquatic club. You may coach boys, or girls, or both. You may coach youngsters or mature persons. You may coach the inexpert or the expert. Some positions may be of short duration and others may extend throughout the entire year. No one formula will apply to all positions; you must be prepared to adapt to any variety of positions.

250

ATTRIBUTES A COACH SHOULD HAVE

An ideal and perfect coach would have all the traits which we are listing in this chapter as desirable. But he does not exist. All have weaknesses as well as strengths; some possess a few qualities in high degree, while others have not developed those particular attributes but excel in others. All are important, and every coach should possess each one in some degree.

One marked difference between coaches relates to a personal philosophy of coaching and the meaning the concept has for the individual coach. One will set winning as the only worthwhile concept, another will consider the primary goals for the swimmer to be enjoyment, self-realization, and learning. A determination of the relative importance of attributes is, therefore, difficult without knowledge of the philosophy which is to be served. However, we believe that the order of importance of qualities is somewhat as they appear in Table 10:1.

TABLE 10:1
DESIRABLE ATTRIBUTES OF THE TEAM COACH

Desirable Attribute	Indications that the Coach has the Attribute
Inspirational leader.	His enthusiasm and desire is contagious. His great interest is obvious. He motivates to maximum efforts. Team spirit is high, team pride is great. Swimmers help each other, divers help each other.
Influential leader.	He sets high conduct standards and requires swimmer commitment. He is firm, fair, and states clearly what he expects. He is able to yield in his opinions when it is advisable. He is not obstinate. He is sensitive to each individual's aspirations and problems. He engenders respect of the team for the coach and for the sport. He motivates members of his team to give maximum effort in an endeavor to win. He emphasizes the importance of individual success to team victory. He teaches that other values are important, that winning unfairly gives a hollow satisfaction, and that arrogance creates hostility. He emphasizes that character, sportsmanship, and individual performance improvement are important objectives.
Efficient teacher.	He leads swimmers to think for themselves, solve problems. He obtains the assistance of others, delegates tasks. He is able to communicate, to explain and be understood. He has knowledge of the techniques of swimming and diving. He is aware of and applies the findings of research. He is flexible, able to adapt to new and better methods. He uses advanced devices (e.g., television instant-replay, tape recorder for his observations during practices and meets).
Diagnostician.	He is able to observe and discern flaws in performance, prescribe corrections. He is able to treat each individual according to his differences from others in abilities and attitudes.
Experimenter-inventor.	He is able to innovate, devise and revise. He originates new dives, better training methods. He critically analyzes and improves upon current methods of meet administration.
Strategist.	He studies opponents and the situation, and assigns swimmers to events wherein their abilities will count the most. He counsels his divers concerning the dives they will choose to perform.

Table 10:1—Desirable Attributes of the Team Coach (continued)

Humorist.	He sees the funny side of happenings. He does not take himself too seriously. His humor relieves tensions.
Promoter.	He is adept in public relations and publicity. He is able to meet with people and to involve people. He makes the program and its values known to the public. He has schedules and meet results presented by news media.

THE FIRST SEASON AS TEAM COACH

When you start a new coaching job, and especially if it is your first experience, there are tasks to perform that will make your efforts more productive and your baptism less traumatic. Following is a table illustrating the more important initial steps that you should take to establish yourself and your program.

TABLE 10:2
FIRST YEAR COACHING TASKS

General Task	Specific Tasks Related to Each General Task
Analyze the situation.	If the organization has had a team in the past, study the performances of the individual team members. Determine the talent you have and the goals you will set. Study the facilities, determine the times the pool is available for practice sessions, and estimate the number of swimmers and divers that can be accommodated during those times. Determine the kind and extent of equipment available and estimate additional needs. Learn what money is available for equipment, travel, awards, and other needs.
Determine existing assets, limitations, and needs.	Learn the administrative pattern of the organization for which you work and your place in the scheme of things. Know the chain of command, procedures which must be followed, your responsibilities and your prerogatives.
Form the squad.	Make a roster of names of team candidates, publicize the schedules for practice and for competition, and encourage swimmers and divers to become candidates for positions on the team. Begin the study of individual candidates for the team, evaluate potentials, and identify team weaknesses.
Plan practices.	Plan and organize practice sessions appropriate to the program and in relation to facilities, equipment, time, assistance, and the number of candidates (see pages 258-261 and Table 10:13).
Obtain help.	Recruit assistance from faculty, organization members, parents, former team members, community members. List the help you will need and decide whom you will request to do each task (Table 10:11).
Establish rapport.	Think carefully on the standards of dress, personal appearance, speech and manners you will advocate. Meet with the team candidates, explain your philosophy, and state clearly what you will require of them in practice effort and what you hope for in team spirit (Table 10:12).

| Obtain publicity. | Establish lines of communication with all kinds of news media. Advertise the schedule of meets, provide information for pre-meet publicity, submit meet summaries. Arrange banquets, award ceremonies. |
| Analyze opponents. | Study the past performances of members of teams against which your team will be competing and, with this knowledge, determine what the goals of the team members must be if they are to be victorious over individual opponents. |

ATTRIBUTES A SWIMMER OR DIVER SHOULD HAVE

A composite of the perfect team member includes several desirable qualities. As in the case of the coach, no one swimmer possesses all of these attributes to high degree, but the better swimmers will have each of them to an appreciable degree. Any rating of them in the order of their importance is vulnerable to challenge, but we are agreed that desire is the most essential ingredient. A swimmer without desire will be a source of frustration to you and, in his effect upon team morale and effort, may hinder you more than he will help. A swimmer who has a consuming desire, even though he is awkward in the performance of stroke techniques, is likely through sheer determination to defeat an opponent who lacks the drive to excel. Moreover, he will try harder, learn more quickly, and get himself in better condition. Following are tables indicating the characteristics a coach hopes to find in candidates for positions on his team.

TABLE 10:3
DESIRABLE ATTRIBUTES OF THE COMPETITIVE SWIMMER

Desirable Attribute	Some Indications That the Swimmer Has the Attribute
Desire.	He has a compulsion to strive, to excel, to win. He is willing to make sacrifices and to give maximum effort in preparation for competition. He is dedicated to maximum effort in competition.
Cardio-respiratory efficiency.	His heartbeat rate is lower and it has greater stroke and volume. He has more capillaries. He recovers quickly after effort, and his pulse rate drops quickly after effort. He is able to obtain "second wind," as his body accommodates to the demands resulting from effort.
Strength.	He has thicker muscle fibers and better muscle tonus.
Flexibility.	His muscles, ligaments, and tendons do not restrict effective movement.
Coordination.	The actions of his body parts are synchronized. He uses only needed muscles. His rhythm is flowing. His breathing is properly timed and efficient.
Technical Skill.	He is efficient in the performance of the techniques of starts, strokes, and turns.
Self-reliance.	He is able to set his own far-reaching goals. He can get himself "up" for a race. He thinks for himself, uses strategy during a race, and does not panic when the unexpected happens.
Emotional control.	He performs better under stress of competition than he does in practice. He does not "psych out."

TABLE 10:4
DESIRABLE ATTRIBUTES OF THE COMPETITIVE DIVER

Desirable Attribute	Some Indications That the Diver Has the Attribute
Desire	He has a compulsion to strive, to excel, and to win.
Self-confidence.	He delights in being a center of attraction. He is at his best when many people are watching him. He does not "freeze."
Mind-muscle coordination.	His muscles react as willed by his mind. His actions are quick.
Flexibility.	His twists are fluid. He assumes the pike position without strain. His entries are with full body extension. He saves his long and short dives.
Strength.	His body motion and actions show controlled power.
Technical skill.	He is efficient in the performance of fundamentals (approach, hurdle, take-off, flight, entry). He has mastery of the techniques of the dives in each group.
Self-reliance.	His practice is as purposeful and as serious when the coach is absent as when he is present. He analyzes and selects his dives wisely.
Dedication.	He is willing to practice under difficult conditions (with swimmers in the same area, and at odd hours) and is willing to endure the monotony of the many repetitions necessary to learn and perfect dives.
Concentration.	He fixes his attention upon the movements comprising the dive.
Patience.	He is willing to master fundamentals before attempting to learn dives.
Emotional control.	He is calm before a dive. He reflects an absence of tension during periods of waiting between dives in competition.
Courage.	He attempts new and difficult dives. He overcomes his fears.

TRAINING THE SWIMMING AND DIVING TEAM

Obviously, as coach your major responsibility is to prepare the members of your team for the competitive challenges to come. The proper performance of this task requires that you do more than tell the candidates to sign their names and come back on the day of the first meet.

What do we mean by training?

To some people, training connotes the services provided by a team athletic trainer, to others it means only the processes of physical conditioning. In this book we use the term to embrace several facets. We define training to include *all* that is done by the coach and by the swimmer and diver in preparation for attainment of best performance in competition. We include conditioning, timing, gearing up, rules, diet, warm-up, phases, fatigue, and staleness.

What do we mean by conditioning?

We define conditioning as the process whereby physiological functions are improved to the point that the athlete performs at a high level, recuperates quickly and has stamina and strength. The onset of fatigue is retarded.

254

What do we mean by pace sense?

We define pace sense as the ability to distribute the available energy somewhat equally throughout the race. The swimmer should "feel" that he is performing at a pace of, let us say, 16 seconds per pool length. It is pathetic to watch a swimmer who has misjudged his pace and for whom the last few yards are an agonizing effort in slow motion, and it is equally pathetic to see a swimmer explode in a strong sprint during the last length of the race and still finish in last place but with an abundance of unexpended energy.

What do we mean by "gearing up?"

We define gearing up as the ability to adjust the rate of muscle action to the rate required by the distance of the race. Rhythms of muscle actions are learned and become firmly established. The swimmer who trains exclusively by swimming long distances will encounter difficulty in a short sprint race because he is unable to adjust to the faster arm stroke and leg kick.

What do we mean by training rules?

We define training rules as regulations pertaining to swimmer conduct and sacrifice. These rules have to do with diet (e.g., eat no greasy foods) and sleep (e.g., must be in bed by 10:00 p.m.); with nonuse of alcohol (no beer, wine, whiskey) and nonprescribed drugs (no LSD); nonuse of tobacco (no smoking); and with kind and extent of outside activities (dancing, skiing). They may regulate swimmer conduct (no swearing) and appearance (no long hair or beards; suits and neckties must be worn on trips).

Although you must suggest the rules that you want to have included, you will be wise to invite discussion by the team members and obtain the agreement of each member to obey the regulations. Parents should be informed about the rules the team has adopted in order that they may assist their sons and daughters to abide by the agreement.

What do we mean by swimmer diet?

We define the swimmer diet as one including the essential food elements but with a higher than normal ratio of proteins (meat, bread, vegetables, eggs), with a lower ratio of fats (25%, or less, of the total of calories in the diet), and one that does not cause stomach upset. Strict diets have no value in themselves. In fact, self-denial of wanted foods and the following of an unfamiliar diet may create tensions that are harmful.

The swimmer's weight should be watched carefully. He will consume more calories than he did before he started training and yet, because he is burning more calories to meet the demands of exercise, he should show little gain in weight. He will be likely to lose weight during the first two or three weeks of training, gain back that loss during the next two or three weeks, and then either maintain a constant weight or gain slightly in weight while training continues.

Although some research indicates that neither the time when a meal is eaten nor what is eaten appreciably affects the quality of performance, the common practice of coaches is to have their swimmers eat at a time from two to four hours before competing. Obviously, however, if final races in an age group competition follow closely upon a day-long series of trail heats, eating will be catch-as-catch-can rather than on a precise schedule or according to a restricted diet plan.

What do we mean by warm-up?

We define warm-up as a method employed to warm the muscles, set action rhythms immediately prior to competition, adjust cardio-respiratory processes to the great demands that follow upon the discharge of the starter's gun, and hasten the onset of second wind.

Research in this general area has resulted in conflicting findings, but studies of warm-up as specifically related to swimming reveal some benefits result from hot showers, calisthenics, massage, and swimming. Common practice among coaches is to have swimmers sprint several pool lengths or partial lengths and to swim one or more single lengths to reaffirm pace and rhythm. Divers engage in flexibility and relaxation exercises and perform practice dives when the rules of the competition permit.

A few deep breaths taken before the race or dive provide two benefits: they have a relaxing effect, and they facilitate breath-holding at the race start and during the springboard dive.

There has been some research indication that, following one or two false starts, heart rate, ventilation, and oxygen absorption are reduced and reaction time is slowed, indicating impairment of benefits gained by warm-up.

What do we mean by phases of training?

We define the phases of training as that which is done during the parts into which a total season may be divided. The common phases are described in the following table.

The length of the swimming season will vary greatly among teams, and you must adapt to the nature of the coaching job you have. Most high school competition is confined within specified starting and ending dates, but some nonschool teams will train continuously throughout the entire year. Whatever the length of season, your objective must be to have your swimmers and divers improve steadily and to bring each individual to his peak level of performance, neither too soon nor too late, at season's end when the most important meets occur.

TABLE 10:5
PHASES OF THE TRAINING SEASON

Season Phase	Major Emphasis During Each Phase	Methods Used to Achieve the Objectives Set for Each Phase
Early preseason.	Emphasis during this phase is upon learning and refining techniques, Laying the groundwork for conditioning, Acquiring all-around abilities, and establishing team morale.	*Specific objectives are achieved by:* Practicing strokes, pacing, starts, turns, springboard diving fundamentals; Isometric, isotonic exercises; Interval training at short distances; Distance swimming, especially butterfly; Swimming all strokes and all distances; and Swimmers helping each other, divers helping each other, and veterans helping novices.
Late preseason.	Emphasis during this phase is upon perfecting techniques, specializing in events, and stressing conditioning.	*Specific objectives are achieved by* practicing strokes, starts, and turns; Pacing in specific events, and refining performances of selected dives, and Stepped-up isometric, isotonic, and interval training.
Competitive season.	Emphasis during this phase is upon continuing rigorous training, Improving performances in events, and Resting.	*Specific objectives are achieved by:* Time trials for team positions; Diving for score as in a meet; and Easing off work on the day before and the day of meet, especially if away from home.
Postseason.	Emphasis during this phase is upon tapering off, and Experimenting.	*Specific objectives are achieved by* de-conditioning gradually, by avoiding abrupt cessation of all physical exercise, and by trying new techniques and new dives.

(Water polo may be an important part of postseason and preseason phases.)

What do we mean by fatigue?

We define fatigue as the normal tiredness which occurs at the end of a race or day and from which recovery is accomplished within minutes after the race or after a night of rest. We define chronic fatigue as excessive tiredness that is caused by day-after-day practice sessions that are so demanding that the rest between days is insufficient for recovery.

What do we mean by staleness?

We define staleness as a physical condition characterized by lethargy and reduced quality of physical performance and resulting from excessive fatigue. We define it also as a state of mind characterized by listlessness, boredom, irritability, and loss of interest and caused by overfatigue or by the monotony of an overlong season. The cure is to lighten practice sessions, emphasize fun-type games, employ new methods to motivate, and avoid day-after-day repetition of the same practice routine.

COACHING THE SWIMMER

There are three methods of conditioning swimmers that are used by almost all coaches. Each makes a singular contribution and all three may be utilized to advantage. If any one of them must be chosen and the other two excluded, we believe that interval training is the one making the greatest contribution. Following is a table that may be used as a guide in the employment of these methods. Each method should be preceded by a warm-up.

TABLE 10:6
SWIMMER CONDITIONING METHODS

Conditioning Method	Desired Primary Outcomes	Information Concerning the Method	Examples
Isometric exercise.	Muscle strength by increasing muscle size.	A muscle used neither shortens nor lengthens in an act of pushing or pulling pressure applied against a fixed object. The position assumed is identical to position of the body part in performing stroke mechanics.	Standing, the swimmer extends his arms forward at shoulder level and presses down upon a fixed shoulder-high surface. Each contraction is sustained for 5-15 seconds and is repeated 5-25 times. Each between-contraction rest period is of the same duration as the length of time of contraction.

Table 10:6–Swimmer Conditioning Methods (continued)

Isotonic exercise.	Endurance (with light weights and many repetitions). Strength (with heavy weights and fewer repetitions).	Muscles contract and expand and joints move. Weights are lifted or pressed upward. It is best that the movement resemble the movement of a body part in performing stroke mechanics.	Similar exercises are devised for each muscle group used in the stroke. Lying on his back with his arms extended beyond his head and parallel to his body, the swimmer grasps a 15-pound bar weight, raises it to position directly overhead, and then returns it slowly to starting position, repeating 25 times.  The usual frequency and amount of isotonic exercise is three days a week, 30 minutes a day.
Interval training (repeat training).	Endurance. Strength.	Bursts of swimming, kicking, or pulling effort are alternated with equal periods of rest. The method may be modified by making rest two or three times as long as effort, and vice versa.	The swimmer swims 100 yards, rests 60 seconds, and repeats 10 times. The swimmer kicks 25 yards, rests 20 seconds, and repeats 20 times. Three swimmers engage in a continuous relay, continuing until each has swum 25 times. For example, swimmer No. 1 swims 25 yards to the shallow end of the pool, No. 2 swims from shallow to deep, and No. 3 swims from deep to shallow. Then the cycle is repeated without pause. The relay may be modified by using 5 or 7 swimmers, by increasing or decreasing the number of repetitions or by increasing or decreasing the distance swum each time.

Planning the swimming practice session

The nature of the practice session on any one day will depend upon the phase of the season, the ages and abilities of the team members, the number of team members, the nature of the facilities and the degree to which they are available, the amount of assistance available, and the number of sessions to be held each day.

Obviously, you will not use the same routines for a group of youngsters in a Parks and Recreation Department Learn-To-Swim program as you would use for a topflight college team. You must use good judgment and limit your requirements to the capabilities of your team candidates.

In general, the tempo of, and the demands made by, the practice session will accelerate as the season progresses. In the beginning, for example, interval training may specify swimming 25 yards ten times; during the competitive season, twenty repetitions of a 100-yard sprint may be required.

A common pattern includes a squad meeting, flexibility exercises, warm-up by exercises or swimming, technique drills, kicking and pulling drills, pacing drills, interval training and, as may be appropriate, swimming time trials and scoring of dives. Candidates for team positions will differ greatly in needs and abilities, and you must make the necessary adaptations to those individual differences. Table 10:7 presents examples of a practice session for one day. (Each may also include exercises, warm-up, technique drills, and pacing drills. High school and college teams probably will use interval training repeats.)

The relative amounts of kicking and pulling practice that you have your free-style swimmers do should be related to research findings which indicate that, in the crawl stroke, from three to four times the amount of energy (oxygen used) is required to move the body at a given speed by kick only as is necessary to move the body at the same speed by arm-pull only. Consequently, most successful coaches assign much more time to pulling practice than they do to kicking practice. Moreover, you will observe that, in distance free-style races, the majority of expert swimmers will emphasize the arm action and will use few or only occasional leg kicks.

TABLE 10:7
SAMPLE ONE-DAY CONDITIONING ROUTINES

Novice team	Good high school or agency (e.g., YMCA) team	Good college or A.A.U. team
One 200-yard swim. Two 50-yard swims. Four 25-yard kick. Four 25-yard pull. Four 25-yard swims.	Five 100-yard sprints. Four 50-yard kick. Four 50-yard pull. Four 50-yard swims. Four 25-yard kick. Six 25-yard pull. Fifteen 25-yard swims.	Twenty 100-yard sprints. Four 50-yard kick. Eight 50-yard pull. Eight 50-yard sprints. Twenty 25-yard sprints.
or	or	or
One 400-yard swim. Two 50-yard kick. Three 50-yard pull. Eight 25-yard sprints.	Two 200-yard swims. One 400-yard kick. One 400-yard pull. Four 100-yard sprints. Ten 25-yard sprints.	One 400-yard swim. One 800-yard kick. One 1200-yard pull. Ten 100-yard swims.

Organizing the practice session

The first thing to do is to group your swimmers by stroke and by swimming speed; at times you will want to segregate those swimming the same stroke, at other times you will prefer to have all the swimmers in a group swimming at the same speed regardless of stroke. Space and time must be utilized to best advantage; your aim is to accommodate the greatest possible number of swimmers without sacrificing efficiency. In order to prevent monotony, daily sessions should be varied.

Chart 10:1 depicts and explains the various methods of organizing swimmers in the water for practice sessions.

CHART 10:1
FORMATIONS FOR PRACTICE SESSIONS

A. Basic Formations

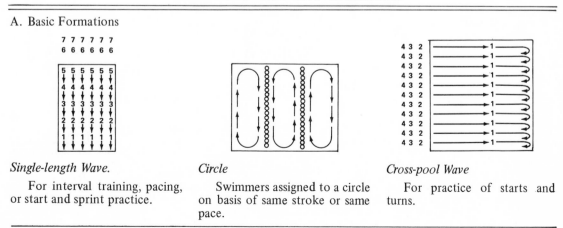

Single-length Wave.

For interval training, pacing, or start and sprint practice.

Circle

Swimmers assigned to a circle on basis of same stroke or same pace.

Cross-pool Wave

For practice of starts and turns.

B. Interval Training

Each group (1's and 2's) continues for an even number of lengths (2, 4, 6, etc.), or for the same number of seconds (30, 60, 120, etc.). Kick, pull or swim may be specified.

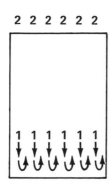 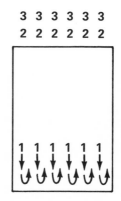

With two swimmers comprising each group, the length of time of rest is equal to the length of time of effort.

With three swimmers comprising each group, the length of time of rest is double the length of time of effort.

Putting two groups at opposite ends of pool is recommended for experienced swimmers; this can cut down rest periods and congestion. Swimmers in group 2 start from one end of pool as soon as swimmers in Group 1 (who started at the other end and will finish at other end) have half-completed the last length of the swim.

C. Continuous Relay

This is a form of interval training; the more swimmers on each team, the greater the rest between swims. Repeats continue until each swimmer has swum a predetermined number of times. Each team may be composed of any odd number of swimmers for odd-length swims, or each team may be composed of any odd or even number of swimmers for swimming relay legs comprised of an even number of pool lengths. The techniques may be used for length-of-pool or cross-pool relays. The illustration below shows an economical use of water space (single length, an odd number of swimmers on each team).

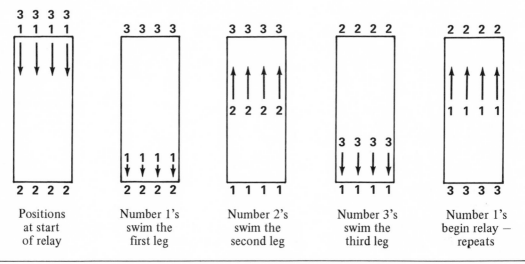

| Positions at start of relay | Number 1's swim the first leg | Number 2's swim the second leg | Number 3's swim the third leg | Number 1's begin relay — repeats |

D. Combination Methods

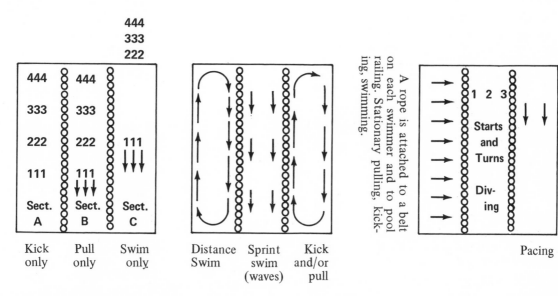

| Kick only | Pull only | Swim only | Distance Swim | Sprint swim (waves) | Kick and/or pull | Pacing |

Do kick assignment in Section A, move to Section B and do pull assignment, move to Section C and do swim assignment.

Teaching the skills for swimming competition

The techniques for performing strokes have been described in Chapter 4. The mechanics of starts and turns are illustrated here. Before teaching, you should read the rule books carefully with reference to requirements stipulated by those rules.

The start from standing position. The freestyle, breaststroke, and butterfly starts require coordination of arm, leg, and body actions in an explosive outward springing effort. The most common type of arm action for the start is shown in Chart 10:2.

The backstroke start. The better the facilities are, the easier the backstroke start is to perform. Grips for the hands and nonslip surfaces for the placement of the feet are important aids. This start also is shown in Charts 10:2 and 10:4.

CHART 10:2
THE RACING START — ACTIONS PRIOR TO WATER ENTRY

Technique	Illustration	Major and/or Common Performance Errors
THE START FOR CRAWL AND BUTTERFLY STROKES, AND FOR BREASTSTROKE A. Assume a standing position in a semicrouch, with bend at hips and knees, balance forward, heels flat, toes over the forward edge of starting stand and hands about 12 inches in front of knees.		A. Assuming a straight standing position with high center of balance. Having the body weight too far forward or too far backward.

261

B. At the starting signal, lower the upper body and head, bend the knees, let the body weight fall forward off balance, raise the shoulders and arms, and begin the arm swing upward, backward, and downward.

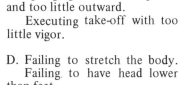

B. Failing to let the body drop lower during arm swing.
  Holding the head too high.

C. Continue the circular arm action vigorously forward and outward as the legs straighten vigorously in a spring to propel the body outward.

C. Having arm swing precede or follow leg spring.
  Springing too much upward and too little outward.
  Executing take-off with too little vigor.

D. Assume a stretched position with extended arms covering the ears and with the body inclined slightly downward.

D. Failing to stretch the body.
  Failing to have head lower than feet.
  Arching body in flight.
  Letting hips sag.

THE START FOR BACKSTROKE:

E. Grasp the starting grips, place the feet against the wall at water level, draw the body into tight tuck with the chin above the knees and eyes looking toward the feet.

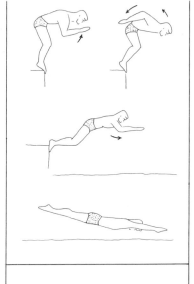

E. Having arms straight and body away from knees.
  Inclining head backward.

F. At the starting signal, vigorously cast the head backward, and the arms sideward and backward.
  Straighten the legs vigorously to thrust the body outward.
  Lift the hips over the water.

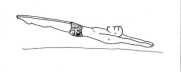

F. Casting the arms forward and downward, with wrists hyperextended.
  Springing upward instead of outward.
  Executing take-off with too little vigor.
  Having arm action precede leg action.

G. Assume a stretch position with the arms covering the ears, eyes looking upward, and the body inclined slightly downward.

G. Overarching the back.
  Inclining head and arms too far backward.
  Bringing chin toward chest.
  Bending hips in pike.
  Failing to have head lower than feet.

The water position. During the dives, the distance achieved varies according to ability and other factors. The dive for free-style and butterfly starts is relatively shallow and short. The dive for the breaststroke start is deeper and longer. It is the comparison between the speed at which the swimmer moves on the surface and the speed at which he moves during the dive that determines his decision as to depth and distance of the dive; the faster the swimming pace of the race, the shallower and shorter the dive is likely to be. Chart 10:3 shows the depths and distances attained by mature experts.*

The breaststroke swimmer seeks to achieve a roller-coaster effect using his body weight to obtain depth and his buoyancy to gain an additional thrust forward as he rises to the surface. Moreover, the breaststroke swimmer is permitted by the rules to execute one and *only* one complete stroke while he is submerged. Chart 10:4 describes the position under the water for all variations cited above.

CHART 10:3
AVERAGE DIVE-DISTANCES ATTAINED BY SUPERIOR COLLEGIATE SWIMMERS*

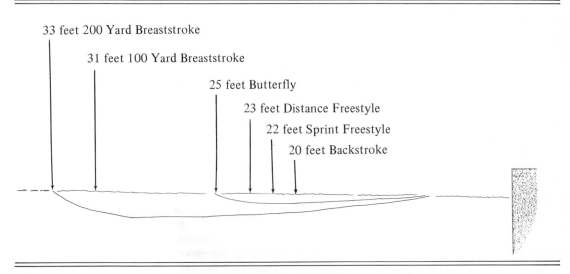

33 feet 200 Yard Breaststroke

31 feet 100 Yard Breaststroke

25 feet Butterfly

23 feet Distance Freestyle

22 feet Sprint Freestyle

20 feet Backstroke

*Data calculated at 1969 NCAA Swimming and Diving Championships

CHART 10:4
THE RACING START — ACTIONS AFTER WATER ENTRY

Technique	Illustration	Major and/or Common Performance Errors
THE START FOR CRAWL AND BUTTERFLY STROKES:		
A. Obtain a depth of 6-14 inches.		A. Making the dive too deep or too shallow.
B. Keep the body in a straight extended position from fingertips to toes.	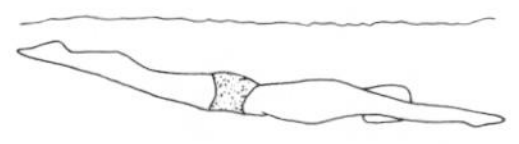	B. Having a back arch, (thus causing the body to surface too soon).
C. Begin kicking as the upward rise begins.	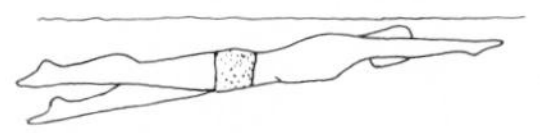	C. Continuing underwater glide after impetus is lost.
D. Pull through with one (crawl) or both (butterfly) arms immediately before surfacing.	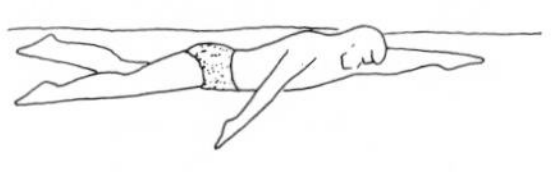	D. Surfacing abruptly (vertically) instead of on a gradual upward plane.
E. Obtain a distance of from 12 feet (youngsters) to 25 feet (college-age experts).		E. Pausing to breathe before beginning the arm stroke.

THE START FOR
BREASTSTROKE:

F. Obtain a depth of 18-30 inches.

F. Making the dive too deep or too shallow.

G. Keep the body in a straight extended position.
   As speed from the dive wanes, pull both arms through to the thighs.
   Take a brief glide.

G. Failing to tuck the chin toward the chest to prevent premature rise upward.
   Failing to glide briefly.

H. Recover the arms to extension forward.
   Deliver a breaststroke kick as the body nears the surface.

H. Kicking before arms are extended forward.
   Kicking when too deep below the surface.

I. Obtain a distance of from 18 feet (youngsters) to 35 feet (college-age experts).

I. Surfacing too soon or too abruptly.

THE START FOR
BACKSTROKE:

J. Obtain a depth of 6-14 inches.

J. Going too deep or too shallow.

K. Keep the body in a straight extended position.

K. Having back arched.
   Pointing fingers downward.
   Having body in semipike with arms extended skyward.

L. Begin the leg kick as upward rise begins.

L. Gliding too long before recovering arms and legs.

M. Pull through with one arm stroke immediately before surfacing.

M. Pulling through too soon before surfacing.

N. Get a distance of from 8 feet (youngsters) to 20 feet (college-age experts).

N. Surfacing too soon or too abruptly.

The turn. There are three distinct turns used in competition, as illustrated and described in Chart 10:5.

Technique	Illustrations	Major and/or Common Performance Errors
THE TUMBLE TURN (FLIP TURN) FOR CRAWL STROKE: A. Prepare to perform a somersault when about 3 feet from the wall. Leave one arm alongside the body, pull the other arm partially or completely through, to thigh.		A. Turning too close to or too far away from the wall.
B. Lower the head and shoulders. Pike at the hips and bend the knees to put the body in tuck position.		B. Failing to put the body in a tuck position.

C. Lift the heels and hips upward vigorously.
   Begin the performance of a one-half body twist.
		C. Failing to bring the chin toward the knees.
		   Failing to thrust the hips and heels upward and toward the wall.

D. Place the feet flat against the wall.
   Cover the ears with the extended arms.
   Continue the half-twist.
		D. Placing only one foot on the wall.
		   Failing to extend the arms.
		   Placing the feet too high or too low on wall.

E. Spring vigorously away from the wall. Complete the half-twist.		E. Springing before the feet are set properly and before the upper body is in a straight position.
F. Stretch to streamline the body in the glide.		F. Failing to straighten the arms and stretch the body. Raising head from between arms during glide.
G. Begin kicking. Pull through with one arm immediately·before surfacing.		G. Beginning arm pull too soon before surfacing or beginning the pull after surfacing.

265

THE TURN FOR BREAST
AND BUTTERFLY STROKES:

H. Continue to stroke until the wall is contacted with the arms extended. Touch with both hands at the same level and at the same time.

H. Gliding into the wall (thus losing the momentum to drive the body to the wall and hold it there).

I. Let the elbows bend as the leg kick forces the body to wall. Bend at the hips and knees to put the body in a tuck.

(A flip turn may be used in butterfly, but the body must be perfectly on the breast when contact is made and when contact is broken.)

I. Failing to bend the elbows at contact with the wall.
    Failing to draw the body into a tight tuck.

J. With the body in close to the wall and in a tight tuck, turn the head and shoulders in one horizontal direction and legs in the other direction. Bring the hands in toward chest.

J. Raising the head too high, causing the feet to sink too low.
    Failing to draw the arms in close to the sides.
    Making the turn without vigor.

K. At the end of the pivot, place the feet flat against the wall and cover the ears with the extended arms.

K. Failing to place both feet properly.
    Placing the feet too high or too low on the wall.

L. Spring vigorously from the wall. Glide briefly with the body streamlined.

L. Springing before the feet are set properly and before the arms are extended and covering the ears.

M. Pull the arms completely through to the sides and glide briefly (breaststroke), or deliver kicks to drive the body to surface (butterfly).

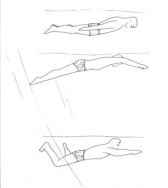

M. Pulling through too soon or too late.

N. Recover the arms to extended position and deliver a frog kick to drive the body to the surface (breaststroke).

N. Arching the back and surfacing too soon.
    Kicking too soon or too late. Beginning a second arm stroke before surfacing.

THE TUMBLE TURN (FLIP TURN) FOR BACKSTROKE:

O. Prepare to somersault backward when about 3 feet from the wall. Continue a vigorous kick. Contact the wall underwater with the palm of one hand and with the fingers pointing toward the pool bottom.

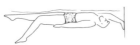

O. Turning too close to, or too far away from, the wall.
Contacting the wall at too high a level.

P. Pike at the hips and bend the knees.
Thrust the knees and feet upward and forward toward the wall as the body somersaults backward.

P. Failing to pike at the hips and bend the knees.
Failing to cast the feet and knees upward and toward the wall with vigor.

Q. Pivot on the shoulders (if the feet circle sideward as the legs are brought toward the wall), or begin a half-twist of upper body (if legs are brought vertically over the body).

Q. Failing to pivot or to start a half-twist.

R. Place the feet flat against the wall. Bring the arms into position to cover the ears. Continue the half-twist.

R. Failing to place both feet properly.
Placing the feet too high or too low on the wall.

S. Streamline the upper body.
Spring vigorously from the wall.
Complete a half-twist.

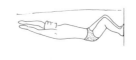

S. Springing before the feet are set properly.
Having the body in semipike or arched position.
Having the hands higher or lower than the shoulders.

T. Begin the leg kick and pull through with one arm immediately before surfacing.

T. Beginning the arm pull too soon before surfacing or beginning the pull after surfacing.

COACHING THE DIVER

Several methods are used to prepare the diver for the demands of competition. All experienced coaches place a high value on flexibility. All recognize that flexibility is of limited usefulness without strength to supplement it — the ability to move gracefully must be combined with the ability to apply controlled power. All recognize the relationship of strength of leg and shoulders to the force and rhythm of the approach, hurdle, and take-off. In short, physical condition plays a vital part in the determination of the quality of diving performance. Table 10:8 indicates some of the possible conditioning procedures.

TABLE 10:8
DIVER-CONDITIONING METHODS

Conditioning Method	Desired Primary Outcomes	Information Concerning the Method	Example of Use of the Method
Running up stairs.	Leg strength.	Leg muscles are developed through effort required to lift body weight. The efficiency of heart, blood vessels, and lungs is increased.	Progression is applied by beginning with a few steps and few repetitions and by increasing assignments as the diver's condition improves.
Jump reach.	Leg strength.	Leg and shoulder muscles are developed through the effort required. Stretch for reach puts the body in full extension.	Standing, the diver uses leg spring and arm swing to attempt to bring the fingers of both hands to touch a lightweight bar suspended at appropriate heights.
Distance running.	General body development. Endurance.	Muscles are developed. The efficiency of heart, blood vessels, and lungs is increased.	The diver begins with short distances and low speeds, and his assignments are increased as his condition improves. Soft surfaces (grass or composition track rather than concrete, gym floor or cinder track) should be used to avoid shin splints.
Rope jumping.	Leg strength. Nerve-muscle coordination.	Muscles are developed. Agility and balance are improved.	A wide variety of children's stunts may be used (e.g., two-foot jumps and skip steps, slow time and quick time, forward and backward rope swing).
Isotonic and isometric exercise.	Muscle strength. Flexibility.	The exercises strengthen specific muscles of back, side, and stomach, and improve mobility and extension in specific joints.	Lying on his back with his arms extended and parallel to his body, the diver raises a bar weight overhead and toward his feet until his chest contacts his thighs. In isotonic and calisthenic exercise, movements should not be explosive lest unrestrained overextension cause the tearing of muscle fibers. Stretching should be felt but pain should not accompany it.
Calisthenic exercise.	Muscle strength. Flexibility.	The purposes are to strengthen specific muscles, stretch muscles, increase range and ease of movements in joints and spine, and emphasize extension of the ankles and toes.	The diver emphasizes bending, extending, and twisting. He continues this type of exercise throughout the season.

Participation in other sports.	General body development.	The purposes are to develop muscles and benefit heart, blood vessels, and lungs. Incidental values may result (e.g., stretching in volleyball spiking and in basketball rebounding).	During the first and last phases of the season, the diver plays non-contact sports that he enjoys, and avoids hazardous sports (e.g., skiing) that may lead to such injuries as ankle sprains and leg fractures.
Trampoline.	General body development.	Position techniques (tuck, pike layout) are learned.	It is primarily during the early preseason and postseason phases of training that the diver utilizes these devices. His purpose is to learn the techniques of new dives before practicing them on the diving board.
Tumbling belt.	Acquisition of new dives.	Extending, twisting, and somersaulting techniques of dives are learned.	

Planning the diving-practice session

At this point, it is appropriate to mention again that the conditions you will face will not be identical in different situations. Specifically, in this instance, the level of divers' abilities in one situation will differ greatly from the level of divers' abilities in another situation. Consequently, no one formula will apply in all cases without modification. What is to be done during the session will vary widely in kind and amount in accordance with the unlike characteristics of the different coaching positions. It will be your task, in each job that you hold, to adapt the information in Table 10:9 to conditions as you find them in that job.

TABLE 10:9
PLANNING THE DIVING PRACTICE SESSION*

Detail to be Considered	Recommendations Concerning the Detail
The frequency of practice sessions.	Diving sessions should be conducted five days per week.
The length of the practice session.	The duration of the practice session should be from one and one-half hour to two hours. The length of time of practice should be the same or slightly less on the day before competition.
The practice of required dives.	The diver should perform two or three repetitions, possibly four or five repetitions, of each dive. He should do all repetitions of one dive, then proceed to the next dive. He should perform the forward, back, and reverse dives in pike or layout position, inward dive in pike position, and the forward with ½ twist in layout position. He should practice them in the group order as listed in the diving tables (forward, back, reverse, inward, twist).
The practice of optional dives.	The diver should perform two or three, and possibly four or five, repetitions of each dive. He should practice them in the group order as listed in the diving tables.
The learning/teaching of new dives.	The diver should learn simple dives first and then proceed to more complex dives. He should first learn dives with headfirst, rather than feetfirst, entry. He should perfect dives on the one-meter board before attempting them on the three-meter board.
The following of an exercise program.	The diver should exercise five days a week, and for five to ten minutes each day before practice on the board. He should place more emphasis on flexibility than on strength.

Table 10:9–Planning the Diving Practice Session (continued)

Exercise on the trampoline.	The diver should place emphasis on diving mechanics rather than on stunts or development of leg strength. Not all coaches agree on its inclusion as a training device. The majority of those who advocate trampoline use recommend a time duration of thirty to sixty minutes, five days a week.
The use of Sand Pit and Diving Belt.	The diver should emphasize fundamentals (approach, hurdle, take-off) and techniques of somersault and twist dives. Gymnastic exercises (tumbling, apparatus) are beneficial.
Observation.	The diver benefits from watching experts in live action or watching movies of experts, and from seeing movies of himself or T-V replay of himself in action.

*Adapted from Lephart, Sigmund A., *A Study of the Diving Training Procedures Used by Outstanding Diving Coaches,* unpublished Master's thesis, University of Illinois, 1962.

Organizing the diving practice session

When too many divers are practicing on one board during a practice session, none will improve greatly and each of them will be unhappy about the small amount of practice he is able to obtain. When the session is haphazard in nature and is without obvious goals to be achieved on that day, the lack of organization will be reflected in the divers' attitudes and slower progress. Table 10:10 shows some of the actions you should be prepared to take to improve the quality of the diving session.

TABLE 10:10
THE ORGANIZATION OF THE DIVING PRACTICE SESSION*

General Actions to be Taken	Specific Actions to Increase Practice Session Benefits
The determination of the number of divers during a practice session.	Six divers can be accommodated with good results during a practice session on one board. More will be accomplished if the number is four or less. The number must be related to the attention the coach gives to each diver (e.g., use of T-V replay; the coach cannot comment on the replay and watch another diver at the same time).
The determination of the time of board-practice.	Preferably, the time of practice should be when swimmers are not practicing (if there is no separate diving area), and when both coach and divers are free of other commitments. A time when the coach can be present is strongly advised (to avoid negligence), but it is possible for capable divers to help each other (divers help each other and depend on each other far more than is true of swimmers).
The assignment of divers to practice times.	Grouping the divers by ability is best but time commitment conflicts (work schedule, school classes, other activities) may prevent this. Divers who are close friends or of the same temperament communicate better and, therefore, letting divers decide with whom they will practice may be quite advantageous.
The statement of the objectives of the practice period.	At the start of the day's practice session, you should make known a general schedule of order in which divers will perform, the plan for the day, and the theme of the session that will apply to all. Because each diver is different, you should tell each one what fundamentals he will stress on that day, what dives he will perform, and how many of each of them. You may have cause to make changes, but you will have made it evident that there was advance planning.

The use of visual aids.	The showing of movies of experts, particularly as loop films, need not alter the time schedule; each diver can view them and relate his own experiences to them, while awaiting his turn on the board. The same is true of photographs and diagrams of correct form.
The scheduling of exercises.	Most daily strength exercises and flexibility exercises should precede the practice session on the diving board.

*Adapted from Lephart, Sigmund A., *A Study of the Diving Training Procedures Used by Outstanding Diving Coaches*, unpublished Master's thesis, University of Illinois, 1962.

Saving long and short dives

While the diver is in flight, actions to save the dive should not include such major ones as assuming a pike position to compensate for a short forward dive in layout position or arching the lower region of the back to compensate for a long forward dive. Acceptable actions include depressions of the head for a short forward dive, elevation of the head for a long forward dive, or depression or elevation of the upper chest or back. If position error is gross, limited elevation or depression of the arms may be used.

As the diver is entering the water, long dives and short dives may be partially saved by underwater actions shown in the following chart.

CHART 10:6
EXAMPLES OF ACTIONS TO SAVE SHORT AND LONG DIVES

A. Short Back Dive or Short Reverse Dive:

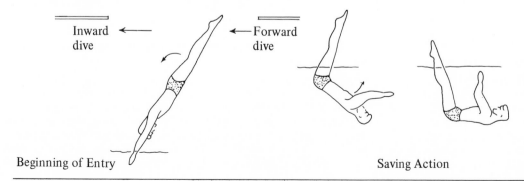

B. Short Inward Dive or Short Forward Dive:

271

Chart 10:6—Examples of Actions to Save Short and Long Dives (continued)

C. Long Back Dive or Long Reverse Dive:

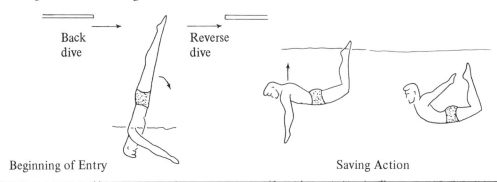

Back dive   Reverse dive

Beginning of Entry   Saving Action

D. Long Inward Dive or Long Forward Dive:

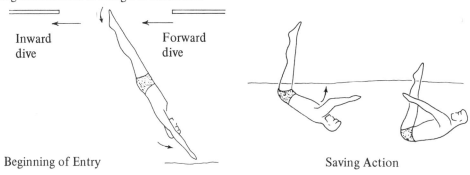

Inward dive   Forward dive

Beginning of Entry   Saving Action

COACHING THE SWIMMING AND DIVING TEAM

Many of the coaching tasks you will perform are related to the total team more than to the swimmer or diver specifically. You will be the general in charge of all the troops. You will be the coordinator who must fit all of the parts into a cohesive unit. You will be the engineer who must see that the machine, as a whole, runs with maximum efficiency.

Recruiting and Utilizing Assistance

Some beginning coaches try to do everything without obtaining help from anyone. One of the reasons is that they fear that status may be impaired and their abilities questioned. Actually, the better coaches are those who have many helpers and thus are free to devote themselves to the more important tasks.

Competence in delegating tasks is a vital part of the utilization of the assistance of others. There must be a clear understanding that the work is to be done as you want it to be done; there must, for example, be no contradiction between instructions given by you to team members and instructions given by a helper. In all matters in which no specific directions have been given by you, the assistant must come to you for direction before acting. Offers for help must be subject to your evaluation and approval; you would not accept an offer to provide transportation of team members if the driver were intoxicated and the automobile were in a dangerous condition. In the main, you will find that people *want* to help and will continue to devote time and effort so long as they feel needed and wanted.

When a job is done, and at times along the way, be sure to express your appreciation. Give praise and acknowledgment on appropriate occasions, and you will find that you have sown the seeds that produce additional willing assistance.

Following is a table that indicates a few of the many tasks that may be delegated in part or in total. You should expand this chart, adding items as they occur to you throughout your coaching career.

TABLE 10:11
PERSONS WHO MAY ASSIST THE COACH

Tasks Other Persons May Perform to Help the Coach	Persons who are Suitable to Perform Particular Tasks					
	Team Manager	Parents and Parents' Committees	Organization Members and Administrators	Candidates Not Selected to Team	Present Team Members	Former Team Members
Coaching					X	X
Record keeping	X			X		
Swimmer timing	X	X	X	X	X	X
Meet officiating		X	X	X		X
Transporting teams		X	X			
Entertaining guests	X	X	X			X
Obtaining awards		X	X			
Writing letters	X		X			
Telephoning	X	X				
Scheduling	X		X			
Obtaining officials	X	X	X			
Planning banquets	X	X	X			
Obtaining publicity	X	X	X			X

Motivating the Swimmer and Diver

In addition to showing interest and enthusiasm, conducting well-organized practice sessions, being victorious in meets, and obtaining publicity for the team, the wise coach will employ additional methods to motivate each individual to greater effort and to build and sustain team morale. Following are some of the things he may do.

TABLE 10:12
METHODS FOR MOTIVATING THE SWIMMER AND DIVER

General Methods to Motivate	Suggestions to the Coach Concerning Specific Methods to Motivate Members of the Team
Establishing Relationship with team members.	Treat all team members alike, show no favoritism, grant no special privileges. Insist on punctuality and regular attendance at practice sessions. Emphasize team-member self-discipline and group commitment to standards. Make practice sessions rigorous; morale is not built on easy training. Set a series of difficult but attainable goals for each individual. Keep graphs of improvement of each swimmer (times) and diver (points). Create an atmosphere of fun and friendliness as well as one of hard work.
Building pride in team and self:	Display awards and citations won by team and individuals. Display the pictures and membership of teams for each year. Maintain an up-to-date school and league record board. In trophy case or on bulletin board, post a picture of Swimmer-of-the-Week.
General.	Publish fact sheets for home meets. Tell about the competing teams, meet time and place, admission prices. Deliver copies to news media, to parents and to all offices and switchboards of the organization sponsoring your team.

Table 10:12–Methods for Motivating the Swimmer and Diver (continued)

At meets.	Construct outcome-prediction charts before the meet. Involve team members in plotting strategy.
	Give dignity to the sport by establishing efficient meet administration.
	Identify swimmers by name plates at lane ends and divers by announcement.
	Have all team members enter onto the deck in a group, require them to sit together rather than with girl friends or scattered among the spectators, and encourage them to cheer for their teammates.
	Supply the announcer with information on records and about individuals.
	Create spectator enthusiasm by keeping them completely informed. Tell them the running score of the meet, the point values of places in events.
	Use an unofficial big-face clock or have the announcer count off the seconds when a record time may be made. Involve the spectator by making him feel he is part of what is going on.
On trips.	Publish an information sheet that tells the time and place of departure, time and place of arrival, where the team will stay, the time and place of the meet, the time of departure for home, and the time of arrival home. Give copies to team members, parents, and to offices and switchboards of the sponsoring organization.
	Cause team members to want to dress neatly, to be well-groomed, and to be considerate of others.
At season-end banquet.	Invite dignitaries to attend, give out awards for the season (inspirational, most improved, highest scholarship, most outstanding), and show movies and still pictures taken during the season.

Selecting Team Personnel

A major problem of the swimming coach is to make the best possible decisions when assigning individuals to the events in which they will compete. In the beginning, he should require that every candidate practice *all* strokes; the stroke which the candidate has chosen to swim may not be the one in which his potential is greatest. Moreover, the versatile swimmer is able to fill a vacancy created by the loss of a team member through illness or other cause.

Racing time trials and diving trials, in which team members vie for positions on the team, serve two purposes. They provide information that is helpful to the coach when he must submit his list of entrants, and they give competitive experience to the team members. These trials should approximate meet conditions; the time for rest between events and the order of events should be as they will be in the meet.

No selection of team members should be made without first constructing a chart of the strengths and weaknesses of the opponent. Based on such information you may, for example, decide to place your best butterfly swimmer, Jones, in the freestyle event because (a) your second-best butterfly swimmer is better than the best opponent in this event, and (b) your freestyle swimmers are weak and entering Jones in this event will add strength.

The major difference between the novice coach and the veteran one is that the latter has acquired an extensive store of knowledge that enables him to know what to anticipate as problems, how to obtain best results from the members of his team, and what decisions to make in each competitive situation. Table 10:13 presents a few ideas that illustrate the kinds of wisdom the coach should acquire and use during his years of coaching experience.

TABLE 10:13
ADDITIONAL COACHING SUGGESTIONS

Classification of Suggestion	Suggestions to the Team Coach Concerning Specific Ways to Make Coaching More Effective
Pertaining to the swimmer:	Make practices organized and demanding. Loafing, standing around, and lazy swimming create boredom. Organize so one group is resting while another is swimming (as in interval training).
During practice.	Although this is the age of specialization, all swimmers should be coached to swim all strokes.
	When coaching on pacing, group together the swimmers who need practice at the same pace.
	Vary the practice routines to keep interest high.
	For a change in routine and for benefits of continuous swimming, use "locomotives": the swimmer sprints for one length, cruises easily for one length, sprints two lengths, cruises two lengths, sprints three, cruises three, sprints four, cruises four, sprints five, cruises five, sprints six, cruises six, sprints seven, cruises seven, sprints eight, cruises eight, and then continues in descending distances from sprint seven and cruise seven down to sprint one and cruise one. You may set the maximum distance at any number of lengths you choose (e.g., 3, 4, 6, etc.) instead of eight.
	Group your swimmers by ability.
	Training is ineffective unless each swimmer expends near-maximum effort. A practice period exceeding 40-50 minutes probably means that the session is too easy.
	Have swimmers swim some single lengths without breathing.
	For continuous relays, make the teams of equal ability.
	In circle swimming, kicking or pulling, put the fastest man in the lead and the others to follow in descending order of speed ability. If there are marked differences in speed ability, permit passing of the slower swimmers by the faster ones.
During competition.	Instruct swimmers to concentrate on and react instantly to the discharge of the starter's gun.
	Instruct swimmers to look underwater to watch opponents on the side away from the breathing side.
	Instruct your swimmer that, if he is slightly behind and wants to pass an opponent, he should accelerate into the turn, come out of the turn fast, and move ahead before his opponent is aware of what is happening; tell him to do this when his opponent is breathing on the side toward your swimmer as they go into the turn, and is breathing on the side away from your swimmer after the turn.
	Instruct swimmers that they are never to glide into a turn or finish.
	Instruct swimmers to think pace and not to be thrown into panic by the opponent who sprints at the start and tires at the finish.
	Do not permit swimmers to shave their legs until just prior to trial heats of the championship meet. Shaving not only allows the swimmer to swim faster — it also causes him to believe he can.
	Although the conventional method for order-placement of men on a freestyle relay team is to have the fastest man swim in anchor (or last) position, consider placing the fastest man in lead-off position to increase the probability that your team will take the lead and the members swimming the following legs will be exposed to less rough water.

Table 10:13—Additional Coaching Suggestions (continued)

Pertaining to the diver:	Do not permit a diver to attempt a dive until you are sure that he knows what he is to do.
	Emphasize quality over quantity in practice dives. Value lies not in how many dives the diver performs but how he does them.
During practice.	Teach the diver to be self-reliant. If he is overly dependent upon you he may feel abandoned if you cannot be at his side when you are serving as a judge or secretary during competition.
	Instruct the diver to work constantly to acquire dives with a degree of difficulty higher than the ones he is able to do.
	Do not teach a new dive until the diver is ready.
	Teach the simpler dives first, then the more difficult.
During competition.	Coach divers to be members of the team. Often, divers consider themselves to be a group apart.
	Instruct the divers, before they turn in the lists of dives they will perform, to check the conditions that will prevail when they dive (lighting, spots on which they will fix eyes, spectator traffic) and to select dives accordingly.
	Instruct divers never to turn in a list of dives hastily or carelessly; the dives they list are the dives they must perform.
	Require your divers to be well-groomed and in attractive trunks, the diver's appearance makes an impression on judges.
	Make it clear to the diver that you are his coach and the only coach to whom he should listen; divers tend to be willing and eager to listen to anyone who will observe them and make comments, with the result that they become confused and unsure if comments vary.
Pertaining to both swimmers and divers.	Post the plan-for-the-day or present it in prepractice squad meeting so each swimmer and diver will know what he is to do and how and when.
During practice.	Coach with vigor and enthusiasm. The swimmers and divers will take their cue from you and respond in kind.
	Coach individuals as well as the team. Each swimmer and diver is different from the others; his structure, his attitudes, his objectives, and his physical condition will be unique to him as an individual. Your task will be to develop each individual to his full potential.
	Schedule the conditioning exercises to precede pool practice.
	With reference to competition, teach swimmers and divers to think for themselves. Teach each to decide what pace he will swim, what dives he will do, and why.
	Be sure that each swimmer and diver is mentally alert and ready.
	As far as is feasible, have all team members eat together and sightsee or go to movies together. This will be more difficult for divers because they must practice at different times than the swimmers.
	When leaving to go on a trip, or when leaving to return home, insist that all team members report to the assembly place on time.
	Recognize the excitable swimmer or diver and watch to see that he does not overextend himself in warm-up before the competition begins. Your manner with this type athlete must be calm.
	Counteract tension in the swimmer or diver by having him take deep breaths before his race or dive, having him exhale underwater as he submerges several times in shallow water, or having him move (the diver may engage in stretching and flexibility exercises, the swimmer may swim with a slow, ultra-loose stroke).
	Speak to every man after his event. Find some reason to praise him. Be vague and general if you must. But do not ignore him.

Postpone serious fault-finding until the next practice session. Be prepared to revive the spirits of a team member who is discouraged by a poor performance in a meet away from home. He may be aware that he was affected by poor visibility on turns, slippery end walls, rough water, overly warm or overly cold water temperatures, a different length of pool, distracting foot traffic or an unfamiliar diving board. But he may not be aware that anything that creates muscular and nervous tensions will rob the body of some of its energy and rhythm. Tensions may result from trying to maintain balance in a jolting bus, from fear of an airplane flight, from wearing insufficient clothing in cold weather, or from walking on slippery snow or ice. A break in the normal daily routine and adjustment to the strange pool also may be causes of tension.

ADMINISTERING A SWIMMING AND DIVING MEET

The things that should be done in planning and conducting a swimming and diving meet are many in number and the planning must begin days, perhaps months, before the day of the competition. Following is a table which shows some of these responsibilities. For the most part, they apply to the management of a championship meet but a portion will apply to a dual meet as well. You should be aware, also, that some of the procedures that must be followed are stated in the various official rule books and in league regulations. You should construct your own chart of duties and add to it continuously throughout your coaching career.

TABLE 10:14
ADMINISTRATIVE TASKS RELATIVE TO SWIMMING MEETS

Order of Performance	Examples of General Tasks	Examples of Specific Tasks
Advance planning.	Obtain approval of employer, association (e.g., State High School) or organization (e.g., AAU).	Set dates, times, and events. Avoid conflicts with other events, and especially with another meet.
	Prepare information bulletins and entry forms.	Explain the events, rules, awards, eligibility, housing, meals, practice times, coaches' meetings. Describe the pool and the diving facilities.
	Obtain publicity information.	Obtain facts on teams and individual entrants, including best individual performances.
Actions prior to meet.	Prepare meet forms.	Have slips or cards for officials, score forms for diving and swimming events, for heat and final events, dive listing, etc.
	Obtain officials.	Contact parents, citizens, faculty, coaches, or local officials' association.
	Arrange for tickets.	Plan for tickets, gate lists, gate passes, passout stamps, and admission of special guests. Obtain ticket sellers and takers and ushers.
	Obtain equipment.	Have a P.A. system, watches, score cards, typewriters, mimeograph machine, tables, chairs, award stand. Have awards ready.
	Print programs.	Include events, entrants, records, pictures.
	Obtain publicity.	Use newspapers, T-V, radio, posters, bulletins, and other media.
	Arrange facilities.	Provide lockers, towels, valuables checking, lost-and-found. Be sure toilets and spectator areas are clean.

Table 10:14—Administrative Tasks Relative to Swimming Meets (continued)

	Arrange hospitality.	Plan transportation, tours, parties, banquets.
	Assign competitors.	Check entry blanks, verify eligibility and dive lists. Assign competitors to heats, lanes, dive flight and order.
Actions during the meet.	Have equipment available.	Have paper forms, starting stands, lane lines, false-start line, backstroke overhead lines, diving flash cards, gun and blank shells, and scoreboard.
	Assign officials.	Issue forms, pencils, watches to them. Assign runners to pick up cards from judges and timers.
	Maintain records.	Mimeograph the results as events are completed.
Actions after the meet.	Check in and store equipment.	Remove equipment from pool and deck. Check in watches, pencils, flash cards.
	Obtain publicity.	Issue mimeographed copies of meet results to news media, or telephone results to media.
	Clean up pool area.	Mop the deck, check toilets, store found articles.
	Complete security.	Clear the area. Lock windows, doors and gates.
	Send summary to teams.	In days immediately after the meet, print a complete meet summary and mail copies to all teams in league.

OFFICIATING

A knowledge of officiating is important to you for three reasons. You will be involved in selecting officials, you may have to instruct and train officials, and you may be an official yourself.

In each of the three cases, certain evidences of competence must prevail lest an otherwise good competition be ruined by wrangling and bitterness caused by officiating errors and injustices.

Each official must know the precise manner in which he is to perform his duties. Each official and coach must know the duties and prerogatives of each officiating position as stipulated by current rules for competition under the jurisdiction of a particular sponsoring organization (e.g., AAU, YMCA, interscholastic, parks and recreation department, local league).

A good official is one who is well-informed, arrives early, has good rapport with coaches and competitors, and is properly attired, alert, decisive, and fair.

The official who must be reprimanded or rejected is one who arrives late, and has accepted the assignment in order to be seen and to talk with spectators rather than to serve in an important capacity. He is unkempt in appearance, inattentive, slow in filling out slips, indecisive, biased, and incompetent because of ignorance of the rules or for reasons of physical impairment.

Meet Officials and Their Duties

Each organization that sponsors a swimming team is almost certain to be governed by "ground rules" which apply to the league in which it participates. Some leagues adhere strictly to the universal one published by the National Collegiate Athletic Association (NCAA) and by the Amateur Athletic Union (AAU). Many agree on modifications in order to adapt to limitations imposed by inadequate facilities, participant ability levels, and lack of money.

In arranging the officials for a meet, you must adjust to the type and level of competition. A championship meet is more complex in organization and requires a far greater number of high quality officials than does a dual meet. Moreover, you may have difficulty in assembling more than a very few for your less important meets. In this instance your salvation lies in the provision that an official may perform more than one duty. Thus, you may arrange that the referee also acts as starter, judge of strokes and turns, and as diving referee and diving secretary. Place judges may serve as take-off judges and as diving judges. One person may be both announcer and scorer. When duties are combined in this manner, the number of officials necessary for a dual meet may be reduced to ten. Combining the duties of place judge and timer is not recommended but, under certain circumstances, you may find this action to be necessary; in this case, the number of officials would be further reduced.

Whenever officials can be obtained in sufficient number, the NCAA Swimming Rules Committee strongly recommends that the procedures specified concerning the duties of judges and timers in championship meets (the ballot system: two judges for each lane and three timers for each lane) should be used for dual meets.

Table 10:15 shows the meet officials and their duties as stipulated by the NCAA Collegiate-Scholastic Swimming Guide. Before undertaking to administer an AAU-sponsored competition, you must consult the AAU swimming rule book.

TABLE 10:15
COLLEGIATE-SCHOLASTIC SWIMMING OFFICIALS AND THEIR DUTIES*

Meet Official and Type of Meet	Duties of Swimming Meet Officials as Stated for Dual and Championship Contests
Referee: Dual and championship meets.	He enforces rules, decides questions not covered by the rules; assigns all officials to their duties; assigns contestants to events; sees that results are announced; prevents delay and prohibits the use of noisemakers, audits scorer's final tabulation; and notifies a disqualified swimmer of his disqualification.
Starter: Dual and championship meets.	He starts each race, declares false start penalties, and discharges the pistol when the leading swimmer has two lengths plus five yards to swim in a distance freestyle race.
Finish judges: Dual meet.	Two are needed to select the winner of first place and one additional judge for each of the other places. First, second, third, and fourth place judges select the swimmers finishing in first, second, third, and fourth places (if the ballot system or automatic judging system is not used).
Championship meet.	Two judges are assigned to each lane. The two lane judges in each lane determine the place won by the swimmer in that lane.
Chief finish judge: Dual and championship meets.	He checks the recorded decisions of place judges. He applies the official rules to resolve disagreements.
Timers: Dual meet.	Three are assigned to time the winner of first place (if the ballot system or an automatic timing device is not used). Each starts his watch on the flash of the starter's pistol and stops it with the finish of the winner of first place.
Championship meet.	Three timers are assigned to each lane. Each of the three timers records the time made by the swimmer in that lane. A fourth (alternate) timer becomes official if one of the original three timers fails to obtain a time.
Chief timer: Dual and championship meets.	He instructs the timers, reads all watches, and records the official time.
Scorer: Dual and championship meets.	He keeps a record of the results of each event and maintains a cumulative score of the meet.

Table 10:15—Collegiate-Scholastic Swimming Officials and Their Duties* (continued)

Chief Recorders:
    Dual and championship meets.

        They determine the finish order of swimmers in a heat or final race by adding the numerical values of the three ballots (two finish judge ballots and one timer ballot in each lane) and record the official time.

Take-off judges:
    Dual and championship meets.

        One is assigned for each relay team.
        Each determines whether a relay take-off is legal. He raises his hand when a violation occurs.

Stroke inspector:
    Dual and championship meets.

        He observes stroke form and raises his hand to signal violation.

Turn judge:
    Dual and championship meets.

        He observes turns made by swimmers and raises his hand to signal a violation.

Clerk of course:
    Dual and championship meets.

        He verifies that the contestants are in the proper lanes.

Announcer:
    Dual and championship meets.

        He announces the results of each event.

Diving referee:
    Dual and championship meets.

        He places the judges in position. He signals the judges to indicate their awards for each dive and announces the judges' awards for the dive. He rules on disqualification, failed dives, and balks.
        He cancels the lowest and highest award (unless there are only three judges). He supervises the computation to obtain final scores and signs the computation sheet.

Diving judges:
    Dual and championship meets.

        A minimum of three for dual meets, from five to ten in championship meets.
        Each appraises each dive and indicates an award for it.

Diving secretary:
    Dual and championship meets.

        He totals the judges' awards (after cancellations), multiplies the sum by the degree of difficulty for the dive, and records and announces the resulting figure. He computes the final scores (see pages 130-132, Chapter 5).

Meet physician:

    Championship meet.

        Though not termed a meet official, he is required for championship meets.
        He determines the fitness of contestants to compete in case of illness or injury and cares for the physical well-being of contestants.

---

*National Collegiate Athletic Association. *Official Collegiate-Scholastic Swimming Guide.* Phoenix, Arizona: College Athletics Publishing Service, 1970, pp. 15-19, 25-29. Used by permission.

WRITTEN ASSIGNMENTS

1. Go to your local swimming organization and obtain a sample team-practice program for one day.

2. Plan the organization of a sample team-practice for one day. Show the organization patterns you will use and what will be done by the swimmers and divers during the session.

3. Prepare a chart designating tasks which other persons may perform for you, or assist in performing, and indicate to what persons these tasks may be delegated.

4. Go to a local swimming organization, study samples and draw facsimiles of cards or slips for finish judges, timer, meet score, diving entry, diving scoring.

5. Study an official rule book and construct a table showing the minimum number of each type of official necessary for conducting a dual meet and the minimum number for a championship meet.

6. Study an official rule book and make a list of the duties to be performed by one official (finish judge, diving judge, timer, starter, etc.).

BEHAVIORAL OBJECTIVES

Many things in this chapter will not seem particularly important until you actually begin to coach. We hope that at that time you will reread this chapter in greater detail. However, we expect our students to prepare for coaching now by studying this chapter and being able to meet the following objectives. You may be asked to do any or all of the tasks below.

1. Suggest eight desirable attributes of the team coach. Select any two and give at least two ways that each attribute is indicated.

2. Name eight steps the coach must take in his first year of coaching.

3. Name the desirable qualities of a competitive swimmer.

4. Name the desirable qualities of a competitive diver.

5. Define these terms:

   training
   conditioning
   pacing
   gearing-up
   swimmer diet
   warm-up
   chronic fatigue
   staleness

6. Name the four phases of the training season and the objectives of each.

7. Diagram single-length wave, the circle, and the cross-pool wave swimming formations.

8. Define interval training and continuous relays. Then, explain how a continuous relay is a form of interval training.

9. Indicate at least five different items to be considered when planning the diving-practice session, adding one recommendation by the authors concerning each of the items.

10. Complete this chart:

Planning For a Swim Meet

	Two General Tasks	Officials Needed for a Dual Meet
Advance Planning	1. 2.	1. 2. 3. 4. 5. 6. 7. 8. 9. 10. 11. 12. 13. 14. 15.
Actions after Meet	1. 2.	

11. Perform, in acceptable form as described in this text, any of these skills:

Racing start (air and water positions) for the crawl stroke sprint.
Racing start (air and water positions) for the breaststroke.
Tumble turn (crawl stroke).
Tumble turn (backstroke).
Racing turn (breaststroke).
Racing start (air and water positions) for the backstroke.

BIBLIOGRAPHY

Amateur Athletic Union of the United States. *Official Swimming, Water Polo, and Diving Rules.* New York: Amateur Athletic Union, 1968.

Armbruster, David A., Robert Allen, and Bruce Harlan. *Swimming and Diving.* St. Louis: The C. V. Mosby Company, 1963.

Clayton, Robert D. *A Programmed Text Containing the Essentials of Physiology of Muscular Exercise.* Minneapolis: Burgess Publishing Company, 1968. Chapters 3, 4, 5, 6.

Counsilman, James E. *The Science of Swimming.* Englewood Cliffs, N.J.: Prentice-Hall, 1968.

Lephart, Sigmund A. "A Study of the Diving Training Procedures Used by Outstanding Diving Coaches." Unpublished Master's Thesis, The University of Illinois, Urbana, 1962.

Meyers, Carlton R., and William H. Sanford. *Swimming and Diving Officiating.* Palo Alto, California: The National Press, 1966.

National Collegiate Athletic Association. *Official Collegiate-Scholastic Swimming Guide.* Phoenix, Arizona: College Athletics Publishing Service, 1969.

Torney, John A., Jr. *Swimming.* New York: McGraw-Hill, 1950.

Torney, John A., Jr. "Officiating a Swimming Meet," *The Scholastic Coach,* 22:32, September, 1952.

PERFORMANCE ANALYSIS SHEET FOR THE
RACING START FOR CRAWL STROKE, BUTTERFLY STROKE AND BREASTSTROKE*

DIRECTIONS: Check √ all items that apply to the performance of this skill. Add other noted errors in the spaces provided.

NAME_____
(of performer)

NAME_____
(of analyzer)

Illustrations of Correct Techniques	Analysis of Performance

_____ The form *is* acceptable.
_____ The form is *not* acceptable because:
_____ Stance too erect.
_____ Weight too far forward.
_____ Weight too far backward.

_____ Body not lowered with arm swing.
_____ Head too high.

_____ Spring too much upward.
_____ Too little effort in spring.
_____ Arms and legs not coordinated.
_____ Body not stretched.
_____ Head not lower than feet.
_____ Body arched.
_____ Hips in pike.

_____ Dive too deep.
_____ Dive too shallow.
_____ Body surfaces too soon.
_____ Glide too short.
_____ Glide too long.

_____ Leg kick started too soon.
_____ Leg kick started too late.
_____ Arm pull started too soon.
_____ Arm pull started too late.

_____ (Other)_____
_____ _____
_____ _____
_____ _____
_____ _____
_____ _____

Breaststroke underwater action

*Method by Barbara J. Sanborn

PERFORMANCE ANALYSIS SHEET FOR THE RACING START FOR BACKSTROKE*

DIRECTIONS: Check √ all items that apply to the performance of this skill. Add other noted errors in the spaces provided.

NAME _____
(of performer)

NAME _____
(of analyzer)

Illustrations of Correct Techniques	Analysis of performance

____ The form *is* acceptable.
____ The form is *not* acceptable because:
    ____ Forehead not drawn to hands.
    ____ Knees not at chest.
    ____ Feet not well-placed.
    ____ Body not drawn upward.

    ____ Spring not vigorous.
    ____ Spring too much upward.
    ____ Arm-cast precedes leg-spring.
    ____ Leg-spring precedes arm-cast.
    ____ Body is over-arched.
    ____ Hips in pike position.
    ____ Hips drag in water.

    ____ Head not lower than feet.
    ____ Arms point toward sky.
    ____ Chin is on chest.
    ____ Fingers point toward pool bottom.

    ____ Dive too deep.
    ____ Dive too shallow.
    ____ Body surfaces too soon.
    ____ Glide too short.
    ____ Glide too long.

    ____ Leg kick started too soon.
    ____ Leg kick started too late.
    ____ Arm pull started too soon.
    ____ Arm pull started too late.

    ____ (Other)_____
____ _____
____ _____
____ _____
____ _____
____ _____

*Method by Barbara J. Sanborn

PERFORMANCE ANALYSIS SHEET FOR THE TUMBLE (FLIP) TURN FOR CRAWL STROKE*

DIRECTIONS: Check √ all items that apply to the performance of this skill. Add other noted errors in the spaces provided.

NAME _____
(of performer)

NAME _____
(of analyzer)

Illustrations of Correct Techniques	Analysis of Performance

_____ The form *is* acceptable.
_____ The form is *not* acceptable because:
_____ Turn begun too soon.
_____ Turn begun too late.
_____ Head and shoulders not lowered.
_____ Hips and heels not raised.
_____ Legs not tucked to body.
_____ Somersault not vigorous.

_____ Too much twist.
_____ Too little twist.
_____ Only one foot on wall.
_____ Feet too high on wall.
_____ Feet too low on wall.

_____ Push-off precedes arm extension.
_____ Head not between extended arms.
_____ Push-off not vigorous.

_____ Body not straight and stretched.
_____ Body not horizontal.

_____ Body surfaces too soon.
_____ Glide is too short.
_____ Glide is too long.

_____ Leg kick started too soon.
_____ Leg kick started too late.
_____ Arm pull started too soon.
_____ Arm pull started too late.

_____ (Other)_____
_____ _____
_____ _____
_____ _____
_____ _____
_____ _____

*Method by Barbara J. Sanborn

PERFORMANCE ANALYSIS SHEET FOR THE TURN FOR
BREASTSTROKE AND BUTTERFLY STROKE

DIRECTIONS: Check √ all items that apply to the performance of this skill. Add other noted errors in the spaces provided.

NAME_____
(of performer)

NAME_____
(of analyzer)

Illustrations of Correct Techniques

Analysis of Performance

_____ The form *is* acceptable.
_____ The form is *not* acceptable because:
    _____ Body glides into wall.
    _____ Elbows remain straight.
    _____ Hand-touch not at same time, same level.

    _____ Body not tucked.
    _____ Head raised too high.
    _____ Body raised too high.
    _____ Turn-around not vigorous.

    _____ Body not settled underwater.
    _____ Only one foot on wall.
    _____ Feet too high on wall.
    _____ Feet too low on wall.

    _____ Push-off precedes arm extension.
    _____ Head not between extended arms.
    _____ Push-off not vigorous.
    _____ Body not perfectly on breast.

    _____ Body not straight and stretched.
    _____ Body not horizontal.

    _____ Body surfaces too soon.
    _____ Glide too short.
    _____ Glide too long.

    _____ Leg kick started too soon.
    _____ Leg kick started too late.
    _____ Arm pull started too soon.
    _____ Arm pull started too late.

    _____ (Other) _____
_____ _____
_____ _____
_____ _____
_____ _____
_____ _____

Butterfly stroke

Breaststroke

PERFORMANCE ANALYSIS SHEET FOR THE TURN FOR BACKSTROKE

DIRECTIONS: Check √ all items that apply to the performance of this skill. Add other noted errors in the spaces provided.

NAME_____
(of performer)

NAME_____
(of analyzer)

Illustrations of Correct
Techniques

Analysis of Performance

_____ The form *is* acceptable.
_____ The form is *not* acceptable because:
    _____ Turn begun too soon.
    _____ Turn begun too late.

    _____ Hand touches wall too high.
    _____ Hand touches wall too low.
    _____ Legs not tucked to body.
    _____ Knees and feet not raised.
    _____ Somersault not vigorous.

    _____ Too much twist.
    _____ Too little twist.
    _____ Only one foot on wall.
    _____ Feet too high on wall.
    _____ Feet too low on wall.

    _____ Push-off precedes arm extension.
    _____ Head not between extended arms.
    _____ Push-off not vigorous.

    _____ Body not straight and stretched.
    _____ Body not horizontal.
    _____ Wrists hyperextended, fingers pointing downward.

    _____ Body surfaces too soon.
    _____ Glide too short.
    _____ Glide too long.

    _____ Leg kick started too soon.
    _____ Leg kick started too late.
    _____ Arm pull started too soon.
    _____ Arm pull started too late.

    _____ (Other)_____

_____ _____
_____ _____
_____ _____
_____ _____
_____ _____

Evaluation of Swimming Skills

The beginning instructor thinks that teaching a class is comparatively easy, if the printed instructions of the organization are followed. This is generally true, but the evaluation of students is often a different story. Not all organizations give precise standards to be met by students — and the objectives and standards of some school programs are even more vague.

WHAT IS INVOLVED IN EVALUATION?

Certain questions plague every aquatic instructor, beginning with, "How good must the student be to pass this course?" This question leads to the practical problem of, "How much time and effort will be devoted to teaching and how much to testing?" Other problems quickly enter the picture. Where is the information concerning the tests? What record forms are available and must these record forms be used? If so, how are they completed? Assuming that you know what to test on, how can the results be recorded in such a manner that you later can tell a student specifically why he did not pass a particular item?

Teaching in a school brings additional problems. Will the ARC (or YMCA) program be followed, or will a local program be developed? Can objectives for the course be devised which meet the purposes of the course? Can they be clearly understood by the students? What is the difference between an "A" student and an "F" student? Will you grade by adherence to a set of standards (and run the risk of all students earning the same grade) or will you use the natural curve method? Regardless of which method of grading you use, what knowledge of elementary statistics will you need to develop the standards and/or to determine letter grades?

As in other chapters of this text, we cannot give the final answers. However, we believe that our suggestions will help meet the problems facing you in a particular situation.

BASIC CONSIDERATIONS BEFORE EVALUATION CAN BEGIN

Before evaluation can be attempted, the instructor must decide: 1) what standards of achievement are expected, and 2) how much time will be devoted to evaluation. Without consideration of these items, meaningful evaluation will be a difficult, if not impossible, process.

The standards of achievement can vary greatly from program to program. The ARC and YMCA have exact listings of skills to be taught; from this, they have developed certain skills which must be "passed."

The instructor is authorized to conduct a specific course and all students in this course are assumed to have the same minimum level of skill at the completion of the course. The problem is that the standard of performance is not always precisely specified; for example, "The student should swim (using various styles or strokes) with proper coordination, breathing, and effective stroking. . ." (ARC, *Swimming and Water Safety Courses,* p. 78).

The great variety of aquatic skills possessed by students in a physical education class makes it virtually impossible to conduct a regular Beginners, Advanced Swimmers, etc. course in school situations. If several instructors are available, then several levels of instruction can be given at once. Because this usually is not feasible, the individual instructor develops his own course with his own standards. The fact that letter grades must be given complicates matters. The beginning instructor is faced with deciding what skills to teach, how well these skills should be mastered, and then how to grade. It is hoped that the remainder of this chapter will help resolve some of these issues.

The other principal question before beginning the evaluation process concerns testing. Some instructors maintain that testing should be done throughout the course. Normally, this means teaching a skill on one day and testing each student during the next one or two sessions. When a student has passed all the skills, he has passed the course. Most of the ARC and YMCA courses are taught in this manner because these organizations provide skill sheets (discussed later) which make daily testing feasible. Testing throughout the course is highly motivating for most students; they see that they are making steady progress. It also provides the instructor with a clear picture of the rate of progress for each student in the class. A student who is having difficulty is easily noted by absence of check marks near his name on the skill sheet.

Another group of instructors maintains that testing during most class sessions is very wasteful of time, and that this time could more profitably be spent in practicing or learning new skills. They emphasize that all aquatic courses are designed to ensure a certain amount of skill at the conclusion of the course, not in the middle. They further say that if the instructor will wait until the end of the course, he will find that two full days of testing will enable all those who should pass to do so.

To aid the beginning instructor in making a decision on this issue, it should be said that the majority of instructors make use of skill sheets and tests throughout any swimming course they conduct. They feel that the advantages of student motivation outweigh any time that is lost in testing. Whatever the decision, testing must be done with a purpose, not just for the sake of testing.

SOURCES OF STANDARDS FOR SWIMMING LIFESAVING COURSES

The instructor's primary responsibility when teaching for an organization (ARC, for example) is to cover exactly the material that is expected and to make certain that the students are qualified according to the standards of that group. Listings of skills and/or evaluation standards are found in these books:

A. Courses taught by the American National Red Cross:
1. *Swimming and Water Safety,* First Edition, 1968. Contains description of basic swimming strokes (sidestroke, elementary backstroke, breaststroke, crawl, back crawl); additional strokes and variations (overarm sidestroke, trudgen strokes, inverted breaststroke, butterfly stroke); related aquatic skills (surface diving, etc.); diving fundamentals (including standing and running front dive); safety in aquatics; survival floating; and artificial respiration. It is the basic source for the Red Cross swimming courses.
2. *Lifesaving and Water Safety,* 1956 Edition. Contains lifesaving skills and techniques for both junior and senior lifesaving courses. Some material included in it is no longer taught, but this is the basic source for both levels of lifesaving.
3. *Swimming and Water Safety Courses,* 1968 Edition. An instructor's manual to be used when teaching any swimming course. It has general information for teaching, plus descriptions of the skills and standards to be taught in each class.
4. *Lifesaving and Water Safety Courses,* 1968 Edition. An instructor's manual to be used when teaching any lifesaving course. It describes each skill, gives teaching suggestions, and indicates the skills (but not standards) for the final examination.

Other informative publications by the Red Cross include:

Teaching Johnny to Swim, 1957 Edition. A booklet for parents which tells them how to teach their child to swim. The skills taught are those in the beginner course.

Survival Swimming, 1961 Edition. Manual for the teacher which describes the basic and advanced survival courses.

Sources for these publications are varied. Most of the above literature is given to the instructor when he or she takes the Water Safety Instructor's course. Replacement copies of some literature is available from local ARC offices. All skill sheets are also available from these local offices.

B. Courses taught by the YMCA:

1. Harold T. Friermood, *New YMCA Aquatic Workbook,* 1965. This is the source of basic information about the philosophy, operation, training of instructors, etc. of the YMCA program. It also contains a listing of skills and standards for each course.

2. Charles Silvia, *Lifesaving and Water Safety Today,* 1965. Contains a description of all skills and tests for the lifesaving course.

These publications are obtained primarily through the local association, but can be ordered from the Association Press, 291 Broadway Street, New York, New York 10007.

C. Courses taught in Canada:

1. Canadian Red Cross Society, *Instructor's Guide and Reference,* (Ottawa: Canadian Red Cross Society), Publication WS202, 1966. A guide describing swimming and lifesaving skills, teaching techniques, and pool and waterfront organization.

2. Joint National Technical Committee, *Canadian Lifeguard Manual,* (Toronto National Lifeguard Service, 550 Church Street, Toronto), 1963. The Canadian YMCA, the Canadian Red Cross, the Royal Life Saving Society, and the Ontario Recreation Directors have combined to form the National Lifeguard Service. This manual effectively describes and illustrates skills, techniques, and knowledges needed by all lifeguards.

D. Courses taught by the Boy Scouts:

1. *Aquatic Program* (New Brunswick, N.J.: Boy Scouts of America), 1965. This booklet describes the swimming, lifesaving, rowing, and canoeing skills taught by the Boy Scouts, plus material on the layout, protection, and administration of lake waterfronts.

RECORDING ACHIEVEMENT

Actually, none of the organizations require that the instructor keep records as the course is being taught, but it is a common sense procedure to do so. Both the ARC and the YMCA provide check sheets which are invaluable. Check sheets have spaces for three main items of information:

1. The name of students in the class,
2. a listing of all of the skills needed to pass the course; and
3. a box for each skill to be checked as it is passed by the student.

Some instructors add two more features to their check sheets:

4. space for comments and/or totals; and
5. a key for the code (Examples: P means passed, P- means poor but passing, Ab means absent, etc.) that might be used.

Chart 11:1 is a reproduction of the Red Cross Beginner Skill Sheet. Instructors in school aquatic programs can easily make similar skill sheets by providing space for the skills and names as these illustrations show. Posting a copy of the skill sheet where all students can see it will prepare them for the next skills to be taught, and will possibly provide motivation.

CHART 11:1
BEGINNER SKILL SHEET*

(For use by currently authorized Red Cross instructor)

- Use the Instructor's Manual – Swimming & Water Safety Courses (ARC 2123) for teaching this course.
- Use check (√) for satisfactory performance in each skill.
- Final grades should be P – passing
  INC – incomplete
- Contact your local chapter for information concerning supplies, recording of activity, certificates.
- Complete and process records promptly.

NAME AND ADDRESS	BREATH HOLDING – 10 SEC. (1)	RHYTHMIC BREATHING – 10 TIMES (2)	PRONE FLOAT (3)	PRONE GLIDE – 10 FT. (4)	BACK FLOAT (5)	BACK GLIDE – 6 FT. (6)	PRONE GLIDE WITH KICK – 20 FT. (7)	BACK GLIDE WITH KICK – 20 FT. (8)	ARM STROKE – 20 FT. (9)	FINNING OR SCULLING – 20 FT. (10)	CRAWL STROKE – 20 YDS. (11)	COMBINED STROKE – 20 YDS. (12)	CHANGE STROKE (BACK) – 10 YDS. (13)	TURNING OVER (14)	CHANGE DIRECTION (15)	LEVELING OVER (16)	JUMP (CHEST DEEP WATER) (17)	JUMP (DEEP WATER) (18)	FRONT DIVE (19)	SAFETY SKILLS (20)	COMBINED SKILLS	FINAL GRADE
1. Carlson, Joyce Ann 1 Stratton Place, City	✓	✓	✓	✓	✓	✓	✓	✓	✓	✓	✓	✓	✓	✓	✓	✓	✓	✓	✓	✓		E
2. Madison, Marian 1969 Husky St., City																						E
3.																						
4.																						
5.																						
6.																						
7.																						
8.																						
9.																						
10.																						
11.																						
12.																						
13.																						
14.																						
15.																						

*American National Red Cross, Form 1382 (Rev. 11-68). Used by permission.

For lifesaving tests, it is possible to develop specific directions which explain what is desired. For example, a test involving the lifesaving entry, approach swim, contact and carry could be done in this fashion.

1. Victim of approximately the same weight as rescuer is in vertical position in deep water, arms at surface, facing shallow end, 5 feet from deep end.
2. Rescuer enters water at shallow end with lifesaving dive. The stopwatch is started with the first movement of the dive.
3. Rescuer may use any stroke in approach but must not take eyes off victim.
4. The approach distance is 60 feet.
5. The rescuer must
   (a) Reverse
   (b) Make front surface approach
   (c) Level victim
   (d) Assume cross-chest carry
         Victim held firmly
         Rescuer's hips placed under victim's back
         Victim must not assist with arms or legs
         Victim's face must not submerge at any time
6. The watch is stopped as rescuer's head crosses pool line at 20 foot mark (length of tow is 40 feet).
7. An elapsed time greater than 60 seconds is failure. Any error in technique (items 2, 3, 5, 6) means automatic failure.

The ARC requires students to achieve a certain number of points in their final test. Points for the above test item can be assigned as follows (assuming the instructor wishes to assign seven points for excellent performance).

35 seconds or less	= 7 points		
36-40 seconds	= 6 points	50-53 seconds	= 3 points
41-45 seconds	= 5 points	54-57 seconds	= 2 points
46-49 seconds	= 4 points	58-60 seconds	= 1 point

COMPLETING AND SUBMITTING RECORDS FOR ARC AND YMCA COURSES

Completing the records is not a difficult process — if directions are followed. One basic rule is that two copies are submitted, with a third copy being retained for your records. Beginning instructors are invariably careless with their own records, but experience will soon show that at least one inquiry (either from the organization or a student) can be expected for each three classes taught. Chart 11:1 (already shown) depicts a typical class record which must be submitted to the authorities. When submitting such a record, the instructor need not check each square (Chart 11:1 line 1). Instead, he may draw a horizontal line indicating that the student has passed all tests (Chart 11:1, line 2).

It is important that instructors sign each form properly and submit it as soon as possible. For ARC courses, the form is submitted to the local chapter. In YMCA courses, the physical director for the local association receives the form and then sends it to the proper headquarters.

There are several "tricks of the trade" which experienced instructors have adopted. These are explained in Table 11:1.

TABLE 11:1
SUGGESTIONS CONCERNING COMPLETING AND SUBMITTING RECORDS

Item	Suggestions
Allowing a student in your class.	It is very important to check the eligibility of each student for each particular course, especially the lifesaving courses which have a requirement concerning age. The problem of what to do with a person who is "almost" the

proper age will always arise. Most instructors will allow the person to enroll if his birthday falls on or before the completion of the course. Some instructors will accept anyone whose birthday falls within three or four weeks of the completion of the course. However, extending the limits invariably causes problems; primarily with someone whose birthday is five or six weeks away. An underage person cannot be officially passed, and if enrolled, there will be a delay in sending the record or changing the age. In the long run, following the requirements exactly is the best procedure for the organization, the student, and you.

Screening the class.

Instructors in ARC and YMCA courses are sometimes judged on the number of students they pass during the season. One way to increase this total is to have all students, regardless of swimming ability, begin in the lowest level and quickly earn all awards up to their true level. While this looks good on the records, it is wasteful on three accounts: 1) most of the instructor's time should be spent teaching, not testing; 2) the student is there to learn new skills, not to enhance someone's reputation as a swimming teacher; and 3) it costs money and time to process the records. Every student on a roster must be recorded, cards issued, etc. This takes the time of several persons, not just the instructor. There is no justification for this practice. A qualified teacher should be able to screen students so that they will start in the proper class and progress normally — not from beginner through advanced swimming in two months.

Using work copy for your records.

Keep one copy of the skill sheet on the clipboard and be unconcerned about its wrinkled appearance. It won't be presentable for submission, but can become the third (personal) copy.

Omission of students from final record sheet.

Most experienced instructors submit records with few, if any, names of students who have failed the course. This does not imply that there are no students in this category! Since the original sheet (which lists the names of all class members) is used as the guide when making the official record, merely omit the names of those who failed when filling out the copies to be sent in.

Distributing award certificates.

If certificates can be given the same day that the class terminates, it minimizes work for the instructor. However, usually there is a delay before the awards are ready for distribution. Experienced instructors soon learn to have each student who will earn a certificate hand in a stamped, self-addressed envelope. After the certificates are returned to the instructor for his signature, it is a simple matter to put them into the envelopes and mail them. It might seem easier and less expensive for the student to call for the certificate at an office, but invariably the awards are not yet ready and this causes consternation to all concerned. Mailing seems to be by far the best answer.

BASIC EVALUATION PROCEDURES IN AN AQUATIC PROGRAM

Constructing Behavioral Objectives. It is extremely difficult to transplant a regulation YMCA or ARC swim program into the average physical education program. The school class is usually so heterogeneous in swimming ability that one instructor cannot properly teach all the levels that are represented. If it is possible to obtain a homogeneous group, or several instructors for the several skill levels, the ARC program is recommended because of its widespread acceptance by the population.

However, the facts are that most instructors in a physical education program have to develop their own courses, using either the ARC or YMCA program as their primary source of skills. In developing his own course, the instructor is at an immediate disadvantage because he must first think of his objectives — and the national groups have already decided upon theirs. Objectives refer to those statements which indicate the course content. The listing of skills to be taught (with their standards of evaluation) are in fact a statement of the objectives of the Red Cross and YMCA programs. The YMCA Minnow Test (Chart 11:2) illustrates this point because it lists the skills, the objective, and test specifications to meet standards.

MINNOW
YMCA Beginner Swimming and Diving Instruction, Practice, and Testing
21 Skills (stunts)

Name
PRINT .... FIRST .... INITIAL .... LAST

Address ....
NUMBER .... STREET

....
CITY .... STATE .... (ZIP)

Phone Number .... Sex: Female ☐ Male ☐

Date of Birth ....
MONTH .... DAY .... YEAR

YMCA or Camp ....

INDIVIDUAL LESSON PLANNING & TEST SHEET
(AT THIS, AND AT EVERY, GRADE LEVEL, INSTRUCT AND REVIEW: DROWNPROOFING TECHNIQUE AND MOUTH-TO-MOUTH RESUSCITATION.)

Date started .... Date completed .... New class assignment ....
(FISH)

Notification to parents .... Award card .... Button .... Emblem ....

Name posted for recognition, permanent record, and aquatic program production report ....

NUMBER			SKILL NAME	OBJECTIVE SUGGESTED	INSTRUCTOR'S LESSON PLAN AND SUGGESTIONS FOR LEAD-UP DEVELOPMENTAL ACTIVITIES (for individual or class)	SKILL TEST SPECIFICATIONS TO MEET STANDARDS	SKILL MASTERED, SHOW DATE AND INITIALS OF INSTRUCTOR, OR CHECK (√)
		1	LOOK AT BOTTOM "See Bottom"	Confidence and adjustment to water		Put face in water and open eyes; look at bottom or object.	
	M	2	RIDE ON FRONT "Aquaplane"	Confidence and adjustment		Permit being pulled on front in glide position by partner, remaining relaxed in streamline position.	
	M	3	KICKING TO WALL ON FRONT "Steamer Idling in Dock"	Leg movements		Flutter kick on front, holding to gutter with both hands, and ability to keep legs at surface 15 seconds.	
S	M	4	FRONT GLIDE AND REGAIN FEET "Coasting on Front"	Initial safety, gliding, and control of body		Push-off, hold face down in glide position for 5 seconds and regain feet properly.	
S	M	5	DIVING GLIDE "Slide-in Dive"	Initial diving		Squatting or kneeling on one knee on edge of pool, or with feet in gutter, push for shallow diving glide.	
	M	6	BUOYANCY FLOAT "Cork"	Breathing and floating skills		Take a long deep breath, reach down and grasp ankles, hold for 10 seconds: + = Rise to surface − = Sink to bottom (Insert over checks)	
	M	7	BACK GLIDE "Coasting on Back"	Initial safety, gliding, and control of body		Push-off on back, hold glide for 3 seconds, regain feet efficiently.	
		8	CRAWL STROKES WITH ROTARY BREATHING	Co-ordination		In waist-deep water, feet on bottom, body bent forward from hips, stroke and breathe in good form.	
		9	BOBBING WITH RHYTHMIC BREATHING	Breathing		In chest-deep water, alternately stand and stoop, getting a breath in through mouth when up, blow out through nose when down.	
S	M	10	RECOVER OBJECT "Duck and Fetch"	Confidence and adjustment		In chest-deep water, reach under water, open eyes, recover object and stand with object.	
S	M	11	PADDLE WITH ARMS "Reach and Pull"	Arm movements		Push-off glide, and paddle 15 feet across pool in shallow water.	
S	M	12	FLUTTER KICK WITH ROTARY BREATHING "Co-ordinate Kicking with Breathing"	Leg movements Breathing Co-ordination		Kick and breathe regularly by rotating the head for intake. Repeat 10 times.	
		13	PLUNGE "Plunging Glide"	Initial diving		Standing on edge or end of pool, swing arms and plunge 15 feet.	
		14	FLUTTER KICK "Steamboat"	Leg movements		Push-off glide and kick 15 feet across pool in shallow water.	
	M	15	JUMPING SURFACE DIVES "Porpoise Dives"	Initial diving		In water chest deep, jump from bottom and execute two surface dives successively touching bottom on each with both hands and feet.	
	M	16	UNDERWATER SWIM "Bottom Search"	Arm movements Confidence		Using breast stroke swim 10 feet across the pool remaining under water.	
	M	17	SWIM 20 FEET "Tadpole Swim"	Co-ordination		Propel across pool in shallow water, any stroke, using arms and legs and getting at least two breaths.	
S	M	18	RHYTHMIC ROTARY BREATHING "Rotary Bubbles"	Breathing		Hands on knees in waist-deep water, turn head for intake through mouth, return head and blow out through nose. Repeat 10 times.	
		19	SAFETY SWIM "Save Yourself"	Co-ordination		Jump feet first into water over head, come up and swim 20 feet to shallow water.	
		20	CHANGE TO RESTING STROKE "Conserve Energy"	Initial safety Body control		Swim on front 20 feet, change and return on back.	
S	M	21	COMBINATION SWIM IN DEEP WATER "Co-ordination Swim"	Co-ordination		Jump feet first into water over head (holding nose if desired), swim 25 feet, any stroke, turn around and return to starting place.	

1 Note: S — Selected skills for instruction and testing used in the 7-item short course.
M — Items used in the 14-item middle length course.
— Items numbered from 1 to 21 are the skills used in the full-length YMCA beginner swimming and diving Minnow grade.

PHYSICAL EDUCATION SUBCOMMITTEE ON AQUATICS
NATIONAL BOARD OF YOUNG MEN'S CHRISTIAN ASSOCIATIONS, U.S.A.
Order from Association Press, 291 Broadway, New York, N.Y. 10007
Minnow Test Sheet PTS 303-TP-1

The primary objective of the YMCA and ARC is the development of aquatic skills. However, school programs customarily have at least two other objectives — attitude and improvement. The instructor must therefore decide before the course which objectives he is seeking and then construct statements which will clearly explain to the students what is being sought.

Quite often the objectives for a unit or course of study are so vague that they do not mean the same thing to all people. For example, one objective of any ARC, YMCA, or school aquatic program is "to swim the breaststroke correctly." Yet, in every lifesaving or WSI class there will be at least one student who uses the scissors rather than the breaststroke kick, or who doesn't glide, or who pulls his arms past the shoulder level. He was "passed" by some instructor earlier — someone who apparently didn't know (or didn't apply) the usual standards for the breaststroke. If the objective was "The student must be able to swim the breaststroke for 50 feet, must use the whip kick, must not pull past the shoulder level, and must glide at least two seconds with his face in the water between strokes," every instructor could probably agree as to what an acceptable stroke should be.

The type of objective just described above is called "behavioral," because it specifically tells what the behavior of the learner should be after he has learned. The objectives found at the end of most chapters in this book illustrate behavioral objectives. Hopefully, these objectives are written so exactingly that all readers will know precisely what we expect of our students. Any student, whether working for a certificate or a grade, wants to know beforehand exactly what he will have to do to pass the course; behavioral objectives give him that information. The ARC and YMCA have both clearly defined the skills to be taught in their courses, but a list of skills does not necessarily ensure that all instructors will apply the same standards.

Behavioral objectives are not easy to construct because they require much thinking and precise writing. The ones presented in the chapters of this text meet the characteristics of good behavioral objectives, as given by Mager (1962, p. 53).

1. A good behavioral objective identifies the behavior to be demonstrated by the learner (i.e., it specifically names and describes the skill).
2. A good behavioral objective states the conditions under which it will occur (i.e., it specifically tells how the learner will be tested).
3. A good behavioral objective indicates a standard of acceptable performance (i.e., it specifically tells what score is required to "pass" the test or it lists specific things that must be done).

Table 11:2 illustrates different types of objectives, with an analysis of the three desirable characteristics.

TABLE 11:2
EXAMPLES OF BEHAVIORAL OBJECTIVES

Behavioral Objective	Characteristics		
	Behavior to be Demonstrated	Condition under which Behavior will occur	Standard of Acceptable Performance
1. From the low board, the student must perform a forward dive, pike position. To pass, the student must use a three-step approach, a vertical hurdle, take-off at 10-20° angle, pike position without bending at knees, nearly vertical entry with legs straight and toes pointed.	Forward dive, pike position	Diving from the low diving board.	Three-step approach, vertical hurdle, take off at 10-20° angle. No bend of knees in pike position. Nearly vertical entry with legs straight and toes pointed. NOTE: Instead, the standard could be: "Score at least 15 pts. (3 judges) in performing the dive." This is explicit enough for experienced judges, but not for novice judges.

Table 11:2—Examples of Behavioral Objectives (continued)

2. Swim the sidestroke 50 yards, using the shallow arm-pull, scissors kick, and minimum glide of two seconds.	Swim sidestroke	Swim 50 yards	Shallow arm-pull, scissors kick, glide of two seconds. NOTE: Instead, the standard could be "Swim 50 feet in eight strokes or less, using the shallow arm-pull and the scissors kick."
3. In a written examination, be able to define "massed" and "distributed" practice, according to the views of the authors of this text.	Defining "massed" and "distributed" practice	Written examination	Massed practice: when a certain amount of practice is given at a certain time. Distributed practice: same amount of time is divided into several days' practice.
4. Demonstrate a favorable attitude toward swimming, as evidenced by voluntarily attending five recreational swim periods.	Favorable attitude toward swimming	Recreational swim period	Voluntary attendance at five sessions.
5. Indicate satisfactory swimming improvement by passing at least eight tests at the end of the course which could not be passed at the beginning.	Satisfactory improvement	Taking tests at the end of the course	Passing eight or more tests that could not be passed at the beginning of the course.

At this point, we suggest rereading the objectives at the end of the chapters. This will provide actual examples of behavioral objectives that meet these characteristics.

The practical value of behavioral objectives to the teacher comes when evaluation of students must be done. The instructor knows exactly what to test on, what type of test will be used, and what score must be earned to achieve a passing grade.

The students should likewise know at the beginning of a course exactly what the objectives are. The job of the instructor is not to fail the students but to help as many as possible achieve the desired standards. Much more motivation comes when the student knows exactly what he must do.

The Importance of, and the Method of Calculating the Mean Score and the Standard Deviation. All systems of evaluation are based on some means of comparison either between test scores or between persons. This comparison can be subjective (based on judgment of the tester) or objective (based on mathematical figures). It is generally agreed that objective evaluation is preferred — yet instructors fear that they lack competence in simple statistical procedures.

Actually, little knowledge of mathematics is required to figure the mean (or average) score of a group, and the standard deviation (how much members of the group vary). The use of these, the mean and standard deviation, is all that is needed to:

1. construct scales which can compare one performance with another; and
2. construct a grading system based on the normal curve.

In view of the fact that grades are ordinarily given in school situations, the ability to construct performance scales and a grading system is desirable. Each of these is explained in detail later in this chapter. However, the instructor must first be able to calculate the mean score and the standard deviation. The material that follows will enable these calculations to be made, but it will not explain the reasoning behind their use. (Think of it as a recipe in a cookbook, not as a scientific study on the chemistry of food.) Even though there are different (and shorter) methods to calculate the mean and standard deviation, the simplest methods are presented here. It is hoped that the reader will consult a book which contains elementary statistics (such as Johnson's and Nelson's *Practical Measurements for Evaluation in Physical Education)* for further explanation.

To find a mean (or average) score of any group of scores, it is merely necessary to add the scores together, and then divide by the number of scores (see calculations, Table 11:3).

The standard deviation tells how far the scores of the group are from the center. In normal groups, most of the scores are in the middle, and there are fewer scores at each end (see Chart 11:4, p. 303). The calculation of the standard deviation is begun by calculating the mean, as described above. Then, each score is squared (see Column 2, Table 11:3). The total of these squared scores is obtained (see bottom of Column 2, Table 11:3). The mean score is squared. Next, the number of scores is divided into the total of the squared scores, and the squared mean is subtracted. The square root of computation thus far becomes the standard deviation (see example at the bottom of Table 11:3). The actual computation of the standard deviation is not nearly as hard as this explanation makes it appear, duplicating the example shown in Table 11:3 will prove this.

TABLE 11:3
CALCULATION OF THE MEAN AND STANDARD DEVIATION

Column 1 Scores on Any Test (or, Average Score on Several Tests)	Column 2 Each Score Squared	Calculations for this Problem
97	97 x 97 = 9409	1. Mean Score =
95	95 x 95 = 9025	
95	etc. 9025	$\dfrac{\text{Total Number of Scores}}{\text{Number of Scores}}$
92	8464	
91	8281	
89	7921	$= \dfrac{1307}{22}$
86	7396	
85	7225	
79	6241	$= \underline{\underline{59.4}}$
64	4096	
63	3969	2. Standard Deviation =
50	2500	
49	2401	$\sqrt{\dfrac{\text{Total of each squared score - Mean}^2}{\text{Number of Scores}}}$
47	2209	
36	1296	
35	1225	$\sqrt{\dfrac{95217 - 59.4^2}{22}} = \sqrt{\dfrac{95217 - 3528.36}{22}}$
34	1156	
34	1156	
34	1156	$\sqrt{4328.04 - 3528.36}$
27	729	
16	256	$*\sqrt{799.68} = \underline{\underline{28.28}}$
9	81	
Total = 1307	Total = 95217	

Number of Scores = 22

$*\sqrt{}$ means to "find the square root" of a number. This is done in the following manner:

$\sqrt{7\,99.6\,800}$ 1. Mark off two places either side of decimal.

$\begin{array}{r} 2 \\ \sqrt{7\,99.6\,800} \\ 2 \quad \underline{4} \\ \overline{399} \end{array}$ 2. Decide what number is closest to the square of 7; answer is 2. Put 2 above 7 and also to the side. Multiply 2 x 2 = 4. Subtract, and bring down the next two numbers.

297

2 8
$\sqrt{799.6800}$
48 4
    ───
    399
    384

3. Double the first number in the answer; put this to the side. Decide what number between 40-50 goes into 399.
Put answer above 99 and beside 4.   8 x 48 = 384.

2 8. 2
$\sqrt{799.6800}$
562 4
     ───
     399
     384
     ─────
     15 68
     11 24
      ────
      4 44

4. Subtract, bring down next two numbers. Double the answer so far (28 x 2 = 56).

2 8. 2 7
$\sqrt{799.6800}$
5647 4
      ───
      399
      384
      ─────
      15 68
      11 24
       ─────
       4 4400
       3 9529
        ──────
        487100

5. Continue as in step 3, using 560-569 into 1568 as the problem.

6. Repeat steps 3, 4, 5 until answer is rounded back to two decimal places.

The Importance and Calculation of Achievement Scales. How do we judge if a person is a good swimmer? Ordinarily we observe him while swimming a particular stroke over a distance and, on the basis of our knowledge and experience, we say that he is of a certain skill level. A beginning instructor simply does not have the knowledge or experience to do this. Compounding the issue might be the fact that several skills may have to be evaluated, and a grade determined.

There are other ways besides observation to judge how skilled a swimmer is. By referring to a table of past scores for this test, we can quickly evaluate a current student. These tables of past scores (which actually list all the possible scores) are called scales (or norms). A scale is composed of a number of scores, one of which tells how good one person is compared to others in the group. For example, if someone can swim 25 yards of the sidestroke taking no more than four strokes, we assume that he is better than someone who takes ten strokes to cover the same distance. Or, someone who can swim 1,000 yards in 20 minutes is considered better than another person from the same group who can only swim 700 yards of the same stroke in 20 minutes.

Crude scales can be made quickly by any instructor by doing the following:

1. Have all students perform the same test following exactly the same procedure.
2. Record the results in some objective fashion (count, time with a watch, etc.).
3. Put the scores in one long list (best scores on top).
4. Note what the top, middle, and bottom scores are. If there are at least 15 in the group, and they are judged to be normal in skill development, then the instructor can use these scores as a means of assigning letter grades *for this group only.*

Establishing scales according to correct statistical procedures is more time-consuming but worthwhile because they can be used for any similar group, regardless of its number or abnormality in skill development. With scales, it is also possible to average certain scores (say, distance swum underwater and the time it takes to swim 50 yards of the back crawl) in order to arrive at one common number for grading purposes.

By a comparatively simple statistical procedure it is possible for an instructor to develop a scale for any test, provided he has a sufficient number of scores. It is desirable to have at least 100 scores from similar subjects, but scales can be made from as few as 30 test scores. (The greater the number of scores, the more assurance the instructor can have that the group is normal. It is possible to combine the scores of several smaller classes into one large group for the purpose of constructing scales if the same test is administered the same way to a similar group.) There are different types of scales which can be used; we recommend the Hull Scale as being the most useful because it provides for a great range of scores (from very high to very low) and yet seems to reward a very good test score with a high number.

To make a Hull Scale (shown in Table 11:4):

1. Find the mean and standard deviation of this test (see Table 11:3 shown earlier).
2. Number along the left margin of a sheet of paper from 100 down to 1. Opposite 50, place the mean score that was calculated.
3. Multiply the standard deviation by 3½. (The number 3½ comes from the fact that in the Hull Scale there are 3½ standard deviations above, and 3½ standard deviations below the mean score if the distribution is normal.)
4. Divide the product obtained (step 3) by 50. (The number 50 indicates the possible points on either side of the mean.)
5. The number derived (step 4) is called a constant and is added to the mean score to find the value for 51. Add it again and the value for 52 is found. Keep adding until the number 100 is reached. To find the value for 49, subtract the constant from the mean. For 48, 47, etc. continue subtracting. If done in a statistically defensible manner (starting with an adequate number of scores that have been obtained under the same conditions of test administration, etc.) the instructor can now take a particular score and say that "Compared to a large normal group, this score of 81 is equal to a Hull score of 61." (Check with Table 11:4 to see if this is correct.)

TABLE 11:4
CALCULATION OF HULL SCORES
(BASED ON DATA PRESENTED IN TABLE 11:3)

Given: Mean = 59.4; Standard Deviation = 28.28

Column 1 Hull Score	Column 2 Scores Achieved by Adding the Constant	Column 3 Scores Achieved by Rounding
100	158.40	158
99	156.42	156
98	154.44	154
97	152.46	153
96	150.48	151
95	148.50	149
94	146.52	147
93	144.54	145
92	142.56	143
91	140.58	141
90	138.60	139
89	136.62	137
88	134.64	135
87	132.66	133
86	130.68	131
85	128.70	129
84	126.72	127
83	124.74	125

Table 11:4–Calculation of Hull Scores (Based on Data Presented in Table 11:3) (continued)

Column 1 Hull Score	Column 2 Scores Achieved by Adding the Constant	Column 3 Scores Achieved by Rounding
82	122.76	123
81	120.78	121
80	118.80	119
79	116.82	117
78	114.84	115
77	112.86	113
76	110.88	111
75	108.90	109
74	106.92	107
73	104.94	105
72	102.96	103
71	100.98	101
70	99.00	99
69	97.02	97
68	95.04	95
67	93.06	93
66	91.08	91
65	89.10	89
64	87.12	87
63	85.14	85
62	83.16	83
61	81.18	81
60	79.20	79
59	77.22	77
58	75.24	75
57	73.26	73
56	71.28	71
55	69.30	69
54	67.32	67
53	65.34	65
52	63.36	63
51	61.38	61
50	59.40	59
49	57.42	57
48	55.44	55
47	53.46	54
46	51.48	52
45	49.50	50
44	47.52	48
43	45.54	46
42	43.56	44
41	41.58	42
40	39.60	40
39	37.62	38
38	35.64	36
37	33.66	34
36	31.68	32
35	29.70	30

Column 1 Hull Score	Column 2 Scores Achieved by Adding the Constant	Column 3 Scores Achieved by Rounding
34	27.72	28
33	25.74	26
32	23.76	24
31	21.78	22
30	19.80	20
29	17.82	18
28	15.84	16
27	13.86	14
26	11.88	12
25	9.90	10
24	7.92	8
23	5.94	6
22	3.96	4
21	1.98	2
20	0.00	0

(No scores below this because the lowest a person can score on this test is 0.)

Calculations for above problem:

1. $\dfrac{\text{Standard deviation x 3.5}}{50} = \dfrac{28.28 \text{ x } 3.5}{50} = \dfrac{98.98}{50} = 1.98$ (Constant)

2. Hull scores of 50 is the mean; therefore, 50 is 59.4 (Column 2)

3. Constant (1.98) is added to mean to get a Hull score of 51 = 1.98 + 59.4 = 61.38 (Column 2)

4. Constant (1.98) is added to Hull score of 51 to get 52 = 1.98 + 61.38 = 63.36 (Column 2)

5. Continue adding constant until Hull score of 100 is reached.

6. Constant (1.98) is subtracted from the mean to get a Hull score of 49 = 59.4 - 1.98 = 57.42 (Column 2)

7. Continue subtracting constant until Hull score (or raw score) of 0 is reached.

8. Round off to nearest whole number (Column 3).

If Hull scales are constructed for a number of tests, it will be possible to average the points earned on different kinds of tests, as shown in Table 11:5. This ability to average different kinds of tests will prove very useful for grading, as will be seen on page 302.

The two important features of achievement scales, then, are that they permit you to evaluate current students on the basis of past students and allow you to average scores from different tests.

Assigning Letter Grades. While grading can be done in several ways, the two methods most used are the "standards" approach, and the "normal curve" approach. The standards approach is characterized by arbitrarily deciding that if all skills are passed, a grade of "A" will be earned; if 90% are passed, a grade of "B" will be earned, etc. (Actually, to give a letter grade using ARC and YMCA standards is impossible, because in both of these organizations all test items must be passed before the certificate is earned. This, in effect, is the pass-or-fail grading system, which is not always appropriate for a school situation.)

The possible grading system described above (all skills passed equals an "A", etc.) has a major flaw. Several students will pass the same percentage of the tests but some of these swimmers will be considerably better than others (as judged by observation). Also, some tests are considerably easier than others. A possible solution is to weight each test according to how difficult you deem it. Examples in a beginning swimmer class: One point for doing the tuck float for five seconds; five points for jumping

TABLE 11:5
AVERAGING HULL SCORES
(HYPOTHETICAL DATA)

Hull Scale Points	Breaststroke Test (Yards per 5 minutes)	Crawl Stroke Test (Seconds per 50 yards)	Underwater Swim Test (feet)
55	200	28.3	
54	195	28.7	80
53	190	29.1	78
52	185	29.8	77
51	180	29.9	76
50	175	30.3	75
49	170	30.7	73
48	165	31.1	72
47	160	31.5	71
46	155	31.9	70

Calculation of average score for a hypothetical swimmer:

Performance	Hull Scale Points
He swam 180 yards breaststroke in 5 min.	51
He swam 50 yards of crawl stroke in 30.7 sec.	49
He swam 70 feet underwater	46
	146

$$146 \div 3 = 46.6 \text{ average}$$

off the high board; ten points for swimming 25 yards underwater. Another example from a college male class:

Test items worth five points:	75 ft. elem. back, 75 ft. side, 75 ft. breast, 75 ft. crawl, 75 ft. trudgen, 75 racing back, etc.
Test itesms worth ten points:	100 yd. elem. back, 100 yd. side, 100 yd. breast, etc.
Test items worth 15 points:	30 ft. under water
Test items worth 20 points:	One-minute vertical tread w/o use of hands
Test items worth 30 points:	450-yard swim, five-minute tread

A system such as shown above will give a wider range of total points and motivate people to master the more difficult skills, not merely a certain percentage of the total items. The basic principle of weighting, then, is that the harder the test item, the more points should be allotted to it.

Instructors who use the standards approach predetermine what the standard shall be for a particular letter grade. If they weight the tests, they may say that 95 points (of a possible 100) would be an "A"; 88-94 = B; 80-87 = C; and 70-80 would be a "D." Anyone below 70 would fail. Or, if Hull scales are used for all tests, an average of 80 or better would be an "A"; 60-79 a "B"; 40-59 a "C"; 20-39 would be a "D"; and below 20 would be a failure. It is possible for an entire class to earn "A" or "B" grades or for most of a very poor class to be in the "D" bracket. Instructors who favor this approach point out that a person who earns a "C" grade in the current class is comparable to a "C" student student two years ago. This leads to consistency in grading.

It is popular to consider the normal curve when assigning grades. (Instructors who favor the standards approach described above will indicate that they have already considered the curve. They say that experience with several similar groups has already shown them how good the "A" student is.) When using the normal curve method, the instructor assumes that his class is normal in ability (some are good students, some are poor, with the majority between the two) and, therefore, the grades should be about what a normal group would receive. There are adequate statistical explanations available in texts (see Johnson-Nelson, Chapter 3) which describe the way a normal group is distributed; generally, we know that the great majority are in the middle, and fewer students are found as we go above and below that middle of the group. The normal curve approach to grading says that if a certain part of the standard deviation is used, it is possible to assign letter grades. The most common standard deviation segments used is 1, as shown in Chart 11:3.

CHART 11:3
ASSIGNING LETTER GRADES BY MEANS OF THE NORMAL CURVE

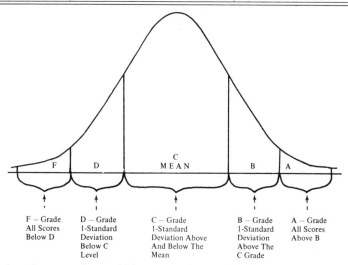

Chart 11:4 shows how letter grades could be assigned, using data presented earlier.

CHART 11:4
EXAMPLE OF ASSIGNING LETTER GRADES BY MEANS OF THE NORMAL CURVE

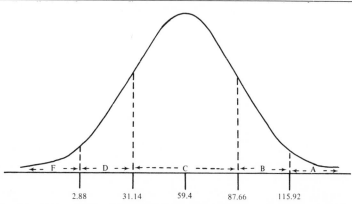

Using data presented earlier (Mean = 59.4, and Standard Deviation = 28.26 (grade based on standard deviation units as shown in Chart 11:3)) the grades would be:

A = 115.92 and up   (116 when rounded off)
B = 87.66 - 115.91   (88-115)
C = 31.14 - 87.65   (31-87)
D =   2.88 - 31.13   (3-30)

Instructors must remember that in some test items, the smaller number is the better score (e.g., swimming a distance in two minutes is better than a time of three minutes). Therefore, before assigning grades, instructors must decide whether high scores are better or worse, and calculate accordingly.

It is entirely possible to combine the use of Hull Scale scores with the normal curve approach to grading. When the averages for all students are found, a mean and standard deviation for the group is calculated. It is then possible to calculate the A, B, C, D, and F grades according to the system described above.

Comments About Evaluation of Students at Private Pools and Country Clubs

The use of the ARC program is quite common in private pools, however, this can lead to complications. These pools are usually the scene of private or semi-private instruction, and while the usual ARC standards can be applied, sometimes there is a considerable amount of pressure exerted by parents to have their children pass the course. While it is a temptation (for job security, if nothing else) to lower the standards to pass some student, this is not the aim of the ARC program. We strongly counsel you to establish high performance norms and be firm in your demand that these standards be met. If you need help in deciding what the norms should be, talk with the local aquatic groups or veteran instructors.

WRITTEN ASSIGNMENTS

1. Talk to a local ARC or YMCA instructor.
   a. What problems with evaluation does he have?
   b. What techniques (e.g., skill sheets, stroke analysis sheets, achievement scales, etc.) does he use?
   c. How does he test — throughout the course, or at the end?
2. Talk to a local school aquatic instructor.
   a. What problems with evaluation does he have?
   b. What techniques (e.g., skill sheets, stroke analysis sheets, achievement scales, etc.) does he use?
   c. How does he test — throughout the course, or at the end?
   d. How does he grade?

BEHAVIORAL OBJECTIVES

After study, we expect students to be able to take a written examination based on the material in this chapter, consisting of defining terms, answering short essay questions, and performing simple mathematical problems.

1. The student must list the two basic questions which are to be considered before evaluation can be attempted and explain why each is important.

2. The student must indicate for which one of these organizations he probably will teach: American National Red Cross, American YMCA, Canadian Red Cross. Then, the student must list, by correct title, the name of those publications of this group which give the skills and/or standards for all their aquatic courses. The address where these publications may be obtained must be given too.

3. When given a list of specific skills, the student must develop a check sheet for any class.

4. When shown samples, the student must be able to properly complete any of the YMCA and ARC aquatic forms normally submitted by an instructor.

5. When given a hypothetical situation, the student must possess the ability to create correctly worded behavioral objectives for a school swimming program.

6. When given hypothetical data, the student must be able to calculate the mean, standard deviation, and Hull scores for any aquatic event involving time or distance.

7. When given a listing of skills, the student must possess the ability to weight different skills according to the basic principle given in this text.

8. When given hypothetical data, the student must be able to determine letter grades according to the "normal curve" method.

BIBLIOGRAPHY

American National Red Cross. *Swimming and Water Safety Courses.* Washington: American National Red Cross, 1968.

Friermood, Harold T. *New YMCA Aquatic Workbook.* New York: The Association Press, 1965.

Johnson, Barry L. and Nelson, Jack K. *Practical Measurements for Evaluation in Physical Education.* Minneapolis: Burgess Publishing Company, 1969.

Mager, Robert F. *Preparing Objectives for Programmed Instruction.* San Francisco: Fearon Publishers, 1962.

Mathews, Donald K. *Measurement in Physical Education.* Philadelphia: W. B. Saunders Company, 1968.

APPENDIX A

SOURCES TO WHICH THE AQUATIC EMPLOYEE MAY APPLY FOR INFORMATION CONCERNING POOL AND BEACH OPERATION IN THE STATE OR TERRITORY IN WHICH HE IS EMPLOYED

Alabama[1]
Division of Public Water Supply
Bureau of Environmental Health
Alabama Department of Public Health
State Office Building
Montgomery, Alabama 36104

Alaska[1]
Branch of Environmental Health
Division of Public Health
Alaska Department of Health and Welfare
Pouch H, Juneau, Alaska 99801

Supervisory Sanitarian
Northern Regional Office
Department of Health and Welfare
604 Barnette Street
Fairbanks, Alaska 99701

Supervisory Sanitarian
South Central Regional Office
338 Denali Street, McKay Bldg.
Anchorage, Alaska 99501

Supervisory Sanitarian
Southeastern Regional Office
Division of Public Health
Pouch J
Juneau, Alaska 99801

Arizona[3]
Division of Water Supply
4019 N. 33rd Avenue
Hayden Plaza West
Phoenix, Arizona 85017

Arkansas[3]
Bureau of Sanitary Engineering
State Board of Health
State Health Building
State Capitol Grounds
Little Rock, Arkansas 72201

California[1]
Bureau of Sanitary Engineering
State Department of Public Health
2151 Berkeley Way
Berkeley, California 94704

Colorado[4]
Division of Engineering and Sanitation
State Department of Health
4210 East 11/th Avenue
Denver, Colorado 80220

Connecticut[3]
Section of Sanitation Services
Division of Laboratory Services
State Department of Health
79 Elm Street
Hartford, Connecticut 06115

Delaware[4]
Division of Sanitary Engineering
State Board of Health
State Health Building
Dover, Delaware 19901

District of Columbia[1]
D. C. Department of Public Health
Water Quality Control Division
801 North Capitol Street N.E.
Washington, D. C. 20002

Florida[4]
Bureau of Sanitary Engineering
State Board of Health
P. O. Box 210
Jacksonville, Florida 32201

Georgia[3]
Environmental Sanitation Service
Georgia Department of Public Health
47 Trinity Avenue S.W.
Atlanta, Georgia 30334

[1]Printed materials available free to employees in the State.

[2]Fee payment is required for printed materials.

[3]Printed materials are available. They may be free or there may be a charge for them.

[4]No printed materials are available at the state level. In some instances, materials are in the process of preparation.

[5]Materials probably are available but this fact is unconfirmed.

Guam[4]
Environmental Health Section
Department of Public Health and Social
   Services
P. O. Box 2816
Agana, Guam 96910

Hawaii[4]
Sanitary Engineering Branch
Environmental Health Division
State Department of Health
P. O. Box 3378
Honolulu, Hawaii 96801

Idaho[3]
Engineering and Sanitation Division
State Department of Health
Capitol Building
Boise, Idaho 83701

Illinois[1]
Bureau of Public Water Supplies
Division of Sanitary Engineering
Department of Public Health
State Office Building
400 South Spring Street
Springfield, Illinois 62706

Indiana[4]
Water Supply Section
Division of Sanitary Engineering
State Board of Health
1330 West Michigan Street
Indianapolis, Indiana 46206

Iowa[5]
State Department of Health
State Office Building
Des Moines, Iowa 50319

Kansas[1]
Program of General Engineering and
   Sanitation
Environmental Health Services
State Department of Health
State Office Building
Topeka Avenue at Tenth
Topeka, Kansas 66612

Kentucky[1]
Sanitary Engineering Program
Division of Environmental Health
State Department of Health
275 East Main Street
Frankfort, Kentucky 40601

Louisiana[1]
Division of Engineering
Bureau of Environmental Health
State Department of Health
Civic Center, P. O. Box 60630
New Orleans, Louisiana 70160

Maine[1]
Division of Sanitary Engineering
Department of Health and Welfare
Bureau of Health
State House
Augusta, Maine 04330

Maryland[1]
Division of General Sanitation
Environmental Health Services
State Department of Health
2305 North Charles Street
Baltimore, Maryland 21218

Massachusetts[5]
Department of Public Health
546 State House
Boston, Massachusetts 02133

Michigan[1]
Division of Engineering
Department of Public Health
3500 North Logan Street
Lansing, Michigan 48914

Minnesota[3]
Section of Water Supply and General
   Engineering
Division of Environmental Sanitation
State Department of Health
University Campus
Minneapolis, Minnesota 55440

Mississippi[4]
Division of Sanitary Engineering
State Board of Health
Felix J. Underwood State Board of Health
   Building
P. O. Box 1700
Jackson, Mississippi 39205

Missouri[1]
Bureau of Water Supply
Division of Health
State Office Building
221 West High Street
Jefferson City, Missouri 65101

Montana[1]
　Division of Environmental Sanitation
　State Board of Health
　Cogswell Building
　Helena, Montana 59601

Nebraska[1]
　Bureau of Environmental Health Services
　State Department of Health
　State House Station, Box 94757
　Lincoln, Nebraska 68509

Nevada[1]
　Bureau of Environmental Health
　State Department of Health and Welfare
　790 Sutro Street
　Reno, Nevada 89503

New Hampshire[1]
　New Hampshire Water Supply and Pollution
　　Control Commission
　61 South Spring Street
　Concord, New Hampshire 03301

New Jersey[1]
　Division of Environmental Health
　State Department of Health
　P. O. Box 1540
　Trenton, New Jersey 08625

New Mexico[3]
　Environmental Services Division
　State Health and Social Services Department
　P. O. Box 2348
　Santa Fe, New Mexico 87501

New York[2]
　Camp and Recreation Section
　Bureau of Food and Recreation Sanitation
　Division of General Engineering and
　　Radiological Health
　845 Central Avenue
　Albany, New York 12206

North Carolina[1]
　Section of Sanitation
　Division of Sanitary Engineering
　State Board of Health
　225 North McDowell Street
　Raleigh, North Carolina 27602

North Dakota[3]
　Sanitary Engineering Services
　State Department of Health
　Capitol Building
　Bismarck, North Dakota 58501

Ohio[1]
　Unit of General Sanitation
　Division of Sanitation
　Bureau of Environmental Health
　State Department of Health
　450 East Town Street
　Columbus, Ohio 43216

Oklahoma[3]
　Water Quality Control Division
　Environmental Health Services
　State Department of Health
　3400 North Eastern
　Oklahoma City, Oklahoma 73105

Oregon[3]
　Sanitary Engineering Division
　State Board of Health
　1400 S.W. Fifth Avenue
　Portland, Oregon 97201

Pennsylvania[3]
　Division of Recreation Sanitation and
　　Environmental Safety
　Bureau of Housing and Environmental
　　Control
　State Department of Health
　State Capitol
　Health and Welfare Building
　Harrisburg, Pennsylvania 17120

REGION I
1400 West Spring Garden Street
Philadelphia, Pennsylvania 19130

REGION II
401 Buttonwood Street
West Reading, Pennsylvania 19601

REGION III
29 Chestnut Street
Lewistown, Pennsylvania 17044

REGION IV
734 West Fourth Street
Williamsport, Pennsylvania 17701

REGION V
300 Liberty Avenue
Pittsburgh, Pennsylvania 15222

REGION VI
996 S. Main Street
Meadville, Pennsylvania 16335

Puerto Rico[4]
  Bureau of Health
  Department of Health
  Ponce de Leon Avenue
  San Juan, Puerto Rico 00908

Rhode Island[3]
  Division of Water Supply Control
  Service of Environmental Health
  State Department of Health
  State Office Building
  Providence, Rhode Island 02903

South Carolina[1]
  Environmental Sanitation Section
  Division of Local Health Services
  State Board of Health
  J. Marion Sims Building
  Columbia, South Carolina 29201

South Dakota[1]
  Water Sanitation Section
  Division of Sanitary Engineering
  State Department of Health
  State Capitol
  Pierre, South Dakota 57501

Tennessee[1]
  Division of Sanitary Engineering
  State Department of Public Health
  Cordell Hull Building
  Sixth Avenue, North
  Nashville, Tennessee 37219

Texas[3]
  Division of Sanitary Engineering
  State Department of Health
  1100 West 49th Street
  Austin, Texas 78756

Utah[1]
  Bureau of Disease Prevention and
    Environmental Control Services
  State Division of Health
  44 Medical Drive
  Salt Lake City, Utah 84113

Vermont[3]
  Division of Sanitary Engineering
  Bureau of Environmental Sanitation
  State Department of Health
  115 Colchester Avenue
  Burlington, Vermont 05402

Virginia[4]
  Bureau of Tourist Establishment
    Sanitation
  State Department of Health
  Madison Building
  Richmond, Virginia 23219

Virgin Islands[4]
  Division of Environmental Health
  Virgin Islands Department of Health
  Charlotte Amalie
  St. Thomas, Virgin Islands 00801

Washington[1]
  Section of Sanitary Engineering
  Division of Environmental Health
  State Department of Health
  Public Health Building
  Olympia, Washington 98501

West Virginia[3]
  General Environmental and Food Control
    Section
  Division of Sanitary Engineering
  State Department of Health
  1800 E. Washington Street
  Charleston, West Virginia 25305

Wisconsin[1]
  Division of Health
  Bureau of Environmental Health
  Department of Health and Social Services
  P. O. Box 309
  Madison, Wisconsin 53701

Wyoming[1]
  Division of Sanitary Engineering
  State Department of Public Health
  State Office Building
  Cheyenne, Wyoming 82001

United States[2]
  U. S. Department of Health, Education and
    Welfare
  Public Health Service
  Bureau of State Services (Community
    Health)
  Washington, D. C. 20201

American Public Health Association, Inc.[2]
1740 Broadway
New York, New York 10019

MONTHLY OPERATION REPORT OF SWIMMING POOLS

NORTH DAKOTA STATE DEPARTMENT OF HEALTH
BISMARCK, NORTH DAKOTA

FOR MONTH OF _____ 19___

POOL _____

CITY _____

CHIEF OPERATOR _____

DATE	HOURS PER DAY POOL OPERATED	MAXIMUM BATHING LOAD	FEMALE BATHERS PER DAY	MALE BATHERS PER DAY	TOTAL NUMBER BATHERS PER DAY	SIDES & BOTTOM OF POOL	SCUM GUTTERS	BATH HOUSE	NEW WATER ADDED IN GALLONS OR INCHES IN POOL	TOTAL HOURS OPERATED/DAY	FILTERS WASHED	ALUM	SODA-ASH OR LIME	AMMONIA TYPE	COPPER SULPHATE	DOSAGE IN	POUNDS FED PER DAY	11 AM DEEP	11 AM SHALLOW	3 PM DEEP	3 PM SHALLOW	8 PM DEEP	8 PM SHALLOW	pH	AM AIR	AM WATER	PM AIR	PM WATER	DATE SAMPLED	PLATE COUNT 1 ML. AGAR 37°C 24+ HRS	MOST PROBABLE NUMBER	REMARKS
	2	3	4	5	6	7	8	9	10	11	12	13	14	15	16	17	18	19	20	21	22	23	24	25	26	27	28	29	30	31	32	
1																																
2																																
3																																
4																																
5																																
6																																
7																																
8																																
9																																
10																																
11																																
12																																
13																																
14																																
15																																
16																																
17																																
18																																
19																																
20																																
21																																
22																																
23																																
24																																
25																																
26																																
27																																
28																																
29																																
30																																
31																																
TOTAL																																
AV.																																
MAX.																																
MIN.																																

Column groups:
BATHING LOAD — columns 3–6
CHECK WHEN CLEANED — columns 7–9
FILTER OPERATION / CHEMICALS PER DAY IN LBS — columns 13–16
DISINFECTION / CHLORINE — columns 17–18
CHLORINE RESIDUAL, PPM — columns 19–24
pH — column 25
AVERAGE TEMPERATURE °F — columns 26–29
BACTERIOLOGICAL ANALYSIS — columns 31–32

311

REFERENCES

Each chapter of this text contains the primary references used for that section. The listing below is an attempt to provide further sources of aquatic information.

AQUATIC BIBLIOGRAPHY

Council for National Cooperation in Aquatics. *Swimming and Diving: A Bibliography.* New York: Association Press, 1968.

AQUATIC ORGANIZATIONS

Council for National Cooperation in Aquatics. Harold Friermood, Executive Director. 51 Clifford Avenue, Pelham, New York 10803

International Academy of Aquatic Art. 403 Iowa Theatre Building, Cedar Rapids, Iowa 52401.

National Lifeguard Service. 550 Church Street, Toronto 5, Ontario, Canada.

National Swimming Pool Institute. 2000 K Street, N. W., Washington, D. C. 20006.

Royal Lifesaving Society of Canada. 550 Church Street, Toronto 5, Ontario, Canada.

ORGANIZATIONS THAT INCLUDE AQUATICS
IN THEIR PROGRAM

American Association for Health, Physical Education and Recreation. 1201 16 Street, N. W., Washington, D. C. 20036.

Amateur Athletic Union of the United States. 231 West 58 Street, New York, New York 10019.

American National Red Cross. 17 and D Streets, N. W., Washington, D. C. 20006.

Boys Clubs of America. 771 First Avenue, New York, New York 10017.

Boy Scouts of America. National Council, U. S. Highway No. 1, New Brunswick, New Jersey 08903.

Canadian Red Cross Society. 460 Jarvis Street, Toronto 5, Ontario, Canada.

Camp Fire Girls, Inc. Division of Program Services, 65 Worth Street, New York, New York 10013.

Girls Clubs of America. 101 Park Avenue, New York, New York 10017.

Girl Scouts of U. S. A. 830 Third Avenue, New York, New York 10022.

Los Angeles County Department of Parks and Recreation. Room 1200, 155 West Washington Boulevard, Los Angeles, California 90015.

National Industrial Recreation Association. 20 North Wacker Drive, Chicago, Illinois 60606.

National Recreation Association. 8 West Eighth Street, New York, New York 10011.

National Safety Council, Inc. 425 North Michigan Avenue, Chicago, Illinois 60611.

National Council of Young Men's Christian Associations. 2160 Yonge Street, Toronto 7, Ontario, Canada.

National Board, Young Women's Christian Association, 600 Lexington Avenue, New York, New York 10022.

National Council, Young Women's Christian Association. 571 Jarvis Street, Toronto, Ontario, Canada.

AQUATIC PUBLISHERS AND PUBLICATIONS

Hoffman Publications, Inc. Sunrise Professional Building, Fort Lauderdale, Florida 33304.

Albert Schoenfield, Publisher. 12618 Killion Street, North Hollywood, California 91607.

Swimming Pool Age (See Hoffman)

Swimming Pool Data and Reference Annual (See Hoffman)

Swimming World and *Junior Swimmer.* (See Schoenfield)

PUBLISHERS AND PUBLICATIONS THAT INCLUDE AQUATICS IN THEIR MATERIAL

Association Press. 291 Broadway, New York, New York 10007.

Athletic Institute. 805 Merchandise Mart, Chicago, Illinois 60654.

Athletic Journal. Athletic Journal Publishing Company. 1719 Howard Street, Evanston, Illinois 60202.

Journal of Canadian Association of Health, Physical Education and Recreation. 168 Isabella Street, Toronto 5, Ontario, Canada.

Journal of Physical Education. Physical Education Society of the Y.M.C.A.'s of North America. 600 Broad Street, Newark, New Jersey 07100.

National Collegiate Athletic Bureau. Box 757, Grand Central Station, New York, New York 10017.

The Physical Educator. 3747 North Linwood Avenue, Indianapolis, Indiana 46218.

Scholastic Coach. Scholastic Magazines, Inc. 50 West 44 Street, New York, New York 10036.

Sportshelf. P. O. Box 634, New Rochelle, New York 10802.

U. S. Naval Institute. Secretary and Treasurer of the United States Naval Institute, Annapolis, Maryland 21402.

RECENT NOTEWORTHY AQUATIC PUBLICATIONS FOR COACHES

Gambril, Donald L. *Swimming.* Pacific Palisades, California: Goodyear Publishing Company, 1969.

O'Brien, Ronald F. *Springboard Diving Fundamentals.* Columbus, Ohio: Charles E. Merrill Publishing Company, 1968.

PERIODICAL REFERENCES

Aitken, Margaret H. "Organizing the College Program to Give Varied Swimming Experiences." *Journal of Health, Physical Education and Recreation* 34 (May, 1963): 29.

Alley, L. E. "An Analysis of Water Resistance and Propulsion in Swimming Crawl Stroke." *Research Quarterly* 23 (October, 1952): 253-270.

Asprey, G. M., Louis E. Alley, and W. W. Tuttle. "Effect of Eating at Various Times on Subsequent Performances in the One-mile Freestyle Swim." *Research Quarterly* 39 (May, 1968): 231.

Balch, Roland E. "College-Run Recreational Swim Program for Fathers and Sons." *Journal of Health, Physical Education and Recreation* 34 (May, 1963): 39.

Ball, J. R. "Effect of Eating Upon Swimming." *Research Quarterly* 33 (May, 1962): 163.

Behrman, Robert M. "Personality Differences Between Nonswimmers and Swimmers." *Research Quarterly* 38 (May, 1967): 163.

Beisman, Gladys L. "No School . . . We're All at the Pool." *Journal of Health, Physical Education and Recreation* 30 (January, 1959): 23.

Bennett, LaVerne M. "A Test of Diving for Use in Beginning Classes." *Research Quarterly* 13 (March, 1942): 109.

Breon, Earl H. "Teaching Oral Resuscitation." *Journal of Health, Physical Education and Recreation* 31 (May, 1960): 34.

Bria, Anthony J. "Games in the Swimming Pool." *Athletic Journal* 48 (October, 1967): 34.

Brown, Richard L. "Finding and Using the Aquatics Resources in Your Own Community." *Journal of Health, Physical Education and Recreation* 34 (May, 1963): 43.

_____. "New Facts on Near Drownings." *Journal of Health, Physical Education and Recreation* 34 (September, 1963): 38.

_____. "Swimming—Sport for the Handicapped." *Journal of Health, Physical Education and Recreation* 24 (April, 1953): 14.

Bullock, Doris L. "Some Basic Skills in the Water." *Journal of Health, Physical Education and Recreation* 28 (January, 1957): 27.

314

Burdeshaw, Dorothy. "Acquisition of Elementary Swimming Skills by Negro and White College Women." *Research Quarterly* 39 (December, 1968): 872.

Burke, Lillian A. C. "The Advanced High School Swimmer." *Journal of Health, Physical Education and Recreation* 19 (November, 1948): 600.

Busch, William M. "Overcoming the Fears of Swimming." *Journal of Health, Physical Education and Recreation* 39 (May, 1968): 75.

_____. "Scuba Diving: Delight or Disaster." *Journal of Health, Physical Education and Recreation* 36 (April, 1965): 81.

Campbell, William R., T. F. Wetzler, J. E. Faber, and J. D. Marshall, Jr. "Iodine—New Disinfectant for your Swimming Pool" *Journal of Health, Physical Education and Recreation* 32 (May-June, 1961): 21.

Capen, Edward K. "Common Sense for Fun on the Water." *Journal of Health, Physical Education and Recreation* 30 (May, 1959): 22.

Carlile, F. "Effect of Preliminary Passive Warming on Swimming Performance." *Research Quarterly* 27 (May, 1956): 143-151.

Carroll, Edwin H. "Red Cross First Aid and Lifesaving Program." *Journal of Health, Physical Education and Recreation* 14 (February, 1943): 99.

Carlson, Joan. "Black Light Your Water Ballet." *Journal of Health, Physical Education and Recreation* 25 (March, 1954): 19.

Casey, Ralph. "Backstroke Swimming." *Journal of Health, Physical Education and Recreation* 30 (March, 1959): 78.

Caulfield, Hal D. "Daily Log and Split-Time Record For Swimmers." *Athletic Journal* 46 (October, 1965): 32.

_____. "Pulse Swimming." *Athletic Journal* 46 (December, 1965): 14.

Clemenger, J. W. "Characteristic Positions in the Field of Aquatics." *Research Quarterly* 11 (May, 1940): 132.

Collins, H. C. and Charles Schlegel. "Elbow Room in the Swimming Pool." *Athletic Journal* 39 (January, 1959): 64.

Costill, David L. "Analysis of the Breast Stroke." *Athletic Journal* 47 (October, 1966): 18.

_____. "Use of a Swimming Ergometer in Physiological Research." *Research Quarterly* 37 (December, 1966): 564.

Counsil, Roger E. "The Dynamics of Entries in Diving." *Athletic Journal* 45 (May, 1965): 14.

Counsilman, James E. "Fatigue and Staleness." *Athletic Journal* 35 (June, 1955): 16.

_____. "Forces in Swimming Two Types of Crawl Stroke." *Research Quarterly* 26 (May, 1955): 127-139.

_____. "Interval Training Applied to Swimming." *Athletic Journal* 42 (September, 1961): 20.

_____. "Principles of Training." *Athletic Journal* 35 (March, 1955): 40.

_____. "The Back Crawl Stroke." *Athletic Journal* 33 (April, 1953): 14.

_____. "The Butterfly Stroke." *Athletic Journal* 33 (February, 1953): 26.

_____. "The Physiological Effects of Training." *Athletic Journal* 35 (February, 1955): 14.

_____. "Isometric and Isotonic Drills for Swimmers." *Jr. Swimmer—Swimming World* 2 (December, 1961): 4.

"Court Decisions Affecting Municipal Swimming Pools." *Swimming Pool Age* 31 (August, 1957): 68.

Craig, A. B. "Underwater Swimming and Drowning." *Journal of Sports Medicine and Physical Fitness* 2 (1962): 23-26.

Cureton, Thomas K. "A Technical Analysis of the World's Greatest Swimmers." *Scholastic Coach* 27 (September, 1957): 38.

_____. "Science Aids Australian Swimmers." *Athletic Journal* 37 (March, 1957): 40.

Curtis, Howard. "Approach to Diving." *Scholastic Coach* 21 (February, 1952): 12.

_____. "Safety in Diving." *Scholastic Coach* 22 (January, 1953): 54.

_____. "The Basic Dives." *Scholastic Coach* 21 (March, 1952): 12.

Daviess, Grace B. "Leadup Steps to Advanced Diving." *Journal of Health, Physical Education and Recreation* 29 (May, 1958): 19.

Davis, Jack F. "Will Your Swimming Classes Make Them Water-safe?" *Journal of Health, Physical Education and Recreation* 30 (April, 1959): 27.

Davis, Michael G. "Put Some Public Relations in Your Swimming." *Athletic Journal* 48 (October, 1967): 37.

deVries, H. A. "A Cinematographical Analysis of the Dolphin Swimming Stroke." *Research Quarterly* 30 (December, 1959): 413.

_____. "Effect of Various Warm-up Procedures on 100-Yard Times of Competitive Swimmers." *Research Quarterly* 30 (March, 1959): 11-20.

Dietrich, Marion. "Canoe in Our Pool." *Journal of Health, Physical Education and Recreation* 29 (February, 1958): 59.

Dillon, Evelyn K. "A Clinic for Swimming Officials." *Journal of Health, Physical Education and Recreation* 18 (March, 1947): 151.

_____. "Swim to Music." *Journal of Health, Physical Education and Recreation* 23 (January, 1952): 17.

Dohrman, Paul. "Water Fistball." *Journal of Health, Physical Education and Recreation* 37 (November-December, 1966): 61.

Dumutru, A. P. and F. G. Hamilton. "Underwater Blackout—A Mechanism of Drowning." *American Academy of General Practice* 29 (1964): 123-125.

Durant, Sue M. "An Analytical Method of Rating Synchronized Swimming Stunts." *Research Quarterly* 35 (May, 1964): 126.

"Effect of Cardiac Conditioning on the Anticipatory, Exercise and Recovery Heart Rates of Young Men." *Journal of Sports Medicine and Physical Fitness* 4 (1964): 79-86.

Empleton, Bernard E. "Water Games Add to Confidence, Control and Competence." *Journal of Health, Physical Education and Recreation* 34 (May, 1963): 37.

Fairbanks, Berthaida. "Teaching How to Swim is Not Enough." *Journal of Health, Physical Education and Recreation* 38 (March, 1967): 38.

Faulkner, John A. "Motivation and Athletic Performance." *Coaching Review* 1 (1963): 3-5.

_____. "Physiology of Swimming." *Research Quarterly* 37 (March, 1966): 41.

_____. and R. M. Dawson. "Pulse Rate After 50-Meter Swims." *Research Quarterly* 37 (May, 1966): 282-284.

Ferguson, Ruth S. "Water Safety for the Physically Handicapped." *Journal of Health, Physical Education and Recreation* 20 (May, 1949): 317.

Ferro, A. P. "Learning to Get Along in the Water." *Journal of Health, Physical Education and Recreation* 37 (April, 1966): 34.

Fleming, Prudence. "Training Women for Competitive Swimming." *Journal of Health, Physical Education and Recreation* 19 (December, 1948): 644.

Foster, Carleton N. and Emmon L. Vernier. "Swimming—A Cooperative Community Enterprise." *Journal of Health, Physical Education and Recreation* 15 (May, 1944): 277.

Fox, Edward L., Robert L. Bartels and Richard W. Bowers. "Comparison of Speed and Energy Expenditure for Two Swimming Turns." *Research Quarterly* 34 (October, 1963): 322.

Fox, M. G. "Swimming Power Test." *Research Quarterly* 28 (October, 1957): 233.

Friermood, Harold T. "Research as an Aid to Improved Instruction in Aquatics Skills." *Journal of Health, Physical Education and Recreation* 34 (May, 1963): 44.

Gabrielson, M. Alexander. "Report of the 1964 Meeting of the Council for National Cooperation in Aquatics." *Journal of Health, Physical Education and Recreation* 36 (April, 1965): 6.

_____. "Swimming Phenomenon." *Journal of Health, Physical Education and Recreation* 35 (September, 1964): 45.

Gentile, Adolph. "Aquatic Games." *Athletic Journal* 48 (April, 1968): 80.

_____. "Comparison of Dry and Wet Body Starts in Swimming." *Athletic Journal* 47 (September, 1966): 76.

Gerard, W. F. "An Improved Swimming Program." *Journal of Health, Physical Education and Recreation* 14 (September, 1943): 386.

Gold, M. and I. F. Waglow. "Swimming Classification Test." *Research Quarterly* 26 (December, 1955): 485.

Grapes, James E. "Two Teams, Two Coaches, Two Hours, One Pool." *Athletic Journal* 48 (March, 1968): 43.

Gross, E. A. and H. L. Thompson. "Relationship of Dynamic Balance to Speed and to Ability in Swimming." *Research Quarterly* 28 (December, 1957): 342.

Gray, Norman A. "Training and Conditioning for Competitive Swimming." *Athletic Journal* 32 (February, 1952): 14.

Groves, William H. "Mechanical Analysis of Diving." *Research Quarterly* 21 (May, 1950): 132.

_____. "Dry Land Workouts for Swimmers." *Journal of Health, Physical Education and Recreation* 37 (April, 1966): 72.

Guenther, Donald P. "Problems Involving Legal Liability." *Journal of Health, Physical Education and Recreation* 20 (October, 1949): 511.

Guerrara, Joseph A. "Year-round School-community Swimming." *Journal of Health, Physical Education and Recreation* 29 (May, 1958): 24.

Gundling, Beulah. "Synchronized Swimming—A Sport and an Art." *Journal of Health, Physical Education and Recreation* 24 (April, 1953): 7.

Handy, Jamison. "The Six-beat Crawl." *Scholastic Coach* 20 (December, 1950): 30.

Harper, Don. "The Physical Principles of Diving." *Athletic Journal* 47 (November, 1966): 34.

Hartlaub, Paul. "Conditioning for Swimming." *Athletic Journal* 39 (October, 1958): 50.

_____. "The Butterfly With a Fishtail Kick." *Athletic Journal* 39 (December, 1958): 30.

Heffner, Fred. "Competitive Use of Pool Facilities." *Athletic Journal* 45 (December, 1964): 38.

_____. "The Swimming Start." *Athletic Journal* 40 (January, 1960): 18.

_____. "Training for Swimmers." *Athletic Journal* 38 (February, 1958): 46.

Hendry, L. B. "A Personality Study of Highly Successful and 'Ideal' Swimming Coaches." *Research Quarterly* 40 (May, 1969): 299.

_____. "Assessment of Personality Traits in the Coach-Swimmer Relationship, and a Preliminary Evaluation of the Father-Figure Stereotype." *Research Quarterly* 39 (October, 1968): 543.

Heusner, William. "Swimming Officiating—Science or Art?" *Journal of Health, Physical Education and Recreation* 32 (May-June, 1961): 32.

_____. "Theoretical Specifications for the Racing Dive: Optimum Angle of Take-Off." *Research Quarterly* 30 (March, 1959): 25.

Hewitt, Jack E. "Aquatics at the National Level." *Journal of Health, Physical Education and Recreation* 22 (April, 1951): 22.

_____. "Fear of the Water." *Journal of Health, Physical Education and Recreation* 18 (May, 1947): 302.

_____ and Robert E. Hazelwood. "Physiological Conditions Associated with Drowning." *Athletic Journal* 25 (September, 1954): 31.

_____. "Swimming Goes to War." *Journal of Health, Physical Education and Recreation* 14 (September, 1943): 354.

Hoffman, H. P. "Breathing in Swimming." *Journal of Health, Physical Education and Recreation* 16 (December, 1945): 573.

Holtz, Doris D. "Safe Boating." *Journal of Health, Physical Education and Recreation* 37 (May, 1966): 38.

Hooley, Agnes M. "Teaching Adult Swimming." *Journal of Health, Physical Education and Recreation* 16 (September, 1945): 404.

Horton, B. T. and M. A. Gabrielson. "Hypersensitiveness to Cold: A Condition Dangerous to Swimmers." *Research Quarterly* 11 (October, 1940): 119-126.

Jacobs, Marshall L. "Turns for the Butterfly and Breaststroke." *Athletic Journal* 41 (November, 1960): 40.

Jacobson, Thomas J. "Coaching the Backstroke Turn." *Athletic Journal* 45 (November, 1964): 18.

_____. "Coaching the Breaststroke Turn." *Athletic Journal* 43 (April, 1963): 66.

_____. "Training for Swimming." *Athletic Journal* 43 (December, 1962): 32.

Jamerson, Dick. "Relay Starts and Racing Turns in Swimming." *Journal of Health, Physical Education and Recreation* 27 (February, 1956): 42.

Jensen, Clayne R. "Comparison of the Dry Body and Wet Body Starts in Swimming." *Research Quarterly* 35 (March, 1964): 81.

_____. "The Controversy of Warm-up." *Athletic Journal* 47 (December, 1966): 24.

_____. "Effects of Five Training Combinations of Swimming and Weight Training on Swimming the Front Crawl." *Research Quarterly* 34 (December, 1963): 471.

_____. "Weight Training for Swimmers?" *Athletic Journal* 44 (October, 1963): 44.

"Job Specifications for Lifeguards." *Swimming Pool Data and Reference Annual* 31 (1964): 171.

Karpovich, P. V. "Respiration in Swimming and Diving." *Research Quarterly* 10 (October, 1939): 3.

_____. "Water Resistance in Swimming." *Research Quarterly* 4 (October, 1933): 28.

Kascle, Clifford. "A Portable Swimming Pool." *Journal of Health, Physical Education and Recreation* 19 (May, 1948): 329.

Kaye, Richard A. "The Use of a Waist-type Flotation Device as an Adjunct in Teaching Beginner Swimming Skills." *Research Quarterly* 36 (October, 1965): 277.

Kelly, Ellen. "Swimming For the Physically Handicapped." *Journal of Health, Physical Education and Recreation* 25 (April, 1954): 12.

Kerns, Virginia. "Parent-Child Swimming Classes." *Scholastic Coach* 21 (June, 1952): 34.

Key, John R. "Relationship Between Load and Swimming Endurance in Humans." *Research Quarterly* 33 (December, 1962): 559.

Keyes, Lynford and Fred R. Lanoue. "Teaching Advanced Watermanship Through Stunts." *Journal of Health, Physical Education and Recreation* 16 (June, 1945): 345.

Kibbe, Sherwin. "How To Succeed in Swimming Without Trying." *Athletic Journal* 46 (September, 1965): 82.

King, W. H., Jr. and L. W. Irwin. "A Time and Motion Study of Competitive Backstroke Swimming Turns." *Research Quarterly* 28 (October, 1957): 257.

Kinsey, Dan. "Optimum Distribution of Effort in the 150-Yard Backstroke." *Research Quarterly* 25 (February, 1945): 40.

_____. "Optimum Distribution of Effort in the 200-Yard Breaststroke." *Research Quarterly* 26 (January, 1946): 39.

Klang, John M. "Coeducational School Swimming." *Athletic Journal* 41 (November, 1960): 44.

Korb, Edward M. "Trends in Camp Aquatics." *Journal of Health, Physical Education and Recreation* 27 (May, 1956): 8.

Kott, John H. "Signal Techniques For Swimming Instruction." *Athletic Journal* 28 (November, 1947): 13.

Lagemann, John K. "Drowned Wearing Life Preserver." *Reader's Digest* (July, 1965): 215-218.

Lanoue, Fred R. "Analysis of the Basic Factors Involved in Fancy Diving." *Research Quarterly* 11 (March, 1940): 102.

_____. "Some Facts on Swimming Cramps." *Research Quarterly* 21 (May, 1950): 153.

_____. "Swimming Through Burning Gasoline or Oil." *Journal of Health, Physical Education and Recreation* 13 (November, 1942): 535.

_____, Lynford Keyes and Lyle Wesler. "Improved Techniques in the Use of Inflated Pants as Life Preservers." *Journal of Health, Physical Education and Recreation* 14 (November, 1943): 494.

Leach, D. Clark. "What the Judges Look For." *Athletic Journal* 35 (January, 1955): 20.

Loeffelbein, Robert L. "Rejuvenate the Swim Program With Guard Ball." *Athletic Journal* 43 (November, 1962): 48.

MacNeill, Lou. "Getting the Most Out of the Least in Swimming." *Athletic Journal* 45 (September, 1964): 70.

Maglischo, C. W. and Maglischo, E. "Comparison of Starts in Swimming." *Research Quarterly* 39 (October, 1968): 604.

Mann, Channing. "Swimming Classes in Elementary Schools On a City-Wide Basis." *Journal of Health, Physical Education and Recreation* 34 (May, 1963): 35.

Martinez, Ray. "Physiological Effects of Swimming 100-Yard Races in Water of Five Temperatures." *64th Proceedings of The College Physical Education Association* (December, 1961): 108-112.

Masilionis, Jeanette. "The Elementary Backstroke For Beginners." *Journal of Health, Physical Education and Recreation* 26 (March, 1955): 312.

Matthews, David O. "Pointers For the Diving Judge." *Athletic Journal* 40 (September, 1959): 85.

_____. "Interval Training In Swimming." *Scholastic Coach* 28 (November, 1958): 42.

McCatty, Cressy A. "Underwater Photography." *Journal of Health, Physical Education and Recreation* 38 (October, 1967): 84.

_____. "Effects of the Use of A Flotation Device in Teaching Nonswimmers." *Research Quarterly* 39 (October, 1968): 621.

Merchant, Frank C. "First Steps in the Water." *Scholastic Coach* 18 (April, 1949): 22.

Merritt, Roy B. "Judging the Dives." *Athletic Journal* 35 (January, 1955): 18.

Merson, Bruce Jr. "Surgical Equipment Goes Athletic." *Athletic Journal* 47 (December, 1966): 22.

Meyer, Hannah. C. "Swimming For the Deaf." *Journal of Health, Physical Education and Recreation* 26 (May, 1955): 12.

Mills, Estel L. "Use the Trampoline to Condition Divers." *Athletic Journal* 48 (January, 1968): 68.

Moench, Frances J. "Safety Precautions vs. Liability." *Journal of Health, Physical Education and Recreation* 13 (February, 1942): 87.

Mohr, Dorothy R. "Needed Aquatic Research." *Journal of Health, Physical Education and Recreation* 28 (May, 1957): 23.

_____ and M. E. Barrett. "Effect of Knowledge of Mechanical Principles in Learning to Perform Intermediate Swimming Skills." *Research Quarterly* 33 (December, 1962): 574.

Montcrief, John, W. R. Morford and M. L. Howell. "Acquisition of Elementary Swimming Skills." *Research Quarterly* 33 (October, 1962): 405.

Morehouse, L. E. "The Respiratory Habits of Trained Swimmers During the Start of a Race." *Research Quarterly* 12 (May, 1941): 186.

_____. "Two Studies in Swimming Starts." *Research Quarterly* 10 (March, 1939): 89.

Morgan, John E. "A Swimming Program for the Whole Community." *Athletic Journal* 27 (June, 1947): 13.

Moriarty, Philip. "Basic Dives Analyzed." *Athletic Journal* 35 (January, 1955): 20.

Murphy, Alvin B. "The Red Cross Swimming Program for the Armed Forces." *Journal of Health, Physical Education and Recreation* 14 (May, 1943): 247.

Nunney, Derek N. "Relation of Circuit Training to Swimming." *Research Quarterly* 31 (May, 1960): 188.

Olszewski, Joe. "Teaching A Youngster to Swim." *Athletic Journal* 44 (November, 1963): 39.

_____. "Three Basics For Instant Swimming." *Athletic Journal* 45 (January, 1965): 26.

Oneil, John J. "Nonschool Facilities For Swimming Instruction." *Journal of Health, Physical Education and Recreation* 39 (September, 1968): 88.

Orphan, Milton Jr. "Motivating Beginners to Increase Learning in the Basic Skills." *Journal of Health, Physical Education and Recreation* 34 (May, 1963): 33.

Papenguth, Dick. "Developing the Average Swimmer." *Athletic Journal* 26 (December, 1945): 18.

_____. "The Flying Breast Stroke." *Athletic Journal* 26 (February, 1946): 10.

_____. "Why We Fly The Breast Stroke." *Athletic Journal* 28 (March, 1948): 50.

Pastore, Edward W. "Community Action Saves Lives." *Journal of Health, Physical Education and Recreation* 27 (May, 1956): 12.

Peek, Clifford. "Hoist The Sails." *Journal of Health, Physical Education and Recreation* 24 (June, 1953): 6.

Peppe, Michael. "Developing Diving Skills." *Journal of Health, Physical Education and Recreation* 27 (March, 1956): 58.

Ploessel, Howard. "A Community Swims at the Pool." *Journal of Health, Physical Education and Recreation* 25 (January, 1954): 22.

Pohndorf, Richard. "No Pool But Spartanburg Swims." *Athletic Journal* 31 (May, 1951): 48.

_____. "Swimming and Fitness." *Journal of Health, Physical Education and Recreation* 35 (January, 1964): 22.

Puff, Don. "Motivating the Swimmer with the Handicap Method." *Athletic Journal* 49 (January, 1969): 114.

Putrin, Johanna. "Personal Water Safety." *Journal of Health, Physical Education and Recreation* 19 (June, 1948): 403.

Rath, Virginia. "Swimming For Polio Patients." *Journal of Health, Physical Education and Recreation* 20 (April, 1949): 275.

Robertson, David H. "Multi-Activity, Year-Round Program for the Senior High School." *Journal of Health, Physical Education and Recreation* 34 (May, 1963): 33.

Ross, Anne. "Teaching Elementary Diving to Small Children." *Journal of Health, Physical Education and Recreation* 18 (March, 1947): 178.

Ruggian, Claude J. "Laboratory Training in Underwater Exercises." *Journal of Health, Physical Education and Recreation* 27 (May, 1956): 14.

Runquist, Kenneth C. "Teaching Arm Action for the Crawl Stroke." *Journal of Health, Physical Education and Recreation* 28 (November, 1957): 42.

Ryan, Jack. "A Pre-Season Training Program for Swimming." *Athletic Journal* 40 (November, 1959): 21.

_____. "Calisthenics for Swimmers." *Athletic Journal* 36 (January, 1956): 16.

_____. "Teaching Skills in Diving." *Athletic Journal* 34 (February, 1954): 38.

_____. "Teaching the Crawl Stroke." *Athletic Journal* 37 (February, 1957): 34 (March, 1957): 16.

_____. "Teach Them How to Turn." *Athletic Journal* 34 (January, 1954): 22.

Sanders, Joan and Doris L. Bulloch. "Experiments in Water Sounds." *Journal of Health, Physical Education and Recreation* 29 (May, 1958): 21.

Savastano, Orland R. and Harold Anderson. "How You Can Plan for an All-Around Aquatics Program." *Swimming Pool Age* 42 (September, 1968): 26.

Schaefer, Mildred A. "Teaching Swimming to the Slow Beginner." *Journal of Health, Physical Education and Recreation* 17 (May, 1946): 280.

Scharf, Raphael J. and William H. King. "Time and Motion Analysis of Competitive Swimming Turns." *Research Quarterly* 35 (March, 1964): 37.

Scheunemann, Virginia Lee. "Bathtub Swimmers." *The Physical Educator* 19 (March, 1962): 12.

Scott, M. G. "Learning Rate of Beginning Swimmers." *Research Quarterly* 25 (March, 1954): 91.

Silvia, Charles E. "Courses Integrating Intellectual Content With Aquatics Skills." *Journal of Health, Physical Education and Recreation* 34 (May, 1963): 31.

Slee, Dennis. "Swimming Program of California High School Coaches." *Athletic Journal* 45 (April, 1965): 34.

Smilgoff, James. "Water Basketball." *Athletic Journal* 36 (November, 1955): 36.

Smith, Alton. "The Coiled Spring Racing Dive." *Athletic Journal* 38 (January, 1958): 51.

Spears, Betty. "Safety at the Camp Waterfront." *Journal of Health, Physical Education and Recreation* 19 (April, 1948): 244.

Stager, A. B. "The Michigan Season Training Plan." *Jr. Swimmer–Swimming World* 2 (June, 1961).

Steinhaus, A. H. and J. E. Norris. "Teaching Neuromuscular Relaxation." *Comparative Research Project 1529, Office of Education, U. S. Department of Health, Education and Welfare, 1964.*

Steve, Alex. "Conditioning Techniques for Competitive Swimmers." *Beach and Pool* 26 (December, 1952): 14.

Swegan, Don and Hugh L. Thompson. "Experimental Research in Swimming." *Scholastic Coach* 28 (April, 1959): 22.

Taylor, Thomas W. "Tuck Float Skills for Beginning Swimmers." *Journal of Health, Physical Education and Recreation* 28 (April, 1957): 18.

"The Nation's Swimming Program." *Athletic Journal* 40 (September, 1959): 42.

Thomas, David G. "Swimming is Easy." *Journal of Health, Physical Education and Recreation* 40 (May, 1969): 74.

Thompson, Hugh L. "Relationship of Dynamic Balance to Speed and To Ability in Swimming." *Research Quarterly* 28 (December, 1957): 342.

_____ and Richard Wells. "A Capsule Swimming Program with Weights." *Athletic Journal* 42 (October, 1961): 41.

_____ and G. Alan Stull. "Effects of Various Training Programs on Speed of Swimming." *Research Quarterly* 30 (December, 1959): 479.

Todd, Frances and Betty Blue. "Teaching Swimming Wholesale." *Journal of Health, Physical Education and Recreation* 25 (October, 1954): 21.

Torney, John A. Jr. "Navy Pilots Must Swim." *Journal of Health, Physical Education and Recreation* 13 (December, 1942): 583.

_____. "Officiating A Swimming Meet." *Scholastic Coach* 22 (September, 1952): 32.

_____. "We Don't Want Still Waters." *Journal of Health, Physical Education and Recreation* 24 (April, 1953): 22.

Vansant, W. Kenneth. "A Wartime Swimming Program for High Schools." *Journal of Health, Physical Education and Recreation* 14 (December, 1943): 521.

Vickers, Betty J. "First Lessons in Synchronized Swimming." *Journal of Health, Physical Education and Recreation* 34 (April, 1963): 33.

Vitti, James J. "Water Baseball." *Athletic Journal* 47 (May, 1967): 52.

Von Wenck, Katherine. "Synchronized Swimming." *Journal of Health, Physical Education and Recreation* 15 (June, 1944): 318.

Walton, Lee A. "Beginning Water Polo." *Journal of Health, Physical Education and Recreation* 37 (October, 1966): 58.

Weber, Ann E. "Standards For Safe Canoeing." *Journal of Health, Physical Education and Recreation* 19 (May, 1948): 338.

Webster, Ted. "Diving Made Easier." *Athletic Journal* 26 (January, 1946): 11.

_____. "Swim and Keep Swimming." *Athletic Journal* 26 (December, 1945): 18.

Wells, L. Janet. "Boating in the School Program." *Journal of Health, Physical Education and Recreation* 29 (May, 1958): 8.

Wetmore, Reagh C. "Artificial Supports for Non-Swimmers." *Athletic Journal* 35 (December, 1954): 19.

_____. "Experimental Data Applied to the Crawl and Breast Strokes." *Athletic Journal* 33 (November, 1952): 30.

Whiting, H. T. A. "Variations in Floating Ability With Age In the Male." *Research Quarterly* 34 (March, 1963): 84.

_____. "Variations in Floating Ability With Age in the Female." *Research Quarterly* 36 (May, 1965): 216.

_____ and D. E. Stembridge. "Personality and the Persistent Non-Swimmer." *Research Quarterly* 36 (October, 1965): 348.

Whitney, Frank. "Our Indoor Swimming Pool." *Journal of Health, Physical Education and Recreation* 29 (May, 1958): 24.

Wild, Charles. "A Swimming Record Board." *Journal of Health, Physical Education and Recreation* 25 (October, 1954): 48.

Will, Helen R. "A Workable Swimming Program." *Journal of Health, Physical Education and Recreation* 14 (June, 1943): 336.

Williams, John H. "Producing Champion Divers." *Athletic Journal* 37 (November, 1956): 6.

Winter, Ford W. "Mechanics of the Tuck Position in Executing the Forward Three and One-Half Somersault." *Athletic Journal* 45 (January, 1965): 19.

Yates, Fern. "Building Swimming Formations." *Journal of Health, Physical Education and Recreation* 14 (May, 1943): 262.

_____. "Teaching Non-Swimmers." *Journal of Health, Physical Education and Recreation* 25 (February, 1954): 11.

_____. "Why Stress Endurance Swimming?" *Journal of Health, Physical Education and Recreation* 27 (May, 1956): 16.

Yost, Charles, P. "How a College Course Develops Aquatics Teaching Abilities." *Journal of Health, Physical Education and Recreation* 34 (May, 1963): 28.

INDEX